Oracle® SQL

INTERACTIVE WORKBOOK

ISBN 0-13-015745-7

90000

9 780130 157454

PRENTICE HALL PTR ORACLE INTERACTIVE WORKBOOKS SERIES

- Baman Motivala
  "Oracle Forms Interactive Workbook"
  0-13-015808-9

- Benjamin Rosenzweig & Elena Silvestrova
  "Oracle PL/SQL"
  0-13-015743-0

- Alex Morrison & Alice Rischert
  "Oracle SQL Interactive Workbook"
  0-13-015745-7

Oracle SQL

INTERACTIVE WORKBOOK

ALEX MORRISON
&
ALICE RISCHERT

PH
PTR

Prentice Hall PTR
Upper Saddle River, New Jersey 07458
www.phptr.com

Library of Congress Cataloging-in-Publication Data

Morrison, Alex.
    Oracle SQL interactive workbook / Alex Morrison, Alice Rischert.
      p. cm.
    Includes bibliographical references and index.
    ISBN 0–13–015745–7
      1. SQL (Computer program language) 2. Oracle (Computer file) I. Rischert, Alice. II. Title.

    QA76.73.S67 M68 2000
    005.75'65--dc21

                                                    00–027499

Editorial/Production Supervisor: *Jan H. Schwartz*
Acquisitions Editor: *Tim Moore*
Development Editor: *Russ Hall*
Marketing Manager: *Bryan Gambrel*
Buyer: *Maura Goldstaub*
Editorial Assistant: *Julie Okulicz*
Cover Design Director: *Jerry Votta*
Cover Designer: *Talar Agasyan*
Art Director: *Gail Cocker-Bogusz*
Web Site Project Manager: *Eileen Clark*
Compositor/Production Services: *Pine Tree Composition, Inc.*

Printed in the United States of America
10 9 8 7 6 5

ISBN 0-13-015745-7

Prentice-Hall International (UK) Limited, *London*
Prentice-Hall of Australia Pty. Limited, *Sydney*
Prentice-Hall Canada Inc., *Toronto*
Prentice-Hall Hispanoamericana, S.A., *Mexico*
Prentice-Hall of India Private Limited, *New Delhi*
Prentice-Hall of Japan, Inc., *Tokyo*
Pearson Education Asia Pte. Ltd.
Editora Prentice-Hall do Brasil, Ltda., *Rio de Janeiro*

For Steve

Alex Morrison

To my daughter, Kirsten, and my parents,
Albert and Hilde Rischert

Alice Rischert

CONTENTS

From the Editor		**xiii**
Foreword		**xv**
Preface		**xix**
Acknowledgments		**xxiii**
About the Authors		**xxv**

Chapter 1 SQL and Data		**1**
LAB 1.1 Data, Databases, and the Definition of SQL		2
	1.1.1 Identify and Group Data	3
	1.1.2 Define a Database and Its Use	3
	1.1.3 Define SQL	3
LAB 1.2 A Case Study Schema Diagram		9
	1.2.1 Define a Schema	11
	1.2.2 Identify a Table and Its Columns	11
	1.2.3 Identify Primary Keys and Foreign Keys	11
LAB 1.3 Referential Integrity and Table Relationships		15
	1.3.1 Define Referential Integrity	17
	1.3.2 Identify Table Relationships	17
LAB 1.4 The SQL*PLUS Environment		20
	1.4.1 Identify Oracle's Client/Server Software	21
	1.4.2 Login and Logout of SQL*Plus	21
CHAPTER 1 Test Your Thinking		26

Chapter 2 SQL: The Basics		**27**
LAB 2.1 The Anatomy of a SELECT Statement		28
	2.1.1 Write a SQL SELECT Statement	32
	2.1.2 Use DISTINCT in a SQL Statement	32
LAB 2.2 Editing a SQL Statement		38
	2.2.1 Edit a SQL Statement Using SQL*Plus Commands	41
	2.2.2 Edit a SQL Statement Using an Editor	41
LAB 2.3 The WHERE Clause: Comparison and Logical Operators		46
	2.3.1 Use Comparison and Logical Operators in a WHERE Clause	53

2.3.2 Use NULL in a WHERE Clause 53

LAB 2.4 The ORDER BY Clause 58
2.4.1 Custom Sort Query Results 59

CHAPTER 2 Test Your Thinking 63

Chapter 3 Character and Number Functions **65**

LAB 3.1 Character Functions 66
3.1.1 Use a Character Function in a SQL Statement 74
3.1.2 Concatenate Strings 75

LAB 3.2 Number Functions 83
3.2.1 Use Number Functions and Perform
Mathematical Computations 87

CHAPTER 3 Test Your Thinking 90

Chapter 4 Date and Conversion Functions **91**

LAB 4.1 Converting from One Datatype to Another 92
4.1.1 Convert from a NUMBER to a CHAR
Datatype and Vice Versa 94
4.1.2 Format Data 95

LAB 4.2 Applying Oracle's Date Format Models 98
4.2.1 Compare a Text Literal to a DATE Column 100
4.2.2 Apply Format Models 100

LAB 4.3 Performing Date and Time Math 110
4.3.1 Understand the SYSDATE Function
and Perform Date Arithmetic 113

LAB 4.4 The NVL and DECODE Functions 116
4.4.1 Replace NULL Values with the NVL Function 119
4.4.2 Utilize the Power of DECODE 119

CHAPTER 4 Test Your Thinking 125

**Chapter 5 Aggregate Functions,
GROUP BY, and HAVING** **127**

LAB 5.1 Aggregate Functions 128
5.1.1 Use Aggregate Functions in a SQL Statement 131

LAB 5.2 The GROUP BY and HAVING Clauses 135
5.2.1 Use the GROUP BY and HAVING Clauses 139

CHAPTER 5 Test Your Thinking 145

Chapter 6 Equijoins **147**

LAB 6.1 The Two Table Join 148

6.1.1 Write Simple Join Constructs 154
6.1.2 Narrow Down Your Result Set 154
6.1.3 Understand the Cartesian Product 155
LAB 6.2 Joining More Than Two Tables 163
6.2.1 Join More Than Two Tables 167
6.2.2 Join with Multicolumn Join Criteria 168
CHAPTER 6 Test Your Thinking 179

Chapter 7 Subqueries **181**

LAB 7.1 Simple Subqueries 182
7.1.1 Write Subqueries in the WHERE
and HAVING Clauses 188
7.1.2 Write Subqueries Returning Multiple Rows 189
7.1.3 Write Subqueries Returning Multiple Columns 190
LAB 7.2 Correlated Subqueries 198
7.2.1 Write Correlated Subqueries 204
7.2.2 Write Correlated Subqueries Using
the EXISTS and NOT EXISTS Operators 204
LAB 7.3 ANY, SOME, and ALL Operators in Subqueries 213
7.3.1 Use the ANY, SOME, and ALL
Operators in Subqueries 216
CHAPTER 7 Test Your Thinking 222

Chapter 8 Set Operators **223**

LAB 8.1 The Power of UNION and UNION ALL 224
8.1.1 Use the UNION and UNION ALL Set
Operators 227
LAB 8.2 The MINUS and INTERSECT Set Operators 233
8.2.1 Use the MINUS Set Operator 237
8.2.2 Use the INTERSECT Set Operator 238
CHAPTER 8 Test Your Thinking 242

Chapter 9 Complex Joins **243**

LAB 9.1 Outer Joins 244
9.1.1 Write Outer Joins with Two Tables 246
9.1.2 Write Outer Joins with Three Tables 247
LAB 9.2 Self-Joins 258
9.2.1 Write Self-Joins and Detect Data
Inconsistencies 259
CHAPTER 9 Test Your Thinking 266

Chapter 10 Insert, Update, and Delete   267

LAB 10.1 Manipulating Data and Transaction Control   268
      10.1.1 Insert Data   277
      10.1.2 Update Data   278
      10.1.3 Delete Data   279

CHAPTER 10 Test Your Thinking   288

Chapter 11 Create, Alter, and Drop Tables   289

LAB 11.1 Creating and Dropping Tables   290
      11.1.1 Create and Drop Tables   297
      11.1.2 Create Constraints   298

LAB 11.2 Altering Tables and Manipulating Constraints   306
      11.2.1 Alter Tables and Manipulate Constraints   312

CHAPTER 11 Test Your Thinking   320

Chapter 12 Views, Indexes, and Sequences   321

LAB 12.1 Creating and Modifying Views   322
      12.1.1 Create, Alter, and Drop Views   324
      12.1.2 Understand the Data Manipulation
            Rules for Views   325

LAB 12.2 Indexes   335
      12.2.1 Create B-Tree Indexes   338
      12.2.2 Understand When Indexes Are Useful   339

LAB 12.3 Sequences   347
      12.3.1 Create and Use Sequences   348

CHAPTER 12 Test Your Thinking   352

Chapter 13 The Data Dictionary
and Dynamic SQL Scripts   353

LAB 13.1 The Oracle Data Dictionary Views   354
      13.1.1 Query the Data Dictionary   357

LAB 13.2 Dynamic SQL Scripts   370
      13.2.1 Write Dynamic SQL Statements   372
      13.2.2 Write Dynamic SQL Scripts   374

CHAPTER 13 Test Your Thinking   390

Chapter 14 Security   391

LAB 14.1 Users, Privileges, Roles, and Synonyms   392
    14.1.1 Create Users, and Grant and Revoke
        Privileges   401
    14.1.2 Create and Use Synonyms   403
    14.1.3 Create User-Defined Roles   403
CHAPTER 14 Test Your Thinking   412

Chapter 15 Advanced SQL Queries   413

LAB 15.1 DECODE Magic and In-line Views   414
    15.1.1 Transpose a Result Set Using
        the DECODE Function   421
    15.1.2 Understand the Danger of Aggregate Functions
        and Write In-line Views   421
LAB 15.2 Hierarchical Queries   429
    15.2.1 Restrict the Result Set in Hierarchical
        Queries   432
    15.2.2 Move Up and Down the Hierarchy Tree   433
CHAPTER 15 Test Your Thinking   441

Chapter 16 SQL Optimization   443

LAB 16.1 The Oracle Optimizer and Writing
  Effective SQL Statements   444
    16.1.1 Analyze Tables and Indexes   453
    16.1.2 Read the Explain Plan   453
    16.1.3 Understand Join Operations
        and Alternate SQL Statements   455
CHAPTER 16 Test Your Thinking   471

Appendix A Answers to Self-Review Questions   473

Appendix B SQL Formatting Guide and SQL*Plus Command Reference   487

Appendix C Student Database Schema   497

Index   507

FROM THE EDITOR

Prentice Hall's Interactive Workbooks are designed to get you up and running fast, with just the information you need, when you need it.

We are certain that you will find our unique approach to learning simple and straightforward. Every chapter of every Interactive Workbook begins with a list of clearly defined Learning Objectives. A series of labs make up the heart of each chapter. Each lab is designed to teach you specific skills in the form of exercises. You perform these exercises at your computer and answer pointed questions about what you observe. Your answers will lead to further discussion and exploration. Each lab then ends with multiple-choice Self-Review Questions, to reinforce what you've learned. Finally, we have included Test Your Thinking projects at the end of each chapter. These projects challenge you to synthesize all of the skills you've acquired in the chapter.

Our goal is to make learning engaging, and to make you a more productive learner.

And you are not alone. Each book is integrated with its own "Companion Web site." The Web site is a place where you can find more detailed information about the concepts discussed in the Workbook, additional Self-Review Questions to further refine your understanding of the material, and perhaps most importantly, where you can find a community of other Interactive Workbook users working to acquire the same set of skills that you are.

All of the Companion Web sites for our Interactive Workbooks can be found at http://www.phptr.com/phptrinteractive.

Timothy C. Moore
V.P., Executive Editor
Prentice Hall PTR

FOREWORD

THE ANCIENT PROBLEM

The year was 1680 AD; the place was the Levant—the eastern shores of the Mediterranean. The political climate was stable enough to allow peaceful trade among nations and the seaports were bustling with merchants who were making profits by expanding their markets outside of their country of origin. They met many challenges in the travel itself, as well as in adapting to other cultures and customs. A major obstacle was communication. How can you sell something if you cannot extol its virtues to your potential customer? Sign language and written language can be quite effective, but are not nearly as personal and understandable as the spoken word. The problem with spoken language in a situation like this is that there are many languages to master. As a seller of goods, your best chance for top sales is to people whose language you know. This was the problem in 1680 AD.

The solution that emerged from this problem in the classical world was one that has been used by people of many lands throughout history. This solution was to use a common language when gathered in a multicultural environment. In the Levant, the language that developed was a combination of Italian, Spanish, French, Greek, Arabic, and Turkish. This language, called *lingua franca*, became a standard in many ports as merchants used it to successfully communicate with their customers and fellow traders. Those who learned and mastered this language became the most effective and successful business people.

THE MODERN-DAY PROBLEM

In today's information technology industry, we face a similar situation. Companies are solving their data management requirements using relational and object-relational databases. Businesses have found these databases to offer the best features and most robust environments. The challenges that companies are facing when using databases are mainly in creating flexible and efficient human interfaces. Customized application development takes much in the way of effort and resources if it is to properly address the requirements of the particular business.

IT professionals who are tasked with creating modern database systems must rely on their training and expertise, both in designing the proper database storage objects and in programming the most efficient application programs. In the recent past, relational and object-relational developers have used procedural programming languages such as COBOL, Fortran, and C to create the programs that access the data. Regardless of the procedural language used, there is an additional language embedded in these procedural programs. This language offers a standard way to define and manipulate the data structures in a relational or object-relational database. It is the lingua franca of database technology—Structured Query Language (SQL). Using SQL, all database developers can create commonly recognized programs for their applications. A standard language means that the written code is commonly recognized and can be easily supported and enhanced. This is the promise of SQL, and this promise has been fulfilled successfully for decades in countless relational database applications.

Therefore, the problem today is not that there is no common language, as was the case in ancient times before lingua franca. The problem today is in the assimilation of the language and its proper use. As the computer industry continues its logarithmic growth, the number of application developers increases similarly. Each new developer that comes into contact with a relational database must be trained in the lingua franca used to access it. In the recent past, with a smaller number of new developers, this was a manageable feat. When a new developer was in training, she or he would learn both a procedural programming language and the database language embedded in it—SQL.

Today, the trend is toward object orientation. Object-oriented analysis, design, and programming has come of age and, according to popular opinion, is now the best way to create computer systems. This means that C++ and Java, which are object-oriented languages, are replacing the traditional procedural languages as the choice for building new systems. This is merely a shift in the main programming language that the developer uses to interface with the user. The core database language, SQL, is still required and of key importance.

However, something has gotten lost in this paradigm shift to object orientation. That something is a solid background in SQL. There are many reasons for this, but the problem persists despite the reasons. IT management professionals everywhere are employing Java programmers who do not have a good grasp of the SQL language. This arrangement works up to a point, but there is, eventually, a collision with a brick wall. In many situations, this consultant has had to break into the SQL code used in a Java program only to find inefficient or incorrect use of the SQL language. Misunderstanding or misuse of the SQL language can have adverse effects on the program's efficiency and, without proper testing, can adversely affect production data systems, many of which are critical to the functioning of the business.

THE MODERN-DAY SOLUTION

The solution to the problem of misunderstanding the lingua franca of databases is simple—an increased focus on learning the abilities of SQL and the correct methods for coding SQL programs. Time and money spent in training on the basics are time and money well spent. There are many ways to learn a subject like SQL. In this writer's experience of over 17 years as a trainer in the IT and other industries, the best learning experience comes from a multifaceted approach. Human beings learn in different ways, and using different approaches to present the same subject ensures that the subject will be mastered. In addition, the repetition of concepts and material in different formats ensures a thorough understanding of the subject.

What Ms. Morrison and Ms. Rischert have accomplished in this book is the epitome of the solution for the misunderstanding of SQL. This book will be useful for seasoned IT professionals who need a refresher on the concepts and thought processes of using SQL, as well as for those who are new to the subject and want to learn it in the right way.

The multifaceted approach that the authors use allows the student of the subject to totally master the basics as well as the best ways to use the language. All core SQL subjects are treated with this approach, which includes a brief description of the concept followed by simple and easy-to-grasp examples. Examples make the concepts real and allow the reader to quickly master the subject.

The very best way to learn the concepts of any new technology is to be tasked with an application development project that uses that technology. However, a project in the real-world work place is not the right place to learn as the stakes are high and the pressure too great. This book gives you a taste of real-world application development needs and processes by assigning a series of labs in each chapter to apply the knowledge gained by the conceptual discussion and examples. The book then provides the solutions to these problems so that you can check your work. Proper use of these sections will lead you to a solid mastery of the language and give you the ability to use this lingua franca successfully to solve real-world business data problems. This type of mastery will serve you well in whatever type of database programming environment you find yourself.

Peter Koletzke
Millennia Vision Corporation
Redwood Shores, CA
February 2000

PREFACE

WHO THIS BOOK IS FOR

The SQL language is the de facto standard language for relational databases. Oracle's database server is the leading relational database on the market today. This book is intended for anyone requiring a background in Oracle's implementation of the SQL language.

The book's exercises build knowledge step by step by introducing you to relational database concepts, the SQL*Plus environment, and the SQL language. Learning involves not just reading about a subject, but also doing it. The book's focus is to give the reader examples of how the SQL language is commonly used, with many exercises reinforcing the learning experience.

Unlike other SQL books, this book is not a reference book. Rather, its emphasis is on the exercises and the learning-by-doing experience. The best way to learn the SQL language is to perform the exercises and compare your answers with the sample answers and accompanying explanations.

HOW THIS BOOK IS ORGANIZED

Each chapter of the book is divided into labs covering a particular topic. The objective of each lab is defined at its beginning, with brief examples that introduce the reader to the covered concepts.

Following the lab's introductory examples are exercises that are the heart of the lab which reinforce and expand the reader's knowledge of the subject.

Each exercise consists of a series of steps to follow to perform specific tasks, or particular questions that are designed to help you discover the important aspects of the SQL language. The answers to these questions are given at the end of the exercises, along with more in-depth discussion of the concepts explored.

After you perform the exercises and compare the answers with the sample queries, answers, and explanations, the lab ends with multiple-choice

Self-Review questions. These are meant to test that you have understood the material covered in the lab. The answers to these questions appear in Appendix A. There are additional Self-Review questions at this book's companion Web site, found at `http://www.phptr.com/Morrison`.

At the end of each chapter, the Test Your Thinking section reinforces the topics learned in labs, and solidifies your skills. The answers to these questions can also be found on the companion Web site for this book.

LAYOUT OF A CHAPTER

Chapter
 Lab
  Exercises
  Exercise Answers with detailed discussion
  Self-Review Questions
 Lab
  Exercises
  Exercise Answers with detailed discussion
  Self-Review Questions
 Test Your Thinking Questions

 The chapters should be completed in sequence because concepts covered in earlier chapters are required for the completion of exercises in later chapters.

ABOUT THE COMPANION WEB SITE

The companion Web site is located at

`http://www.phptr.com/Morrison`

Here you will find three very important things:

1. Installation files you need before you begin reading the workbook.
2. Answers to the Test Your Thinking questions.
3. Additional Self-Review questions.

INSTALLATION FILES

All of the exercises and questions are based on a sample schema called STUDENT. The files required to install this STUDENT schema and the installation instructions can be downloaded from the Web site.

TEST YOUR THINKING

The answers to the Test Your Thinking sections are also found at the Web site. These answers will be textual or in the form of downloadable files.

ADDITIONAL SELF-REVIEW QUESTIONS

The Web site will have many other features, such as additional Self-Review questions, a message board, and periodically updated information about the book.

Visit the companion Web site and download the required files before starting the labs and exercises.

WHAT YOU'LL NEED

To complete the exercises you need the following:

The Oracle® database software

Oracle's SQL*Plus software

Access to the WWW and installation files from the companion Web site

ORACLE8 Oracle8 is Oracle's relational database software and its flagship product. You can use either Oracle Personal Edition or Oracle Enterprise Edition. Oracle 8.1.5 Enterprise Edition was used to create the exercises for this book, but subsequent versions should be compatible.

ACCESS TO THE WWW You will need access to the Internet and the WWW so that you can access the companion Web site.

```
http://www.phptr.com/Morrison
```

Here you will find files that are necessary to install the sample STUDENT schema.

ABOUT THE STUDENT SCHEMA

Throughout this workbook, you access data from a sample schema called STUDENT, which contains information about a computer education program. The schema was designed to record data about instructors, courses, students, and their respective enrollments and grades.

After you download the installation files to transfer the schema into your Oracle database, you will be able to follow the exercises in the workbook. In Chapter 1, "SQL and Data," you are introduced to the relational concepts necessary to read the schema diagram. Appendix C, "Student Database Schema," shows you a graphical representation of the schema and useful descriptive information about each table and column.

CONVENTIONS USED IN THIS BOOK

There are several conventions used in this book to make your learning experience easier. These are explained here.

 This icon denotes advice and useful information about a particular topic or concept from the authors to you, the reader.

 This icon flags tips that are especially helpful tricks that will save you time or trouble, for instance, a shortcut for performing a particular task or a method that the authors have found useful.

 Computers are delicate creatures and can be easily damaged. Likewise, they can be dangerous to work on if you're not careful. This icon flags information and precautions that not only save you headaches in the long run, but may even save you or your computer from harm.

Passages referring to the book's companion Web site are flagged with this icon. The companion Web site once again is located at:

    http://www.phptr.com/Morrison

ACKNOWLEDGMENTS

First and foremost, I would like to thank the entire Prentice Hall/PTR team for helping to pull this book together, in particular, Ralph Moore with his endless patience and encouragement in the early writing of this book; Russ Hall who picked up where Ralph left off, carrying on in the same steady, jovial manner; Tim Moore as Acquisitions Editor and chief taskmaster; Pete Cassidy as Technical Editor; and Jan Schwartz, Production Editor, for explaining—over and over again—how the whole process works.

Second, I'd like to thank my many colleagues who are wise and learned in the ways of Oracle and SQL, particularly Potter Palmer, without whose faith in me I would never have undertaken this project. Also, thanks to Christine Moran and Wayne Henry for their helpful comments after working through the exercises in the early chapters of the book.

Third, I'd like to thank the other authors in the Oracle Interactive Workbook series, all of whom deserve equal credit for bringing the entire series to fruition. I'm particularly indebted to Douglas Scherer for the opportunity to crowd my life with yet another project, and to my co-author, Alice Rischert, for being the unceasing perfectionist.

Fourth, there are numerous people in my life that make a big difference every day—they know who they are. Among them are my mother, father, sister, and brother, and Angela Vance who has seen me come so far.

And last but hardly least, there is Steve who is so many things to me, more than he will ever know, and who knew more about why I should co-author this book than I did. I'm glad I listened to him.

Alex Morrison

This book would not have been possible without encouragement and support from a number of individuals.

I am very grateful to my co-chair of Columbia University's database track, colleague and friend, Douglas Scherer, for inviting me to write this book. Peter Koletzke, co-author of the *Oracle Designer Handbook* and *Oracle Developer Advanced Forms and Reports,* has been a wonderful friend, instructor, and supporter for so many years. My co-author, Alex Morrison, provided many valuable comments and edits that significantly improved the initial drafts of the book. Despite many out-of-town trips, vacations, and, finally, a broken leg, Alex pulled through to see this book completed.

Thanks also to Russ Hall, the Prentice Hall Development Editor whose humor and encouragement kept my spirits up, despite constant deadlines looming over my head, and to Ralph Moore, the initial Development Editor on the project, who crafted the style and provided the help to get this project off the ground. Tim Moore, Acquisitions Editor at Prentice Hall, and Jan Schwartz, Production Editor, were instrumental in getting this book out on time. Pete Cassidy, the Technical Editor, provided a number of useful suggestions and valuable feedback, despite his demanding travel schedule. Thanks also to Sol Morse for reading some of the initial chapters.

Many of my students, my colleagues at Columbia University, and at XWare, Inc. have unwittingly contributed to this book. Their questions, problems, and challenges provided the framework for some of the material. Thanks also to Lonnie Blackwood for allowing me to take the necessary time off to finish this book.

Espie Lising, Trisha Choi, Balo Garcia, Dr. Raymond Garcia, and Marisue Rodriguez have given me invaluable support and inspiration over the last few years. My parents, sisters Irene and Christa, and my brother Guenter deserve a great deal of thanks for all their support, advice, and encouragement. Finally, I owe most of my thanks to my daughter, Kirsten, for going to bed early—without too many complaints, and for interrupting me whenever she thought I needed a break.

Alice Rischert

ABOUT THE AUTHORS

Alex Morrison

Alex Morrison's computing career began with the Arts & Entertainment Cable Network. She attended Columbia University's CTA program, earning a certificate in Relational Database and Structured Design, later returning to teach SQL. She has since worked for various consulting companies as a systems analyst, team leader, and project manager, helping to build international financial systems in the U.S., Canada, and South America. Currently she applies her extensive knowledge of Oracle SQL and project management in the world of Internet development at Concrete Media in New York City.

She lives in Greenwich Village with her partner, Steve, and the occasional cockroach.

Alice Rischert

Alice Rischert is the co-chair of Columbia University's Database Application Development and Design track at the Computer Technology and Application program, where she also teaches classes in Oracle SQL, PL/SQL, and database design. She currently consults on data warehouse and Internet/intranet projects. Ms. Rischert has worked as product manager, database administrator, project manager, and data architect for a number of companies in the U.S., Europe, and Asia. Ms. Rischert has also been a presenter at Oracle conferences on SQL and PL/SQL topics. She holds an MBA from Pforzheim University, Germany.

C H A P T E R   1

SQL AND DATA

CHAPTER OBJECTIVES

In this chapter, you will learn about:

- ✔ Data, Databases, and the Definition of SQL — Page 2
- ✔ A Case Study Schema Diagram — Page 9
- ✔ Referential Integrity and Table Relationships — Page 15
- ✔ The SQL*Plus Environment — Page 20

What is SQL? SQL (pronounced *sequel*) is an acronym for *Structured Query Language,* a standardized language used to access and manipulate data. Before you begin to use SQL, however, you must learn about data and how it is designed and organized for use in a database. You will then learn how to use SQL to access that data.

Organizing data into a *schema diagram* is necessary for good software development. Before you begin to write SQL, it is important you first understand the components of a schema diagram.

Also in this chapter, you will be introduced to Oracle's SQL*Plus tool, which gives you access to the Oracle database. After you have performed the exercises in this chapter, you will have a good grasp of the basics of data, databases, database design, and SQL*Plus, and you will be well on your way to unleashing the power of your Oracle database.

L A B   1 . 1

DATA, DATABASES, AND THE DEFINITION OF SQL

LAB OBJECTIVES

After this lab, you will be able to:

✔ Identify and Group Data
✔ Define a Database and Its Use
✔ Define SQL

Data is all around you—you make use of it every day. Your hair may be brown; your flight leaves from gate K10; you try to get up in the morning at 6:30 A.M. Storing this data in related groups and making the connections among them are what databases are all about.

A database is a collection of grouped data that can be shared among users. For example, database systems organize and maintain patient data in a hospital, bank accounts in a bank, or inventory in a warehouse. A Database Management System (DBMS) is software that organizes the data in a meaningful way. Among its functions are controlling access to data, managing one or more concurrent users, and providing security. A Relational Database Management System (RDBMS) provides all of this functionality. In addition, it organizes groups of data into *tables,* and each table consists of *columns* and *rows.* These columns and rows are specifically designed to uniquely identify rows and eliminate duplication of data, providing the power of the relational database.

SQL is used to communicate specifically with a relational database. It is an industry-wide standard, based on rules developed in the 1970's by IBM's E.F. Codd, making it portable across all relational database products on the market today. It is an interactive language that comes in three flavors: DML, or data manipulation language; DDL, or data definition language; and DCL, or data control language. DML, DDL, and DCL commands help a user query, manipulate, define, and control the data in a RDBMS.

LAB 1.1 EXERCISES

1.1.1 IDENTIFY AND GROUP DATA

a) Give three examples of types of data.

_____

_____

b) What groupings of data do you use in your daily life?

_____

_____

1.1.2 DEFINE A DATABASE AND ITS USE

a) Give an example of a database system you use outside of the workplace, and explain how it helps you.

_____

_____

b) How is data organized in a relational database?

_____

_____

1.1.3 DEFINE SQL

a) What is SQL and why is it useful?

_____

_____

The following two questions will pose a challenge to anyone not yet familiar with SQL. For question b, think about what the command on the left is trying to accomplish.

b) Try to match each of the SQL commands on the left with a verb from the list on the right.

1. CREATE   _____   a. manipulate
2. INSERT   _____   b. define
3. GRANT   _____   c. control

_____

_____

c) Why do you think it is important to control access to data in a database?

_____

_____

LAB 1.1 EXERCISE ANSWERS

1.1.1   ANSWERS

a)   Give three examples of types of data.

Answer: The answer to this question will vary depending on your choices.

A circle, square, and triangle are all data about geometrical shapes. Your mother, father, and sister is data about your immediate family members. Fiction, comedy, cookbook, and computer are all data about types of books.

b)   What groupings of data do you use in your daily life?

Answer: The answer to this question will vary depending on your situation.

I use my address book daily. It contains addresses and phone numbers of friends and relatives. I also keep a running to-do list of tasks at work, which groups together the tasks I have completed, as well as separately grouping those tasks I have yet to do.

When grouping data, each piece of data should be related to the others. A person's physical appearance is typically described by more than just brown hair; they may also have green eyes, be six feet tall, and be of the female sex. In my address book, I group together a person's name, their address, and telephone number. I may keep a separate address book for my business contacts that would group together the person's name, company name, work telephone number, fax number, and e-mail address.

1.1.2 ANSWERS

a) Give an example of a database system you use outside of the workplace, and explain how it helps you.

Answer: The answer to this question will vary depending on your situation.

When I'm in a record store, I often use a computerized information kiosk to search for information about an album, such as where it is located in the store. Another example is an ATM machine, where I can inquire about my account balance.

b) How Is data organized in a relational database?

Answer: Data is organized by placing like pieces of information together in a table, organized into columns and rows.

■ FOR EXAMPLE

The data found in a library is typically organized in several ways to facilitate finding a book. Searching for a book by title might yield the following excerpt of data:

Title	Author	ISBN#	Genre	Location_ID
Computer's Life, A	Jeff Smith	0-11-124456-2	Computer	D11
Desk Work	Robert Jones	0-11-223754-3	Fiction	H24
Let's Go to the Beach	Mark Porter	0-11-922256-8	Juvenile	J3
From Here to There	Gary Mills	0-11-423356-5	Fiction	H24

This group of information contains data specific to books. The data is organized into columns and rows; the columns represent a type of data (title vs. genre), while the rows contain data. A table in a database is organized the same way. You might call this table book as it contains information related to books only. Each intersection of a column and row in a table represents a value. Searching for a book by location might yield this excerpt of data:

Location_ID	Floor	Section	Shelf
D11	1	3	1
H24	2	2	3
J3	3	1	1

This set of columns and rows represents another database table called location, with information specific to locations in a library. The advantage to storing information about books and their locations separately is that information is not repeated unnecessarily, and maintenance of the data is much easier.

For instance, two books have the same location_id, H24. If the floor, section, and shelf information were also stored in the book table, this information would be repeated for each of the two book rows. If the floor of location_id H24 changes, both of the rows in book would have to change. Instead, by storing the location information separately, the floor information only has to change once in the location table.

The two tables have a common column between them, namely location_id. In a relational database, SQL can be used to query information from more than one table at a time, making use of the common column they contain by performing a *join*. The join allows you to query both the book and location tables to return a list of books listing the floors, sections, and shelves where they are located. You will learn how to write joins in Chapter 6, "Equijoins."

Each of these columns contains a different kind of data, which can be classified by a *datatype*. For instance, values in the location_id column of the location table contain both letters and numbers, also called *alphanumeric* data, and could be stored in a column of datatype VARCHAR2(10). This means up to 10 alphanumeric characters (letters or numbers) may be stored in this column. Another datatype, the CHAR datatype, also stores alphanumeric data, but is a fixed-length datatype and pads any unused space in the column with blanks until it reaches the defined column length.

The floor, section, and shelf columns all contain numbers, and could be stored as either a NUMBER or VARCHAR2 datatype. Oracle also provides a DATE datatype, which stores both the date and time.

The SQL language is sanctioned by ANSI, an acronym for the American National Standards Institute. ANSI determines standards on all aspects of the SQL language, including datatypes. However, most relational database products, including Oracle, have their own extensions to the ANSI standard, providing additional functionality within their respective products by further extending the use of SQL.

1.1.3 ANSWERS

a) What is SQL and why is it useful?

Answer: SQL is a standardized relational database access language. It is useful because it allows a user to query, manipulate, define, and control data in a RDBMS.

b) Try to match each of the SQL commands on the left with a verb from the list on the right:

Answer: The following shows how these commands match with the appropriate verb:

1. CREATE	__b__	a. manipulate
2. INSERT	__a__	b. define
3. GRANT	__c__	c. control

DML (data manipulation language) is used to *manipulate* data, with the SELECT, INSERT, UPDATE, and DELETE commands. DDL (data definition language) is used to *define* objects such as tables with the CREATE, ALTER, and DROP commands. DCL (data control language) is used to *control* access privileges in a RDBMS, such as with the commands GRANT and REVOKE to give or remove privileges. These SQL commands are written and executed against the database using a software program. In this workbook, Oracle's SQL*Plus program is used to communicate these commands to the RDBMS. The use of SQL*Plus and SQL commands will be covered in Lab 1.4 and subsequent chapters.

c) Why do you think it is important to control access to data in a database?

Answer: Data can contain sensitive information to which some users should have limited access privileges. Some users may be allowed to query certain data but not change it, while others are allowed to add data to a database, but not delete it. By controlling access to data, the security of the data is assured for all users.

LAB 1.1 SELF-REVIEW QUESTIONS

In order to test your progress, you should be able to answer the following questions.

1)   A university's listing of students and the classes they are enrolled in is an example of a database system.
     a) _____ True
     b) _____ False

2)   A table contains both columns and rows.
     a) _____ True
     b) _____ False

3)   SQL is software that interacts with a relational database.
     a) _____ True
     b) _____ False

4)   More than one user cannot be connected to a database at the same time.
     a) _____ True
     b) _____ False

Quiz answers appear in Appendix A, Section 1.1.

L A B   1 . 2

A CASE STUDY SCHEMA DIAGRAM

LAB OBJECTIVES

After this lab, you will be able to:

✔   Define a Schema
✔   Identify a Table and Its Columns
✔   Identify Primary Keys and Foreign Keys

Throughout this series of Oracle Interactive Workbooks, the database for a school's computer education program is used as a case study upon which all exercises are based. The *schema diagram* is a model of data that reflects a business, depicting the relationships among data in a database. The name of the case study schema diagram is Student. Please see Appendix C, "Student Database Schema," for a graphical representation of the schema diagram.

TABLES AND COLUMNS

The schema diagram depicts the design of a relational database that contains data about the computer education program. Each box in the diagram represents a *table* in the database, and each table has a name at the top, namely STUDENT, SECTION, and INSTRUCTOR, which identifies each as containing the student, section, and instructor data, respectively.

A table name must be unique within a database schema, should not be abbreviated, cannot have spaces in it, and should describe the nature of the data contained within it.

Each table contains a list of columns. There is always at least one, and usually many more, columns in a table. Columns tell you what pieces of data are stored in each table. The order of the columns is unimportant because SQL allows you to display data in any order you choose. A column name must be unique within a table. The name should also accurately describe the nature of the data it contains. By default, Oracle creates table and column names in upper case and does not allow spaces.

Next to each column there are different symbols. These symbols were drawn by the software tool that produced this schema diagram. There are other software programs that produce schema diagrams, each using its own notation, so you will see different symbols outside of this workbook.

NULL VERSUS NOT NULL

The circle (O) symbol on the schema diagram indicates a column may allow NULL values. A NULL value is an unknown value. A space or value of zero is not the same as NULL. When a column in a row is defined as allowing NULL values, it means a NULL value in that column in any row of the table is acceptable. The asterisk (*) on the schema diagram indicates a column is defined as NOT NULL, and therefore must always contain a value.

THE PRIMARY KEY

The hash (#) symbol denotes a table's *primary key*. For example, the student_id column in the student table is the primary key of the table. Every value in the student_id column is unique; no duplicates are allowed. A primary key is a column, or combination of columns, which uniquely identifies a row in a table, and cannot be NULL. Oracle does not require that every table have a primary key, and there may be cases where it is not appropriate to have one. However, it is strongly recommended that most tables have a primary key. Also, a table can have only one primary key, consisting of one or more columns.

THE FOREIGN KEY

A table may also have zero, one or more *foreign keys*. A foreign key is defined as being a column, or columns, in the *child* table. This column refers back to the primary key of another table, referred to as the *parent* table. The parent table may even be the same table as the child table. These two tables, or sometimes one table, are said to have a *parent–child relationship*.

LAB 1.2 EXERCISES

1.2.1 DEFINE A SCHEMA

LAB
1.2

a) What does the Student schema diagram represent?

_____

_____

b) Does the Student schema tell you where a student lives? Explain.

_____

_____

1.2.2 IDENTIFY A TABLE AND ITS COLUMNS

a) What are three common elements of relational tables?

_____

_____

b) What four columns are common to all tables in the Student schema diagram?

_____

_____

1.2.3 IDENTIFY PRIMARY KEYS AND FOREIGN KEYS

a) What is the primary key of the course table?

_____

_____

b) How many primary keys does the enrollment table have? Name the column(s).

_____

_____

c) How many foreign keys does the section table have?

_____

_____

d) What are a primary key's identifying characteristics?

_____

_____

LAB 1.2 EXERCISE ANSWERS

1.2.1 ANSWERS

a) What does the Student schema diagram represent?

Answer: The Student schema diagram is a graphical representation of tables in a relational database.

A schema diagram is a useful tool during the software development life-cycle. Unabbreviated, English-like words should be used to name tables and columns so that anyone, whether developer or end-user, can look at a schema diagram and grasp the meaning of data, and the relationships among them, represented there. Developers study it to understand the design of a database, long before they put hands to keyboard to develop a system, and end-users use it to understand how their data is stored.

b) Does the Student schema tell you where a student lives? Explain.

Answer: No. The Student schema diagram tells you how data is organized in a relational database: the names of tables, the columns in those tables, and the relationship among them. It cannot tell you what actual data looks like.

You use the SQL language to interact with a relational database in order to view the data stored in tables.

1.2.2 ANSWERS

a) What are three common elements of relational tables?

Answer: A table has a name, which is unique within a database schema; a table has one or more columns; a table usually has a primary key.

b) What four columns are common to all tables in the Student schema diagram?

Answer: The four columns are created_by, created_date, modified_by, modified_date.

Database tables are often created with columns similar to these four to create an *audit trail*. These columns are designed to identify who first created or last modified a row of a table, and when the action occurred. You will learn how to fill in these values automatically by writing *triggers* in the *Oracle PL/SQL Interactive Workbook* (Benjamin Rosenzweig and Elena Silvestrova; Prentice Hall, 2000).

1.2.3 ANSWERS

a) What is the primary key of the course table?

Answer: The primary key of the course table is the column course_no.

b) How many primary keys does the enrollment table have? Name the column(s).

Answer: A table can have only one primary key. The primary key of the enrollment table consists of the two columns student_id and section_id.

As mentioned earlier, a primary key uniquely identifies a single row in a table. In the case of the enrollment table, two columns uniquely identify a row. This is referred to as a *composite* or *concatenated* primary key. There is one primary key on the enrollment table, but it consists of two columns.

c) How many foreign keys does the section table have?

Answer: Two. The foreign keys of the section table are course_no and instructor_id.

Note, the primary key of the section table is a single column, namely section_id. Two of the columns in the table, course_no and section_no, also uniquely identify a row, but section_id has been created instead. This column is called a *synthetic key* because it does not have any meaning to the user, and is not subject to updates. This replacement of the *natural pri-*

mary key with a synthetic key is a necessary database design technique to avoid primary keys that are subject to change.

d)   What are a primary key's identifying characteristics?

Answer: A primary key uniquely identifies a row in a table, and the column or columns of the primary key are defined as NOT NULL.

Notice that on the schema diagram the primary key in every table is denoted with a hash symbol. By default, the one or more columns comprising the primary key of a table cannot be null. All columns of a primary key must have values in order to maintain the rule of uniqueness.

LAB 1.2 SELF-REVIEW QUESTIONS

In order to test your progress, you should be able to answer the following questions.

1)   What role(s) does the student_id column play in the grade table? Check all that apply.
a) _____ Part of composite primary key
b) _____ Primary key
c) _____ Foreign key

2)   The grade_type table does not allow values to be NULL in any column.
a) _____ True
b) _____ False

3)   The number of columns in a table matches the number of rows in that table.
a) _____ True
b) _____ False

4)   The section table has no foreign key columns.
a) _____ True
b) _____ False

5)   A table can contain 10 million rows.
a) _____ True
b) _____ False

6)   A primary key may contain NULL values.
a) _____ True
b) _____ False

Quiz answers appear in Appendix A, Section 1.2.

L A B   1 . 3

REFERENTIAL INTEGRITY AND TABLE RELATIONSHIPS

LAB OBJECTIVES

After this lab, you will be able to:

✔   Define Referential Integrity
✔   Identify Table Relationships

As you learned in Lab 1.2, a primary key is important to uniquely identify a row in a table. You also learned about the relationship of foreign keys to primary keys, the glue that holds together relationships among tables in a relational database. This is referred to as *referential integrity*.

Referential integrity ensures that each value in a foreign key column of the child table links back to a matching primary key value in the parent table. The primary key values are the *domain* of values for the foreign key column. That is, the primary key values are the only acceptable values that may appear in the foreign key column in the other table. For example, the only acceptable values for the foreign key column zip of the student table are the available values of the primary key column zip in the zipcode table.

Referential integrity does not allow deletion in a parent table of a primary key value that exists in a child table as a foreign key value. This would create *orphan rows* in the child table.

The lines connecting tables on the schema diagram depict the *table relationships* in the database. For instance, in the schema diagram, the line leading from the course table ends at the section table with a *crow's feet* notation. The relationship between these tables is said to be a *one-to-many* relationship; one row in the course table may refer to one or many rows in the section table. This means a course can have zero, one, or more sections. (A section represents a specific class of a particular course, taught by a specific instructor, and students can only be enrolled in sections, not courses.) Conversely, every section must have a corresponding row in the course table.

Relationships between tables are based on *business rules*. In this case, the business rule is that a course can exist without a section, but a section cannot exist unless it is assigned to a course. All of the relationships on the schema diagram, except those labeled CRSE_CRSE_FK and INST_ZIP_FK, are considered *mandatory* relationships. This dictates that the foreign key columns in the child table must contain a value (must not be NULL) and that value must correspond to a row in the parent table via its primary key.

On the schema diagram the course table has a dotted line that starts and terminates at the course table. The first characteristic, that of the line being dotted, indicates the relationship is *optional*. An optional relationship means the columns making up the foreign key may either contain a value, or they may be NULL. The meaning in the case of the course table is a course may have a prerequisite. If it does, then the course that is the prerequisite must be a course already listed in the course table. Alternatively, the course may be a first semester course that does not have a prerequisite. In this case, the prerequisite column is NULL.

RECURSIVE RELATIONSHIP

Another characteristic, that of the line starting and ending at the same table, designates a *recursive relationship*, or a *self-referencing relationship*. As the term implies, a column in the course table refers back to another column in the same table. In this case, the prerequisite column refers back to the course_no column, which provides the domain of values for the prerequisite column. A prerequisite is only valid if it is a valid course number in the course table.

LAB 1.3 EXERCISES

1.3.1 DEFINE REFERENTIAL INTEGRITY

a) Will a foreign key column in a table accept any data value? Explain.

_____

_____

b) From what domain of values (what column in what table) do you think the prerequisite column of the course table gets its values?

_____

_____

1.3.2 IDENTIFY TABLE RELATIONSHIPS

a) Explain the relationship(s) the enrollment table has to other table(s).

_____

_____

b) If the relationship between the zipcode and student tables were optional, what would have to change in the student table?

_____

_____

LAB 1.3 EXERCISE ANSWERS

1.3.1 ANSWERS

a) Will a foreign key column in a table accept any data value? Explain.

Answer: No. A foreign key must use the values of the primary key it references as its domain of values.

b) From what domain of values (what column in what table) do you think the prerequisite column of the course table gets its values?

Answer: From the course_no column in the course table.

RECURSIVE RELATIONSHIP

As the term implies, a column in the course table refers back to another column in the table. In this case, the prerequisite column refers back to the course_no column, which provides the domain of values for the prerequisite column. A prerequisite is valid only if it is also a valid course number in the course table.

1.3.2 ANSWERS

a) Explain the relationship(s) the enrollment table has to other table(s).

Answer: The student table and the section table are the parent tables of the enrollment table. The relationship signifies a student may be enrolled in zero, one, or many sections. A particular student can be enrolled in a section only once, otherwise the unique combination of the two columns would be violated. The combination of these two foreign key columns represents the primary key of the enrollment table.

The enrollment table is also a parent table of the grade table. For each section a particular student may have zero, one, or multiple grades. The primary key columns of the enrollment table (student_id and section_id) are foreign keys in the grade table that become part of the grade table's composite primary key. This signifies you may have grades in the grade table only if you are enrolled, but it is possible not to have any grades for a particular section.

In some cases, the foreign keys become part of a table's primary key, as in the enrollment table. If a composite primary key contains many columns, a synthetic key may be created for simplicity.

b)   If the relationship between the zipcode and student tables were optional, what would have to change in the student table?

Answer: The foreign key column zip in the student table would have to be defined as allowing NULL values. It is currently defined as NOT NULL.

LAB 1.3 SELF-REVIEW QUESTIONS

In order to test your progress, you should be able to answer the following questions.

1)   If a table is a child table in three different one-to-many relationships, how many foreign key columns does it have?
a) _____ One
b) _____ Three
c) _____ Possibly more than three

2)   Referential integrity requires the relationship between foreign key and primary key to maintain values from the same domain.
a) _____ True
b) _____ False

3)   A foreign key may be NULL.
a) _____ True
b) _____ False

4)   Orphan rows are not allowed in the relational model.
a) _____ True
b) _____ False

Quiz answers appear in Appendix A, Section 1.3.

LAB 1.4

THE SQL*PLUS ENVIRONMENT

> ## LAB OBJECTIVES
>
> After this lab, you will be able to:
>
> ✔   Identify Oracle's Client/Server Software
> ✔   Login and Logout of SQL*Plus

Oracle's software runs in many different environments. The most common is the client/server environment, where one or more client computers communicate with one or more servers. In this type of environment, Oracle's SQL*Plus tool resides on a client computer; the Oracle RDBMS software resides on a server. Another piece of Oracle software, called SQL*Net, or Net8, depending on your version of Oracle, provides the standard communication protocol between the client and the server. SQL*Plus may also be run in a *standalone* environment where the client and database software reside on the same physical machine.

In the midst of all this software lies the SQL language. DDL, DML, or DCL commands are sent from the client software, also known as the *front end*, to the server, or *back end*. These commands send instructions to the server to tell it what services to provide. The server responds by sending back a *result* to the client, where it is displayed by the SQL*Plus software.

USER ID AND PASSWORD

SQL*Plus is the tool used throughout this workbook to communicate with the Oracle database. To connect to the database and communicate via SQL*Plus, you must have a user id that has been created for you. For the purposes of all examples in this workbook, you use the user id STUDENT and the password LEARN.

LAB 1.4 EXERCISES

1.4.1 IDENTIFY ORACLE'S CLIENT/SERVER SOFTWARE

a) Identify which piece of Oracle software is the client, which is the server, and how they communicate with each other.

_____

_____

b) What is the role of SQL between client and server?

_____

_____

1.4.2 LOGIN AND LOGOUT OF SQL*PLUS

a) Start SQL*Plus and type STUDENT in the User Name field on the Log On window. Click OK without entering a password. What happens?

_____

_____

b) Once you have logged in to SQL*Plus with the user id STUDENT and password LEARN, what information does SQL*Plus automatically provide you with?

_____

_____

c) What do you learn when you type DESCRIBE student?

_____

_____

d) Type the following command and describe what you see: SHOW SQLPROMPT.

_____

_____

e) Describe what happens when you type the command EXIT.

_____

_____

LAB 1.4 EXERCISE ANSWERS

1.4.1 ANSWERS

a) Identify which piece of Oracle software is the client, which is the server, and how they communicate with each other.

Answer: SQL*Plus is the client software and the Oracle RDBMS is the server software. In a client/server environment, SQL*Net or Net8 is the communication protocol.

b) What is the role of SQL between client and server?

Answer: SQL commands are issued from the client, telling the server to perform specific actions. The server sends back the results of those instructions to the client software, where they are displayed.

1.4.2 ANSWERS

a) Start SQL*Plus and type STUDENT in the User Name field on the Log On window. Click OK without typing a password. What happens?

Answer: SQL*Plus prompts you again to enter your password.

b) Once you have logged in to SQL*Plus with the user id STUDENT and password LEARN, what information does SQL*Plus automatically provide you with?

Answer: The version of SQL*Plus you are using; the current date and time; Oracle copyright information; the version of the Oracle database you are connected to; the version of PL/SQL you are using.

Now that you have logged into SQL*Plus, you have successfully established a connection with the Oracle database as the user STUDENT. The client and the server may now communicate with each other. Note that the user id and password are not case sensitive.

PL/SQL is another Oracle language addressed in a separate Interactive Workbook in this series—*Oracle PL/SQL Interactive Workbook* (Benjamin Rosenzweig and Elena Silvestrova; Prentice Hall, 2000).

c) What do you learn when you type DESCRIBE student and press Enter?

Answer: You find out about the structure of the student table, specifically its column names, whether those columns are nullable or not, and the datatype of each column.

To write SQL statements, you need to know a table's column names and their datatypes. The SQL*Plus DESCRIBE command displays this information.

Many SQL*Plus commands may be abbreviated. For instance, DESCRIBE may be shortened to DESC, and DEFINE may be shortened to DEF. Retype the command from Question c using this abbreviation, and compare the results.

SQL*Plus is not case sensitive; the user id, password, and SQL*Plus commands may all be entered in either upper or lowercase, or a combination of the two. Throughout this book, they are in upper case for easy identification. You will learn in the next chapter about formatting your SQL statements, and when it is appropriate to capitalize words.

d) Type the following command, press Enter, and describe what you see:
SHOW SQLPROMPT.

Answer: The sqlprompt "SQL>" is displayed back to you. It tells you the current "prompt" setting.

The SQL *prompt* is the symbol next to the cursor indicating you may begin to type. This is the default prompt for SQL*Plus. You may change the default prompt by using the SQL*Plus SET command.

■ *FOR EXAMPLE*

Type the following command and press Enter, and notice what happens:

```
SET SQLPROMPT MYSESSION>
```

The prompt changes from SQL> to MYSESSION>. You have just changed a part of your SQL*Plus environment. In fact, there are many *environmental variables* you can change to customize your SQL*Plus environment. Type the following command and press Enter:

SHOW ALL

This command displays all of the SQL*Plus environmental variables and their current settings. Using the SET command, many of them can be changed to suit your needs for a SQL*Plus *session,* which is defined as the time in between when you login and logout of SQL*Plus. When you start your next SQL*Plus session, however, all commands will be set back to their defaults. Later you will learn to create a file that sets SQL*Plus environmental variables to your liking at the beginning of each session.

LAB 1.4

It is important to note here that SQL*Plus commands, such as SHOW and DESCRIBE, are *not* part of the SQL language. You will begin to type SQL commands using the SQL*Plus tool in Chapter 2, "SQL: The Basics."

e) Describe what happens when you type the command EXIT and press Enter.

Answer: You exit the SQL*Plus program.

Your SQL*Plus client session has ended, and the user STUDENT is no longer connected to the database. However, there may be other clients connected to the Oracle database; the server software continues to run, regardless of whether a client is connected to it or not.

 All commands in SQL*Plus require the user to press the Enter key to execute them. The reminder to press the Enter key will not be included in the rest of the examples and exercises in this workbook.

LAB 1.4 SELF-REVIEW QUESTIONS

In order to test your progress, you should be able to answer the following questions.

1) The DESC command displays column names of a table.
   a) _____ True
   b) _____ False

2) Anyone can connect to an Oracle database as long as they have the SQL*Plus software.

   a) _____ True

   b) _____ False

3) The SQL*Plus command SHOW USER displays your login name.

   a) _____ True

   b) _____ False

4) Typing SHOW RELEASE at the prompt displays the version number of SQL*Plus you are using.

   a) _____ True

   b) _____ False

Quiz answers appear in Appendix A. Section 1.4.

C H A P T E R   1

TEST YOUR THINKING

In this chapter you have learned about data, how data is organized in tables, and how the relationships among them are depicted in a schema diagram. Based on your newly-acquired knowledge, design a schema diagram based on the fictional ACME Construction Company. Draw on your own work experience to design the components below.

1) Draw boxes for these three tables: employee, position, and department.

2) Create at least 4 columns for each of the tables, and designate a primary key for each table. All columns should indicate whether they allow NULL values or not.

3) Create relationships among the tables that make sense to you. At least one table should have a self-referencing relationship. Hint: Be sure to include the necessary foreign key columns.

CHAPTER 2

SQL: THE BASICS

CHAPTER OBJECTIVES

In this chapter, you will learn about:

- ✔ The Anatomy of a SELECT Statement   Page 28
- ✔ Editing a SQL Statement   Page 38
- ✔ The WHERE Clause: Comparison
  and Logical Operators   Page 46
- ✔ The ORDER BY Clause   Page 58

Now that you are familiar with the concepts of databases, schema diagrams, and SQL*Plus, you will learn how to write SQL *statements*, or *queries*, to retrieve the data. SQL statements can range from very simple to highly complex; they can be four words long, or 400 words long. In this chapter, you begin by writing simple SQL statements, but you will build longer, more complex SQL statements very quickly.

L A B   2 . 1

THE ANATOMY OF A SELECT STATEMENT

> ## LAB OBJECTIVES
>
> After this lab, you will be able to:
>
> ✔ Write a SQL SELECT Statement
> ✔ Use DISTINCT in a SQL Statement

THE SELECT STATEMENT

When you write SQL query, it is usually to answer a question, such as "How many students live in New York?", or "Where, and at what time, does the Unix class meet?" A SQL *SELECT statement,* or SQL *query,* is used to answer these questions. A SELECT statement can be broken down into a minimum of two parts: the *SELECT list* and the *FROM clause*. The SELECT list usually consists of the column or columns of a table from which you want to display data. The FROM clause states on what table this column or columns are found. Later in this chapter, you will learn some of the other clauses that can be used in a SELECT statement.

Before formulating the SELECT statement, you must first determine the table where the information is located.

■ FOR EXAMPLE

A study of the schema diagram reveals that the course table provides descriptions of courses. The following SELECT statement provides a list of course descriptions:

```
SELECT description
  FROM course
```

The SELECT list contains the single column, description, which provides this information. The FROM clause references the course table which contains the description column. When this statement is executed, the result set is a list of course descriptions:

```
DESCRIPTION
----------------------------------------------------
DP Overview
Intro to Computers
...
JDeveloper Techniques
DB Programming in Java

30 rows selected.
```

Many of the result sets displayed throughout this workbook do not display all the rows. This is denoted with a line of "..." in the middle of the output. Typically, you will see the beginning and the ending rows of the result set, and the number of rows returned.

You may notice that SQL*Plus sometimes does not show the number of rows returned by the query, however. It depends on the feedback settings for your SQL*Plus session. It is particularly useful to set the feedback to 1, which displays the feedback line even when there is only one row returned. You will find this setting useful if any of the rows return NULLs which display as a blank; otherwise, you may think it is not a row or value. To always display the exact number of rows returned, enter the SQL*Plus command: SET FEEDBACK 1.

To retrieve a list of course descriptions and the cost of each course, include the cost column in the SELECT list:

```
SELECT description, cost
  FROM course
DESCRIPTION              COST
-----------------------  ----
DP Overview              1195
Intro to Computers       1195
...
JDeveloper Techniques    1195
DB Programming in Java

30 rows selected.
```

When you want to display more than one column in the SELECT list, separate the columns with commas. It is good practice to include a space after the comma for readability. The order of columns in a SELECT list will determine the order in which the columns are displayed in the output.

You can also select all columns in a table with the asterisk (*) wildcard character. This is handy so you don't have to type all columns in the SELECT list. The columns are displayed in the order in which they are defined in the table. This is the same order you see when you use the DESCRIBE command in SQL*Plus.

```
SELECT *
  FROM course
```

You will notice that the SQL statements presented in this and all other Oracle Interactive Workbooks in this series follow a common format. Refer to Appendix B, "SQL Formatting Guide and SQL*Plus Command Reference," for the formatting guidelines used throughout. A standard format enhances the clarity and readability of your SQL statements, and helps you detect errors more easily.

Oracle is not case sensitive. The use of upper case for SELECT, FROM, and other Oracle keywords is for emphasis only, and distinguishes them from table and column names which are in lower case letters.

SQL*Plus does not require a new line for each clause, but it requires the use of a semicolon at the end of each SQL statement to execute the statement. Alternatively, the forward slash may be used on a separate line. The SQL*Plus commands discussed in Chapter 1 are not SQL commands, and therefore do not require a semi-colon or forward slash.

ELIMINATING DUPLICATES WITH DISTINCT

The use of DISTINCT in the SELECT list eliminates duplicate data in the result set.

■ FOR EXAMPLE

The following SELECT statement retrieves all instructor zip codes for each of the rows in the instructor table:

```
SELECT last_name, zip
  FROM instructor
LAST_NAME                        ZIP
------------------------        -----
Hanks                            10015
Wojick                           10025
```

```
Schorin                 10025
Pertez                  10035
Morris                  10015
Smythe                  10025
Chow                    10015
Lowry                   10025
Frantzen                10005
Willig
```

10 rows selected.

Notice that there are 10 rows, yet only nine instructors have zip codes. Instructor Irene Willig has a NULL value in the zip column. If you want to show only the distinct zip codes of the table, you write the following SELECT statement. The last row shows the NULL value.

```
SELECT DISTINCT zip
   FROM instructor
 ZIP
 -----
 10005
 10015
 10025
 10035
```

5 rows selected.

By definition, a NULL is an unknown value, and a NULL does not equal another NULL. However, there are exceptions: If you write a SQL query using DISTINCT, SQL will consider a NULL value equal to another NULL value.

From Chapter 1, "SQL and Data," you already know that a primary key is always unique, or distinct. Therefore, the use of DISTINCT in a SELECT list containing the primary key column(s) is unnecessary. The zip column in the instructor table is not the primary key, and can therefore contain duplicate values.

LAB 2.1 EXERCISES

2.1.1 WRITE A SQL SELECT STATEMENT

a) Write a SELECT statement to list the first and last names of all students.

_____

_____

b) Write a SELECT statement to list all cities, states, and zip codes.

_____

_____

c) Describe the result set of the following SQL statement:

```
SELECT *
  FROM grade_type
```

_____

_____

2.1.2 USE DISTINCT IN A SQL STATEMENT

a) Why are the result sets of each of the following SQL statements the same?

```
SELECT letter_grade
  FROM grade_conversion

SELECT DISTINCT letter_grade
  FROM grade_conversion
```

_____

_____

b) Explain the result set of the following SQL statement:

```
SELECT DISTINCT cost
   FROM course
```

_____

_____

c) Explain what happens, and why, when you execute the following SQL statement:

```
SELECT DISTINCT course_no
   FROM class
```

_____

_____

LAB 2.1 EXERCISE ANSWERS

2.1.1 ANSWERS

a) Write a SELECT statement to list the first and last names of all students.

Answer: The SELECT list contains the two columns in the student table that provide the first and last names of students; the FROM clause contains the student table where these columns are found.

```
SELECT first_name, last_name
   FROM student
FIRST_NAME                   LAST_NAME
-----------------------      -----------------------
George                       Eakheit
Leonard                      Millstein
...
Kathleen                     Mastandora
Angela                       Torres

268 rows selected.
```

b) Write a SELECT statement to list all cities, states, and zip codes.

Answer: The SELECT list contains the three columns in the zipcode table that provide the city, state, and zip code; the FROM clause contains the zipcode table where these columns are found.

```
SELECT city, state, zip
  FROM zipcode
CITY                           ST ZIP
------------------------------ -- -----
Santurce                       PR 00914
North Adams                    MA 01247
...
New York                       NY 10005
New York                       NY 10035

227 rows selected.
```

c) Describe the result set of the following SQL statement:

```
SELECT *
  FROM grade_type
```

Answer: All columns and rows of the grade_type table are returned in the result set.

```
GR DESCRIPTION
CREATED_BY                           CREATED_D
-- -------------------------------------------- --
------------------------------ -------
MODIFIED_BY                          MODIFIED_
------------------------------ ---------
FI Final
MCAFFREY                             31-DEC-98
MCAFFREY                             31-DEC-98

MT Midterm
MCAFFREY                             31-DEC-98
MCAFFREY                             31-DEC-98

QZ Quiz
MCAFFREY                             31-DEC-98
MCAFFREY                             31-DEC-98

HM Homework
MCAFFREY                             31-DEC-98
MCAFFREY                             31-DEC-98
```

```
PA Participation
MCAFFREY                          31-DEC-98
MCAFFREY                          31-DEC-98

PJ Project
MCAFFREY                          31-DEC-98
MCAFFREY                          31-DEC-98

6 rows selected.
```

Notice here that the result set is difficult to read when data "wraps" itself onto the next line. This will often occur when your SELECT statement contains multiple columns. To help you view the output more easily, SQL*Plus offers a number of formatting commands.

THE SQL*PLUS COLUMN AND FORMAT COMMANDS

The SQL*Plus COLUMN command allows you to specify format attributes for specific columns.

■ *FOR EXAMPLE*

Because the SQL statement contains three long alphanumeric columns, format each using these SQL*Plus commands:

```
COL description FORMAT A13
COL created_by FORMAT A8
COL modified_by FORMAT A8
```

When you re-execute the SQL statement, the result is more readable:

```
SELECT *
  FROM grade_type
GR DESCRIPTION    CREATED_ CREATED_D MODIFIED MODIFIED_
-- ------------- -------- --------- -------- ---------
FI Final          MCAFFREY 31-DEC-98 MCAFFREY 31-DEC-98
MT Midterm        MCAFFREY 31-DEC-98 MCAFFREY 31-DEC-98
QZ Quiz           MCAFFREY 31-DEC-98 MCAFFREY 31-DEC-98
HM Homework       MCAFFREY 31-DEC-98 MCAFFREY 31-DEC-98
PA Participation  MCAFFREY 31-DEC-98 MCAFFREY 31-DEC-98
PJ Project        MCAFFREY 31-DEC-98 MCAFFREY 31-DEC-98

6 rows selected.
```

If the values in the columns do not fit into the space allotted, the data will wrap within the column. To clear all the column formatting, execute the CLEAR COLUMNS command in SQL*Plus.

For more SQL*Plus commands, see Appendix B, "SQL Formatting Guide and SQL*Plus Command Reference."

2.1.2 ANSWERS

a) Why are the result sets of each of the following SQL statements the same?

```
SELECT letter_grade
  FROM grade_conversion
```

```
SELECT DISTINCT letter_grade
  FROM grade_conversion
```

Answer: The result sets are the same because the data values in the letter_grade column in the grade_conversion table are not repeated; the letter_grade column is the primary key of grade_conversion, so by definition its values are already distinct.

b) Explain the result set of the following SQL statement:

```
SELECT DISTINCT cost
  FROM course
```

Answer: The result set contains four rows of distinct costs in the course table, including the NULL value.

```
    COST
-----------
      1095
      1195
      1595


4 rows selected.
```

There is one row in the course table containing a NULL value in the cost column. Even though NULL is an unknown value, DISTINCT recognizes one or more NULL values in a column as a distinct value when returning a result set.

c) Explain what happens, and why, when you execute the following SQL statement:

```
SELECT DISTINCT course_no
  FROM class
```

Answer: Oracle returns an error because a table called class does not exist.

```
FROM class
      *
ERROR at line 2:
ORA-00942: table or view does not exist
```

The asterisk in the error messgae indicates the error in the query. SQL is an exacting language. As you learn to write SQL, you will inevitably make mistakes. It is important to pay attention to the error messages returned to you from the database to learn from and correct your mistakes. This Oracle error message tells you that you referenced a table or a view (discussed in Chapter 12, "Views, Indexes, and Sequences") that does not exist in this database schema. Correct your SQL statement and execute it again.

LAB 2.1 SELF-REVIEW QUESTIONS

In order to test your progress, you should be able to answer the following questions.

1) Columns selected from a table in a SELECT list must be separated by commas.
   a) _____ True
   b) _____ False

2) A SELECT list may contain all the columns in a table.
   a) _____ True
   b) _____ False

3) The asterisk may be used as a wildcard in the FROM clause.
   a) _____ True
   b) _____ False

4) The following statement contains an error:

```
SELECT courseno
  FROM course
```

   a) _____ True
   b) _____ False

Quiz answers appear in Appendix A, Section 2.1.

LAB 2.2

EDITING A SQL STATEMENT

LAB OBJECTIVES

After this lab, you will be able to:

✔   Edit a SQL Statement Using SQL*Plus Commands
✔   Edit a SQL Statement Using an Editor

EDITING WITH SQL*PLUS COMMANDS

By now you may have noticed that typing the same SQL statement over and over again to make a small change quickly becomes very tedious. You can use SQL*Plus's *line editor* to change your statement, indicating which line to change, then use a command to execute the change.

■ *FOR EXAMPLE*

At the SQL prompt, type and execute the following statement to retrieve a list of course numbers:

```
SELECT course_no
  FROM course
```

If you want to retrieve a list of descriptions instead, simply change the word `course_no` to `description` using the line editor. To understand how the line editor works, first look at what SQL statement is in the *buffer*. Type the word `LIST` at the SQL prompt:

```
LIST
1 SELECT course_no
2*  FROM course
```

The SQL buffer retains the last SQL statement you typed in SQL*Plus. The LIST command, or simply the letter L, will list the contents of the buffer. The asterisk next to the number 2 indicates this is the current line in the buffer. To make a change, indicate to the line editor which line to make current. To change it to the first line, type the number 1 at the SQL prompt:

```
1* SELECT course_no
```

Just the first line of the two-line statement is displayed, and the asterisk indicates this is now the current line in the buffer. You can make a change to that line with the CHANGE command:

```
CHANGE/course_no/description
```

The newly-changed line is presented back to you:

```
1* SELECT description
```

The CHANGE command is followed by a forward slash, followed by the text you want to change, and separated from the new text with another forward slash. The abbreviated command for the CHANGE command is the letter C.

You are now ready to execute your statement to produce the new result set.

Because you are not typing the statement for the first time, you cannot use the semicolon. Type a forward slash to execute the statement instead. The forward slash will always execute the current SQL statement in the buffer.

*Remember that certain commands you've learned so far, such as the LIST command, are not SQL, but SQL*Plus commands. Only SQL statements are saved in the buffer, never SQL*Plus commands.*

Refer to Appendix B for a list of other useful SQL*Plus editing commands and tips.

USING AN EDITOR

Although handy, using SQL*Plus's line editor capabilities can still be tedious, especially as your SQL statements grow in size and complexity. You may also want to save some statements for later use. This is where a *text editor* becomes useful. A text editor is a software program with no ability to format the text, such as with boldface or italics. Notepad, a text editor that comes with the Microsoft operating systems, is one example of a text editor, and referenced in this workbook. Any other text editor will work just as well.

For more about setting the default editor in SQL*Plus, see Appendix B.

To use a text editor in SQL*Plus, simply execute the EDIT command. This command will *invoke*, or open, the default editor currently set in SQL*Plus. When you use the EDIT command at the SQL prompt, SQL*Plus will stay open in the background and your text editor will be in the foreground, automatically displaying the SQL statement in the buffer. The file already has a name, which can also be set as a default in SQL*Plus. For quick editing of statements, simply make your changes here, Save the file, and exit Notepad, which brings you back to SQL*Plus. If you wish to save the file for future reference, while still in Notepad select Save As to save the file with a different name and any extension you wish. It is common to save the file with a .sql extension.

Notice that when you invoke an editor, the SQL statement ends with a forward slash on a separate line at the end. SQL*Plus adds this character to the file so the file can be executed in SQL*Plus.

■ FOR EXAMPLE

Type the following statement:

```
SELECT *
  FROM course
```

Now edit the file in Notepad and select Save As to save the file with the name myfile.sql. Exit Notepad, and type and execute a new, different SQL statement:

```
SELECT state
  FROM zipcode
```

This statement is now in the buffer; however, you can execute a different SQL statement, such as the one you saved in myfile.sql, with the START command.

```
START myfile
```

The statement in the file runs, producing a result set. Because the file already contains a forward slash, the SQL statement is executed automatically. If you save myfile with an extension other than .sql, you must type the file name and extension with the START command. If you want to change myfile again, simply type the following:

```
EDIT myfile
```

Notepad will open with myfile.sql containing your SQL statement.

LAB 2.2 EXERCISES

2.2.1   EDIT A SQL STATEMENT USING SQL*PLUS COMMANDS

Type and execute the following SQL statement:

```
SELECT employer
  FROM student
```

a) Using SQL*Plus commands, change the column employer to registration_date, and execute the statement again.

_____

_____

b) Using SQL*Plus commands, add a second column, phone, to the statement you changed. Display the phone column first, then the registration_date column, in the result set.

_____

_____

2.2.2   EDIT A SQL STATEMENT USING AN EDITOR

a) Invoke the editor and change the statement in your buffer to the following. Then save the file and execute it in SQL*Plus.

```
SELECT salutation, first_name, last_name, phone
  FROM instructor
```

_____

_____

b) Edit the preceding statement, which is now in your buffer; save it as inst.sql, and use the START command to execute it in SQL*Plus.

_____

_____

c) Edit inst.sql; save it as inst.x, and use the START command to execute it in SQL*Plus.

_____

_____

LAB 2.2 EXERCISE ANSWERS

2.2.1 ANSWERS

Type and execute the following SQL statement:

```
SELECT employer
  FROM student
```

a) Using SQL*Plus commands, change the column employer to registration_date, and execute the statement again.

Answer: Select the first line in the buffer, then use the CHANGE command to change employer to registration_date.

Type 1 to select the first line in the buffer:

1* SELECT employer

Then use the CHANGE command:

```
C/employer/registration_date
```

Type L to list the changed statement:

```
1 SELECT registration_date
2*   FROM student
```

b) Using SQL*Plus commands, add a second column, phone, to the state-ment you changed. Display the phone column first, then the registra-tion_date column, in the result set.

Answer: You must again select the first line in the buffer, then use the CHANGE com-mand to add the phone column to the SELECT list.

Type 1 to select the first line in the buffer:

```
1* SELECT registration_date
```

Then use the CHANGE command:

```
C/SELECT/SELECT phone,
```

Here, the CHANGE command will replace SELECT with SELECT phone, (including the comma), changing your statement to the following:

```
1 SELECT phone, registration_date
2*   FROM student
```

The result set will display phone first, then registration date:

```
PHONE             REGISTRAT
---------------   ---------
201-555-5555      18-FEB-93
201-555-5555      22-FEB-93
...
718-555-5555      22-FEB-93
718-555-5555      28-JAN-93

268 rows selected.
```

The CHANGE command looks for the first occurrence, from left to right, of the text you wish to change. When it locates it, it replaces this occurrence with the new text you wish to change it to.

2.2.2 ANSWERS

a) Invoke the editor and change the statement in your buffer to the following. Then save the file and execute it in SQL*Plus.

```
SELECT salutation, first_name, last_name, phone
  FROM instructor
```

Answer: Use the EDIT *command to edit the file, and execute the changed statement in SQL*Plus with the forward slash.*

b) Edit the preceding statement, which is now in your buffer; save it as inst.sql, and use the START command to execute it in SQL*Plus.

Answer: Use the EDIT *command to edit the file, and save it as inst.sql. Execute the changed statement in SQL*Plus with the* START *command.*

c) Edit inst.sql; save it as inst.x, and use the START command to execute it in SQL*Plus.

Answer: At the SQL prompt, type EDIT; *edit the file in your editor; save the file as inst.x; exit the editor; type* START inst.x *to execute the changed statement.*

Because you saved the file with an extension other than .sql, you must explicitly reference both the file name and its extension. If you want to edit this file, you must type EDIT inst.x at the SQL prompt.

LAB 2.2 SELF-REVIEW QUESTIONS

In order to test your progress, you should be able to answer the following questions.

1) You can save a SQL statement to the buffer for it to be referenced later.
  a) _____ True
  b) _____ False

2) You can execute a SQL statement with either the semicolon or the forward slash.
  a) _____ True
  b) _____ False

3) You cannot save a .sql file to the A: drive.
  a) _____ True
  b) _____ False

4) The START command can execute what is in the buffer.
   a) _____ True
   b) _____ False

Quiz answers appear in Appendix A, Section 2.2.

L A B   2 . 3

THE WHERE CLAUSE: COMPARISON AND LOGICAL OPERATORS

LAB OBJECTIVES

After this lab, you will be able to:

✔   Use Comparison and Logical Operators
in a WHERE Clause
✔   Use NULL in a WHERE Clause

The *WHERE clause,* also called the *predicate,* provides the power to narrow down the scope of data retrieved. In fact, most SQL statements you write will contain a WHERE clause.

COMPARISON OPERATORS

Comparison operators compare *expressions.* An expression can be a column of any datatype, a *string* or *text literal* (sometimes referred to as a *text constant* or *character literal*), a number, or any combination of these. An expression can also be a *function* or *mathematical computation,* which you will learn about in Chapter 3, "Character and Number Functions." An expression always results in a value.

TESTING FOR EQUALITY AND INEQUALITY

Comparison operators compare one expression with another expression. One of the most commonly used comparison operators is the *equal* operator, denoted by the = symbol.

■ *FOR EXAMPLE*

If you are asked to provide the first name, last name, and phone number of a teacher with the last name of Schorin, you write the following SQL statement:

```
SELECT first_name, last_name, phone
  FROM instructor
 WHERE last_name = 'Schorin'
FIRST_NAME LAST_NAME  PHONE
---------- ---------- ----------
Nina       Schorin    2125551212
```

1 row selected.

Here, the column `last_name` is the left side of the equation, the text literal `'Schorin'` the right. Single quotes are used around the text literal `'Schorin'`. This statement will only retrieve rows from the instructor table that satisfy this condition in the WHERE clause. In this case, only one row is retrieved.

When you describe the instructor table, you see the datatype of the last_name column is VARCHAR2. This means the data contained in this column is alphanumeric. When two values are compared to each other they must be of the same datatype; otherwise, Oracle returns an error. You will learn more about converting from one datatype to another in Chapter 4, "Date and Conversion Functions."

SQL is case insensitive when it comes to column names, table names, and keywords such as SELECT. But when you compare a text literal to a database column, the case of the data must match exactly. The syntax of the following statement is correct, but it does not yield any rows:

```
SELECT first_name, last_name, phone
  FROM instructor
 WHERE last_name = 'schorin'
```

no rows selected

Just as equality is useful, so is inequality.

```
SELECT first_name, last_name, phone
  FROM instructor
 WHERE last_name <> 'Schorin'
FIRST_NAME LAST_NAME  PHONE
---------- ---------- ----------
Fernand    Hanks      2125551212
```

```
Tom        Wojick      2125551212
...
Marilyn    Frantzen    2125551212
Irene      Willig      2125551212
```

9 rows selected.

All rows, except the one with the last name of 'Schorin' are retrieved. In-equality can also be expressed with the != notation.

THE GREATER THAN AND LESS THAN OPERATORS

The comparison operators >, <, >=, <= can all be used to compare values in columns. In the following example, the >=, or *greater than or equal to,* operator is used to retrieve a list of course descriptions whose cost is greater than or equal to 1195:

```
SELECT description, cost
  FROM course
 WHERE cost >= 1195
DESCRIPTION                      COST
------------------------------   ----
DP Overview                      1195
Intro to Computers               1195
...
Database System Principles       1195
JDeveloper Techniques            1195
```

26 rows selected.

The value 1195 is not enclosed in single quotes because it is a number literal.

THE BETWEEN COMPARISON OPERATOR

The BETWEEN operator tests for a range of values:

```
SELECT description, cost
  FROM course
 WHERE cost BETWEEN 1000 AND 1100
DESCRIPTION                      COST
------------------------------   --------
Unix Tips and Techniques         1095
Intro to Internet                1095
Intro to the Basic Language      1095
```

3 rows selected.

BETWEEN is inclusive of both values defining the range; the result set includes courses that cost 1000 and 1100, and everything in between. BETWEEN is most useful for number and date comparisons. Date comparisons are discussed in Chapter 4, "Date and Conversion Functions."

THE IN OPERATOR

The IN operator works with a *list of values,* separated by commas, contained within a set of parentheses. The following query looks for courses where the cost is either 1095 or 1595.

```
SELECT description, cost
  FROM course
 WHERE cost IN (1095, 1595)
```

DESCRIPTION	COST
Structured Programming Techniques	1595
Unix Tips and Techniques	1095
Intro to Internet	1095
Intro to the Basic Language	1095

4 rows selected.

THE LIKE OPERATOR

Another very useful comparison operator is LIKE which performs pattern-matching using the percent (%) or underscore (_) characters as wildcards. The percent wildcard is used to denote multiple characters, while the underscore wildcard is used to denote single characters. The following statement retrieves rows where the last name begins with the letter S, and ends in anything else:

```
SELECT first_name, last_name, phone
  FROM instructor
 WHERE last_name LIKE 'S%'
```

FIRST_NAME	LAST_NAME	PHONE
Nina	Schorin	2125551212
Todd	Smythe	2125551212

2 rows selected.

The % character may be placed at the beginning, end, or anywhere within the literal text, but always within the single quotes. This is also true of the underscore wildcard character, as in this statement:

```
SELECT first_name, last_name
  FROM instructor
```

```
WHERE last_name LIKE '_o%'
FIRST_NAME               LAST_NAME
------------------------- ---------
Tom                      Wojick
Anita                    Morris
Charles                  Lowry
```

3 rows selected.

The WHERE clause returns only rows where the last name begins with any letter, but the second letter must be a lower case "o". The rest of the last name is irrelevant.

 All the previously mentioned operators can be negated with the NOT comparison operator, for example, NOT BETWEEN, NOT IN, NOT LIKE.

Note, in the following SQL statement, the last_name column used in the WHERE clause is not shown in the SELECT list. There is no rule about columns in the WHERE clause having to exist in the SELECT list.

```
SELECT phone
  FROM instructor
 WHERE last_name NOT LIKE 'S%'
```

LOGICAL OPERATORS

For the ultimate power in the WHERE clause, comparison operators can be combined with the help of the *logical operators* AND and OR. These logical operators are also referred to as *boolean operators*. They group expressions, all within the same WHERE clause of a single SQL statement.

■ FOR EXAMPLE

The following SQL query combines two comparison operators with the help of the AND boolean operator. The result shows rows where a course is between 1000 and 1100, and the course description starts with the letter I:

```
SELECT description, cost
  FROM course
 WHERE cost BETWEEN 1000 AND 1100
   AND description LIKE 'I%'
DESCRIPTION                           COST
------------------------------------- ---------
Intro to Internet                     1095
Intro to the Basic Language           1095
```

2 rows selected.

With just the BETWEEN operator in the WHERE clause, the result set contains three rows. With the addition of the AND description LIKE 'I%', the result is further reduced to two rows.

PRECEDENCE OF LOGICAL OPERATORS

When AND and OR are used together in a WHERE clause, the AND operator always takes precedence over the OR operator, meaning the AND conditions are evaluated first. If there are multiple operators of the same precedence, the left operator is executed before the right. You can manipulate the precedence in the WHERE clause with the use of parentheses. In the following SQL statement, the AND and OR logical operators are combined:

```
SELECT description, cost, prerequisite
  FROM course
 WHERE cost = 1195
   AND prerequisite = 20
   OR prerequisite = 25
```

DESCRIPTION	COST	PREREQUISITE
Hands-On Windows	1195	20
Structured Analysis	1195	20
Project Management	1195	20
GUI Programming	1195	20
Intro to SQL	1195	20
Intro to the Basic Language	1095	25
Database System Principles	1195	25

7 rows selected.

The above SQL statement chooses any record that has either a cost of 1195 and a prerequisite of 20, or just has a prerequisite of 25 no matter what the cost. The sixth row, Intro to the Basic Language, is selected because it satisfies the OR expression.

Here is the same SQL statement, but with parentheses to group the expressions in the WHERE clause:

```
SELECT description, cost, prerequisite
  FROM course
 WHERE cost = 1195
   AND (prerequisite = 20
       OR prerequisite = 25)
```

DESCRIPTION	COST	PREREQUISITE
Database System Principles	1195	25
Hands-On Windows	1195	20
Structured Analysis	1195	20
Project Management	1195	20
GUI Programming	1195	20
Intro to SQL	1195	20

6 rows selected.

The first expression selects only courses where the cost is equal to 1195. If the prerequisite is either 25 or 20, then the second condition is also true. Both expressions need to be true for the row to be displayed. These are the basic rules of logical operators. If two conditions are combined with the AND operator, both conditions must be true; if two conditions are connected by the OR operator, only one of the conditions need be true for the record to be selected.

The result set returns six rows instead of seven. The order in which items in the WHERE clause are evaluated is changed by the use of parentheses, and changes the result set. To ensure that your SQL statements are clearly understood, it is always best to use parentheses.

EVALUATING NULL VALUES

Recall from Chapter 1, "SQL and Data," that NULL means an *unknown* value. A value either *is* or *is not* known; something cannot be *equal* to an unknown value. The IS NULL and IS NOT NULL operators evaluate whether a data value is NULL or not. The following SQL statement returns courses that do not have a prerequisite:

```
SELECT description
  FROM course
 WHERE prerequisite IS NULL
DESCRIPTION
--------------------
DP Overview
Intro to Computers
Java for C/C++ Programmers
Operating Systems

4 rows selected.
```

LAB 2.3 EXERCISES

2.3.1 USE COMPARISON AND LOGICAL OPERATORS IN A *WHERE* CLAUSE

a) Write a SELECT statement to list the last names of students living either in zip code 10048, 11102, or 11209.

_____

_____

b) Write a SELECT statement to list the first and last names of instructors with the letter "i" (either upper case or lower case) in their last name, living in the zip code 10025.

_____

_____

c) Does the following statement contain an error? Explain.

```
SELECT last_name
  FROM instructor
 WHERE created_date = modified_by
```

_____

_____

2.3.2 USE *NULL* IN A *WHERE* CLAUSE

a) Write a SELECT statement to list descriptions of courses with prerequisites, and cost less than 1100.

_____

_____

b) Write a SELECT statement to list the cost of courses without a prerequisite; do not repeat the cost.

_____

_____

LAB 2.3 EXERCISE ANSWERS

2.3.1 ANSWERS

a) Write a SELECT statement to list the last names of students living either in zip code 10048, 11102, or 11209.

Answer: The SELECT statement selects a single column, and uses the IN comparison operator in the WHERE clause.

```
SELECT last_name
  FROM student
 WHERE zip IN ('10048', '11102', '11209')
LAST_NAME
-------------------------
Lefkowitz
McLean
Allende
Williams
Winnicki
Wilson
Masser

7 rows selected.
```

The statement can also be written using the equal operator (=), in combination with the logical operator OR, and yield the same result set:

```
SELECT last_name
  FROM student
 WHERE zip = '10048'
    OR zip = '11102'
    OR zip = '11209'
```

There will be times when a SELECT statement can be written more than one way. The preceding statements are logically equivalent.

b) Write a SELECT statement to list the first and last names of instructors with the letter "i" (either upper case or lower case) in their last name, living in the zip code 10025.

Answer: The SELECT statement selects two columns, and uses the LIKE, =, and the AND and OR logical operators, combined with parentheses, in the WHERE clause.

```
SELECT first_name, last_name
  FROM instructor
```

```
WHERE (last_name LIKE '%i%' OR last_name LIKE '%I%')
   AND zip = '10025'
FIRST_NAME                           LAST_NAME
-------------------------- --------------
Tom                                  Wojick
Nina                                 Schorin

2 rows selected.
```

The LIKE operator must be used twice in this example because there is no way of knowing whether there is an upper or lower case 'i' anywhere in the last name. You must test for both conditions, which cannot be done using a single LIKE operator. If one of the OR conditions is true, the expression is true.

c) Does the following statement contain an error? Explain.

```
SELECT last_name
  FROM instructor
 WHERE created_date = modified_by
```

Answer: Yes. The two columns in the WHERE clause are not the same datatype, and the Oracle database returns an error when this statement is executed.

2.3.2 ANSWERS

a) Write a SELECT statement to list descriptions of courses with prerequisites, and cost less than 1100.

Answer: The SELECT statement selects a single column, and uses the IS NOT NULL and less than (<) comparison operators in the WHERE clause.

```
SELECT description
  FROM course
 WHERE prerequisite IS NOT NULL
   AND cost < 1100
DESCRIPTION
-------------------------
Unix Tips and Techniques
Intro to Internet
Intro to the Basic Language

3 rows selected.
```

b) Write a SELECT statement to list the cost of courses without a prerequisite; do not repeat the cost.

Answer: The SELECT statement selects a single column in combination with DISTINCT, and uses the IS NULL comparison operator in the WHERE clause.

```
SELECT DISTINCT cost
  FROM course
 WHERE prerequisite IS NULL
COST
---------
     1195
     1595
```

`2 rows selected.`

LAB 2.3 SELF-REVIEW QUESTIONS

In order to test your progress, you should be able to answer the following questions.

1) Comparison operators always compare two values.
   a) _____ True
   b) _____ False

2) The BETWEEN operator uses a list of values.
   a) _____ True
   b) _____ False

3) The following statement is incorrect:

```
SELECT first_name, last_name
  FROM student
 WHERE employer = NULL
```

   a) _____ True
   b) _____ False

4) The following statement is incorrect:

```
SELECT description
  FROM course
 WHERE cost NOT LIKE (1095, 1195)
```

   a) _____ True
   b) _____ False

5) The following statement is incorrect:

```
SELECT city
  FROM zipcode
 WHERE state != 'NY'
```

      a) _____ True
      b) _____ False

Quiz answers appear in Appendix A, Section 2.3.

L A B   2 . 4

THE ORDER BY CLAUSE

LAB OBJECTIVES

After this lab, you will be able to:

✔ Custom Sort Query Results

Recall from Chapter 1, "SQL and Data," that data is not stored in a table in any particular order. In all of the examples used thus far, the result sets display data in the order in which they happen to be returned from the database. However, you may want to view data in a certain order. The ORDER BY clause orders the data any way you wish.

■ *FOR EXAMPLE*

The following statement retrieves a list of course numbers and descriptions for courses without a prerequisite, in alphabetical order by their descriptions:

```
SELECT course_no, description
  FROM course
 WHERE prerequisite IS NULL
 ORDER BY description
COURSE_NO DESCRIPTION
--------- -------------------------
       10 DP Overview
       20 Intro to Computers
      146 Java for C/C++ Programmers
      310 Operating Systems

4 rows selected.
```

Even though the column called description is used in the SELECT list, it does not need to be, in order to be used in the ORDER BY clause.

By default, when the ORDER BY is used, the result set is sorted in *ascending* order; or you can be explicit by adding the abbreviation ASC after the column. If descending order is desired, the abbreviation DESC is used after the column in the ORDER BY clause:

```
SELECT course_no, description
  FROM course
 WHERE prerequisite IS NULL
 ORDER BY description DESC
COURSE_NO DESCRIPTION
--------- -------------------------
      310 Operating Systems
      146 Java for C/C++ Programmers
       20 Intro to Computers
       10 DP Overview

4 rows selected.
```

A result set can be sorted by more than one column. The columns you wish to sort by need only be included in the ORDER BY clause, separated by commas. The ORDER BY clause is always the last clause in an SQL statement.

LAB 2.4 EXERCISES

2.4.1 CUSTOM SORT QUERY RESULTS

a) Write a SELECT statement to list each city in New York State or Connecticut, sorted in ascending order by zip code.

_____

_____

b) Write a SELECT statement to list course descriptions and their prerequisite course numbers, in ascending order by description. Do not list courses without a prerequisite.

_____

_____

c) Show the salutation, first and last name of students with the last name Grant. Order the result by salutation in descending order, and the first name in ascending order.

_____

_____

LAB 2.4 EXERCISE ANSWERS

2.4.1 ANSWERS

a) Write a SELECT statement to list each city in New York State or Connecticut, sorted in ascending order by zip code.

Answer: The SELECT statement selects two columns, uses the equal operator and OR logical operator to combine expressions in the WHERE clause, and uses ORDER BY with a single column to sort the results in ascending order.

```
SELECT city, zip
  FROM zipcode
 WHERE state = 'NY'
    OR state = 'CT'
 ORDER BY zip
CITY                           ZIP
------------------------       -----
Ansonia                        06401
Middlefield                    06455
...
Hicksville                     11802
Endicott                       13760

142 rows selected.
```

Alternatively, the WHERE clause can be written as:

```
WHERE state IN ('NY', 'CT')
```

b) Write a SELECT statement to list course descriptions and their prerequisite course numbers, in ascending order by description. Do not list courses without a prerequisite.

Answer: The SELECT statement selects two columns, uses the IS NOT NULL comparison operator in the WHERE clause, and uses ORDER BY with a single column to sort the results in ascending order.

```
SELECT description, prerequisite
  FROM course
 WHERE prerequisite IS NOT NULL
 ORDER BY description
DESCRIPTION                        PREREQUISITE
---------------------------------  ------------
Advanced Java Programming                   122
```

```
Advanced Unix Admin                          132
...
Structured Programming Techniques            204
Unix Tips and Techniques                     134
```

```
26 rows selected.
```

c) Show the salutation, first and last name of students with the last name Grant. Order the result by salutation in descending order, and the first name in ascending order.

Answer: The ORDER BY clause contains two columns, the salutation and the first name. The salutation is sorted first in descending order. Within each salutation, the first name is sorted in ascending order.

```
SELECT salutation, first_name, last_name
  FROM STUDENT
 WHERE LAST_NAME = 'Grant'
ORDER BY salutation DESC, first_name ASC
SALUT FIRST_NAME                 LAST_NAME
----- ------------------------- ---------
Ms.   Eilene                    Grant
Ms.   Verona                    Grant
Mr.   Omaira                    Grant
Mr.   Scott                     Grant
```

```
4 rows selected.
```

LAB 2.4 SELF-REVIEW QUESTIONS

In order to test your progress, you should be able to answer the following questions.

1) The following is the correct order of all clauses in this SELECT statement:

```
SELECT ...
  FROM ...
 ORDER BY ...
 WHERE ...
```

    a) _____ True
    b) _____ False

2) You must explicitly indicate whether an ORDER BY is ascending or descending.
    a) _____ True
    b) _____ False

3) The following statement is correct:

```
SELECT *
  FROM instructor
 ORDER BY phone
```

> **a)** _____ True
> **b)** _____ False

Quiz answers appear in Appendix A, Section 2.4.

C H A P T E R   2

TEST YOUR THINKING

1) Invoke an editor from SQL*Plus; create a file called first.sql containing an SQL statement that retrieves data from the course table for courses that cost 1195, and whose descriptions start with 'Intro', sorted by their prerequisites.

2) Create another file called second.sql that retrieves data from the student table for students whose last names begin with 'A', 'B', or 'C', and who work for 'Competrol Real Estate', sorted by their last names.

3) Create yet another file called third.sql that retrieves all the descriptions from the grade_type table, for rows that were modified by the user MCAFFREY.

4) Execute each of the files, in the order they were created, in SQL*Plus.

CHAPTER 3

CHARACTER AND NUMBER FUNCTIONS

CHAPTER OBJECTIVES

In this chapter, you will learn about:

✔ Character Functions   Page 66
✔ Number Functions   Page 83

Functions are a useful part of the SQL language. They can transform data in a way that is different from the way it is stored in a database. This chapter details the most important Oracle character and number functions.

A function is a type of formula whose result is one of two things: either a *transformation,* such as changing the name of a student to upper case letters, or *information,* such as the length of a word in a column. Most functions share similar characteristics, including a name, and typically at least one *input parameter,* or *argument,* inside a pair of matching parentheses:

```
function_name(input_parameter)
```

All functions in this chapter and Chapter 4, "Date and Conversion Functions," are performed on a single row. This is in contrast to *aggregate functions,* which are performed against multiple rows. You will learn about aggregate functions in Chapter 5, "Aggregate Functions, GROUP BY, and HAVING."

L A B   3 . 1

CHARACTER
FUNCTIONS

LAB OBJECTIVES

After this lab, you will be able to:

✔ Use a Character Function in a SQL Statement
✔ Concatenate Strings

All character functions require alphanumeric input parameters. The input can be a *text* or *character literal*, sometimes referred to as a *string* or *text constant,* or a column of datatype VARCHAR2 or CHAR. Text literals are always surrounded by single quotes.

THE LOWER FUNCTION

The LOWER function transforms data into lower case. In the following SELECT statement, both a column name and a text constant are used separately with the LOWER function:

```
SELECT state, LOWER(state), LOWER('State')
  FROM zipcode
ST LO LOWER
-- -- -----
PR pr state
MA ma state
...
NY ny state
NY ny state

227 rows selected.
```

The first column in the SELECT list shows you the state column without any transformation. The second column uses LOWER to transform the state column of the zipcode table into lower case letters in the result set. The third column of the SELECT list transforms the text literal 'State' into lower case letters. Constants used in SELECT statements are repeated for every row of resulting output.

THE LPAD AND RPAD FUNCTIONS

The LPAD and RPAD functions also transform data: they *left pad* and *right pad* strings, respectively. When you pad a string, you add to it. These functions can add characters, symbols, or even spaces to strings in your result set. They distinguish themselves from the LOWER function because they take more than one parameter as their input.

■ FOR EXAMPLE

This SELECT statement displays cities right padded with asterisks, and states left padded with a dash:

```
SELECT RPAD(city, 20, '*') "City Name",
       LPAD(state, 10, '-') "State Name"
  FROM zipcode
City Name            State Name
-------------------- ----------
Santurce************ --------PR
North Adams********* --------MA
...
New York************ --------NY
New York*********** --------NY

227 rows selected.
```

In the preceding example, the SELECT list is split into two lines. This is perfectly acceptable formatting, and makes the SELECT statement easy to read. If the SELECT list is written on one line, the list eventually wraps, making the statement more difficult to read. By putting elements in the SELECT list on separate lines, you control exactly when the next line begins, and indent it properly below the line above it.

The city column is right padded with the '*' character, up to a length of 20 characters. The state column is left padded with '-', up to a total length of ten characters. Both the LPAD and RPAD functions use three parameters, separated by commas. The first input parameter accepts either a text literal or a column of datatype VARACHAR2 or CHAR. The second argument specifies the total length the string should be padded. The third optional argument indicates the character the string should be padded with. If this parameter is not specified, the string is padded with spaces by default, as in this example:

```
SELECT LPAD(city, 20) as "City Name", state
  FROM zipcode
City Name               ST
-------------------- --
           Santurce PR
       North Adams MA
...
           New York NY
           New York NY

227 rows selected.
```

The syntax for the LPAD and RPAD functions is this:

```
LPAD(char1, n [, char2])
RPAD(char1, n [, char2])
```

Char1 is the string to perform the function on, n represents the length the string should be padded to, and char2 is the optional parameter (denoted by the brackets) used to specify which character(s) to pad the string with.

In the previous two examples, two forms of a column alias are used to take the place of the column name in the result set. A column alias can be used in the SELECT list to alias a column or value. A column alias, in conjunction with the SQL*Plus COLUMN command, makes result sets much easier to read.

An alias may also contain one or more words in double quotes. Double quotes are useful when you want to display an alias in exact case. To format the column in SQL*Plus, you must specify the alias in quotes as well. For example: COL "Last Name" FORMAT A25.

Alternatively, the word "as" can follow the column being selected, and precede the alias name.

THE SUBSTR FUNCTION

SUBSTR is another function that transforms a string, returning a *substring*, or *subset* of a string, based on its input parameters.

■ *FOR EXAMPLE*

The following SELECT statement displays student last names, the *first* five characters of those last names, and the *remaining* characters of those last names in the third column:

```
SELECT last_name,
       SUBSTR(last_name, 1, 5),
       SUBSTR(last_name, 6)
  FROM student
```

LAST_NAME	SUBST	SUBSTR(LAST_NAME,6)
Eakheit	Eakhe	it
Millstein	Mills	tein
...		
Mastandora	Masta	ndora
Torres	Torre	s

268 rows selected.

The SUBSTR function's first input parameter is a string; the second is the start position of the subset; the third is optional, indicating the length of the subset. If the third parameter is not used, the default is to display the remainder of the string. Here is the syntax for SUBSTR:

```
SUBSTR(char1, n [, n])
```

THE INSTR FUNCTION

INSTR, meaning *in string,* looks for the occurrence of a string inside another string, returning the number of the position where the string starts.

■ *FOR EXAMPLE*

The following SELECT statement results in course descriptions and the position in which the first occurrence of the string 'er' starts, if at all, in the description column:

```
SELECT description, INSTR(description, 'er')
  FROM course
```

DESCRIPTION	INSTR(DESCRIPTION,'ER')
DP Overview	6
Intro to Computers	16
...	
JDeveloper Techniques	9
DB Programming in Java	0

30 rows selected.

As you can see in the first row of the result set, the string 'er' starts in the sixth position of the course name. INSTR can take two other optional input parameters. The syntax for INSTR is:

```
INSTR(char1, char2 [,n1 [, n2]])
```

The third parameter allows you to specify the start position for the search. The fourth parameter specifies which occurrence of the string to look for. When these optional parameters are not used, the default value is 1.

THE DUAL TABLE

Dual is a table unique to Oracle. It contains a single row and a single column called 'dummy', and holds no significant data of its own. It can be used in conjunction with functions to select values that do not exist in tables, such as today's date, or text literals. A single row is always returned in the result set.

■ *FOR EXAMPLE*

The following SQL statement selects a text literal from dual using the LENGTH function, which determines the length of a string:

```
SELECT LENGTH('Hello there')
  FROM dual
```

LENGTH('HELLOTHERE')
11

1 row selected.

FUNCTIONS IN WHERE AND ORDER BY CLAUSES

The use of functions is not restricted to the SELECT list; they are also used in other SQL clauses. In a WHERE clause, a function restricts the output to rows that only evaluate to the result of the function. In an ORDER BY clause, rows are sorted based on the result of a function.

■ *FOR EXAMPLE*

This SELECT statement uses the SUBSTR function in the WHERE clause to search for student last names that begin with the string 'Mo':

```
SELECT first_name, last_name
  FROM student
 WHERE SUBSTR(last_name, 1, 2) = 'Mo'
```

FIRST_NAME	LAST_NAME
Edgar	Moffat
Angel	Moskowitz
Vinnie	Moon
Bernadette	Montanez

4 rows selected.

Alternatively, you can achieve the same result by replacing the SUBSTR function with this WHERE clause:

```
WHERE last_name LIKE 'Mo%'
```

The following SQL statement selects student first and last names, where the first name has a period in the second position only, and orders the result set based on the length of student last names:

```
SELECT first_name, last_name
  FROM student
 WHERE SUBSTR(first_name, 2, 2) = '.'
 ORDER BY LENGTH(last_name)
```

FIRST_NAME	LAST_NAME
D.	Orent
J.	Dalvi
...	
V.	Greenberg
V.	Saliternan

12 rows selected.

CONCATENATION

Concatenation *puts together* strings to become one. Strings can be concatenated to produce a single column in the result set. There are two methods of concatenation in Oracle: one is with the CONCAT function, the other is with the || symbol, also known as two *vertical bars* or *pipes*.

■ FOR EXAMPLE

When you want to concatenate cities and states together using the CONCAT function, you write it this way:

```
SELECT CONCAT(city, state)
  FROM zipcode
CONCAT(CITY,STATE)
---------------------------
SanturcePR
North AdamsMA
...
New YorkNY
New YorkNY

227 rows selected.
```

The result set is difficult to read without spaces between cities and states. The CONCAT function takes only two parameters, so to add spaces between the strings using CONCAT is complex. By using the || symbol, you can easily concatenate several strings:

```
SELECT city||state||zip
  FROM zipcode
CITY||STATE||ZIP
----------------------------------
SanturcePR00914
North AdamsMA01247
...
New YorkNY10005
New YorkNY10035

227 rows selected.
```

For a result set that is easier to read, concatenate the strings with spaces, and separate the city and state columns with a comma:

```
SELECT city||', '||state||' '||zip
  FROM zipcode
```

```
CITY||','||STATE||''||ZIP
-------------------------
Santurce, PR  00914
North Adams, MA  01247
...
New York, NY  10005
New York, NY  10035
```

227 rows selected.

THE TRANSLATE FUNCTION

The TRANSLATE function provides a one-for-one character substitution, using *if then else* logic. For instance, it allows you to determine if all the phone numbers in the student table follow the same ###-###-#### format. In the following example, TRANSLATE substitutes the '#' character for every character from '0' to '9'. *If* the character in the phone column of the student table is a hyphen (-), *then* it is substituted with the same character. All numbers and hyphens in the phone column are translated to either '#' or '-'. To check if the hyphens are also placed at the correct positions, use TRANSLATE to convert the characters, and then the values are checked against the '###-###-####' format.

```
SELECT phone
  FROM student
 WHERE TRANSLATE(
       phone, '0123456789-',
             '##########-') <> '###-###-####'
```

no rows selected

If any phone number had been entered as 'abc-ddd-efgh', '555-1212', or any other format, the query would have returned the row with the incorrect phone format.

The following is the syntax for the TRANSLATE function:

```
TRANSLATE(char, if, then)
```

THE REPLACE FUNCTION

The REPLACE function literally *replaces* a string with another string, unlike TRANSLATE which replaces a single character. In the following example, when the string 'hand' is found within the string 'My hand is asleep', it is replaced by the string 'foot':

```
SELECT REPLACE('My hand is asleep', 'hand', 'foot')
  FROM dual
```

```
REPLACE('MYHANDISA
------------------
My foot is asleep
```

```
1 row selected.
```

The following is the syntax for the REPLACE function:

```
REPLACE(char, if, then)
```

The second parameter looks to see `if` a string exists within the first parameter. If so, `then` it displays the third parameter. `If` the second parameter is not found, `then` the original string is displayed:

```
SELECT REPLACE('My hand is asleep', 'x', 'foot')
  FROM dual
REPLACE('MYHANDISA
------------------
My hand is asleep
```

```
1 row selected.
```

LAB 3.1 EXERCISES

3.1.1 USE A CHARACTER FUNCTION IN A SQL STATEMENT

a) Execute the following SQL statement. Based on the result, what is the purpose of the UPPER function?

```
SELECT state, UPPER(state), UPPER('State')
  FROM zipcode
```

_____

_____

b) Execute the following SQL statement. Based on the result, what is the purpose of the INITCAP function?

```
SELECT description "Description",
       INITCAP(description) "Initcap Description"
  FROM course
 WHERE description LIKE '%SQL%'
```

_____

_____

c) Write the question for the SQL statement below.

```
SELECT last_name
  FROM instructor
 WHERE LENGTH(last_name) >= 6
```

_____

_____

d) Describe the result of the SQL statement below. Pay particular attention to the negative number parameter.

```
SELECT SUBSTR('12345', 3),
       SUBSTR('12345', 3, 2),
       SUBSTR('12345', -4, 3)
  FROM dual
```

_____

_____

e) Based on the result of the following SQL statement, describe the purpose of the LTRIM and RTRIM functions.

```
SELECT zip, LTRIM(zip, '0'), RTRIM(ZIP, '4')
  FROM zipcode
 ORDER BY zip
```

_____

_____

3.1.2 CONCATENATE STRINGS

a) Write a SELECT statement that returns each instructor's last name, followed by a comma and a space, followed by the instructor's first name, all in a single column in the result set.

_____

_____

b) Using functions in the SELECT list, WHERE, and ORDER BY clauses, write the SELECT statement that returns course numbers and course descriptions from the course table, and looks exactly like the following result set:

```
204.......Intro to SQL
130.......Intro to Unix
230.......Intro to Internet
20........Intro to Computers
25........Intro to Programming
120.......Intro to Java Programming
240.......Intro to the Basic Language

7 rows selected.
```

_____

_____

LAB 3.1 EXERCISE ANSWERS

3.1.1 ANSWERS

a) Execute the following SQL statement. Based on the result, what is the purpose of the UPPER function?

```
SELECT state, UPPER(state), UPPER('State')
  FROM zipcode
```

Answer: The UPPER function transforms a string of any case into upper case.

```
ST UP UPPER
-- -- -----
PR PR STATE
MA MA STATE
...
NY NY STATE
NY NY STATE

227 rows selected.
```

The UPPER function, as you might expect, has the opposite effect of the LOWER function. It is very common for data entry to be performed by several people. This leads to inconsistent use of case in a database. The UPPER and LOWER functions transform the data as you select it so you don't have to worry about how the data is stored.

b) Execute the following SQL statement. Based on the result, what is the purpose of the INITCAP function?

```
SELECT description "Description",
       INITCAP(description) "Initcap Description"
  FROM course
 WHERE description LIKE '%SQL%'
```

> *Answer: The INITCAP function capitalizes the first letter of a word and forces the remaining characters to lower case.*

The result set contains two rows, one displaying a course description as it appears in the database, and one displaying each word with only the first letter capitalized. Notice that INITCAP forces any capitalized words, such as PL/SQL or SQL, to be in lower case.

```
Description                 Initcap Description
-------------------------   -------------------------
Intro to SQL                Intro To Sql
PL/SQL Programming          Pl/Sql Programming

2 rows selected.
```

c) Write the question for the SQL statement below.

```
SELECT last_name
  FROM instructor
 WHERE LENGTH(last_name) >= 6
```

> *Answer: Show the last name of any instructor whose last name is six characters or longer.*

```
LAST_NAME
-------------------------
Wojick
Schorin
...
Frantzen
Willig

7 rows selected.
```

The LENGTH function returns the length of a string, and like the INSTR function, always returns a number. The LENGTH function takes only a single input parameter, as in the following syntax:

```
LENGTH(char)
```

d) Describe the result of the SQL statement below. Pay particular attention to the negative number parameter.

```
SELECT SUBSTR('12345', 3),
       SUBSTR('12345', 3, 2),
       SUBSTR('12345', -4, 3)
  FROM dual
```

> *Answer: The first column takes the characters starting from position three until the end, resulting in the string '345'. The second SUBSTR function also starts at position three but ends after two characters, and therefore returns '34'. The third column has a negative number as the first parameter. It counts from the end of the string to the left four characters; the string starts at position 2, and shows three characters '234'.*

```
SUB SU SUB
--- -- ---
345 34 234
```

```
1 row selected.
```

e) Based on the result of the following SQL statement, describe the purpose of the LTRIM and RTRIM functions.

```
SELECT zip, LTRIM(zip, '0'), RTRIM(ZIP, '4')
  FROM zipcode
 ORDER BY zip
```

> *Answer: The LTRIM and RTRIM functions left trim and right trim strings, trimming based on the function's parameters.*

```
ZIP    LTRIM RTRIM
-----  ----- -----
00914  914   0091
01247  1247  01247
...
43224  43224 4322
48104  48104 4810
```

```
227 rows selected.
```

LTRIM and RTRIM are the opposite of LPAD and RPAD because they *trim,* or remove, unwanted characters, symbols, or spaces in strings. With the three columns in the result set side by side, you see the differences: the first column shows zip without modification, the second with zip left-trimmed of its 0s, and the third with zip right-trimmed of its 4s. Here is the syntax for the LTRIM and RTRIM functions:

```
LTRIM(char1 [, char2])
RTRIM(char1 [, char2])
```

The optional parameter `char2` is used to specify which character to trim from the string. If `char2` is not specified, then the string is trimmed of spaces.

NESTED FUNCTIONS

Functions can be *nested* within each other. Nested functions are evaluated starting from the inner function and working outward. The following example shows you the city column formatted in upper case, right padded with periods.

```
SELECT RPAD(UPPER(city), 20,'.')
   FROM zipcode
 WHERE state = 'CT'
RPAD(UPPER(CITY),20,
--------------------
ANSONIA.............
MIDDLEFIELD.........
...
STAMFORD............
STAMFORD............

19 rows selected.
```

Here is a more complicated but useful example. You may have noticed in the student table that middle initials are entered in the same column as the first name. To separate the middle initial from the first name, nest the SUBSTR and INSTR functions. First, determine the position of the middle initial's period in the first_name column with the INSTR function. From this position, deduct the number one. This brings you to the position before the period, where the middle initial starts, which is where you want the SUBSTR function to start. The WHERE clause only selects rows where the third or any subsequent character of the first name contains a period.

For example, in the record 'Austin V.', the position of the '.' is 9, but you need to start at 8 to include the middle initial letter. To list the first name without the middle initial, start with the first character of the string and end the result before the position where the middle initial starts. The key is to determine the ending position of the string with the INSTR function, and count back two characters.

```
SELECT first_name,
       SUBSTR(first_name, INSTR(first_name, '.')-1) mi,
       SUBSTR(first_name, 1, INSTR(first_name, '.')-2)
       first
  FROM student
 WHERE INSTR(first_name, '.') >= 3
```

FIRST_NAME	MI	FIRST
Austin V.	V.	Austin
John T.	T.	John
...		
Suzanne M.	M.	Suzanne
Rafael A.	A.	Rafael

7 rows selected.

When using nested functions, a common pitfall is to misplace matching parentheses, or forget the second half of the pair altogether. Start by writing a nested function from the inside out. Count the number of left parentheses, and make sure it matches the number of right parentheses you have.

It's easy to confuse character functions. When deciding which one to use, ask yourself exactly what is needed in your result set. Are you looking for the position of a string in a string? Do you need to produce a subset of a string? Do you need to know how long a string is? Do you need to replace a string with something else?

3.1.2 ANSWERS

a) Write a SELECT statement that returns each instructor's last name, followed by a comma and a space, followed by the instructor's first name, all in a single column in the result set.

Answer: The instructor last name, a comma and a space, and the instructor first name are all concatenated using the || symbol.

```
SELECT last_name||', '||first_name
  FROM instructor
LAST_NAME||','||FIRST_NAME
--------------------------
Hanks, Fernand
Wojick, Tom
...
Frantzen, Marilyn
Willig, Irene

10 rows selected.
```

b) Using functions in the SELECT list, WHERE, and ORDER BY clauses, write the SELECT statement that returns course numbers and course descriptions from the course table, and looks exactly like the following result set:

```
204.......Intro to SQL
130.......Intro to Unix
230.......Intro to Internet
20........Intro to Computers
25........Intro to Programming
120.......Intro to Java Programming
240.......Intro to the Basic Language

7 rows selected.
```

Answer: The RPAD function right pads the course_no column with periods, up to 10 characters long; it is then concatenated with the description column. The INSTR function is used in the WHERE clause to filter on descriptions starting with the string 'Intro'. The LENGTH function is used in the ORDER BY clause to sort the result set by ascending (shortest to longest) description length.

```
SELECT RPAD(course_no, 10, '.')||description
  FROM course
 WHERE INSTR(description, 'Intro') = 1
 ORDER BY LENGTH(description)
```

The same result can be obtained without the use of a function, as in the following WHERE clause:

```
WHERE description LIKE 'Intro%'
```

As you can see, concatenation combined with functions is a powerful way to quickly produce result sets that are useful and easy to read.

LAB 3.1 SELF-REVIEW QUESTIONS

In order to test your progress, you should be able to answer the following questions.

1) Functions that operate on single values may only have one input parameter.
   a) _____ True
   b) _____ False

2) The dual table can be used for testing functions.
   a) _____ True
   b) _____ False

3) The same function can be used twice in a SELECT statement.
   a) _____ True
   b) _____ False

4) The following SELECT statement contains an error:
```
SELECT UPPER(description)
  FROM LOWER(course)
```
   a) _____ True
   b) _____ False

5) The RTRIM function is useful for eliminating extra spaces in a string.
   a) _____ True
   b) _____ False

6) Which one of the string functions below tells you how many characters are in a string?
   a) _____ INSTR
   b) _____ SUBSTR
   c) _____ LENGTH
   d) _____ REPLACE

Quiz answers appear in Appendix A, Section 3.1.

L A B   3 . 2

NUMBER FUNCTIONS

LAB OBJECTIVES

After this lab, you will be able to:

✔ Use Number Functions and Perform
Mathematical Computations

Number functions are valuable tools for operations such as rounding numbers or computing the absolute value of a number. There are several number functions in Oracle, some of which are discussed here.

THE ABS FUNCTION

The ABS function computes the *absolute value* of a number, measuring its magnitude:

```
SELECT 'The absolute value of -29 is '||ABS(-29)
  FROM dual
'THEABSOLUTEVALUEOF-29IS'||ABS(
-------------------------------
The absolute value of -29 is 29

1 row selected.
```

ABS takes only a single input parameter, and its syntax is this:

```
ABS(value)
```

THE SIGN FUNCTION

The SIGN function tells you the *sign* of a value, returning a number 1 for positive numbers, −1 for negative numbers, or 0 for a zero. The following example compares SIGN with the ABS function:

```
SELECT -14, SIGN(-14), SIGN(14), SIGN(0), ABS(-14)
  FROM dual
     -14 SIGN(-14) SIGN(14)    SIGN(0)  ABS(-14)
--------- --------- -------- ---------- ---------
     -14        -1        1          0        14
```

1 row selected.

SIGN also takes only a single input parameter, and its syntax is this:

```
SIGN(value)
```

Most single row functions, with few exceptions such as NVL (discussed in Chapter 4), return NULL when a NULL is the input parameter.

THE MOD FUNCTION

MOD is a function returning the *modulus,* or the remainder, of a value divided by another value. It takes two input parameters, as in this SELECT statement:

```
SELECT MOD(20, 7)
  FROM dual
 MOD(20,7)
----------
         6
```

1 row selected.

The MOD function divides 20 by 7; the quotient is 2, returning a remainder of 6. Here is the syntax for MOD:

```
MOD(value, divisor)
```

ROUND VERSUS TRUNC

ROUND and TRUNC are two useful functions that *round* and *truncate* (or cut off) values, respectively, based on a given number of digits of precision.

■ FOR EXAMPLE

The following SELECT statement illustrates the use of ROUND and TRUNC, which both take two input parameters:

```
SELECT 222.34501,
       ROUND(222.34501,2),
       TRUNC(222.34501,2)
  FROM dual
222.34501 ROUND(222.34501,2) TRUNC(222.34501,2)
--------- ------------------ ------------------
222.34501             222.35             222.34

1 row selected.
```

Here, ROUND(2.34501,2) rounds the number 2.34501 to two digits to the right of the decimal, rounding the result *up* to 2.35, following the normal convention for rounding. In contrast, TRUNC has cut off all digits beyond two digits to the right of the decimal, resulting in 2.34. ROUND and TRUNC can be used to affect the *left* side of the decimal as well by passing a negative number as a parameter:

```
SELECT 222.34501,
       ROUND(222.34501,-2),
       TRUNC(222.34501,-2)
  FROM dual
222.34501 ROUND(222.34501,-2) TRUNC(222.34501,-2)
--------- ------------------- -------------------
222.34501                 200                 200

1 row selected.
```

Here is the syntax for both ROUND and TRUNC:

```
ROUND(value [, precision])
TRUNC(value [, precision])
```

Numbers with decimal places may be rounded to whole numbers by omitting the second parameter, or specifying a precision of 0:

```
SELECT 2.617, ROUND(2.617), TRUNC(2.617)
  FROM dual
```

```
2.617 ROUND(2.617) TRUNC(2.617)
----- ------------ ------------
2.617            3            2
```

```
1 row selected.
```

ARITHMETIC OPERATORS

The four mathematical operators, addition, subtraction, multiplication, and division, may be used in a SQL statement, and can be combined.

■ FOR EXAMPLE

Here, each of the four computations is used with course costs. Notice that one of the distinct course costs is NULL. Any computation with a NULL value yields another NULL.

```
SELECT DISTINCT cost, cost + 10,
       cost - 10, cost * 10, cost / 10
   FROM course
```

COST	COST+10	COST-10	COST*10	COST/10
1095	1105	1085	10950	109.5
1195	1205	1185	11950	119.5
1595	1605	1585	15950	159.5

```
4 rows selected.
```

Parentheses are used to group computations, indicating precedence of the operators.

The following SELECT statement returns distinct course costs increased by 10%. The computation within the parentheses is evaluated first, followed by the addition of the value in the cost column, resulting in a single number:

```
SELECT DISTINCT cost + (cost * .10)
   FROM course
COST+(COST*.10)
---------------
        1204.5
        1314.5
        1754.5
```

```
4 rows selected.
```

NULL values can be replaced with a default value. You will learn about this topic in Chapter 4.

LAB 3.2 EXERCISES

3.2.1 USE NUMBER FUNCTIONS AND PERFORM MATHEMATICAL COMPUTATIONS

a) Describe the effect of the negative precision as a parameter of the ROUND function in the following SQL statement.

```
SELECT 10.245, ROUND(10.245, 1), ROUND(10.245, -1)
  FROM dual
```

_____

_____

b) Write a SELECT statement that displays distinct course costs. In a separate column, show the cost increased by 75%, and round the decimals to the nearest dollar.

_____

_____

c) Write a SELECT statement that displays distinct numeric grades from the grade table, and half those values expressed as a whole number in a separate column.

_____

_____

LAB 3.2 EXERCISE ANSWERS

3.2.1 ANSWERS

a) Describe the effect of the negative precision as a parameter of the ROUND function in the following SQL statement.

```
SELECT 10.245, ROUND(10.245, 1), ROUND(10.245, -1)
  FROM dual
```

Answer: A negative precision rounds digits to the left of the decimal point.

```
10.245 ROUND(10.245,1) ROUND(10.245,-1)
--------- --------------- ----------------
10.245          10.2                 10
```

1 row selected.

A negative precision can also be used in the TRUNC function, as in the following example:

```
SELECT 10.245, TRUNC(10.245, 1), TRUNC(10.245, -1)
  FROM DUAL
   10.245 TRUNC(10.245,1) TRUNC(10.245,-1)
--------- --------------- ----------------
   10.245          10.2                 10
```

1 row selected.

The ROUND and TRUNC functions can also use a column of DATE datatype as a parameter. This topic is covered in Chapter 4.

b) Write a SELECT statement that displays distinct course costs. In a separate column, show the cost increased by 75%, and round the decimals to the nearest dollar.

Answer: The SELECT statement uses multiplication and the ROUND function.

```
SELECT DISTINCT cost, cost*1.75, ROUND(cost*1.75)
  FROM course
     COST COST*1.75 ROUND(COST*1.75)
--------- --------- ----------------
     1095   1916.25             1916
     1195   2091.25             2091
     1595   2791.25             2791
```

4 rows selected.

c) Write a SELECT statement that displays distinct numeric grades from the grade table, and half those values expressed as a whole number in a separate column.

Answer: The SELECT statement uses division to derive the value that is half the original value. That value becomes the input parameter for the ROUND function, without specifying a precision, to display the result as a whole number.

```
SELECT DISTINCT numeric_grade, ROUND(numeric_grade / 2)
  FROM grade
```

```
NUMERIC_GRADE ROUND(NUMERIC_GRADE/2)
------------- ----------------------
           70                     35
           71                     36
...
           98                     49
           99                     50
```

30 rows selected.

Here, a mathematical computation is combined with a function. Be sure to place computations correctly, either inside or outside the parentheses of a function, depending on the desired result. In this case, if the / 2 were on the outside of the ROUND function, a very different result occurs, not the correct answer to the task that was posed.

LAB 3.2 SELF-REVIEW QUESTIONS

In order to test your progress, you should be able to answer the following questions.

1) Number functions can be nested.
   a) _____ True
   b) _____ False

2) Number functions can use a string as an input parameter.
   a) _____ True
   b) _____ False

3) The ROUND function can take only the NUMBER datatype as a parameter.
   a) _____ True
   b) _____ False

4) The following SELECT statement is incorrect:
```
SELECT capacity - capacity
  FROM section
```
   a) _____ True
   b) _____ False

5) What does the following function return?
```
SELECT LENGTH(NULL)
  FROM dual
```
   a) _____ 4
   b) _____ 0
   c) _____ Null

Quiz answers appear in Appendix A, Section 3.2.

C H A P T E R   3

TEST YOUR THINKING

1) Write the SELECT statement that returns the following output. Be sure to use spaces and punctuation exactly as you see them.

```
Instructor: R. Chow...... Phone: 212-555-1212
Instructor: M. Frantzen.. Phone: 212-555-1212
Instructor: F. Hanks..... Phone: 212-555-1212
Instructor: C. Lowry..... Phone: 212-555-1212
Instructor: A. Morris.... Phone: 212-555-1212
Instructor: G. Pertez.... Phone: 212-555-1212
Instructor: N. Schorin... Phone: 212-555-1212
Instructor: T. Smythe.... Phone: 212-555-1212
Instructor: I. Willig.... Phone: 212-555-1212
Instructor: T. Wojick.... Phone: 212-555-1212
```

2) Rewrite the following query to replace all occurrences of the string 'Unix' with 'Linux'.

```
SELECT 'I develop software on the Unix platform'
  FROM dual
```

3) Determine which student does not have the first initial of her/his last name capitalized. Show the student_id and last name.

4) Check if any of the phone numbers in the instructor table have been entered in the (###)###-#### format.

C H A P T E R 4

DATE AND CONVERSION FUNCTIONS

CHAPTER OBJECTIVES

In this chapter, you will learn about:

- ✔ Converting From One Datatype to Another   Page   92
- ✔ Applying Oracle's Date Format Masks   Page   98
- ✔ Performing Date and Time Math   Page   110
- ✔ The NVL and DECODE Functions   Page   116

In this chapter, you explore the Oracle conversion functions that allow you to convert a literal or column from one datatype to another. Like character and number functions, date and conversion functions are single row functions. The SQL novice often finds date and conversion functions challenging; the many examples in the labs help you master these functions and avoid the common pitfalls.

Furthermore, you gain an understanding of Oracle's unique date format, and apply date functions in calculations. You gain experience using the NVL function to replace NULLs with default values. As you become more proficient with SQL, the DECODE function becomes one of your favorites, allowing you to perform powerful *if then else* comparisons.

L A B   4 . 1

CONVERTING FROM ONE DATATYPE TO ANOTHER

LAB OBJECTIVES

After this lab, you will be able to:

✔ Convert From a NUMBER to a CHAR Datatype and Vice Versa
✔ Format Data

You know the good old phrase, "You can't compare apples to oranges." SQL works just the same way. When you compare the datatype of a literal or column to the datatype of another literal or column, Oracle cannot always convert from one datatype to the other. It is preferable to explicitly specify the conversion with a function to avoid any ambiguities or errors when your SQL statement is executed.

DATATYPE CONVERSION

In the following SQL statement, the WHERE clause compares a text literal to the column course_no, which is of NUMBER datatype.

```
SELECT course_no, description
  FROM course
 WHERE course_no = '350'
COURSE_NO DESCRIPTION
--------- -------------------------------------------
      350 JDeveloper Lab


1 row selected.
```

From the result set, you see that Oracle implicitly makes the conversion between the text literal and the column course_no. However, it is preferable to explicitly convert the values. The following WHERE clause accomplishes the conversion:

```
WHERE course_no = TO_NUMBER('350')
```

Table 4.1 provides you with an overview of the three most commonly used Oracle conversion functions. In this lab you will concentrate on the TO_NUMBER and the TO_CHAR conversion functions, and in Lab 4.2 on TO_DATE together with the TO_CHAR conversion function.

Table 4.1 ■ Common Datatype Conversion Functions

Function	Purpose
TO_NUMBER	Converts a VARCHAR2 or CHAR to a NUMBER.
TO_CHAR	Converts a DATE or NUMBER to a VARCHAR2.
TO_DATE	Converts a VARCHAR2, CHAR, or NUMBER to a DATE.

FORMATTING DATA

The conversion functions are not only useful for comparison between different datatypes, but also for formatting data. In the next SQL statement you see how a *format mask* can be applied using the TO_CHAR function. To display a formatted result for the cost column, for instance, you can apply the format mask '999,999'. The cost is then formatted with a comma separating the thousands.

```
SELECT course_no, cost,
       TO_CHAR(cost ,'999,999') formatted
  FROM course
 WHERE course_no < 25
COURSE_NO      COST FORMATTED
--------- --------- -----------
       10      1195     1,195
       20      1195     1,195

2 rows selected.
```

The conversion function used in the SELECT statement does not modify the values stored in the database, but rather performs a "temporary" conversion for the purpose of executing the statement. The result of the conversion is displayed in the result set only. In Chapter 2, "SQL: The Basics," you learned about the SQL*Plus COLUMN FORMAT command. The following example achieves the same result.

```
COL cost FORMAT 999,999
SELECT course_no, cost,
       TO_CHAR(cost ,'999,999') formatted
  FROM course
 WHERE course_no < 25
COURSE_NO      COST FORMATTE
---------  -------- --------
       10     1,195    1,195
       20     1,195    1,195
```

2 rows selected.

However, if you execute the SQL statement from a program other than SQL*Plus, the COLUMN command is not available, and you must use the TO_CHAR function.

Table 4.2 provides an overview of the most popular NUMBER format models that can be applied with the TO_CHAR function. Notice that rounding can also be accomplished using a format model.

TABLE 4. 2 ■ Common Number Format Models

Format Mask	Example	Result
999,990.99	.45	0.45 — Note the leading zero
$99,999.99	1234	$1,234.00
999	123.59	124 — Note the rounding

LAB 4.1 EXERCISES

4.1.1 CONVERT FROM A CHAR TO A NUMBER DATATYPE AND VICE VERSA

Type and execute the following query:

```
SELECT zip, city
  FROM zipcode
 WHERE zip = 10025
```

a) Rewrite the query using the TO_CHAR function in the WHERE clause.

_____

_____

b) Rewrite the query using the TO_NUMBER function in the WHERE clause.

4.1.2 FORMAT DATA

a) Format the cost of course number 330 to display the cost with a leading dollar sign, a comma to separate the thousands, and include cents.

b) List the course number and cost of courses that cost more than 1500. As a third column, show the cost increased by 15%. Display the result with a leading dollar sign, separate the thousands, and round to the nearest dollar.

LAB 4.1 EXERCISE ANSWERS

4.1.1 ANSWERS

Type and execute the following query:

```
SELECT zip, city
  FROM zipcode
 WHERE zip = 10025
```

a) Rewrite the query using the TO_CHAR function in the WHERE clause.

Answer: The TO_CHAR function converts the number literal to a VARCHAR2 datatype, which makes it equivalent to the VARCHAR2 datatype of the zip column.

```
SELECT zip, city
  FROM zipcode
 WHERE zip = TO_CHAR(10025)
```

```
ZIP    CITY
----   ---------
10025  New York
```

1 row selected.

b) Rewrite the query using the TO_NUMBER function in the WHERE clause.

Answer: The VARCHAR2 datatype of the zip column is converted to a NUMBER datatype by applying the TO_NUMBER function. Oracle then compares it to the number literal 10025.

```
SELECT zip, city
  FROM zipcode
 WHERE TO_NUMBER(zip) = 10025
ZIP    CITY
-----  --------
10025  New York
```

1 row selected.

When you compare the results of the SQL statements from answers a and b, they are identical. Answer b is less desirable because a function is applied to a database column in the WHERE clause. This disables the use of any *indexes* that may exist on the zip column, causing Oracle to perform a *full table scan*. Applying functions to database columns in the SELECT clause does not affect performance. You will learn about indexes in Chapter 12, "Views, Indexes, and Sequences," and about performance considerations in Chapter 16, "SQL Optimization."

4.1.2 ANSWERS

a) Format the cost of course number 330 to display the cost with a leading dollar sign, a comma to separate the thousands, and include cents.

Answer: The TO_CHAR function, together with the format mask in the SELECT clause of the statement, achieves the desired formatting.

```
SELECT course_no, cost,
       TO_CHAR(cost, '$999,999.99')Formatted
  FROM course
 WHERE course_no = 330
COURSE_NO      COST FORMATTED
---------  --------- ------------
      330       1195    $1,195.00
```

1 row selected.

b) List the course number and cost of courses that cost more than 1500. As a third column, show the cost increased by 15%. Display the result with a leading dollar sign, separate the thousands, and round to the nearest dollar.

Answer: An increase of 15% means a multiplication of the column cost by 1.15. You can either round to the nearest dollar by using the ROUND function or use the format mask to omit the cents.

```
SELECT course_no, cost oldcost, cost*1.15 newcost,
       TO_CHAR(cost*1.15, '$999,999') formatted,
       TO_CHAR(ROUND(cost*1.15), '$999,999.99')
       rounded
  FROM course
 WHERE cost > 1500
```

COURSE_NO	OLDCOST	NEWCOST	FORMATTED	ROUNDED
80	1595	1834.25	$1,834	$1,834.00

1 row selected

LAB 4.1 SELF-REVIEW QUESTIONS

In order to test your progress, you should be able to answer the following questions. There may be more than one correct answer, so choose all that apply.

1) Which SQL statements result in an error?
   a) _____ SELECT TO_CHAR('123') FROM dual
   b) _____ SELECT TO_CHAR(123) FROM dual
   c) _____ SELECT TO_NUMBER('001.99999') FROM dual
   d) _____ SELECT TO_NUMBER('A123') FROM dual
   e) _____ SELECT TO_CHAR('A123') FROM dual
   f) _____ SELECT TO_NUMBER(' 000123 ') FROM dual

2) Which of the following NUMBER format masks is valid?
   a) _____ SELECT TO_CHAR(1.99,'9,9999.9X') FROM dual
   b) _____ SELECT TO_CHAR(1.99,'A99.99) FROM dual
   c) _____ SELECT TO_CHAR(1.99,'$000.99') FROM dual
   d) _____ SELECT TO_CHAR(1.99,'999.99') FROM dual
   e) _____ SELECT TO_CHAR(1.99,'.99') FROM dual

3) Explicit datatype conversion is preferable to Oracle's implicit conversion.
   a) _____ True
   b) _____ False

4) Conversion functions are single row functions.
   a) _____ True
   b) _____ False

Quiz answers appear in Appendix A, Section 4.1.

LAB 4.2

APPLYING ORACLE'S DATE FORMAT MODELS

LAB OBJECTIVES

After this lab, you will be able to:

✔ Compare a Text Literal to a DATE Column
✔ Apply Format Models

The Oracle DATE datatype consists of a *date and time stamp*. Oracle stores dates in an internal format that keeps track of the century, year, month, day, hour, minute, and second. When you query a DATE column, Oracle typically displays it in the default DD-MON-YY format, such as 25-FEB-00.

■ *FOR EXAMPLE*

To change the display format of the column registration_date in the following query, you use the TO_CHAR function together with a format model, also referred to as a format mask. The result shows the registration_date in both the default date format and in the MM/DD/YYYY format.

```
SELECT last_name, registration_date,
       TO_CHAR(registration_date, 'MM/DD/YYYY')
  FROM student
 WHERE registration_date = '22-JAN-99'
LAST_NAME                      REGISTRAT TO_CHAR(RE
------------------------------ --------- ----------
Landry                         22-JAN-99 01/22/1999
```

```
Olvsade                    22-JAN-99 01/22/1999
...
Walter                     22-JAN-99 01/22/1999
Mierzwa                    22-JAN-99 01/22/1999
```

8 rows selected.

In the WHERE clause, the text literal '22-JAN-99' is compared to the DATE column registration_date. Oracle implicitly performs a conversion of the text literal to the DATE datatype because the text literal is in the default date format. If the text literal is in a different format, the TO_DATE function must be applied, together with the format mask to tell Oracle how to translate the text literal.

It is best to explicitly use the TO_DATE function when converting a text literal such as '22-JAN-99'. Always include a four-digit year to avoid any ambiguities.

The next SQL statement shows you an example of a text literal that is *not* in the default date format. Oracle cannot perform an implicit conversion of the text literal '01/22/1999'; it must be explicitly converted to a DATE datatype, telling Oracle how to interpret it using the format mask MM/DD/YYYY.

```
SELECT last_name, registration_date,
       TO_CHAR(registration_date, 'MM/DD/YYYY')
  FROM student
 WHERE registration_date =
       TO_DATE('01/22/1999', 'MM/DD/YYYY')
```

Table 4.3 provides an overview of DATE format masks. This list is not complete, but it gives you a good idea of the most commonly used DATE format masks. You will gain experience using some of them in this lab.

TABLE 4.3 ■ Common Date Format Models

Format Mask	Example	Result
DD-Mon-YYYY HH24:MI:SS	12-APR-99 17:00:00	12-Apr-1999 17:00:00 — Note: The case matters!
MM/DD/YYYY HH:MI pm	12-APR-99 17:00:00	04/12/1999 5:00 pm
Day	12-APR-99 17:00:00	Monday
DY	12-APR-99 17:00:00	MON
Qth YYYY	12-APR-99 17:00:00	2nd 1999 — Note: This shows the 2nd quarter of 1999.

LAB 4.2 EXERCISES

4.2.1 COMPARE A TEXT LITERAL TO A DATE COLUMN

a) Display the course number, section id, and starting date and time for sections that are taught on May 4, 1999.

b) Show the student records that were modified before January 25, 1999. Display the date the record was modified and each student's first and last name concatenated in one column.

4.2.2 APPLY FORMAT MODELS

a) Display the course number, section id, and starting date and time for sections that start on Tuesdays.

b) List the section id and starting date and time for all sections that begin and end in July 1999.

c) Determine the day of the week for December 31, 1899.

LAB 4.2 EXERCISE ANSWERS

4.2.1 ANSWERS

a) Display the course number, section id, and starting date and time for sections that are taught on May 4,1999.

Answer: To compare a text literal with a DATE column, use the TO_DATE function. To display a DATE column in any format, use the TO_CHAR function.

```
SELECT course_no, section_id,
       TO_CHAR(start_date_time, 'DD-MON-YYYY HH24:MI')
  FROM section
 WHERE start_date_time >= TO_DATE('04-MAY-99')
   AND start_date_time < TO_DATE('05-MAY-99')
COURSE_NO SECTION_ID TO_CHAR(START_DAT
--------- ---------- -----------------
       25         88 04-MAY-1999 09:30
      100        144 04-MAY-1999 09:30
      120        149 04-MAY-1999 09:30
      122        155 04-MAY-1999 09:30

4 rows selected.
```

In the WHERE clause the text literal '04-May-99' is transformed into a DATE datatype. If no format mask for the time is specified, Oracle assumes the time is midnight, which is 12:00:00 A.M., or 00:00:00 military time (HH24 time format mask). The WHERE clause retrieves only those rows where the start_date_time column has values on or after '04-MAY-1999 12:00:00 A.M.' and before '05-MAY-1999 12:00:00 A.M.'

You do not need to specify a format mask in the WHERE clause because the text literals are in the Oracle date default format mask. The rows also display the starting date and time using the TO_CHAR function.

The query returns the same result when the following WHERE clause is used instead, but Oracle has to perform the implicit conversion of the text literal into a DATE datatype:

```
WHERE start_date_time >= '04-MAY-99'
  AND start_date_time < '05-MAY-99'
```

THE TRUNC FUNCTION

Alternatively, you can use the TRUNC function on the start_date_time column, which interprets the time stamp as 12:00:00 A.M.

```
SELECT course_no, section_id,
       TO_CHAR(start_date_time,
       'DD-MON-YYYY HH24:MI')
  FROM section
 WHERE TRUNC(start_date_time) = '04-MAY-99'
```

When you modify a column with a function in the WHERE clause, as in the previous statement, you cannot take advantage of an index should one exist on the column.

The next statement does not return the desired rows. Only rows that have a start_date_time of midnight on May 4, 1999 qualify.

```
SELECT course_no, section_id,
       TO_CHAR(start_date_time,
       'DD-MON-YYYY HH24:MI')
  FROM section
 WHERE start_date_time = '04-MAY-99'
```

no rows selected

b) Show the student records that were modified before January 25, 1999. Display the date the record was modified and each student's first and last name concatenated in one column.

Answer: The query compares the modified date to the text literal. The text literal may be in either the Oracle default format or, better yet, formatted with the TO_DATE function and the appropriate format model.

```
SELECT first_name||' '||last_name fullname,
       modified_date
  FROM student
 WHERE modified_date <
       TO_DATE('01/25/1999','MM/DD/YYYY')
FULLNAME                          MODIFIED_
------------------------------    ---------
J. Landry                         22-JAN-99
Judith Olvsade                    22-JAN-99
...
Larry Walter                      22-JAN-99
Catherine Mierzwa                 22-JAN-99
```

8 rows selected.

It is best to explicitly use the TO_DATE function to convert the text literal into a DATE datatype using the format mask 'MM/DD/YYYY'. It does not really matter which format mask you use as long as you inform Oracle how to interpret it.

When you consider the year 2000 problem, it is best to always include the century when you are working with a DATE datatype.

The Whole Truth

Date Formats and the Year 2000: If you don't explicitly specify a century, Oracle assumes the current century. After the year 2000, the text literal '26-JAN-99' is translated as January 26, 2099. To avoid this problem, always specify a four-digit year.

Alternatively, Oracle has created the RR year format that masks the two-digit year to the closest century. Years from 50 to 99 are assumed to be from 1950 until 1999. Years from 00 to 49 are considered 2000 until 2049. To modify the Oracle default mask from DD-MON-YY to DD-MON-RR, until you log off SQL*Plus, you can issue the SQL command ALTER SESSION at the SQL*Plus prompt:

```
ALTER SESSION SET NLS_DATE_FORMAT = 'DD-MON-RR'
```

Visit the companion Web site for this book, located at http://www.phptr.com/Morrison, to find out how to permanently change the format mask for your individual system environment.

4.2.2 ANSWERS

a) Display the course number, section id, and starting date and time for sections that start on Tuesdays.

Answer: The correct answer uses one of the day of the week format masks. The SQL statement shows all the sections that start on Tuesday by using the DY format mask which displays the abbreviated day of the week in capitalized letters.

```
SELECT course_no, section_id,
       TO_CHAR(start_date_time, 'DY DD-MON-YYYY')
  FROM section
 WHERE TO_CHAR(start_date_time, 'DY') = 'TUE'
COURSE_NO SECTION_ID TO_CHAR(START_D
--------- ---------- ---------------
       25         88 TUE 04-MAY-1999
      100        144 TUE 04-MAY-1999
      120        149 TUE 04-MAY-1999
      122        155 TUE 04-MAY-1999
```

4 rows selected.

THE FILL MODE

Some of the format masks are tricky. For example, if you choose the 'Day' format mask, you must specify the correct case and omit the extra blanks. The following query does not return any rows.

```
SELECT course_no, section_id,
       TO_CHAR(start_date_time, 'Day DD-Mon-YYYY')
  FROM section
 WHERE TO_CHAR(start_date_time, 'Day') = 'Tuesday'
```

no rows selected

Use the *fill* mode (fm) with the format mask to suppress the extra blanks:

```
SELECT course_no, section_id,
       TO_CHAR(start_date_time, 'Day DD-Mon-YYYY')
  FROM section
 WHERE TO_CHAR(start_date_time, 'fmDay') = 'Tuesday'
COURSE_NO SECTION_ID TO_CHAR(START_DATE_TI
--------- ---------- ---------------------
       25         88 Tuesday    04-May-1999
      100        144 Tuesday    04-May-1999
```

```
      120            149 Tuesday    04-May-1999
      122            155 Tuesday    04-May-1999
```

4 rows selected.

In the following query, notice that the extra blanks between the month and date are omitted in the fourth column using the fill mode:

```
SELECT course_no, section_id,
       TO_CHAR(start_date_time, 'Month DD'),
       TO_CHAR(start_date_time, 'fmMonth DD')
  FROM section
 WHERE TO_CHAR(start_date_time, 'fmDay') = 'Tuesday'
COURSE_NO SECTION_ID TO_CHAR(STAR TO_CHAR(STAR
--------- ---------- ------------ ------------
       25         88 May          04 May 4
      100        144 May          04 May 4
      120        149 May          04 May 4
      122        155 May          04 May 4
```

4 rows selected.

b) List the section ID and starting date and time for all sections that begin and end in July 1999.

Answer: There are often several different solutions that may deliver the same result set. Look at the various solutions and the pitfalls.

SOLUTION ONE:

```
SELECT section_id,
       TO_CHAR(start_date_time, 'DD-MON-YYYY HH24:MI:SS')
  FROM section
 WHERE start_date_time >= TO_DATE('07/01/1999', 'MM/DD/YYYY ')
   AND start_date_time <  TO_DATE('08/01/1999', 'MM/DD/YYYY')
SECTION_ID TO_CHAR(START_DATE_T
---------- --------------------
        81 24-JUL-1999 09:30:00
        85 14-JUL-1999 10:30:00
...
       147 24-JUL-1999 09:30:00
       153 24-JUL-1999 09:30:00
```

14 rows selected.

Based on the output, you see that solution one takes the time stamp into consideration.

Always think about the time stamp when you compare dates. Also note that a function applied to a database column disables the use of any indexes that may exist on the column. (See Chapter 12, "Views, Indexes, and Sequences" and Chapter 16, "SQL Optimization.")

The following query will *not* yield the correct result if you have a section that starts on July 31, 1999 at 18:00. The TO_DATE function converts the string to a DATE datatype and sets the time stamp to 12:00:00 A.M. Therefore, a section starting on July 31, 1999 at 18:00 is not considered part of the range.

```
SELECT section_id,
       TO_CHAR(start_date_time, 'DD-MON-YYYY HH24:MI:SS')
  FROM section
 WHERE start_date_time BETWEEN
       TO_DATE('07/01/1999', 'MM/DD/YYYY')
   AND TO_DATE('07/31/1999', 'MM/DD/YYYY')
```

SOLUTION TWO:

This solution includes the 24-hour time format mask.

```
SELECT section_id,
       TO_CHAR(start_date_time, 'DD-MON-YYYY HH24:MI:SS')
  FROM section
 WHERE start_date_time BETWEEN
       TO_DATE('07/01/1999', 'MM/DD/YYYY')
   AND TO_DATE('07/31/1999 23:59:59', 'MM/DD/YYYY HH24:MI:SS')
```

This WHERE clause can also be used to obtain the correct result:

```
WHERE TRUNC(start_date_time) BETWEEN
      TO_DATE('07/01/1999', 'MM/DD/YYYY')
  AND TO_DATE('07/31/1999', 'MM/DD/YYYY')
```

The query ignores the date and time stamp on the column start_date_time completely, and also returns the correct answer.

The following WHERE clause also returns the correct result because the literals are in the correct Oracle default format mask. However, it is best not to rely on Oracle's implicit conversion, and to specify the conversion function together with the four-digit year.

```
WHERE TRUNC(start_date_time) BETWEEN
      '1-JUL-99' AND '31-JUL-99'
```

Be sure to choose the correct datatype conversion function in your WHERE clause.

Another common source of errors when using dates is using the wrong datatype conversion function, as illustrated in this example:

```
SELECT section_id,
       TO_CHAR(start_date_time, 'DD-MON-YYYY HH24:MI:SS')
  FROM section
 WHERE TO_CHAR(start_date_time, 'DD-MON-YYYY HH24:MI:SS')
       >= '01-JUL-1999 00:00:00'
   AND TO_CHAR(start_date_time, 'DD-MON-YYYY HH24:MI:SS')
       <= '31-JUL-1999 23:59:59'
SECTION_ID TO_CHAR(START_DATE_T
---------- --------------------
        79 14-APR-1999 09:30:00
        80 24-APR-1999 09:30:00
...
       155 04-MAY-1999 09:30:00
       156 15-MAY-1999 09:30:00

78 rows selected.
```

The column start_date_time is converted to a character column in the WHERE clause, and then compared to the text literal. The problem is that the dates are no longer compared; instead the character representation of the text literal and the character representation of the contents of the column start_date_time are in the format 'DD-MON-YYYY HH24:MI:SS'. A column value such as '14-APR-1999 09:30:00' is inclusive of the text literals '01-JUL-1999 00:00:00' and '31-JUL-1999 23:59:59', because the column value 1 falls within the range of the characters 0 and 3. Therefore the condition is true and the record returned.

To illustrate the effect of character comparisons further, look at the next two examples. The first checks whether the number 3 is between the numbers 10 and 35, and subsequently does not return a row. This check is performed against the dual table and no row returned because the condition is not true.

```
SELECT *
  FROM dual
 WHERE 3 BETWEEN 10 AND 35
```

no rows selected

The next example is the same condition, but this time the numbers are enclosed by quotes making them *text literals*. Now the row is selected because the text literal '3' is considered between '10' and '35'.

```
SELECT *
  FROM dual
 WHERE '3' BETWEEN '10' AND '35'
D
-
X
```

1 row selected.

The same holds true when you copy the text literals from the previous example into the SQL query following.

```
SELECT *
  FROM dual
 WHERE '14-APR-1999 09:30:00' BETWEEN
       '01-JUL-1999 00:00:00'
   AND '31-JUL-1999 23:59:59'
D
-
X
```

1 row selected.

c) Determine the day of the week for December 31, 1899.

Answer: The day of the week is Sunday. You need to nest conversion functions by using the TO_DATE function to convert the text literal to a DATE datatype, then the TO_CHAR function to display the day of the week.

You translate the text literal '31-DEC-1899' using the format mask 'DD-MON-YYYY' into the Oracle DATE datatype. Then apply the TO_CHAR formatting function to convert the date into any format you wish, in this case to show the day of the week.

```
SELECT TO_CHAR(TO_DATE('31-DEC-1899', 'DD-MON-YYYY'),'Dy')
  FROM dual
```

```
TO_
--
Sun
```

```
1 row selected.
```

LAB 4.2 SELF-REVIEW QUESTIONS

In order to test your progress, you should be able to answer the following questions.

1) The TRUNC function on a date without a format model truncates the time stamp to 12:00:00 A.M.
    a) _____ True
    b) _____ False

2) Converting a text literal to a DATE format requires using the TO_CHAR function.
    a) _____ True
    b) _____ False

3) The format mask 'Dy' displays Monday as follows:
    a) _____ MON
    b) _____ Monday
    c) _____ MONDAY
    d) _____ Mon

4) Choose the format mask that displays "December 31st, 1999".
    a) _____ DD-MON-YYYY
    b) _____ MONTH DDth, YYYY
    c) _____ fmMONTH DD, YYYY
    d) _____ Monthfm DDth, YYYY
    e) _____ fmMonth ddth, yyyy

Quiz answers appear in Appendix A, Section 4.2.

LAB 4.3

PERFORMING DATE AND TIME MATH

LAB OBJECTIVES

After this lab, you will be able to:

✔ Understand the SYSDATE Function and Perform Date Arithmetic

---

The SYSDATE function returns the computer operating system's current date and time, and does not take any parameters.

```
SELECT SYSDATE
  FROM dual
SYSDATE
---------
21-NOV-99


1 row selected.
```

Using the SYSDATE function, you can determine the number of days until the year 2001. This is done by subtracting January 1, 2001 from the current date with the following query:

```
SELECT TO_DATE('01-JAN-2001','DD-MON-YYYY') - TRUNC(SYSDATE) int,
       TO_DATE('01-JAN-2001','DD-MON-YYYY') - SYSDATE dec
  FROM dual
      INT        DEC
--------- ---------
      407 406.04851


1 row selected.
```

To perform any date calculation, the column or text literal must be converted into the Oracle DATE datatype. For the first column, the text literal '01-JAN-2001' is converted into a DATE datatype using the format mask. The time stamp of the text literal '01-JAN-2001' is set to 00:00:00 military time or 12:00:00 A.M. because the time is not specified. From this converted date, the operating system's date is deducted. SYSDATE is nested inside the TRUNC function which truncates the time stamp. The column returns 407 days.

The second column does not use the TRUNC function on SYSDATE, therefore the time stamp is factored into the calculation. The difference is now expressed in both days and time, in decimal format.

THE ROUND FUNCTION

The ROUND function allows you to round days, months, or years. The following SQL statement shows you the current date and time in the first column using the TO_CHAR function and a format mask. The next column shows the current date and time rounded to the next day. If the time stamp is at or past 12:00 noon, it rounds to the next day. The last column displays the date rounded to the nearest month using a format mask.

```
SELECT TO_CHAR(SYSDATE,'DD-MON-YYYY HH24:MI') now,
       TO_CHAR(ROUND(SYSDATE), 'DD-MON-YYYY HH24:MI') day,
       TO_CHAR(ROUND(SYSDATE, 'MM'), 'DD-MON-YYYY HH24:MI') mon
  FROM dual
```

NOW	DAY	MON
21-NOV-1999 22:55	22-NOV-1999 00:00	01-DEC-1999 00:00

```
1 row selected.
```

PERFORMING ARITHMETIC ON DATES

From the previous example on calculating the number of days until the year 2001, you know that you can perform arithmetic on a DATE datatype. In the following example, three hours are added to the current date and time. To determine tomorrow's date and time, simply add the number 1 to the SYSDATE function.

```
SELECT TO_CHAR(SYSDATE, 'MM/DD HH24:MI:SS') now,
      TO_CHAR(SYSDATE+3/24, 'MM/DD HH24:MI:SS') now_plus_3hrs,
      TO_CHAR(SYSDATE+1, 'MM/DD HH24:MI:SS') tomorrow
  FROM dual
```

```
NOW             NOW_PLUS_3HRS   TOMORROW
--------------  --------------  --------------
11/21 22:56:54  11/22 01:56:54  11/22 22:56:54
```

1 row selected.

Oracle has a number of functions to perform specific date calculations. To determine the date of the first Sunday of the year 2000, use the NEXT_DAY function as in the following SELECT statement.

```
SELECT TO_CHAR(TO_DATE('31-DEC-1999','DD-MON-YYYY'),
       'DD-MON-YYYY DY') "New Year's Eve",
       TO_CHAR(NEXT_DAY(TO_DATE('31-DEC-1999',
       'DD-MON-YYYY'),
       'SUNDAY'), 'DD-MON-YYYY DY') next_sunday
  FROM dual
```
New Year's Eve   NEXT_SUNDAY
```
---------------  ---------------
```
31-DEC-1999 FRI 02-JAN-2000 SUN

1 row selected.

The text string '31-DEC-1999' is first converted to a date. To determine the date of the next Sunday, the NEXT_DAY function is applied. Lastly, format the output with a TO_CHAR format mask to display the result in the 'DD-MON-YYYY DY' format.

Table 4.4 lists a number of useful date functions. You will use these functions to solve the following exercises.

TABLE 4.4 ■ Date Functions

Function	Purpose
ADD_MONTHS(date, integer)	Adds or subtracts number of months from a certain date.
LAST_DAY(date)	Returns the last date of the month.
MONTHS_BETWEEN(date2, date1)	Determines the number of months between dates. Unlike the other date functions, this function returns a NUMBER.
NEW_TIME(date, current time zone, new time zone)	Returns the date and time in another other time zone, for example, EST (Eastern Standard Time), PST (Pacific Standard Time), PDT (Pacific Daylight Time).
NEXT_DAY(date, day of the week)	Returns the first day of the week that is later than the date passed.

LAB 4.3 EXERCISES

4.3.1   UNDERSTAND THE *SYSDATE* FUNCTION AND PERFORM DATE ARITHMETIC

a) Determine the number of days between February 13, 1964 and the last day of the same month and year.

_____

_____

b) Compute the number of months between August 17, 2003 and September 29, 1999.

_____

_____

c) List the course number and starting date and time for courses meeting in location 'L500'. Display the date and time in EST and PST time zones.

_____

_____

LAB 4.3 EXERCISE ANSWERS

4.3.1   ANSWERS

a) Determine the number of days between February 13, 1964 and the last day of the same month and year.

Answer: First convert the text literal 13-FEB-1964 to a date. Then use the LAST_DAY function. The date returned is February 29, 1964 as 1964 was a leap year. The difference between the two dates is 16 days.

```
SELECT LAST_DAY(TO_DATE('13-FEB-1964','DD-MON-YYYY'))
       lastday,
       LAST_DAY(TO_DATE('13-FEB-1964','DD-MON-YYYY'))
       - TO_DATE('13-FEB-1964','DD-MON-YYYY') days
  FROM dual
```

```
LASTDAY          DAYS
---------  ---------
29-FEB-64         16
```

1 row selected.

The LAST_DAY function takes a single parameter, and accepts only a column of DATE datatype or a text literal that can be implicitly converted to a date.

b) Compute the number of months between August 17, 2003 and September 29, 1999.

Answer: The simplest solution is to use the MONTHS_BETWEEN function to compute the value.

```
SELECT MONTHS_BETWEEN(TO_DATE('17-AUG-2003','DD-MON-YYYY'),
       TO_DATE('29-SEP-1999','DD-MON-YYYY')) months
  FROM dual
MONTHS
--------------
46.612903
```

1 row selected.

The MONTHS_BETWEEN function takes two dates as its parameters, and returns a NUMBER.

c) List the course number and starting date and time for courses meeting in location 'L500'. Display the date and time in EST and PST time zones.

Answer: The function NEW_TIME requires three parameters. The first parameter is the date you want to convert; the second parameter is the time zone on which the date is based; the third parameter is the time zone in which you want the result to be displayed.

```
SELECT course_no,
       TO_CHAR(start_date_time,
       'DD-MON-YYYY HH:MI PM') est,
       TO_CHAR(NEW_TIME(start_date_time,
       'EST','PST'),
       'DD-MON-YYYY HH:MI PM') pst
  FROM section
 WHERE location = 'L500'
```

```
COURSE_NO   EST                 PST
----------  ------------------- -------------------
       230  07-MAY-1999 09:30 AM 07-MAY-1999 06:30 AM
       100  24-JUL-1999 09:30 AM 24-JUL-1999 06:30 AM
```

2 rows selected.

LAB 4.3 SELF-REVIEW QUESTIONS

In order to test your progress, you should be able to answer the following questions.

1) Using the ADD_MONTHS function, you can subtract months from a given date.

   a) _____ True
   b) _____ False

2) Which one of the following solutions adds 15 minutes to a given date?

   a) _____ SELECT SYSDATE+1/96 FROM dual
   b) _____ SELECT SYSDATE+1/128 FROM dual
   c) _____ SELECT TO_DATE(SYSDATE+1/128) FROM dual
   d) _____ SELECT TO_CHAR(SYSDATE+1/128,
               'DD-MON-YYYY 24HH:MI') FROM dual

3) Choose the date that is calculated by the following query:

```
SELECT NEXT_DAY(TO_DATE('02-JAN-2000 SUN',
       'DD-MON-YYYY DY'), 'SUN')
  FROM dual
```

   a) _____ Sunday January 2, 2000
   b) _____ Monday January 3, 2000
   c) _____ Sunday January 9, 2000
   d) _____ None of the above dates
   e) _____ Invalid query

4) The following query gives you which of the following results?

```
SELECT ROUND(TO_DATE('2000/1/31 11:59',
       'YYYY/MM/DD HH24:MI'))
  FROM dual
```

   a) _____ Returns an Oracle error message
   b) _____ 30-JAN-00
   c) _____ 31-JAN-00
   d) _____ 01-FEB-00

Quiz answers appear in Appendix A, Section 4.3.

L A B   4 . 4

THE NVL AND DECODE FUNCTIONS

LAB OBJECTIVES

After this lab, you will be able to:

✔ Replace NULL Values with the NVL Function
✔ Utilize the Power of DECODE

THE NVL FUNCTION

The NVL function replaces a NULL value with a default value. NULLs represent a special challenge when used in calculations. A computation with an unknown value yields another unknown value, as you see in the following example.

```
SELECT 60+60+NULL
  FROM dual
60+60+NULL
----------
```

1 row selected.

To avoid this problem, use the NVL function; it substitutes the NULL for another value.

```
NVL(input_expression, substitution_expression)
```

The NVL function requires two parameters: an input expression (i.e., a column, literal, or a computation), and a substitution expression. If the input expression does *not* contain a null value, the input parameter is returned. If the input parameter does contain a NULL value, then the substitution parameter is returned.

In the following example, the substitution value is the number literal 1000. The NULL is substituted with 1000, resulting in the output 1120.

```
SELECT 60+60+NVL(NULL,1000)
  FROM dual
```
60+60+NVL(NULL,1000)

**   1120**

1 row selected.

When you substitute a value, the datatype of the substituted value must agree with the datatype of the input parameter. The next example uses the NVL function to substitute any NULL values with 'Not Applicable' in the prerequisite column when the course has no prerequisite. An error is encountered when the statement is executed because the datatypes of the two parameters do not agree. The substitution parameter is a text literal, and the column prerequisite is defined as a NUMBER.

```
SELECT course_no, description,
       NVL(prerequisite,'Not Applicable') prereq
  FROM course
 WHERE course_no IN (20,100)
```
NVL(prerequisite,'Not Applicable')
**   ***

ERROR at line 2:
ORA-01722: invalid number

The error indicates Oracle cannot convert the text literal 'Not Applicable' into a NUMBER. To overcome this problem, transform the output of the prerequisite column into a VARCHAR2 datatype using the TO_CHAR function.

```
SELECT course_no, description,
       NVL(TO_CHAR(prerequisite),'Not Applicable') prereq
  FROM course
 WHERE course_no IN (20,100)
```

COURSE_NO	DESCRIPTION	PREREQ
100	Hands Windows	20
20	Intro to Computers	Not Applicable

2 rows selected.

THE DECODE FUNCTION

The DECODE function substitutes values based on a condition using *if then else* logic. If a value is equal to another value, then the substitution value is returned. If the value compared is not equal to any of the listed expressions, a default value can be returned. The syntax code for the DECODE function is:

```
DECODE (if_expr, equals_search,
        then_result [,else_default])
```

Note the search and result values can be repeated.

In the following query the text literals 'New York' and 'New Jersey' are returned when the state is equal to 'NY' or 'NJ' respectively. If the value in the state column is other than 'NY' or 'NJ', a NULL value is returned. In the second DECODE function, when the state is not equal to 'NY' or 'NJ', the *else* condition is executed. In the case of 'CT', the function returns the value 'Other'.

**LAB
4.4**

■ *FOR EXAMPLE*

```
SELECT DISTINCT state,
       DECODE(state, 'NY', 'New York',
                     'NJ', 'New Jersey') no_default,
       DECODE(state, 'NY', 'New York',
                     'NJ', 'New Jersey',
                           'OTHER') with_default
  FROM zipcode
 WHERE state IN ('NY','NJ','CT')
ST NO_DEFAULT WITH_DEFAU
-- ---------- ----------
CT            Other
NJ New Jersey New Jersey
NY New York    New York

3 rows selected.
```

The DECODE function does not allow greater than or less than comparisons; however, combining the DECODE function with the SIGN function overcomes this shortcoming.

■ *FOR EXAMPLE*

The following SELECT statement combines the DECODE and SIGN functions to display the course cost as 500 for courses that cost less than 1595. If the course cost is greater than or equal to 1595, then the actual cost is displayed. The DECODE function checks if the calculation result equals –1. If so, then the function returns 500, otherwise the regular cost is shown. See Chapter 15, "Advanced SQL Queries" for more on the DECODE and SIGN Functions.

```
SELECT course_no, cost,
       DECODE(SIGN(cost-1595),-1, 500, cost) newcost
  FROM course
 WHERE course_no IN (80, 20, 135, 450)
```

COURSE_NO	COST	NEWCOST
20	1195	500
80	1595	1595
135	1095	500
450		

4 rows selected.

LAB 4.4 EXERCISES

4.4.1 REPLACE *NULL* VALUES WITH THE *NVL* FUNCTION

a) List the last name, first name, and phone number of students who do not have a phone number. Display '212-555-1212' for the phone number.

_____

_____

b) For course numbers 430 and greater, show the course cost. Add another column reflecting a discount of 10% off the cost. Substitute any NULL values in the cost column with the number 1000.

_____

_____

4.4.2 UTILIZE THE POWER OF *DECODE*

a) For course numbers 20, 120, 122, and 132, display the description, course number, and prerequisite course number. If the prerequisite is course number 120, display 200; if the prerequisite is 130, display 'N/A'. For courses with no prerequisites, display 'None'. Otherwise, list the current prerequisite. The result should look like the one listed below.

```
COURSE_NO DESCRIPTION                          ORIGINAL NEW
--------- ----------------------------- --------- ----
      132 Basics of Unix Admin               130 N/A
      122 Intermediate Java Programming      120 200
      120 Intro to Java Programming           80 80
       20 Intro to Computers                     None

4 rows selected.
```

b) Display the student id, zip code, and phone number for students with student ids 145, 150, or 325. For those students living in the 212 area code and in zip code 10048, display 'North Campus'. List students living in the 212 area code but in a different zip code as 'West Campus'. Display students outside the 212 area code as 'Off Campus'. The result should look like the following result set. Hint: The solution to this query requires nested DECODE statements.

```
STUDENT_ID ZIP   PHONE              LOC
---------- ----- ---------------- ------------
       145 10048 212-555-5555      North Campus
       150 11787 718-555-5555      Off Campus
       325 10954 212-555-5555      West Campus

3 rows selected.
```

c) Display all the different salutations used in the instructor table. Order them alphabetically except for female salutations, which should be listed first. Hint: Use the DECODE function in the ORDER BY clause.

LAB 4.4 EXERCISE ANSWERS

4.4.1 ANSWERS

a) List the last name, first name, and phone number of students who do not have a phone number. Display '212-555-1212' for the phone number.

Answer: There are two solutions to obtain the desired result. The first determines the rows with a NULL phone number using the IS NULL operator. Then you apply the NVL function to the column with the substitution string '212-555-1212'. The second solution uses the NVL function in both the SELECT and WHERE clauses.

```
SELECT first_name||' '|| last_name name,
       phone oldphone,
       NVL(phone, '212-555-1212') newphone
  FROM student
 WHERE phone IS NULL
NAME                          OLDPHONE        NEWPHONE
------------------------      --------------- ------------
Peggy Noviello                                212-555-1212

1 row selected.
```

You can also retrieve the same rows by applying the NVL function in the WHERE clause.

```
SELECT first_name||' '|| last_name name,
       phone oldphone,
       NVL(phone, '212-555-1212') newphone
  FROM student
 WHERE NVL(phone, 'NONE')='NONE'
NAME                          OLDPHONE        NEWPHONE
------------------------      --------------- ------------
Peggy Noviello                                212-555-1212

1 row selected.
```

b) For course numbers 430 and greater, show the course cost. Add another column reflecting a discount of 10% off the cost. Substitute any NULL values in the cost column with the number 1000.

Answer: Substitute 1000 for the NULL value, using the NVL function, before applying the discount calculation. Otherwise, the calculation yields a NULL.

```
SELECT course_no, cost,
       NVL(cost,1000)*0.9 new
  FROM course
```

```
WHERE course_no >= 430
COURSE_NO      COST      NEW
---------  ---------  ---------
      430       1195     1075.5
      450                   900
```

```
2 rows selected.
```

4.4.2 ANSWERS

a) For course numbers 20, 120, 122, and 132, display the description, course number, and prerequisite course number. If the prerequisite is course number 120, display 200; if the prerequisite is 130, display 'N/A'. For courses with no prerequisites, display 'None'. Otherwise, list the current prerequisite. The result should look like the one listed below.

```
COURSE_NO DESCRIPTION                       ORIGINAL NEW
--------- ------------------------------   --------- ----
      132 Basics of Unix Admin                   130 N/A
      122 Intermediate Java Programming          120 200
      120 Intro to Java Programming               80 80
       20 Intro to Computers                         None
```

Answer: The solution uses the DECODE function together with different datatypes and shows how to test for NULLs.

```
SELECT course_no, description, prerequisite original,
       DECODE(prerequisite, 120, '200',
                            130,'N/A',
                            NULL, 'None',
                                 prerequisite) new
  FROM course
 WHERE course_no IN (20, 120, 122, 132)
 ORDER BY course_no DESC
```

The solution is best approached in several steps. The prerequisite column is of datatype NUMBER. If you replace it in the DECODE function with another NUMBER for prerequisite 120, Oracle expects to continue to convert to the same datatype for all subsequent replacements. Therefore you need to type the number 200 with quotes to predetermine the datatype as a VARCHAR2.

For any records that have a NULL prerequisite, "None" is displayed. Although one NULL does not equal another NULL, for the purpose of the DECODE function, NULL values are treated as equals.

b) Display the student id, zip code, and phone number for students with student ids 145, 150, or 325. For those students living in the 212 area code and in zip code 10048, display 'North Campus'. List students living in the 212 area code but in a different zip code as 'West Campus'. Display students outside the 212 area code as 'Off Campus'. The result should look like the following result set. Hint: The solution to this query requires nested DECODE statements.

```
STUDENT_ID ZIP   PHONE            LOC
---------- ----- ---------------- ------------
       145 10048 212-555-5555     North Campus
       150 11787 718-555-5555     Off Campus
       325 10954 212-555-5555     West Campus

   3 rows selected.
```

LAB
4.4

Answer: DECODE statements are nested inside each other; the output from one DECODE is an input parameter in a second DECODE function.

```
SELECT student_id, zip, phone,
       DECODE(SUBSTR(phone, 1, 3), '212',
                  DECODE(zip, '10048', 'North Campus',
                                       'West Campus'),
           'Off Campus') loc
  FROM student
 WHERE student_id IN (150, 145, 325)
```

c) Display all the different salutations used in the instructor table. Order them alphabetically except for female salutations, which should be listed first. Hint: Use the DECODE function in the ORDER BY clause.

Answer: The DECODE function is used in the ORDER BY clause to substitute a number for all female salutations, thereby listing them first when executing the ORDER BY clause.

```
SELECT DISTINCT salutation
  FROM instructor
 ORDER BY DECODE(salutation, 'Ms', 1,
                             'Mrs', 1,
                             'Miss', 1)

SALUT
-----
Ms
Dr
Hon
Rev
```

```
Mr
```

```
5 rows selected.
```

LAB 4.4 SELF-REVIEW QUESTIONS

In order to test your progress, you should be able to answer the following questions.

1) A calculation with a NULL always yields another NULL.
   a) _____ True
   b) _____ False

2) The NVL function can substitute one datatype with another datatype.
   a) _____ True
   b) _____ False

3) The NVL function updates the data in the database.
   a) _____ True
   b) _____ False

4) The DECODE function is an *if then else* function in the SQL language.
   a) _____ True
   b) _____ False

5) The DECODE function cannot be used in the WHERE clause of a SQL statement.
   a) _____ True
   b) _____ False

Quiz answers appear in Appendix A, Section 4.4.

LAB
4.4

CHAPTER 4

TEST YOUR THINKING

1) Display all the sections where classes start at 10:30 A.M.

2) Write the query to accomplish the result below. The output shows you all the days of the week where sections 82, 144 and 107 start. Note the order of the days.

```
DAY SECTION_ID
--- ----------
Mon         82
Tue        144
Wed        107
```

3) Select the distinct course costs of all the courses. If the course cost is unknown, substitute a zero. Format the output with a leading $ sign, and separate the thousands with a comma. Display two digits after the decimal point. The query's output should look like the following result:

```
COST
-----------
     $0.00
 $1,095.00
 $1,195.00
 $1,595.00
```

4) What, if anything, is wrong with the following SQL statement?

```
SELECT zip + 100
    FROM zipcode
```

5) For the students enrolled on January 30, 1999, display the columns student_id and enroll_date.

CHAPTER 5

AGGREGATE FUNCTIONS, GROUP BY, AND HAVING

CHAPTER OBJECTIVES

In this chapter, you will learn about:

✔ Aggregate Functions   Page 128
✔ The GROUP BY and HAVING Clauses   Page 135

In the last two chapters, you learned about character functions, number functions, date functions, and conversion functions, all *single row* functions. In this chapter, you will learn about *aggregate functions*, which work on *groups of rows*. The most commonly used aggregate functions are discussed in this chapter.

Functions are a useful tool for transforming and interpreting data in a way that makes it easier to read and understand. By mastering aggregate functions, you are well on your way to mastering the SQL language.

L A B   5 . 1

AGGREGATE FUNCTIONS

LAB OBJECTIVES

After this lab, you will be able to:

✔ Use Aggregate Functions in a SQL Statement

Aggregate functions do just as you would expect: they *aggregate*, or group together, data to produce a single result. Questions such as "How many students are registered?", and "What is the average cost of a course?" can be answered by using aggregate functions. You count the individual students to answer the first question, and you calculate the average cost of all courses to answer the second. In each case, the result is a single answer based on several rows of data.

THE COUNT FUNCTION

One of the most common aggregate functions is the COUNT function, which takes a single parameter. The parameter can be a column in a table of any datatype, and can even be the asterisk (*) wildcard.

■ *FOR EXAMPLE*

The following SELECT statement returns the number of rows in the enrollment table:

```
SELECT COUNT(*)
  FROM enrollment
COUNT(*)
---------
      226

1 row selected.
```

This use of the COUNT function is useful for determining whether a table has data or not. If the result set returns the number 0 when using COUNT(*), it means there are no rows in the table, even though the table exists.

COUNT can also be used with a database column as a parameter. The difference is that COUNT(*) counts rows that contain NULL values, whereas COUNT with a column excludes rows that contain NULLs.

```
SELECT COUNT(final_grade), COUNT(section_id), COUNT(*)
  FROM enrollment
COUNT(FINAL_GRADE) COUNT(SECTION_ID)  COUNT(*)
------------------ ------------------ ---------
                 1                226       226
```

`1 row selected.`

The final_grade column in the enrollment table allows NULL values, and there is only one row with a final_grade. Therefore the result of the function is 1. The COUNT(section_id) returns the same number as the COUNT(*) because the section_id column contains no NULLs.

DISTINCT is often used in conjunction with aggregate functions to operate on distinct values within a group of values:

```
SELECT COUNT(DISTINCT section_id), COUNT(section_id)
  FROM enrollment
COUNT(DISTINCTSECTION_ID) COUNT(SECTION_ID)
------------------------- -----------------
                       64               226
```

`1 row selected.`

There are 226 rows in the enrollment table, but 64 distinct section_ids. Several students are enrolled in the same section, therefore a section exists more than once in the enrollment table.

THE SUM FUNCTION

The SUM function adds values together for a group of rows. The following example returns the total capacity of all sections. If any capacity contains a NULL, these values are ignored.

```
SELECT SUM(capacity)
  FROM section
```

```
SUM(CAPACITY)
-------------
         1652
```

1 row selected.

THE AVG FUNCTION

The AVG function returns the average within a group of rows. In the following example, the average capacity of each section is computed. Any NULLs in the capacity column are ignored. To substitute NULLs with a zero, use the NVL function.

```
SELECT AVG(capacity), AVG(NVL(capacity,0))
  FROM section
AVG(CAPACITY) AVG(NVL(CAPACITY,0))
------------- --------------------
    21.179487             21.179487
```

1 row selected.

In this case, there are no sections with a capacity of NULL, therefore, the result is the same as without the NVL function.

THE MIN AND MAX FUNCTIONS

The MIN and MAX functions are opposites of each other, providing the minimum and maximum values, respectively, in a group of rows:

```
SELECT MIN(capacity), MAX(capacity)
  FROM section
MIN(CAPACITY) MAX(CAPACITY)
------------- -------------
           10            25
```

1 row selected.

Both functions can take not just a NUMBER datatype as a parameter, but, like COUNT, a column in a table of any datatype. The *minimum* or *maximum* value of a character datatype column can also be evaluated. For instance, the capital letter "A" is equal to the ASCII value 65, "B" is 66, and so on. Lowercase letters, numbers, and characters all have their own ASCII values. Therefore, MIN and MAX can be used to evaluate characters:

```
SELECT MIN(description), MAX(description)
  FROM course
```

```
MIN                            MAX
-------------------------------------------------------
Advanced Java Programming Unix Tips and Techniques

1 row selected.
```

LAB 5.1 EXERCISES

5.1.1 USE AGGREGATE FUNCTIONS IN A SQL STATEMENT

a) Write a SELECT statement to determine how many courses do not have a prerequisite.

_____

_____

b) Write a SELECT statement to determine the total number of students enrolled in the program. Count students only once, no matter how many courses they are enrolled in.

_____

_____

c) Determine the average cost for all courses. If the course cost contains a NULL value, substitute the value 0.

_____

_____

d) Write a SELECT statement to determine the date of the most recent enrollment.

_____

_____

LAB 5.1 EXERCISE ANSWERS

5.1.1 ANSWERS

a) Write a SELECT statement to determine how many courses do not have a prerequisite.

Answer: The COUNT function is used to count the number of rows in the course table where the prerequisite is null.

```
SELECT COUNT(*)
  FROM course
 WHERE prerequisite IS NULL
COUNT(*)
---------
        4
```

```
1 row selected.
```

b) Write a SELECT statement to determine the total number of students enrolled. Count students only once, no matter how many courses they are enrolled in.

Answer: DISTINCT is used in conjunction with the COUNT function to count distinct students, regardless of how many times they appear in the enrollment table.

```
SELECT COUNT(DISTINCT student_id)
  FROM enrollment
COUNT(DISTINCTSTUDENT_ID)
-------------------------
                      165
```

```
1 row selected.
```

c) Determine the average cost for all courses. If the course cost contains a NULL value, substitute the value 0.

Answer: The NVL function substitutes any NULL value with a zero, and is nested inside the AVG function.

```
SELECT AVG(NVL(cost, 0))
  FROM course
AVG(NVL(COST,0))
----------------
          1158.5
```

```
1 row selected.
```

If you do not substitute the NULLs for the zero value, the average course cost returns a different, more accurate, result.

```
SELECT AVG(cost)
  FROM course
AVG(COST)
---------
1198.4483

1 row selected.
```

d) Write a SELECT statement to determine the date of the most recent enrollment.

Answer: The MAX function determines the most recent enroll_date in the enrollment table.

```
SELECT MAX(enroll_date)
  FROM enrollment
```

LAB 5.1 SELF-REVIEW QUESTIONS

In order to test your progress, you should be able to answer the following questions.

1) How many of these functions are aggregate functions: AVG, COUNT, SUM, ROUND?
   a) _____ One
   b) _____ Two
   c) _____ Three
   d) _____ Four

2) Choose the correct question for the SQL statement below.

```
SELECT NVL(MAX(modified_date),
       TO_DATE('12-MAR-2005', 'DD-MON-YYYY'))
  FROM enrollment
```

   a) _____ Display the date when a student record was last modified.
   b) _____ Display the date a student record was last modified. Replace any NULL with the date March 12, 2005.
   c) _____ Show the date a record in the enrollment table was last modified. If the result returns a NULL value, display March 12, 2005.
   d) _____ For all the enrollment records show the date 12-Mar-2005.

3) An aggregate function can be performed on a single row.
   a) _____ True
   b) _____ False

4) The following SQL statement contains an error:

```
SELECT AVG(*)
  FROM course
```

   a) _____ True
   b) _____ False

5) The following SQL statement determines the average of all capacities in a section.

```
SELECT AVG(DISTINCT capacity)
  FROM section
```

   a) _____ True
   b) _____ False

6) The following SQL statement contains an error.

```
SELECT SUM(capacity*1.5)
  FROM section
```

   a) _____ True
   b) _____ False

Quiz answers appear in Appendix A, Section 5.1.

LAB 5.2

THE GROUP BY AND HAVING CLAUSES

LAB OBJECTIVES

After this lab, you will be able to:

✔ Use the GROUP BY and HAVING Clauses

THE GROUP BY CLAUSE

Aggregate functions are often used with other columns in a SELECT list. This tells the database you want the information *grouped* by other columns. When you do this, the GROUP BY clause must be used to present the information in the output.

■ FOR EXAMPLE

The GROUP BY clause is similar to the DISTINCT clause. The two queries below return the same result.

```
SELECT DISTINCT location
  FROM section

SELECT location
  FROM section
 GROUP BY location
LOCATION
------------
H310
L206
...
M311
```

**LAB
5.2**

M500

12 rows selected.

Using the COUNT function, the following query returns the total number of locations in the section table; the second query returns the total number of distinct locations.

```
SELECT COUNT(location) AS "Total Locations"
  FROM section
```

Total Locations

            78

1 row selected.

```
SELECT COUNT(DISTINCT location)
       AS "Total Distinct Locations"
  FROM section
```

Total Distinct Locations

                     12

1 row selected.

When you want to determine how many sections use this location, use an aggregate function in the SELECT list, and use the GROUP BY clause.

```
SELECT location AS "Location",
       COUNT(location) AS "Total"
  FROM section
 GROUP BY location
```

Location	Total
H310	1
L206	1
...	
M311	3
M500	1

12 rows selected.

With the GROUP BY clause, the row count for each distinct location is determined. When you group data by a specific element in combination with an aggregate function, you are grouping by distinct values.

If you do not include the GROUP BY clause, the following occurs:

```
SELECT location AS "Location",
       *
ERROR at line 1:
ORA-00937: not a single-group group function
```

Oracle returns an error message, indicating it does not know how to process this additional column in the result set. To avoid this error, use the GROUP BY clause, and include all columns in the SELECT list, except aggregate functions. In the following example, there are two columns in the SELECT list that are not aggregate functions, and, therefore, they are included in the GROUP BY clause:

```
SELECT location "Location",
       COUNT(location) "Total Locations",
       capacity "Capacity",
       SUM(capacity) "Total Capacity"
  FROM section
 GROUP BY location, capacity
```

Location	Total Locations	Capacity	Total Capacity
H310	1	15	15
L206	1	15	15
L210	5	15	75
L210	5	25	125
...			
M311	3	25	75
M500	1	25	25

```
19 rows selected.
```

Locations are now repeated because there is more than one distinct capacity within a location in some cases. In the third and fourth rows of the output, this is interpreted as "Location L210 appears 10 times in the section table, 5 times with a capacity of 15 for a total of 75 students, and another 5 times with a capacity of 25 for a total of 125 students".

GROUP BY plays another role: it also *orders* data. Do not confuse the ORDER BY clause, discussed in Chapter 2, "SQL: The Basics," with the GROUP BY clause. The ORDER BY clause is used when you want to change the sort order of the grouping. The ORDER BY must *follow* the GROUP BY in the SELECT statement. The columns used in the ORDER BY clause *must* appear in the SELECT list, which is unlike the normal use of ORDER BY. In the following example, the result is sorted in descending order by the total capacity. Note that you can also use the column alias in the ORDER BY clause.

```
SELECT location "Location",
       COUNT(location) "Total Locations",
       capacity "Capacity",
       SUM(capacity) "Total Capacity"
  FROM section
 GROUP BY location, capacity
 ORDER BY "Total Capacity" DESC
```

THE HAVING CLAUSE

The purpose of the HAVING clause is to eliminate groups, just as the WHERE clause is used to eliminate rows. Using the previous example, use the HAVING clause to restrict the result set to locations with a total capacity of more than 75 students.

```
SELECT location "Location",
       COUNT(location) "Total Locations",
       capacity "Capacity",
       SUM(capacity) "Total Capacity"
  FROM section
 GROUP BY location, capacity
HAVING SUM(capacity) > 75
```

Location	Total Locations	Capacity	Total Capacity
L210	5	25	125
L214	10	15	150
L214	5	25	125
L507	13	25	325
L509	20	25	500

5 rows selected.

An aggregate function is used in the HAVING clause to show rows where the total of distinct capacities for each location is greater than 75.

THE WHERE AND HAVING CLAUSES

The HAVING clause eliminates groups that do not satisfy its condition. However, the WHERE clause eliminates rows *before* the GROUP BY and HAVING clauses are applied:

```
SELECT location "Location",
       COUNT(location) "Total Locations",
       capacity "Capacity",
       SUM(capacity) "Total Capacity"
  FROM section
 WHERE section_no = 3
```

```
GROUP BY location, capacity
HAVING SUM(capacity) > 75
Location Total Locations  Capacity Total Capacity
-------- ---------------- --------- --------------
L507                    4        25            100
L509                    7        25            175
```

2 rows selected.

The WHERE clause is executed by the database first, narrowing the result set to locations for the third section of a course. Next, the result is grouped by the columns listed in the GROUP BY clause; and lastly, the HAVING condition is tested against the groups.

LAB 5.2 EXERCISES

5.2.1 USE THE *GROUP BY* AND *HAVING* CLAUSES

a) Show a list of prerequisites, and count how many times each appears in the course table.

_____

_____

b) Write a SELECT statement showing student ids and the number of courses they are enrolled in. Show only those enrolled in more than two classes.

_____

_____

c) Write a SELECT statement that displays the average room capacity for each course. Display the average expressed to the nearest whole number in another column. Use column aliases for each column selected.

_____

_____

d) Write the same SELECT statement as in the previous question except for classes with exactly two sections. Hint: Think about the relationship between the course and section tables, specifically how many times a course can be represented in the section table.

_____

_____

LAB 5.2 EXERCISE ANSWERS

5.2.1 ANSWERS

a) Show a list of prerequisites, and count how many times each appears in the course table.

Answer: The COUNT function and GROUP BY clause are used to count distinct prerequisites. The last row of the result set shows the number of prerequisites with a NULL value.

```
SELECT prerequisite, COUNT(*)
  FROM course
 GROUP BY prerequisite
```

PREREQUISITE	COUNT(*)
10	1
20	5
...	
350	2
420	1
	4

17 rows selected.

b) Write a SELECT statement showing student ids and the number of courses they are enrolled in. Show only those enrolled in more than two classes.

Answer: To obtain the distinct students, use the student_id column in the GROUP BY clause. For each of the groups, count records for each student with the COUNT function. Eliminate only those students enrolled in more than two sections from the groups with the HAVING clause.

```
SELECT student_id, COUNT(*)
  FROM enrollment
 GROUP BY student_id
HAVING COUNT(*) > 2
STUDENT_ID  COUNT(*)
----------  ---------
       124         4
       184         3
...
       238         3
       250         3
```

7 rows selected.

The HAVING clause can also use multiple operators to further eliminate groups, as in this example:

```
SELECT location "Location",
       COUNT(location) "Total Locations",
       capacity "Capacity",
       SUM(capacity) "Total Capacity"
  FROM section
 WHERE section_no = 3
 GROUP BY location, capacity
HAVING (SUM(capacity) > 75
       AND location LIKE 'L5%9')
```

The columns used in the HAVING clause must be found in the GROUP BY clause or must be aggregate functions.

c) Write a SELECT statement that displays the average room capacity for each course. Display the average expressed to the nearest whole number in another column. Use column aliases for each column selected.

Answer: The SELECT statement uses the AVG function and the ROUND function. The GROUP BY clause ensures that the average capacity is displayed for each course.

```
SELECT course_no "Course #",
       AVG(capacity) "Avg. Capacity",
       ROUND(AVG(capacity)) "Rounded Avg. Capacity"
  FROM section
 GROUP BY course_no
Course # Avg Capacity Rounded Avg Capacity
-------- ------------ --------------------
      10           15                   15
      20           20                   20
      25    22.777778                   23
```

. . .

```
350      21.666667                    22
420             25                    25
450             25                    25
```

28 rows selected.

The previous SQL statement uses nested functions. Nested functions always work from the inside out, so the AVG(capacity) is evaluated first, and its result is the parameter for ROUND(). ROUND's optional *precision* parameter is not used, so the result of AVG(capacity) rounds to a precision of 0, or no decimal places.

Aggregate functions can also be nested, as in the following example. The query returns the largest number of students per section:

```
SELECT MAX(COUNT(*))
  FROM ENROLLMENT
 GROUP BY SECTION_ID
```

d) Write the same SELECT statement as in the previous question except for classes with exactly two sections. Hint: Think about the relationship between the course and section tables, specifically how many times a course can be represented in the section table.

Answer: The HAVING clause is added to limit the result set to courses appearing exactly twice.

```
SELECT course_no "Course #",
       AVG(capacity) "Avg. Capacity",
       ROUND(AVG(capacity)) "Rounded Avg. Capacity"
  FROM section
 GROUP BY course_no
HAVING COUNT(*) = 2
```

Course #	Avg. Capacity	Rounded Avg. Capacity
132	25	25
145	25	25
146	20	20
230	13.5	14
240	12.5	13

5 rows selected.

The HAVING clause counts courses in this SELECT statement because a course appears twice in the section table when it has two sections. Notice the COUNT(*) function in the HAVING clause does not appear as part of the SELECT list. You can eliminate any groups in the HAVING clause using aggregate functions that are not part of the SELECT list.

LAB 5.2 SELF-REVIEW QUESTIONS

In order to test your progress, you should be able to answer the following questions.

1) Which column(s) must be included in the GROUP BY clause of the following SELECT statement?

```
SELECT NVL(MAX(final_grade),0), section_id,
       MAX(created_date)
  FROM enrollment
 GROUP BY _____
```

      a) _____ final_grade
      b) _____ section_id
      c) _____ created_date
      d) _____ All three
      e) _____ None

2) You can combine DISTINCT and a GROUP BY clause in the same SELECT statement.
      a) _____ True
      b) _____ False

3) There is an error in the following SELECT statement.

```
SELECT COUNT(student_id)
  FROM enrollment
 WHERE COUNT(student_id) > 1
```

      a) _____ True
      b) _____ False

4) How many rows in the following SELECT statement will return a NULL prerequisite?

```
SELECT prerequisite, COUNT(*)
  FROM course
 GROUP BY prerequisite
```

a) _____ None
b) _____ One

5) Determine the error in the following SELECT statement.

```
SELECT COUNT(*)
  FROM section
 GROUP BY course_no
```

a) _____ No error
b) _____ Line 1
c) _____ Line 2
d) _____ Line 3

Quiz answers appear in Appendix A, Section 5.2.

CHAPTER 5

TEST YOUR THINKING

1) List the order in which the WHERE, GROUP BY, and HAVING clauses are executed by the database in the following SQL statement.

```
SELECT section_id, COUNT(*), final_grade
  FROM enrollment
 WHERE TRUNC(enroll_date) >
       TO_DATE('2/16/1999', 'MM/DD/YYYY')
 GROUP BY section_id, final_grade
HAVING COUNT(*) > 5
```

2) Display a count of all the different course costs in the course table.

3) Determine the number of students living in zip code 10025.

4) Show all the different companies for which students work. Display only companies where more than four students are employed.

5) List how many sections each instructor teaches.

6) Formulate the question for the following statement:

```
SELECT COUNT(*), start_date_time, location
  FROM section
 GROUP BY start_date_time, location
HAVING COUNT(*) > 1
```

7) Determine the highest grade achieved for the midterm within each section.

CHAPTER 6

EQUIJOINS

CHAPTER OBJECTIVES

In this chapter, you will learn about:

- ✔ The Two Table Join   Page 148
- ✔ Joining More Than Two Tables   Page 163

So far, you have written SQL statements against a single table. In this chapter you learn about joining tables, one of the most important aspects of relational databases and the SQL language. A join creates a connection between tables. The *equijoin* is by far the most common form of join. Equijoins are based on equality of values in one or more columns. You will learn about other types of joins in Chapter 9, "Complex Joins."

L A B   6 . 1

THE TWO TABLE JOIN

LAB OBJECTIVES

After this lab, you will be able to:

✔ Write Simple Join Constructs
✔ Narrow Down Your Result Set
✔ Understand the Cartesian Product

One of the advantages of the relational model is you need to store and update data in only one place. Should the description of a course change, the update needs to happen only in the description column in the course table. In this lab, you join information from two tables into one meaningful result.

■ *FOR EXAMPLE*

Suppose you want to list the course number, course description, section number, location, and instructor_id for each section. This data is found in two separate tables: the course number and description are in the course table; the section table contains the course number, section number, location, and instructor_id. One approach is to query the individual tables and record the results on paper, then match every course number in the course table with the corresponding course number in the section table. The other approach is to formulate a SQL statement that accomplishes the join for you.

Following is an excerpt of the course and section tables. The last table shows the result of the join.

Course Table

Course_no Primary Key	Description	~~~	Modified_date
10	DP Overview	~~~	05-APR-99
20	Intro to Computers	~~~	05-APR-99
25	Intro to Programming	~~~	05-APR-99
80	Structured Programming Techniques	~~~	05-APR-99
100	Hands-On Windows	~~~	05-APR-99
~~	~~~	~~~	~~~

Section Table

Section_id	Course_no Foreign Key	Section_no	~~~	Location
80	10	2	~~~	L214
81	20	2	~~~	L210
82	20	4	~~~	L214
83	20	7	~~~	L509
84	20	8	~~~	L210
85	25	1	~~~	M311
86	25	2	~~~	L210
87	25	3	~~~	L507
88	25	4	~~~	L214
89	25	5	~~~	L509
90	25	6	~~~	L509
91	25	7	~~~	L210
92	25	8	~~~	L509
93	25	9	~~~	L507
141	100	1	~~~	L214
~~	~~~	~~~	~~~	~~~

Resulting Query Output

Course_no	Section_no	Description	Location	Instructor_ID
10	2	DP Overview	L214	102
20	2	Intro to Computers	L210	103
20	4	Intro to Computers	L214	104

(continued)

Resulting Query Output (continued)

Course_no	Section_no	Description	Location	Instructor_ID
20	7	Intro to Computers	L509	105
20	8	Intro to Computers	L210	106
25	1	Intro to Programming	M311	107
25	2	Intro to Programming	L210	108
25	3	Intro to Programming	L507	101
25	4	Intro to Programming	L214	102
25	5	Intro to Programming	L509	103
25	6	Intro to Programming	L509	104
25	7	Intro to Programming	L210	105
25	8	Intro to Programming	L509	106
25	9	Intro to Programming	L507	107
100	1	Hands-On Windows	L214	102
~~	~~~	~~~	~~~	~~~

For course number 10, one section exists in the section table. The result of the match is one row. Course number 20, Intro to Computers, has multiple rows in the section table because there are multiple classes for the same course. Note that course number 80, Structured Programming Techniques, has no matching entry in the section table. Therefore, this row is not in the result.

FORMULATE THE SQL STATEMENT

To write the SQL join statement, first choose the columns you want to include in the result. Next, determine the tables to which the columns belong. Then, identify the common columns between the tables.

Lastly, determine if there is a one-to-one relationship, or a one-to-many relationship among the column values. Joins are typically used to join between the primary key and the foreign key. In the previous example, the course_no column in the course table is the primary key; the column course_no in the section table, the foreign key. This represents a one-to-many relationship among the columns.

When you join tables related through a many-to-many relationship, it yields a *Cartesian product*. There is more on the Cartesian product farther along in this chapter.

When writing an equijoin, list the tables separated by a comma in the FROM clause.

```
SELECT course.course_no, section_no, description,
       location, instructor_id
  FROM course, section
 WHERE course.course_no = section.course_no
```

The WHERE clause formulates the join criteria, using the common columns between the tables. Since this is an equijoin, the values in the common columns must equal each other for a row to be displayed in the result set. Each course_no value from the course table must match a course_no value from the section table. To differentiate between columns of the same name, *qualify* the columns by prefixing the column with the table name and a period. Otherwise, Oracle returns an error—"column ambiguously defined."

Instead of displaying the course_no column from the course table in the SELECT list, you can use the course_no column from the section table. Because it is an equijoin, it returns the same result.

The Whole Truth

The order in which the tables are listed in the FROM clause can have an effect on the efficiency of the SQL statement, but it has no effect on the query result. You will learn about this in Chapter 16, "SQL Optimization."

TABLE ALIAS

Instead of using the table name as a prefix to differentiate between the columns, you can use a *table alias* which qualifies the table using a short abbreviation.

■ *FOR EXAMPLE*

```
SELECT c.course_no, s.section_no, c.description,
       s.location, s.instructor_id
  FROM course c, section s
 WHERE c.course_no - s.course_no
```

The table alias names are arbitrary. However, you cannot use any Oracle reserved words. It is best to keep the name short and simple, as in this example. The course table has the alias c, and the section table has the alias s.

To easily identify the source table of a column and to improve the readability of a join statement, it is best to qualify all column names with the table alias. This also avoids any future ambiguities that may arise if a new column is added later to a table that has the same column name as another column in another table. Without a qualified table alias, a subsequently issued SQL statement referencing both tables results in the Oracle error message "column ambiguously defined."

NULLS AND JOINS

In an equijoin, a NULL value in the common column has a different effect on the result. Look at the foreign key column zip on the instructor table which allows NULLs.

■ FOR EXAMPLE

First, query the records with a NULL value.

```
SELECT instructor_id, zip, last_name, first_name
  FROM instructor
 WHERE zip IS NULL
```

INSTRUCTOR_ID	ZIP	LAST_NAME	FIRST_NAME
110		Willig	Irene

1 row selected.

Next, formulate the join to the zipcode table via the zip column. Observe that instructor Irene Willig does not appear in the result.

```
SELECT i.instructor_id, i.zip, i.last_name, i.first_name
  FROM instructor i, zipcode z
 WHERE i.zip = z.zip
```

INSTRUCTOR_ID	ZIP	LAST_NAME	FIRST_NAME
101	10015	Hanks	Fernand
105	10015	Morris	Anita
109	10015	Chow	Rick
102	10025	Wojick	Tom
103	10025	Schorin	Nina
106	10025	Smythe	Todd
108	10025	Lowry	Charles
107	10005	Frantzen	Marilyn

```
      104 10035 Pertez       Gary
```

9 rows selected.

A NULL value is not equal to any other value, including another NULL value. In this case, the zip code of Irene Willig's record is NULL, therefore, this row is not included in the result.

CARTESIAN PRODUCT

The Cartesian product is rarely useful in the real world. It usually indicates either the WHERE clause has no joining columns, or that multiple rows from one table match multiple rows in another table, that is, a many-to-many relationship.

■ *FOR EXAMPLE*

To illustrate the multiplication effect of a Cartesian product, the following query joins the instructor table with the section table. The instructor table contains 10 rows, the section table has 78 rows. The multiplication of all the possible combinations results in 780 rows.

```
SELECT COUNT(*)
  FROM section, instructor
COUNT(*)
---------
      780
```

Below is a partial listing of the rows showing all the different combinations of values between the two tables.

```
SELECT s.instructor_id s_instructor_id,
       i.instructor_id i_instructor_id
  FROM section s, instructor i
S_INSTRUCTOR_ID I_INSTRUCTOR_ID
--------------- ---------------
            101             101
            101             101
            101             101
            101             101
            101             101
            101             101
            101             101
            101             101
            101             101
            101             102
```

101	102
101	102
108	110
101	110

...

`780 rows selected.`

LAB 6.1 EXERCISES

6.1.1 WRITE SIMPLE JOIN CONSTRUCTS

a) For all students, display last name, city, state, and zip code. Show the result ordered by zip code.

_____

_____

b) Select the first and last names of all enrolled students, and order by the last name in ascending order.

_____

_____

6.1.2 NARROW DOWN YOUR RESULT SET

a) Execute the following SQL statement. Explain your observations about the WHERE clause and the resulting output.

```
SELECT c.course_no, c.description, s.section_no
  FROM course c, section s
 WHERE c.course_no = s.course_no
   AND c.prerequisite IS NULL
 ORDER BY c.course_no, s.section_no
```

_____

_____

b) Select the student id, course number, enrollment date, and section id for students who enrolled in course number 20 on January 30, 1999.

_____

_____

6.1.3 UNDERSTAND THE CARTESIAN PRODUCT

a) Select the students who live in the same zip code as their instructors. What do you observe?

_____

_____

LAB 6.1 EXERCISE ANSWERS

6.1.1 ANSWERS

a) For all students, display last name, city, state, and zip code. Show the result ordered by zip code.

Answer: The common column between the zipcode table and the student table is the zip column. The zip column in both the student and zipcode tables is defined as NOT NULL. For each row in the zipcode table there may be zero, one, or multiple students living in one particular zip code. For each student's zip code there must be one matching row in the zipcode table. Only those records that satisfy the equality condition of the join are returned.

```
SELECT s.last_name, s.zip, z.state, z.city
  FROM student s, zipcode z
 WHERE s.zip = z.zip
 ORDER BY s.zip
LAST_NAME                      ZIP   ST CITY
------------------------------ ----- -- ----------------
Norman                         01247 MA North Adams
Kocka                          02124 MA Dorchester
...
Gilloon                        43224 OH Columbus
```

```
Snow                          48104 MI Ann Arbor
```

268 rows selected.

Because the zip column has the same name in both tables, you must qualify the column. For simplicity, it is best to use an alias instead of the full table name, because it saves you a lot of typing. The ORDER BY clause lists the s.zip column, as does the SELECT clause. Choosing the z.zip column instead of s.zip in the SELECT list or ORDER BY clause produces the same result because the values in the two columns have to be equal to be included in the result.

b) Select the first and last names of all enrolled students, and order by the last name in ascending order.

Answer: You need to join the enrollment and student tables. Only students who are enrolled have one or multiple rows in the enrollment table.

```
SELECT s.first_name, s.last_name, s.student_id
  FROM student s, enrollment e
 WHERE s.student_id = e.student_id
 ORDER BY s.last_name
FIRST_NAME LAST_NAME  STUDENT_ID
---------- ---------- ----------
Mardig     Abdou             119
Suzanne M. Abid              257
...
Salewa     Zuckerberg        184
Salewa     Zuckerberg        184
Salewa     Zuckerberg        184
Freedon    annunziato        206
```

226 rows selected.

Note that student Salewa Zuckerberg with student_id 184 is returned three times. This is because Salewa Zuckerberg is enrolled in three sections. When the section_id column is included in the SELECT list, this fact becomes self-evident in the result set.

However, if you are not interested in the section_id, and you want to only list the names without the duplication, use DISTINCT in the SELECT statement.

```
SELECT DISTINCT s.first_name, s.last_name, s.student_id
  FROM student s, enrollment e
 WHERE s.student_id = e.student_id
 ORDER BY s.last_name
```

The student_id column is required in the SELECT clause because there may be students with the same first and last name but who are, in fact, different individuals. The student_id column differentiates between these students.

You may also notice that the student with the last name 'annunziato' is the last row. Because the last name is in lowercase, it has a higher sort order.

6.1.2 ANSWERS

a) Execute the following SQL statement. Explain your observations about the WHERE clause and the resulting output.

```
SELECT c.course_no, c.description, s.section_no
  FROM course c, section s
 WHERE c.course_no = s.course_no
   AND c.prerequisite IS NULL
 ORDER BY c.course_no, section_no
```

Answer: This query adds a condition to the WHERE clause in addition to the join. It restricts the rows to classes that have no prerequisite. The result is ordered by the course number and the section number.

COURSE_NO	DESCRIPTION	SECTION_NO
10	DP Overview	2
20	Intro to Computers	2
...		
146	Java for C/C++ Programmers	2
310	Operating Systems	1

8 rows selected.

The course and section tables are joined to obtain the section_no; it requires the equality of values for the course_no columns in both tables. The courses without a prerequisite are determined by querying the course table with the IS NULL operator as an additional condition in the WHERE clause.

b) Select the student id, course number, enrollment date, and section id for students who enrolled in course number 20 on January 30, 1999.

Answer: The section and enrollment tables are joined through their common column: section_id. This column is the primary key in the section table, and the foreign key column in the enrollment table. The rows are restricted to those records that have a course number of 20 and an enrollment date of January 30, 1999 by using the WHERE clause conditions.

```
SELECT e.student_id, s.course_no,
       TO_CHAR(e.enroll_date,'MM/DD/YYYY HH:MI PM'),
       e.section_id
  FROM enrollment e, section s
 WHERE e.section_id = s.section_id
   AND s.course_no = 20
   AND e.enroll_date >= TO_DATE('01/30/1999','MM/DD/YYYY')
   AND e.enroll_date < TO_DATE('01/31/1999','MM/DD/YYYY')
```

STUDENT_ID	COURSE_NO	TO_CHAR(ENROLL_DATE	SECTION_ID
103	20	01/30/1999 10:18 AM	81
104	20	01/30/1999 10:18 AM	81

2 rows selected.

6.1.3 ANSWERS

a) Select the students who live in the same zip code as their instructors. What do you observe?

Answer: When you join the student and instructor tables, there is a many-to-many relationship. A student may have zero, one, or multiple instructors, and one instructor teaches zero, one, or multiple students.

```
SELECT s.student_id, i.instructor_id,
       s.zip, i.zip
  FROM student s, instructor i
 WHERE s.zip = i.zip
```

STUDENT_ID	INSTRUCTOR_ID	ZIP	ZIP
223	108	10025	10025
223	106	10025	10025
223	103	10025	10025
223	102	10025	10025
163	108	10025	10025
163	106	10025	10025
163	103	10025	10025
163	102	10025	10025
399	108	10025	10025

```
         399               106 10025 10025
         399               103 10025 10025
         399               102 10025 10025
```

12 rows selected.

At a first look, this example and the result may not strike you as a Cartesian product because the WHERE clause contains a join criteria. However, this relationship does not follow the primary key/foreign key path, and therefore a Cartesian product is possible. A look at the schema diagram reveals that no primary key/foreign key relationship exists between the two tables. To further illustrate the many-to-many relationship between the zip columns, select those students and instructors living in zip code 10025 in separate SQL statements.

```
SELECT student_id, zip
  FROM student
 WHERE zip = '10025'
```
STUDENT_ID ZIP
```
---------- -----
       223 10025
       163 10025
       399 10025
```

3 rows selected.

```
SELECT instructor_id, zip
  FROM instructor
 WHERE zip = '10025'
```
INSTRUCTOR_ID ZIP
```
------------- -----
          102 10025
          103 10025
          106 10025
          108 10025
```

4 rows selected.

These results validate the solution's result set: the Cartesian product shows the three student rows multiplied by the four instructors, which results in twelve possible combinations. You can rewrite the query to include the DISTINCT keyword to select only the distinct student_ids. The query can also be written with a *subquery* construct, which avoids the Cartesian product. You will learn about this in Chapter 7, "Subqueries."

JOINING ALONG THE PRIMARY/FOREIGN KEY PATH

You can also join along the primary/foreign key path by joining the student table to the enrollment table, then to the section table, and lastly to the instructor table. This involves a multi-table join, discussed in Lab 6.2. However, the result is different from the Cartesian product result because it shows only instructors who teach a section in which the student is enrolled. In other words, an instructor living in zip code 10025 is included in the result only if the instructor teaches that student also living in the same zip code. This is in contrast to the Cartesian product example, which shows all of the instructors and students living in the same zip code, whether the instructor teaches this student or not.

LAB 6.1 SELF-REVIEW QUESTIONS

In order to test your progress, you should be able to answer the following questions.

1) Find the error(s) in the following SQL statement.

```
1 SELECT stud.last_name, stud.first_name,
2         stud.zip, zip.zip, zip.state, zip.city,
3         TO_CHAR(stud.student_id)
4   FROM student stud, zipcode zip
5  WHERE stud.student_id = 102
6     AND zip.zip = '11419'
7     AND zip.zip = s.zip
```

a) _____ No error
b) _____ This is not an equijoin
c) _____ Line 1, 2, 3
d) _____ Line 4
e) _____ Line 5, 6
f) _____ Line 7

2) Find the error(s) in the following SQL statement.

```
1 SELECT s.*, zipcode.zip,
2         DECODE(s.last_name, 'Smith', szip,
3                UPPER(s.last_name))
4   FROM student s, zipcode
5  WHERE stud.zip = zipcode.zip
6     AND s.last_name LIKE 'Smi%'
```

a) _____ Line 1 and 2
b) _____ Line 1 and 4

   c) _____ Line 3
   d) _____ Line 2 and 5
   e) _____ Line 4

3) A table alias is the name of a duplicate table stored in memory.
   a) _____ True
   b) _____ False

4) To equijoin a table with another means to compare common column values.
   a) _____ True
   b) _____ False

5) Find the error(s) in the following SQL statement.

```
1 SELECT TO_CHAR(w.modified_date, 'dd-mon-yyyy'),
2        t.grade_type_code, description,
3        TO_NUMBER(TO_CHAR(number_per_section))
4   FROM grade_type t, grade_type_weight w
5  WHERE t.grade_type_code = w.grade_type_code_cd
6    AND ((t.grade_type_code = 'MT'
7        OR t.grade_type_code = 'HM'))
8    AND t.modified_date >=
9        TO_DATE('01-JAN-1999', 'DD-MON-YYYY')
```

   a) _____ Line I and 8
   b) _____ Line 4
   c) _____ Line 5
   d) _____ Line 6 and 7
   e) _____ Line 5, 6, 7

6) Given two tables, tI and t2, and their records shown below, which result will be returned?

```
SELECT t1.val, t2.val, t1.name, t2.location
  FROM t1, t2
 WHERE t1.val = t2.val
```

Table TI

VAL	NAME
A	Jones
B	Smith
C	Zeta
	Miller

Table T2

VAL	LOCATION
A	San Diego
B	New York
B	New York
	Phoenix

```
              a) _____
V  V  NAME              LOCATION
-  -  ----------        ---------
A  A  Jones             San Diego
B  B  Smith             New York
B  B  Smith             New York
      Miller            Phoenix
              b) _____
V  V  NAME              LOCATION
-  -  ----------        ---------
A  A  Jones             San Diego
B  B  Smith             New York
B  B  Smith             New York
              c) _____  None of the above
```

Quiz answers appear in Appendix A, Section 6.1.

L A B   6 . 2

JOINING MORE THAN TWO TABLES

LAB OBJECTIVES

After this lab, you will be able to:

✔   Join More than Two Tables
✔   Join With Multicolumn Join Criteria

You often have to join more than two tables to determine the answer to a query. In this lab, you will practice these types of joins. Additionally, you will join tables with multicolumn keys.

THREE OR MORE TABLE JOINS

The join example in Lab 6.1 involves two tables: the course and section tables. To include the instructor's first and last name, you need to join to a third table, the instructor table.

The following query is from Lab 6.1. The result of the join is listed for you once more.

```
SELECT c.course_no, s.section_no, c.description,
       s.location, s.instructor_id
  FROM course c, section s
 WHERE c.course_no = s.course_no
```

The result from Lab 6.1 lists the courses with assigned sections.

Course_no	Section_no	Description	Location	Instructor_ID
10	2	DP Overview	L214	102
20	2	Intro to Computers	L210	103
20	4	Intro to Computers	L214	104
20	7	Intro to Computers	L509	105
20	8	Intro to Computers	L210	106
25	1	Intro to Programming	M311	107
25	2	Intro to Programming	L210	108
25	3	Intro to Programming	L507	101
25	4	Intro to Programming	L214	102
25	5	Intro to Programming	L509	103
25	6	Intro to Programming	L509	104
25	7	Intro to Programming	L210	105
25	8	Intro to Programming	L509	106
25	9	Intro to Programming	L507	107
100	1	Hands-On Windows	L214	102
~~	~~~	~~~	~~~	~~~

The Instructor Table

Instructor_ID	Last_name	First_name	~~~
101	Hanks	Fernand	~~~
102	Wojick	Tom	~~~
103	Schorin	Nina	~~~
104	Pertez	Gary	~~~
105	Morris	Anita	~~~
106	Smythe	Todd	~~~
109	Chow	Rick	~~~
108	Lowry	Charles	~~~
107	Frantzen	Marilyn	~~~
110	Willig	Irene	~~~

To construct the join to the instructor table, determine the common column. The instructor_id is the foreign key in the section table and the primary key in the instructor table. Every row in the section table with a value for the instructor_id column must have one corresponding row in the instructor table. A particular instructor_id in the instructor table may have zero, one, or multiple rows in the section table.

To formulate the SQL statement, follow the same steps performed in Lab 6.1. First, determine the columns and tables needed for output. Then, confirm whether a one-to-one or a one-to-many relationship exists between the tables to accomplish the join.

```
SELECT c.course_no, s.section_no, c.description, s.location,
       s.instructor_id, i.last_name, i.first_name
  FROM course c, section s, instructor i
 WHERE c.course_no = s.course_no
   AND s.instructor_id = i.instructor_id
```

The join yields the following result.

Resulting Query Output

Course_ no	Section_ no	Description	Location	Instructor_ID	Last_ name	First_ name
10	2	DP Overview	L214	102	Wojick	Tom
20	2	Intro to Computers	L210	103	Schorin	Nina
20	4	Intro to Computers	L214	104	Pertez	Gary
20	7	Intro to Computers	L509	105	Morris	Anita
20	8	Intro to Computers	L210	106	Smythe	Todd
25	1	Intro to Programming	M311	107	Frantzen	Marilyn
25	2	Intro to Programming	L210	108	Lowry	Charles
25	3	Intro to Programming	L507	101	Hanks	Fernand
25	4	Intro to Programming	L214	102	Wojick	Tom
25	5	Intro to Programming	L509	103	Schorin	Nina
25	6	Intro to Programming	L509	104	Pertez	Gary
25	7	Intro to Programming	L210	105	Morris	Anita
25	8	Intro to Programming	L509	106	Smythe	Todd
25	9	Intro to Programming	L507	107	Frantzen	Marilyn
100	1	Hands-On Windows	L214	102	Wojick	Tom
~~	~~~	~~~	~~~	~~~	~~~	~~~

MULTICOLUMN JOINS

The basic steps of the multicolumn join do not differ from the previous examples. The only variation is to make multicolumn keys part of the join criteria.

One of the multikey column examples in the schema is the grade table. The primary key of the table, which represents the columns that uniquely identify each record, are the columns student_id, section_id, grade_code_occurrence, and grade_type_code. The grade table also has two foreign keys: the grade_type_code column which references the grade_type table, and the multicolumn foreign key student_id and section_id which reference the enrollment table.

Examine a set of sample records for a particular student to understand the data in the table. The student with id 220 is enrolled in section_id 119, and has nine records in the grade table: four homework assignments (HM), two quizzes (QZ), one midterm (MT), one final examination (FI), and one participation (PA) grade.

```
SELECT student_id, section_id, grade_type_code type,
       grade_code_occurrence no,
       numeric_grade indiv_gr
  FROM grade
 WHERE student_id = 220
   AND section_id = 119
```

STUDENT_ID	SECTION_ID	TY	NO	INDIV_GR
220	119	FI	1	85
220	119	HM	1	84
220	119	HM	2	84
220	119	HM	3	74
220	119	HM	4	74
220	119	MT	1	88
220	119	PA	1	91
220	119	QZ	1	92
220	119	QZ	2	91

9 rows selected.

In the next example, the grade table is joined to the enrollment table to include the enroll_date column.

```
SELECT g.student_id, g.section_id,
       g.grade_type_code type,
```

```
        g.grade_code_occurrence no,
        g.numeric_grade indiv_gr,
        TO_CHAR(e.enroll_date, 'MM/DD/YY') enrolldt
   FROM grade g, enrollment e
WHERE g.student_id = 220
   AND g.section_id = 119
   AND g.student_id = e.student_id
   AND g.section_id = e.section_id
STUDENT_ID SECTION_ID TY         NO  INDIV_GR ENROLLDT
---------- ---------- --  --------- --------- --------
       220        119 FI          1        85 02/16/99
       220        119 HM          1        84 02/16/99
       220        119 HM          2        84 02/16/99
       220        119 HM          3        74 02/16/99
       220        119 HM          4        74 02/16/99
       220        119 MT          1        88 02/16/99
       220        119 PA          1        91 02/16/99
       220        119 QZ          1        92 02/16/99
       220        119 QZ          2        91 02/16/99
```

9 rows selected.

To join between the tables enrollment and grade, use both the section_id and student_id columns. These two columns represent the primary key of the enrollment table and foreign key of the grade table, thus a one-to-many relationship between the tables.

The values for the enroll_date column are repeated, because for each individual grade you have one row showing the enroll_date in the enrollment table.

LAB 6.2 EXERCISES

6.2.1 JOIN MORE THAN TWO TABLES

a) Display the student_id, course number, and section number of enrolled students where the instructor of the section lives in zip code 10025. Additionally, the course should not have any prerequisites.

b) Produce the mailing addresses for instructors who taught sections starting in June of 1999.

_____

_____

c) List the student ids of enrolled students living in Connecticut.

_____

_____

6.2.2 JOIN WITH MULTICOLUMN JOIN CRITERIA

a) Show all the grades student Fred Crocitto received for section_id 86.

_____

_____

b) List the final examination grades for all enrolled Connecticut students of course number 420. Note final examination does not mean final grade.

_____

_____

c) Display the last_name, student_id, percent_of_final, grade_type_code, and grade for students who received a grade of 80 or less for their class project (grade_type_code = 'PJ'). Order the result by student last name.

_____

_____

LAB 6.2 EXERCISE ANSWERS

6.2.1 ANSWERS

a) Display the student_id, course number, and section number of enrolled students where the instructor of the section lives in zip code 10025. Additionally, the course should not have any prerequisites.

Answer: This query involves joining four tables. The course number is found in the section and course tables, the prerequisite in the course table. To determine the zip code of an instructor, use the instructor table. To choose only enrolled students, join to the enrollment table.

```
SELECT c.course_no, s.section_no, e.student_id
  FROM course c, section s, instructor i, enrollment e
 WHERE c.prerequisite IS NULL
   AND c.course_no = s.course_no
   AND s.instructor_id = i.instructor_id
   AND i.zip = '10025'
   AND s.section_id = e.section_id
```

COURSE_NO	SECTION_NO	STUDENT_ID
10	2	128
146	2	117
146	2	140
...		
20	8	158
20	8	199

12 rows selected.

To obtain this result, build the four-table join just like any other join, step-by-step. First start with one of the tables, such as the course table.

```
SELECT course_no
  FROM course
 WHERE prerequisite IS NULL
```

For each of these courses you find the corresponding sections when you join the course table with the section table.

```
SELECT c.course_no, s.section_no
  FROM course c, section s
 WHERE c.prerequisite IS NULL
   AND c.course_no = s.course_no
```

Then include instructors who live in zip code 10025. The common column between section and instructor is instructor_id.

```
SELECT c.course_no, s.section_no
  FROM course c, section s, instructor i
 WHERE c.prerequisite IS NULL
   AND c.course_no = s.course_no
   AND s.instructor_id = i.instructor_id
   AND i.zip = '10025'
```

Finally, join to the results of the enrollment table via the section_id column, which leads you to the solution shown previously.

b) Produce the mailing addresses for instructors who taught sections starting in June of 1999.

Answer: This solution requires the join of three tables: you join the instructor, section, and zipcode tables to produce the mailing list.

```
SELECT i.first_name || ' ' ||i.last_name name,
       i.street_address, z.city || ', ' || z.state
       || ' ' || i.zip "City State Zip",
       TO_CHAR(s.start_date_time, 'MM/DD/YY') start_dt,
       section_id sect
  FROM instructor i, section s, zipcode z
 WHERE i.instructor_id = s.instructor_id
   AND i.zip = z.zip
   AND s.start_date_time >=
       TO_DATE('01-JUN-1999','DD-MON-YYYY')
   AND s.start_date_time <
       TO_DATE('01-JUL-1999','DD-MON-YYYY')
```

NAME	STREET_ADDRESS	City State Zip	START_DT	SECT
Fernand Hanks	100 East 87th	New York, NY 10015	06/02/99	117
Anita Morris	34 Maiden Lane	New York, NY 10015	06/11/99	83
Anita Morris	34 Maiden Lane	New York, NY 10015	06/12/99	91
Anita Morris	34 Maiden Lane	New York, NY 10015	06/02/99	113
...				
Gary Pertez	34 Sixth Ave	New York, NY 10035	06/12/99	90
Gary Pertez	34 Sixth Ave	New York, NY 10035	06/10/99	120
Gary Pertez	34 Sixth Ave	New York, NY 10035	06/03/99	143
Gary Pertez	34 Sixth Ave	New York, NY 10035	06/12/99	151

17 rows selected.

One of the first steps in solving this query is to determine the columns and tables involved. Look at the schema diagram, or refer to the table and column comments in Appendix C, "Student Database Schema."

In this example, the instructor's last name, first name, street address, and zip code columns are found in the instructor table. The city, state, and zip are columns in the zipcode table. The join also needs to include the section table because the column start_date_time lists the date and time on which the individual sections started. The next step is to determine the common columns. The zip column is the common column between the instructor and zipcode tables. For every value in the zip column of the instructor table you have one corresponding zip value in the zipcode table. For every value in the zipcode table there may be zero, one, or multiple records in the instructor table. The join returns only the matching records.

The other common column is the instructor_id in the section and instructor tables. Only instructors who teach have a record in the section table. Any section that does not have an instructor assigned is not taught.

Looking at the result, notice there are instructors teaching multiple sections. To see only the distinct addresses, use the DISTINCT keyword, and drop the start_date_time and section_id columns from the SELECT list.

c) List the student ids of enrolled students living in Connecticut.

Answer: Only students enrolled in classes are in the result; any student who does not have a record in the enrollment table is not considered enrolled. The student_id is the common column between the student and enrollment tables. The state column is in the zipcode table. The common column between the student and the zipcode tables is the zip column.

```
SELECT s.student_id
  FROM student s, enrollment e, zipcode z
 WHERE s.student_id = e.student_id
   AND s.zip = z.zip
   AND z.state = 'CT'
STUDENT_ID
-----------
       220
       270
       270
...
       210
       154

13 rows selected.
```

Because students can be enrolled in more than one class, add the DIS-TINCT keyword if you want to display each student_id once.

6.2.2 ANSWERS

a) Show all the grades student Fred Crocitto received for section_id 86.

Answer: The grades for each section and student are stored in the grade table. The primary key of the grade table is the student_id, section_id, grade_type_code, and grade_code_occurrence columns. This means a student, such as Fred Crocitto, has multiple grades for each section and grade type.

```
SELECT s.first_name|| ' '|| s.last_name name,
       e.section_id, g.grade_type_code,
       g.numeric_grade grade
  FROM student s, enrollment e, grade g
 WHERE s.last_name = 'Crocitto'
   AND s.first_name ='Fred'
   AND e.section_id = 86
   AND s.student_id = e.student_id
   AND e.student_id = g.student_id
   AND e.section_id = g.section_id
```

NAME	SECTION_ID	GR	GRADE
Fred Crocitto	86	FI	85
...			
Fred Crocitto	86	QZ	90
Fred Crocitto	86	QZ	84
Fred Crocitto	86	QZ	97
Fred Crocitto	86	QZ	97

11 rows selected.

To build up the SQL statement step by step, you may want to start with the student table and select the record for Fred Crocitto.

```
SELECT last_name, first_name
  FROM student
 WHERE last_name = 'Crocitto'
   AND first_name = 'Fred'
```

Next, choose the section with the id of 86 in which Fred is enrolled. The common column between the two tables is student_id.

```
SELECT s.first_name||' '|| s.last_name name,
       e.section_id
```

```
 FROM student s, enrollment e
WHERE s.last_name = 'Crocitto'
  AND s.first_name = 'Fred'
  AND e.section_id = 86
  AND s.student_id = e.student_id
```

Lastly, retrieve the individual grades from the grade table. The common columns between the grade table and the enrollment table are section_id and student_id. They represent the primary key in the enrollment table, and are foreign keys in the grade table. Both columns need to be in the WHERE clause.

Expanding on the above query, add the description column of the grade_type_table for each grade_type_code together with the course number. The common column between the tables grade and grade_type is grade_type_code. Add the description column to the SELECT list, and prefix the grade_type_code column to indicate from which table the column is selected.

```
SELECT s.first_name||' '|| s.last_name name,
       e.section_id, g.grade_type_code grade,
       g.numeric_grade, gt.description
  FROM student s, enrollment e, grade g, grade_type gt
 WHERE s.last_name = 'Crocitto'
   AND s.first_name = 'Fred'
   AND e.section_id = 86
   AND s.student_id = e.student_id
   AND e.student_id = g.student_id
   AND e.section_id = g.section_id
   AND g.grade_type_code = gt.grade_type_code
```

To also show the course_no column, join to the section table via the enrollment table column section_id.

```
SELECT s.first_name||' '|| s.last_name name,
       e.section_id, g.grade_type_code,
       g.numeric_grade grade, gt.description,
       sec.course_no
  FROM student s, enrollment e, grade g, grade_type gt,
       section sec
 WHERE s.last_name = 'Crocitto'
   AND s.first_name = 'Fred'
   AND e.section_id = 86
   AND s.student_id = e.student_id
   AND e.student_id = g.student_id
   AND e.section_id = g.section_id
```

```
   AND g.grade_type_code = gt.grade_type_code
   AND e.section_id = sec.section_id
NAME              SECTION_ID GR GRADE DESCRIPTION    COURSE_NO
--------------    ---------- -- ----- -----------    ----------
Fred Crocitto             86 FI    85 Final                 25
...
Fred Crocitto             86 QZ    90 Quiz                  25
Fred Crocitto             86 QZ    84 Quiz                  25
Fred Crocitto             86 QZ    97 Quiz                  25
Fred Crocitto             86 QZ    97 Quiz                  25
```

11 rows selected.

b) List the final examination grades for all enrolled Connecticut students of course number 420. Note final examination does not mean final grade.

Answer: This answer requires joining five tables. The required joins are: the zipcode table with the student table to determine the Connecticut students; the student and enrollment tables to determine the section_ids in which the students are enrolled. From these section_ids you only include sections where the course number equals 420. This requires a join of the enrollment table to the section table. Lastly, the enrollment table needs to be joined to the grade table to display the grades.

```
SELECT e.student_id, sec.course_no, g.numeric_grade
  FROM student stud, zipcode z,
       enrollment e, section sec, grade g
 WHERE stud.zip = z.zip
   AND z.state = 'CT'
   AND stud.student_id = e.student_id
   AND e.section_id = sec.section_id
   AND e.section_id = g.section_id
   AND e.student_id = g.student_id
   AND sec.course_no = 420
   AND g.grade_type_code = 'FI'
STUDENT_ID COURSE_NO NUMERIC_GRADE
---------- --------- -------------
       196       420            84
       198       420            85
```

2 rows selected.

You may list any of the columns you find relevant to solving the query. For this solution, the columns student_id, course_no, and numeric_grade were chosen.

c) Display the columns last_name, student_id, percent_of_final, grade_type_code, and grade for students who received a grade of 80 or less for their class project (grade_type_code = 'PJ'). Order the result by student last name.

Answer: Join the tables grade_type_weight, grade, enrollment, and student.

The column percent_of_final_grade of the grade_type_weight table stores the weighted percentage a particular grade has on the final grade. The foreign key columns of the grade table are grade_type_code and section_id; these columns represent the primary key of the grade_type_weight table. The grade table already lists the section_id and student_id for each grade_type, together with the occurrence.

To include the student's last name, you have two choices. Either follow the primary and foreign key relationships by joining the tables grade and enrollment via the student_id and section_id columns, and then join the enrollment table to the student table via the student_id column, or skip the enrollment table and join grade directly to the student table via the student_id. Examine the first option of joining to the enrollment table and then to the student table.

```
SELECT g.student_id, g.section_id,
       gw.percent_of_final_grade pct, g.grade_type_code,
       g.numeric_grade grade, s.last_name
  FROM grade_type_weight gw, grade g,
       enrollment e, student s
 WHERE g.grade_type_code = 'PJ'
   AND gw.grade_type_code = g.grade_type_code
   AND gw.section_id = g.section_id
   AND g.numeric_grade <= 80
   AND g.section_id = e.section_id
   AND g.student_id = e.student_id
   AND e.student_id = s.student_id
 ORDER BY s.last_name
```

STUDENT_ID	SECTION_ID	PCT	GR	GRADE	LAST_NAME
245	82	75	PJ	77	Dalvi
176	115	75	PJ	76	Satterfield
244	82	75	PJ	76	Wilson
248	155	75	PJ	76	Zapulla

4 rows selected.

SKIPPING THE PRIMARY/FOREIGN KEY PATH

The second choice is to join the student_id from the grade table directly to the student_id of the student table, thus skipping the enrollment table entirely. The following query returns the same result.

```
SELECT g.student_id, g.section_id,
       gw.percent_of_final_grade pct, g.grade_type_code,
       g.numeric_grade grade, s.last_name
  FROM grade_type_weight gw, grade g,
       student s
 WHERE g.grade_type_code = 'PJ'
   AND gw.grade_type_code = g.grade_type_code
   AND gw.section_id = g.section_id
   AND g.numeric_grade <= 80
   AND g.student_id = s.student_id
 ORDER BY s.last_name
```

STUDENT_ID	SECTION_ID	PCT	GR	GRADE	LAST_NAME
245	82	75	PJ	77	Dalvi
176	115	75	PJ	76	Satterfield
244	82	75	PJ	76	Wilson
248	155	75	PJ	76	Zapulla

4 rows selected.

This shortcut is perfectly acceptable, even if it does not follow the primary/foreign key relationship path. In this case, you can be sure not to build a Cartesian product as you can guarantee only one student_id in the student table for every student_id in the grade table.

LAB 6.2 SELF-REVIEW QUESTIONS

In order to test your progress, you should be able to answer the following questions.

1) Which SQL statement shows the sections that have instructors assigned to them?
   a) _____

```
SELECT c.course_no, s.section_id, i.instructor_id
  FROM course c, section s, instructor i
 WHERE c.course_no = s.course_no
   AND i.instructor_id = s.section_id
```

b) _____

```
SELECT c.course_no, s.section_id, i.instructor_id
  FROM course c, section s, instructor i
 WHERE c.course_no = s.course_no
   AND i.instructor_id = s.instructor_id
```

c) _____

```
SELECT course_no, section_id, instructor.instructor_id
  FROM section, instructor
 WHERE instructor.instructor_id = section.section_id
```

d) _____

```
SELECT c.section_id, i.instructor_id
  FROM course c, instructor i
 WHERE i.instructor_id = c.section_id
```

2) How do you resolve the Oracle error `ORA-00918: column ambiguously defined`?
   a) _____ Correct the join criteria
   b) _____ Add the proper column alias
   c) _____ Rewrite the query
   d) _____ Add the correct table alias
   e) _____ Correct the spelling of the column name

3) Joins involving multiple columns must always follow the primary/foreign key relationship path.
   a) _____ True
   b) _____ False

4) Find the error(s) in the SQL statement below.

```
1 SELECT g.student_id, s.section_id,
2        g.numeric_grade, s.last_name
3   FROM grade g,
4        enrollment e, student s
5  WHERE g.section_id = e.section_id
6    AND g.student_id = e.student_id
7    AND s.student_id = e.student_id
8    AND s.student_id = 248
9    AND e.section_id = 155
```

a) _____ Line 1
b) _____ Line 5
c) _____ Line 6
d) _____ Line 5, 6
e) _____ Line 1, 5, 6
f) _____ No error

Quiz answers appear in Appendix A, Section 6.2.

CHAPTER 6

TEST YOUR THINKING

1) Select the course description, section_no, and location for sections meeting in location L211.

2) Show the course description, course number, starting date and time of the courses Joseph German is taking.

3) List the instructor id, last name of the instructor, and section_id of sections where class participation contributes to 25% of the total grade. Order the result by the instructor's last name.

4) Display the first and last names of students who received 99 or more points on their class project.

5) Select the grades for quizzes of students living in zip code 10956.

6) List the course number, section number, and instructor first and last names of classes with course number 350 as a prerequisite.

7) Write the questions for the following two SELECT statements. Explain the difference between the two results.

```
SELECT stud.student_id, i.instructor_id,
       stud.zip, i.zip
  FROM student stud, instructor i
 WHERE stud.zip = i.zip

SELECT stud.student_id, i.instructor_id,
       stud.zip, i.zip
  FROM student stud, enrollment e, section sec,
       instructor i
 WHERE stud.student_id = e.student_id
   AND e.section_id = sec.section_id
   AND sec.instructor_id = i.instructor_id
   AND stud.zip = i.zip
```

C H A P T E R 7

SUBQUERIES

CHAPTER OBJECTIVES

In this chapter, you will learn about:

- ✔ Simple Subqueries   Page 182
- ✔ Correlated Subqueries   Page 198
- ✔ ANY, SOME, and ALL Operators in Subqueries   Page 213

A subquery is a SELECT statement nested in the WHERE or HAVING clause of another SQL statement. It allows you to use the output from one query as the input of another SQL statement. Subqueries make it easy to break down problems into logical and manageable pieces. Although subqueries can be nested several levels deep, it is impractical beyond four or five levels.

Subqueries can also be formed in the FROM clause of a SQL statement. These types of queries are referred to as *in-line views*. You will learn about these queries in Chapter 15, "Advanced SQL Queries."

L A B   7 . 1

SIMPLE SUBQUERIES

LAB OBJECTIVES

After this lab, you will be able to:

- ✔ Write Subqueries in the WHERE and HAVING Clauses
- ✔ Write Subqueries Returning Multiple Rows
- ✔ Write Subqueries Returning Multiple Columns

Subqueries are not used just in SELECT statements, but also in other SQL statements that allow subqueries, for example, the WHERE clause of DELETE statements, the SET and WHERE clause of UPDATE statements, or part of the SELECT clause of INSERT statements. You use these SQL statements in Chapter 10, "INSERT, UPDATE, and DELETE Statements."

In this workbook, the subquery is referred to as the *inner query*, and the surrounding statement as the *outer query*. In the simple *non-correlated* subquery, the inner query is executed once, before the execution of the outer query. This is in contrast to the *correlated subquery*, where the inner query executes repeatedly. You will learn to write correlated subqueries in Lab 7.2.

SIMPLE SUBQUERIES

The simple subquery is probably the most frequently used type of subquery. It allows you to break down a problem into individual pieces and solve it by nesting the queries.

■ *FOR EXAMPLE*

When you want to show the courses with the lowest course cost, you can write two separate queries. First, determine the lowest cost by applying the aggregate function MIN to the cost column of the course table.

```
SELECT MIN(cost)
  FROM course
MIN(COST)
---------
     1095
```

1 row selected.

Then, write another SELECT statement that retrieves courses equaling the cost.

```
SELECT course_no, description, cost
  FROM course
 WHERE cost = 1095
```

COURSE_NO	DESCRIPTION	COST
135	Unix Tips and Techniques	1095
230	Intro to Internet	1095
240	Intro to the Basic Language	1095

3 rows selected.

The subquery construct simplifies the writing of two separate queries and recording the intermediate result. The following SQL statement nests the query determining the lowest course cost in the WHERE clause of the other query.

```
SELECT course_no, description, cost
  FROM course
 WHERE cost =
       (SELECT MIN(cost)
          FROM course)
```

COURSE_NO	DESCRIPTION	COST
135	Unix Tips and Techniques	1095
230	Intro to Internet	1095
240	Intro to the Basic Language	1095

3 rows selected.

NESTING MULTIPLE SUBQUERIES

You can nest one subquery within another subquery. The innermost query is always evaluated first, then the next higher one, and so on. The result of each subquery is fed into the enclosing statement.

■ FOR EXAMPLE

Determine the last and first names of students enrolled in section number 8 of course number 20.

```
SELECT last_name, first_name
  FROM student
 WHERE student_id IN
       (SELECT student_id
          FROM enrollment
         WHERE section_id IN
               (SELECT section_id
                  FROM section
                 WHERE section_no = 8
                   AND course_no = 20))
```

LAST_NAME	FIRST_NAME
Limate	Roy
Segall	J.

2 rows selected.

The innermost nested subquery is executed first; it determines the section_id for section number 8 and course number 20. The surrounding query uses this resulting section_id in the WHERE clause to select student_ids from the enrollment table. These student_id rows are fed to the outermost SELECT statement. For these student_ids, the first and last names from the student table are displayed.

You cannot use the ORDER BY clause inside a subquery.

SUBQUERIES RETURNING MULTIPLE ROWS

Subqueries can return one or multiple rows. If a subquery returns a single row, the = operator may be used for comparison with the subquery. If multiple records are returned, the IN operator must be used, otherwise Oracle returns an error message.

■ FOR EXAMPLE

The following query displays the course number, description, and cost of courses with a cost equal to the highest cost of all the courses. The highest cost requires the use of the aggregate function MAX. As you recall from Chapter 5, "Aggregate Functions, GROUP BY, and HAVING," aggregate functions always return one row. The subquery returns the single value 1595. All the rows of the course table are compared to this value to see if any rows have the same course cost. Only one record in the course table equals this cost.

```
SELECT course_no, description, cost
  FROM course
 WHERE cost =
       (SELECT MAX(cost)
          FROM course)
```

COURSE_NO DESCRIPTION	COST
80 Structured Programming Techniques	1595

1 row selected.

The next SQL statement is an example of a subquery that returns several rows.

```
SELECT course_no, description, cost
  FROM course
 WHERE cost =
       (SELECT cost
          FROM course
         WHERE prerequisite = 20)
```
ERROR at line 4:
ORA-01427: single-row subquery returns more than one row

Multiple records of the subquery satisfy the criteria of a prerequisite course number equal to 20. Therefore, Oracle returns an error message. To eliminate the error, change the = operator of the outer query to the IN operator. The IN operator compares a list of values for equivalency. If any of the values in the list satisfies the condition, the record is included in the result set.

```
SELECT course_no, description, cost
  FROM course
 WHERE cost IN
       (SELECT cost
          FROM course
         WHERE prerequisite = 20)
```

COURSE_NO DESCRIPTION	COST
10 DP Overview	1195

```
    20 Intro to Computers                    1195
...
   122 Intermediate Java Programming          1195
   100 Hands-On Windows                       1195
```

25 rows selected.

You can also negate the subquery, and not include records in the result, by applying the NOT IN operator.

```
SELECT course_no, description, cost
  FROM course
 WHERE cost NOT IN
       (SELECT cost
          FROM course
         WHERE prerequisite = 20)
COURSE_NO DESCRIPTION                        COST
--------- --------------------------------- ---------
       80 Structured Programming Techniques  1595
      135 Unix Tips and Techniques           1095
      230 Intro to Internet                  1095
      240 Intro to the Basic Language        1095
```

4 rows selected.

Instead of performing equality or non-equality conditions, you may need to perform >, <, >=, or <= comparisons against a set of rows. In Lab 7.3, you apply the ALL, ANY, and SOME operators to perform such comparisons.

SUBQUERIES AND JOINS

Sometimes subqueries using the IN or = operator can be expressed as joins if the subquery does not contain an aggregate function.

■ *FOR EXAMPLE*

The following query can be transformed into an equijoin. Oracle sometimes performs this conversion implicitly as part of its optimization strategy if the primary and foreign keys exist on the table, and the join does not cause a Cartesian product.

```
SELECT course_no, description
  FROM course
 WHERE course_no IN
       (SELECT course_no
```

```
      FROM section
     WHERE location = 'L211')
COURSE_NO DESCRIPTION
--------- ------------------------------
      142 Project Management
      125 JDeveloper
      122 Intermediate Java Programming
```

3 rows selected.

Here is the same query now expressed as an equijoin:

```
SELECT c.course_no, c.description
  FROM course c, section s
 WHERE c.course_no = s.course_no
   AND s.location = 'L211'
```

SUBQUERIES RETURNING MULTIPLE COLUMNS

SQL allows you to compare multiple columns in the WHERE clause to multiple columns of a subquery. The values in the columns must match both sides of the equation in the WHERE clause for the condition to be true. This means the datatype, number of columns, and order of columns must match.

■ FOR EXAMPLE

For each section, determine the students with the highest grade for their project (PJ). The following query does not accomplish this goal. It returns the highest project grade for each section, but does not list the individual student(s).

```
SELECT section_id, MAX(numeric_grade)
  FROM grade
 WHERE grade_type_code = 'PJ'
 GROUP BY section_id
SECTION_ID MAX(NUMERIC_GRADE)
---------- ------------------
        82                 77
        88                 99
...
       149                 83
       155                 92
```

8 rows selected.

The following query obtains the desired result by transforming the query into a subquery. The outer query displays the desired student_id column, and the WHERE clause compares the column pairs against the column pairs in the subquery.

```
SELECT student_id, section_id, numeric_grade
  FROM grade
 WHERE grade_type_code = 'PJ'
   AND (section_id, numeric_grade) IN
       (SELECT section_id, MAX(numeric_grade)
          FROM grade
         WHERE grade_type_code = 'PJ'
         GROUP BY section_id)
```

STUDENT_ID	SECTION_ID	NUMERIC_GRADE
245	82	77
166	88	99
...		
232	149	83
105	155	92

8 rows selected.

The execution steps are just like the previous simple subqueries. First, the innermost query is executed, determining the highest grade for each section. Then the pairs of columns are compared. If the column pair matches, Oracle displays the record.

LAB 7.1 EXERCISES

7.1.1 WRITE SUBQUERIES IN THE *WHERE* AND *HAVING* CLAUSES

a) Write a SQL statement that displays the first and last names of students who registered first.

_____

_____

b) Show the sections with the lowest course cost and a capacity equal to or lower than the average capacity. Also display the course description, section number, capacity, and cost.

_____

_____

c) Select the course number and total capacity for each course. Show only the courses with a total capacity less than the average capacity of all the sections.

_____

_____

d) Choose the most ambitious students: display the student_id for students enrolled in the most sections.

_____

_____

7.1.2 WRITE SUBQUERIES RETURNING MULTIPLE ROWS

a) Select the student_id and section_id of enrolled students living in zip code 06820.

_____

_____

b) Display the course number and course description of the courses taught by instructor Fernand Hanks.

_____

_____

c) Select the last name and first name of students not enrolled in any class.

_____

_____

7.1.3 WRITE SUBQUERIES RETURNING MULTIPLE COLUMNS

a) Determine the student_id and last name of students with the highest final_grade for each section. Include the section_id and the final_grade column in the result.

_____

_____

b) Select the sections where the capacity equals the number of students enrolled.

_____

_____

LAB 7.1 EXERCISE ANSWERS

7.1.1 ANSWERS

a) Write a SQL statement that displays the first and last names of students who registered first.

Answer: The query is broken down into logical pieces by first determining the earliest registration date of all students. The aggregate function MIN obtains the result in the subquery. The oldest date is compared to the registration_date column for each student, and only records that are equal to the same date and time are returned.

```
SELECT first_name, last_name
  FROM student
 WHERE registration_date =
       (SELECT MIN(registration_date)
          FROM student)
```

FIRST_NAME	LAST_NAME
J.	Landry
Judith	Olvsade
...	
Larry	Walter
Catherine	Mierzwa

8 rows selected.

b) Show the sections with the lowest course cost and a capacity equal to or lower than the average capacity. Also display the course description, section number, capacity, and cost.

Answer: First, break down the solution into individual queries. Start by determining the average capacity of all sections and the lowest course cost of all courses. To compare both cost and capacity against the subqueries, the section and course tables require a join.

```
SELECT c.description, s.section_no, c.cost, s.capacity
  FROM course c, section s
 WHERE c.course_no = s.course_no
   AND s.capacity <=
       (SELECT AVG(capacity)
          FROM section)
   AND c.cost =
       (SELECT MIN(cost)
          FROM course)
```

DESCRIPTION	SECTION_NO	COST	CAPACITY
Intro to Internet	1	1095	12
Intro to Internet	2	1095	15
...			
Unix Tips and Techniques	2	1095	15
Unix Tips and Techniques	4	1095	15

6 rows selected.

c) Select the course number and total capacity for each course. Show only the courses with a total capacity less than the average capacity of all the sections.

Answer: To determine the total capacity per course, use the SUM function to add the values in the section table's capacity column. Compare the total capacity for each course to the average capacity for all sections, and return those courses that are less.

```
SELECT course_no, SUM(capacity)
  FROM section
 GROUP BY course_no
HAVING SUM(capacity) <
       (SELECT AVG(capacity)
          FROM section)
```

COURSE_NO	SUM(CAPACITY)
10	15
144	15

2 rows selected.

The solution shows only those courses and their respective capacities that satisfy the condition in the HAVING clause.

To determine the solution, first write the individual queries and then combine them. The following query first determines the capacity for each course.

```
SELECT course_no, SUM(capacity)
  FROM section
 GROUP BY course_no
```

COURSE_NO	SUM(CAPACITY)
10	15
20	80
...	
420	25
450	25

28 rows selected.

The average capacity for all sections is easily obtained using the AVG function.

```
SELECT AVG(capacity)
  FROM section
```

AVG(CAPACITY)
21.179487

1 row selected.

d) Choose the most ambitious students: display the student_id for students enrolled in the most sections.

Answer: A count of records for each student in the enrollment table shows how many sections each student is enrolled in. Determine the most number of enrollments per student by nesting the aggregate functions MAX and COUNT.

```
SELECT student_id, COUNT(*)
  FROM enrollment
 GROUP BY student_id
HAVING COUNT(*) =
       (SELECT MAX(COUNT(*))
          FROM enrollment
        GROUP BY student_id)
```

```
STUDENT_ID  COUNT(*)
----------  ---------
       124         4
       214         4
```

2 rows selected.

To reach the subquery solution, determine the number of enrollments for each student.

```
SELECT COUNT(*)
  FROM enrollment
 GROUP BY student_id
COUNT(*)
---------
       2
       1
...
       2
       2
```

165 rows selected.

The second query combines two aggregate functions to determine the highest number of sections any student is enrolled in. This subquery is then applied in the HAVING clause of the solution.

```
SELECT MAX(COUNT(*))
  FROM enrollment
 GROUP BY student_id
MAX(COUNT(*))
-------------
            4
```

1 row selected.

7.1.2 ANSWERS

a) Select the student_id and section_id of enrolled students living in zip code 06820.

Answer: The IN operator is necessary because the subquery returns multiple rows.

```
SELECT student_id, section_id
  FROM enrollment
 WHERE student_id IN
       (SELECT student_id
          FROM student
         WHERE zip = '06820')
STUDENT_ID SECTION_ID
---------- ----------
       240         81
```

1 row selected.

Alternatively, you can achieve the same result using an equijoin.

```
SELECT e.student_id, e.section_id
  FROM enrollment e, student s
 WHERE e.student_id = s.student_id
   AND s.zip = '06820'
```

   b) Display the course number and course description of the courses taught by instructor Fernand Hanks.

      Answer: To determine the courses taught by this instructor, nest multiple subqueries. This question can also be solved using an equijoin.

```
SELECT course_no, description
  FROM course
 WHERE course_no IN
       (SELECT course_no
          FROM section
         WHERE instructor_id IN
               (SELECT instructor_id
                  FROM instructor
                 WHERE last_name = 'Hanks'
                   AND first_name = 'Fernand'))
COURSE_NO DESCRIPTION
--------- ----------------------------
       25 Intro to Programming
      240 Intro to the Basic Language
...
      120 Intro to Java Programming
      122 Intermediate Java Programming
```

9 rows selected.

The alternative solution is an equijoin:

```
SELECT c.course_no, c.description
  FROM course c, section s, instructor i
 WHERE c.course_no = s.course_no
   AND s.instructor_id = i.instructor_id
   AND i.last_name = 'Hanks'
   AND i.first_name = 'Fernand'
```

   c)   Select the last name and first name of students not enrolled in any class.

Answer: Use the NOT IN operator to eliminate those student IDs not found in the en-rollment table. The result is a listing of students with no rows in the enrollment table. They may be newly registered students that have not yet enrolled in any courses.

```
SELECT last_name, first_name
  FROM student
 WHERE student_id NOT IN
       (SELECT student_id
          FROM enrollment)
```

LAST_NAME	FIRST_NAME
Eakheit	George
Millstein	Leonard
...	
Larcia	Preston
Mastandora	Kathleen

103 rows selected.

You may wonder why the solution does not include the DISTINCT keyword in the subquery. It is not required and does not alter the result, nor change the efficiency of the execution. Oracle automatically eliminates duplicates in a list of values as a result of the subquery.

7.1.3 ANSWERS

   a)   Determine the student_id and last name of students with the highest final_grade for each section. Include the section_id and the final_grade column in the result.

Answer: The solution requires pairs of columns to be compared. First, determine the subquery to show the highest grade for each section. Then match the result to the columns in the outer query.

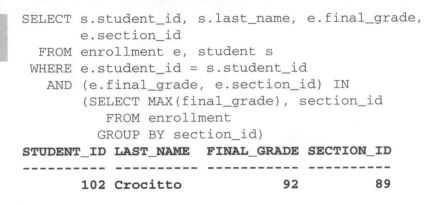

```
SELECT s.student_id, s.last_name, e.final_grade,
       e.section_id
  FROM enrollment e, student s
 WHERE e.student_id = s.student_id
   AND (e.final_grade, e.section_id) IN
       (SELECT MAX(final_grade), section_id
          FROM enrollment
         GROUP BY section_id)
```

STUDENT_ID	LAST_NAME	FINAL_GRADE	SECTION_ID
102	Crocitto	92	89

```
1 row selected.
```

Note, there is no need to add a table alias to the subquery. Table aliases in subqueries are typically only used in correlated subqueries or in subqueries that contain joins. Correlated subqueries are discussed in Lab 7.2.

b) Select the sections where the capacity equals the number of students enrolled.

Answer: The subquery determines the number of enrolled students per section. The resulting set is then compared to the column pair of section_id and capacity.

```
SELECT section_id, capacity
  FROM section
 WHERE (section_id, capacity) IN
       (SELECT section_id, COUNT(*)
          FROM enrollment
         GROUP BY section_id)
```

SECTION_ID	CAPACITY
99	12

```
1 row selected.
```

LAB 7.1 SELF-REVIEW QUESTIONS

In order to test your progress, you should be able to answer the following questions.

1) The ORDER BY clause is not allowed in subqueries.

    a) _____ True

    b) _____ False

2) Subqueries are used only in SELECT statements.
   a) _____ True
   b) _____ False

3) The most deeply nested, non-correlated subquery, always executes first.
   a) _____ True
   b) _____ False

4) Find the error(s) in this SQL statement:

```
1   SELECT *
2     FROM student
3    WHERE (SELECT student_id
4             FROM enrollment
5            WHERE section_id) = student_id
```

   a) _____ Line 3, 4, 5
   b) _____ No Error
   c) _____ Line 3
   d) _____ Line 5

5) What operator would you choose to prevent this Oracle error message?
   ORA-01427: single-row subquery returns more than one row
   a) _____ Use the >= operator
   b) _____ Use the = operator
   c) _____ Use the IN operator
   d) _____ Use the <= operator

6) Subqueries can return multiple rows and columns.
   a) _____ True
   b) _____ False

Quiz answers appear in Appendix A, Section 7.1.

LAB 7.2

CORRELATED SUBQUERIES

LAB OBJECTIVES

After this lab, you will be able to:

✔ Write Correlated Subqueries
✔ Write Correlated Subqueries Using the EXISTS and NOT EXISTS Operators

---

CORRELATED SUBQUERIES

Correlated subqueries are probably one of the most powerful, yet initially very difficult, concepts of the SQL language. Correlated subqueries are different from the simple subqueries discussed so far because they allow you to reference columns used in the outer query. The *correlation* is achieved by executing the inner query once for each row in the outer query.

■ *FOR EXAMPLE*

In the previous lab, one example illustrates how to determine the students with the highest grade for their project (PJ), within their respective sections. The solution is accomplished with the IN operator to compare column pairs. The following SELECT statement repeats the solution.

```
SELECT student_id, section_id, numeric_grade
  FROM grade
 WHERE grade_type_code = 'PJ'
   AND (section_id, numeric_grade) IN
       (SELECT section_id, MAX(numeric_grade)
```

```
      FROM grade
     WHERE grade_type_code = 'PJ'
     GROUP BY section_id)
```

Here is the query rewritten as a correlated subquery.

```
SELECT student_id, section_id, numeric_grade
  FROM grade outer
 WHERE grade_type_code = 'PJ'
   AND numeric_grade =
       (SELECT MAX(numeric_grade)
          FROM grade
         WHERE grade_type_code = outer.grade_type_code
           AND section_id = outer.section_id)
```

STUDENT_ID	SECTION_ID	NUMERIC_GRADE
245	82	77
166	88	99
...		
232	149	83
105	155	92

8 rows selected.

This query is a correlated subquery because the inner query refers to columns from the outer query. The grade table is the *parent query*, or the outer query. For simplicity, a table alias of *outer* is used.

Now you can refer to columns of the outer query using the alias. In this example, the values of the column section_id of the outer query are compared to the values of the inner query. The inner query determines the highest grade for each respective section_id.

STEPS PERFORMED BY THE CORRELATED SUBQUERY

To select the correct records, the following steps are performed by Oracle.

1. Select a row from the outer query.
2. Determine the value of the correlated column(s).
3. For each record of the outer query, the inner query is executed.

> 4.   The result of the inner query is then fed to the outer query and evaluated. If it satisfies the criteria, the row is returned for output.
>
> 5.   The next record of the outer query is selected and steps 2 through 4 are repeated until all the records of the outer query are evaluated.

Here are the steps in more detail.

STEP 1: SELECT A ROW FROM THE OUTER QUERY

Choose the records in the outer query where the grade_type_code equals 'PJ'. For each of these records, evaluate the inner query.

```
SELECT student_id, section_id, numeric_grade
  FROM grade outer
 WHERE grade_type_code = 'PJ'
STUDENT_ID SECTION_ID NUMERIC_GRADE
---------- ---------- -------------
       105        155            92
       111        133            90
...
       245         82            77
       248        155            76
```

21 rows selected.

STEP 2: DETERMINE THE VALUE OF THE CORRELATED COLUMN

Starting with student_id 105, the value of the correlated column outer.section_id equals 155. For the column outer.grade_type_code the value is 'PJ'.

STEP 3: EXECUTE THE INNER QUERY

Based on the correlated column values, the inner query is executed.

```
SELECT MAX(numeric_grade)
  FROM grade
 WHERE grade_type_code = 'PJ'
   AND section_id = 155
MAX(NUMERIC_GRADE)
------------------
                92
```

1 row selected.

STEP 4: EVALUATE THE CONDITION
Because the numeric_grade equals 92, the row for student_id 105 evaluates to true and is included in the result.

STEP 5: REPEAT STEPS 2 THROUGH 4 FOR EACH SUBSEQUENT ROW
Evaluate the next row with student_id 111 and section_id 133. Again, the inner query is executed. The highest grade for the section happens to be 92, but student 111 does not have a numeric_grade equal to this value. Therefore, the row is not returned. Each row of the outer query repeats these steps until all the rows are evaluated.

```
SELECT MAX(numeric_grade)
  FROM grade
 WHERE grade_type_code = 'PJ'
   AND section_id = 133
MAX(NUMERIC_GRADE)
------------------
                92

1 row selected.
```

Unlike the regular subquery where the inner query is evaluated once, the correlated subquery executes the inner query repeatedly, once for each row in the outer table.

THE EXISTS OPERATOR

The EXISTS operator is used for correlated subqueries. It tests if the subquery returns at least one row. The EXISTS operator returns either true or false, never unknown. Because EXISTS tests only if a row exists, the columns shown in the SELECT list are irrelevant. Typically you use a text literal such as '1' or 'X'.

■ *FOR EXAMPLE*

Display the instructor_id, last, and first name of instructors assigned to at least one section. The following correlated subquery displays instructors where the instructor_id has a matching row in the section table.

```
SELECT instructor_id, last_name, first_name, zip
  FROM instructor i
 WHERE EXISTS
       (SELECT 'X'
          FROM section
         WHERE i.instructor_id = instructor_id)
```

INSTRUCTOR_ID	LAST_NAME	FIRST_NAME	ZIP
101	Hanks	Fernand	10015
102	Wojick	Tom	10025
103	Schorin	Nina	10025
104	Pertez	Gary	10035
105	Morris	Anita	10015
106	Smythe	Todd	10025
108	Lowry	Charles	10025
107	Frantzen	Marilyn	10005

8 rows selected.

The query can also be written using the IN operator.

```
SELECT instructor_id, last_name, first_name, zip
  FROM instructor
 WHERE instructor_id IN
       (SELECT instructor_id
          FROM section)
```

Alternatively, you can write this query with an equijoin.

```
SELECT DISTINCT i.instructor_id, i.last_name,
       i.first_name, i.zip
  FROM instructor i, section s
 WHERE i.instructor_id = s.instructor_id
```

THE NOT EXISTS OPERATOR

The NOT EXISTS operator is the opposite of the EXISTS operator; it tests if a matching row cannot be found.

■ *FOR EXAMPLE*

Display the instructor_id, last, and first name of instructors *not* assigned to any section.

```
SELECT instructor_id, last_name, first_name, zip
  FROM instructor i
 WHERE NOT EXISTS
       (SELECT 'X'
          FROM section
         WHERE i.instructor_id = instructor_id)
```

INSTRUCTOR_ID	LAST_NAME	FIRST_NAME	ZIP
109	Chow	Rick	10015
110	Willig	Irene	

2 rows selected.

You cannot rewrite this particular query using an equijoin, but you can rewrite it with the NOT IN operator. But the NOT IN operator does not always yield the same result as you see in the following example.

NOT EXISTS VERSUS NOT IN

Display the instructor_id, first name, last name, and zip columns from the instructor table where there is no corresponding zip code in the zip-code table. Note the zip column in the instructor table allows NULL values.

USING NOT EXISTS

```
SELECT instructor_id, last_name, first_name, zip
  FROM instructor i
 WHERE NOT EXISTS
       (SELECT 'X'
          FROM zipcode
         WHERE i.zip = zip)
```

INSTRUCTOR_ID	LAST_NAME	FIRST_NAME	ZIP
110	Willig	Irene	

1 row selected.

USING NOT IN

```
SELECT instructor_id, last_name, first_name, zip
  FROM instructor
 WHERE zip NOT IN
       (SELECT zip
          FROM zipcode)
```
no rows selected

As you can see, the difference between NOT EXISTS and NOT IN lies in the way NULL values are treated. Instructor Irene Willig's zip column contains a NULL value. The NOT EXISTS operator tests for NULL values, the NOT IN operator does not.

LAB 7.2 EXERCISES

7.2.1 WRITE CORRELATED SUBQUERIES

a) Write a correlated subquery to display the section_id and course number of sections with less than two students enrolled. Remember to include sections that have no students enrolled!

_____

_____

b) Show the sections where the enrollment exceeds the capacity of the section, using a correlated subquery.

_____

_____

7.2.2 WRITE CORRELATED SUBQUERIES USING THE *EXISTS* AND *NOT EXISTS* OPERATORS

a) Write a SQL statement to determine the total number of students enrolled using the EXISTS operator. Count students enrolled in more than one course as one.

_____

_____

b) Show the student_id, last name and first name of students registered for three or more classes.

_____

_____

c) Which courses do not have sections assigned? Use a correlated subquery in the solution.

_____

_____

d) Which sections have no students enrolled? Use a correlated subquery in the solution, and order the result by the course number in ascending order.

_____

_____

LAB 7.2 EXERCISE ANSWERS

7.2.1 ANSWERS

a) Write a correlated subquery to display the section_id and course number of sections with less than two students enrolled. Remember to include sections that have no students enrolled!

Answer: Use the section table to test for all the sections in the enrollment table for which no enrollments exist.

```
SELECT section_id, course_no
  FROM section s
 WHERE 2 >
       (SELECT COUNT(*)
          FROM enrollment
         WHERE section_id = s.section_id)
```

SECTION_ID	COURSE_NO
79	350
80	10
145	100
149	120

27 rows selected.

This solution compares the number literal 2 to the result of the COUNT(*) function in the subquery for each section_id row. If no enrollment is found for the particular section, the COUNT function returns a zero; the section satisfies the criteria that 2 is greater than zero and is included in the result set.

You can write two queries to verify that the result is correct. First, write a query that shows sections where the enrollment is less than 2 students. This query returns 13 rows.

```
SELECT section_id, COUNT(*)
  FROM enrollment
 GROUP BY section_id
HAVING COUNT(*) < 2
SECTION_ID  COUNT(*)
---------- ---------
        80         1
        96         1
...
       145         1
       149         1
```

13 rows selected.

Then write a second query to show the sections without any enrollments, that is, the section_id does not exist in the enrollment table. To determine these sections, you can use the NOT IN operator because the section_id in the enrollment table is defined as NOT NULL.

```
SELECT section_id
  FROM section
 WHERE section_id NOT IN
       (SELECT section_id
          FROM enrollment)
SECTION_ID
----------
        79
        93
...
       136
       139
```

14 rows selected.

The combination of the 13 and 14 rows from the last two queries return a combined total of 27, as in the exercise solution.

Alternatively, you can combine the results of the two queries with the UNION operator discussed in Chapter 8, "Set Operators."

b) Show the sections where the enrollment exceeds the capacity of the section, using a correlated subquery.

Answer: The correlated query solution executes the outer query's GROUP BY clause first; then for every group, the subquery is executed to determine if it satisfies the condition in the HAVING clause. Only sections where the number of enrolled students exceeds the capacity for the respective section are returned for output.

LAB
7.2

```
SELECT section_id, COUNT(*)
  FROM enrollment e
 GROUP BY section_id
HAVING COUNT(*) >
       (SELECT capacity
          FROM section
         WHERE e.section_id = section_id)
```

SECTION_ID	COUNT(*)
101	12

1 row selected.

Alternatively, this can be solved using an equijoin and an aggregate function. The enrollment count is evaluated in the HAVING clause, and compared with the capacity.

```
SELECT e.section_id, COUNT(*), s.capacity
  FROM enrollment e, section s
 WHERE e.section_id = s.section_id
 GROUP BY e.section_id, s.capacity
HAVING COUNT(*) > s.capacity
```

SECTION_ID	COUNT(*)	CAPACITY
101	12	10

1 row selected.

When you join tables and apply aggregate functions, be sure the resulting rows provide the correct result of the aggregate function. For a more comprehensive explanation on this topic, see Chapter 15, "Advanced SQL Queries."

7.2.2 ANSWERS

a) Write a SQL statement to determine the total number of students enrolled using the EXISTS operator. Count students enrolled in more than one course as one.

Answer: For every student, the query checks to see if a row exists in the enrollment table. If this is true, the record is part of the result set. After Oracle determines all the rows that satisfy the EXISTS condition, the aggregate function COUNT is applied to determine the total number of students.

```
SELECT COUNT(*)
  FROM student s
 WHERE EXISTS
       (SELECT NULL
          FROM enrollment
         WHERE student_id = s.student_id)
COUNT(*)
---------
      165
```

```
1 row selected.
```

The same result can be obtained with the next query. Because the enrollment table may contain multiple student_ids if the student is enrolled in several sections, you need to count the distinct occurrences of the student_id to obtain the correct result.

```
SELECT COUNT(DISTINCT student_id)
  FROM enrollment
COUNT(DISTINCT STUDENT_ID)
--------------------------
                       165
```

```
1 row selected.
```

b) Show the student_id, last name, and first name of students registered for three or more classes.

Answer: There are four possible solutions: two of them use a correlated subquery; one uses an equijoin; another uses the IN operator with a subquery.

SOLUTION 1: CORRELATED SUBQUERY

```
SELECT first_name, last_name, student_id
  FROM student s
```

```
WHERE EXISTS
       (SELECT NULL
          FROM enrollment
         WHERE s.student_id = student_id
         GROUP BY student_id
        HAVING COUNT(*) >= 3)
```

FIRST_NAME	LAST_NAME	STUDENT_ID
Daniel	Wicelinski	124
Roger	Snow	238
...		
Salewa	Zuckerberg	184
Yvonne	Williams	214

7 rows selected.

For each record in the student table, the inner query is executed to determine if the student_id occurs three or more times in the enrollment table. The inner query's SELECT clause lists the NULL keyword whereas in the previous examples, a text literal was selected. It is completely irrelevant what columns are selected in the subquery with the EXISTS and NOT EXISTS operators as these operators only check for the existence or nonexistence of rows.

SOLUTION 2: EQUIJOIN

```
SELECT first_name, last_name, student_id
  FROM enrollment e, student s
 WHERE e.student_id = s.student_id
 GROUP BY first_name, last_name, s.student_id
HAVING COUNT(*) >= 3
```

This solution joins the student and enrollment tables. Students enrolled multiple times are grouped into one row, and the COUNT function counts the occurrences of each student's enrollment record. Only those having three or more records in the enrollment table are included.

Although Solution 2 achieves the correct result, you need to be aware of the dangers of aggregate functions in joins. You learn about this issue in Chapter 15, "Advanced SQL Queries."

SOLUTION 3: IN SUBQUERY
This subquery returns only student_ids with three or more enrollments. The result is then fed to the outer query.

```
SELECT first_name, last_name, student_id
  FROM student
```

```
WHERE student_id IN
        (SELECT student_id
           FROM enrollment
          GROUP BY student_id
         HAVING COUNT(*) >= 3)
```

**LAB
7.2**

SOLUTION 4: ANOTHER CORRELATED SUBQUERY

The number literal 3 is compared to the result of the correlated subquery. It counts the enrollment records for each individual student. This solution is similar to the solution in Exercise 7.2.1a.

```
SELECT last_name, first_name, student_id
  FROM student s
 WHERE 3 <= (SELECT COUNT(*)
               FROM enrollment
              WHERE s.student_id = student_id)
```

c) Which courses do not have sections assigned? Use a correlated subquery in the solution.

Answer: For every course in the course table, the NOT EXISTS condition probes the section table to determine if a row with the same course number exists. If the course number is not found, the WHERE clause evaluates to true and the record is included in the result set.

```
SELECT course_no, description
  FROM course c
 WHERE NOT EXISTS
        (SELECT 'X'
           FROM section
          WHERE c.course_no = course_no)
```

COURSE_NO DESCRIPTION
```
--------- --------------------------------
       80 Structured Programming Techniques
      430 JDeveloper Techniques
```

2 rows selected.

Note you can also write the query as follows:

```
SELECT course_no, description
  FROM course c
 WHERE NOT EXISTS
        (SELECT 'X'
           FROM section s
          WHERE c.course_no = s.course_no)
```

The section table uses the table alias s which the s.course_no column refers to. This alias is not required; it simply clarifies the column's source table. When you use column(s) without an alias, it is understood that the column(s) refers to the table in the current subquery. However, you must use a table alias for the c.course_no column, otherwise the query is not correlated.

As an alternative, the same result can be obtained using the NOT IN operator. Because the course_no column in the section table is defined as NOT NULL, the query returns the same result.

```
SELECT course_no, description
  FROM course
 WHERE course no NOT IN
       (SELECT course_no
          FROM section)
```

d) Which sections have no students enrolled? Use a correlated subquery in the solution, and order the result by the course number in ascending order.

Answer: The result contains only rows where the section_id does not exist in the enrollment table. The inner query executes for each row of the outer query.

```
SELECT course_no, section_id
  FROM section s
 WHERE NOT EXISTS
       (SELECT NULL
          FROM enrollment
         WHERE s.section_id = section_id)
 ORDER BY course_no
```

COURSE_NO	SECTION_ID
25	93
124	129
...	
350	79

14 rows selected.

You can achieve the same result using the NOT IN operator because the section_id column in the enrollment table is defined as NOT NULL.

```
SELECT course_no, section_id
  FROM section
```

```
WHERE section_id NOT IN
      (SELECT section_id
         FROM enrollment)
ORDER BY course_no
```

LAB 7.2 SELF-REVIEW QUESTIONS

In order to test your progress, you should be able to answer the following questions.

1) The NOT EXISTS operator tests for occurrences of NULLs.
  a) _____ True
  b) _____ False

2) In a correlated subquery the inner query is executed repeatedly.
  a) _____ True
  b) _____ False

3) The operators IN and EXISTS are equivalent.
  a) _____ True
  b) _____ False

4) The ORDER BY clause is allowed in the inner query of a correlated subquery.
  a) _____ True
  b) _____ False

5) Determine the correct question for the following SQL statement.

```
SELECT student_id, section_id
  FROM enrollment e
 WHERE NOT EXISTS
       (SELECT '1'
          FROM grade g
        WHERE e.section_id = section_id)
          AND e.student_id = student_id)
```

  a) _____ Show the enrolled students and their respective sections which have grades assigned.
  b) _____ Determine the students and their sections where no grades have been assigned.
  c) _____ Determine which students are not enrolled.
  d) _____ Determine the students that are not enrolled and do not have grades.
  e) _____ This is an invalid query.

Quiz answers appear in Appendix A, Section 7.2.

L A B   7 . 3

ANY, SOME, AND ALL OPERATORS IN SUBQUERIES

> ## LAB OBJECTIVES
>
> After this lab, you will be able to:
>
> ✔ Use the ANY, SOME, and ALL Operators in Sub-
>   queries

You are already familiar with the IN operator, which compares a list of values for equality. The ANY, SOME, and ALL operators are related to the IN operator as they also compare against a list of values. Additionally, these operators allow >, <, >=, and <= comparisons.

The ANY operator checks whether *any* value in the list makes the condition true. The ALL operator returns rows if the condition is true for *all* the values in the list. The SOME operator is identical to ANY and the two can be used interchangeably. Before applying these operators to subqueries, examine the effect of these operators on a simple list of values.

■ FOR EXAMPLE

This query retrieves all the grades received for section_id 84.

```
SELECT section_id, numeric_grade
  FROM grade
 WHERE section_id = 84
```

```
SECTION_ID NUMERIC_GRADE
---------- -------------
        84            88
        84            99
        84            77
        84            88
```

4 rows selected.

The familiar IN operator in the next SQL statement chooses all the grades that are either equal to 77 *or* equal to 99.

```
SELECT section_id, numeric_grade
  FROM grade
 WHERE section_id = 84
   AND numeric_grade IN (77, 99)
```

```
SECTION_ID NUMERIC_GRADE
---------- -------------
        84            99
        84            77
```

2 rows selected.

If you want to perform a comparison such as less than (<) against a list of values, use either the ANY, SOME, or ALL operator.

ANY AND SOME

This SQL query looks for any rows where the value in the numeric_grade column is less than either value in the list.

```
SELECT section_id, numeric_grade
  FROM grade
 WHERE section_id = 84
   AND numeric_grade < ANY (80, 90)
```

```
SECTION_ID NUMERIC_GRADE
---------- -------------
        84            88
        84            88
        84            77
```

3 rows selected.

The query returns the numeric_grade values 77 and 88. For the rows with the numeric_grade of 88, the condition is true for the value 90, not for the value 80. However, because the condition needs to be true for *any* of the records compared in the list, the record is included in the result.

The following query performs a greater than comparison with the ANY operator.

```
SELECT section_id, numeric_grade
  FROM grade
 WHERE section_id = 84
   AND numeric_grade > ANY (80, 90)
SECTION_ID NUMERIC_GRADE
---------- -------------
        84            88
        84            99
        84            88
```

3 rows selected.

In this result, since the records with the numeric_grade 88 are greater than 80, they are included. The numeric_grade of 99 is greater than both 80 and 90, and, therefore, is also included in the result set, although just one of the conditions is sufficient to be included in the result set.

The ANY operator with the = operator is the equivalent of the IN operator. There are no rows that have a numeric_grade of either 80 or 90.

```
SELECT section_id, numeric_grade
  FROM grade
 WHERE section_id = 84
   AND numeric_grade = ANY (80, 90)
```

no rows selected

The following query is the logical equivalent to the IN operator.

```
SELECT section_id, numeric_grade
  FROM grade
 WHERE section_id = 84
   AND numeric_grade IN (80, 90)
```

no rows selected

ALL

The ALL operator returns true if *every* value in the list satisfies the condition. In the following example, all the records in the grade table must be

LAB
7.3

less than 80 *and* 90. This condition is true only for the row with the numeric_grade value of 77, which is less than both 80 and 90.

```
SELECT section_id, numeric_grade
  FROM grade
 WHERE section_id = 84
   AND numeric_grade < ALL (80, 90)
SECTION_ID NUMERIC_GRADE
---------- -------------
        84            77
```

1 row selected.

A SQL statement using <> ALL is equivalent to NOT IN.

```
SELECT section_id, numeric_grade
  FROM grade
 WHERE section_id = 84
   AND numeric_grade <> ALL (80, 90)
SECTION_ID NUMERIC_GRADE
---------- -------------
        84            88
        84            99
        84            77
        84            88
```

4 rows selected.

 Whenever a subquery with the ALL operator fails to return a row, the query is automatically true. This is different from the ANY operator, which returns false.

LAB 7.3 EXERCISES

7.3.1 USE THE *ANY, SOME,* AND *ALL* OPERATORS IN SUBQUERIES

a) Write a SELECT statement to display the student_id, section_id, and grade of students who received a final examination grade better than *all* of their individual homework grades.

_____

_____

b) Based on the result of question a, what do you observe about the row with the student_id 102 and the section_id 89?

_____

_____

c) Select the student_id, section_id, and grade of students who received a final examination grade better than *any* of their individual homework grades.

_____

_____

d) Based on question c, explain the result of the row with the student_id 102 and the section_id 89.

_____

_____

LAB 7.3 EXERCISE ANSWERS

7.3.1 ANSWERS

a) Write a SELECT statement to display the student_id, section_id, and grade of students who received a final examination grade better than *all* of their individual homework grades.

Answer: A correlated subquery is used to compare each individual student's final examination grade with his or her respective homework grades for a particular section. The output includes only those records where the final examination grade is higher than all of the homework grades.

```
SELECT student_id, section_id, numeric_grade
  FROM grade g
 WHERE grade_type_codc = 'FI'
   AND numeric_grade > ALL
       (SELECT numeric_grade
          FROM grade
         WHERE grade_type_code = 'HM'
           AND g.section_id = section_id
           AND g.student_id = student_id)
```

```
STUDENT_ID SECTION_ID NUMERIC_GRADE
---------- ---------- -------------
       102         89            92
       124         83            99
       143         85            92
...
       215        156            90
       283         99            85
```

96 rows selected.

To verify the result, use the student_id 143 and section_id 85 as an example. The highest grade for all of the homework is 91 and the lowest is 81. The grade achieved in the final examination is 92.

```
SELECT student_id, section_id, grade_type_code,
       MAX(numeric_grade) max, MIN(numeric_grade) min
  FROM grade
 WHERE student_id = 143
   AND section_id = 85
   AND grade_type_code IN ('HM', 'FI')
 GROUP BY student_id, section_id, grade_type_code
STUDENT_ID SECTION_ID GR        MAX       MIN
---------- ---------- -- --------- ---------
       143         85 FI         92        92
       143         85 HM         91        81
```

2 rows selected.

The student 143 enrolled in section 85 is correctly selected for output as it satisfies the condition that the final examination grade be greater than *all* of the homework grades.

b) Based on the result of question a, what do you observe about the row with the student_id 102 and the section_id 89?

Answer: Whenever the subquery with the ALL operator fails to return a row, the query is automatically true. Therefore, this student is also included in the result set.

The interesting aspect of the relationship between ALL and NULLs is that here the student for this section has no homework grades, yet the row is returned for output.

```
SELECT student_id, section_id, grade_type_code,
       MAX(numeric_grade) max, MIN(numeric_grade) min
  FROM grade
```

```
WHERE student_id = 102
   AND section_id = 89
   AND grade_type_code IN ('HM', 'FI')
 GROUP BY student_id, section_id, grade_type_code
```

STUDENT_ID	SECTION_ID	GR	MAX	MIN
102	89 FI		92	92

1 row selected.

LAB
7.3

   c) Select the student_id, section_id, and grade of students who received a final examination grade better than *any* of their individual homework grades.

     Answer: The ANY operator together with the correlated subquery achieves the desired result.

```
SELECT student_id, section_id, numeric_grade
  FROM grade g
 WHERE grade_type_code = 'FI'
   AND numeric_grade > ANY
       (SELECT numeric_grade
          FROM grade
         WHERE grade_type_code = 'HM'
           AND g.section_id = section_id
           AND g.student_id = student_id)
```

STUDENT_ID	SECTION_ID	NUMERIC_GRADE
102	86	85
103	81	91
143	85	92
...		
283	99	85
283	101	88

157 rows selected.

Examine the grades for the homework and the final for student_id 102 and section_id 86. This student's final grade of 85 is better than the homework grade of 82. The ANY operator tests for an OR condition, so the student and section are returned because only one of the homework grades has to satisfy the condition.

```
SELECT student_id, section_id, grade_type_code,
       numeric_grade
  FROM grade
```

```
WHERE student_id = 102
  AND section_id = 86
  AND grade_type_code IN ('HM', 'FI')
GROUP BY student_id, section_id, grade_type_code,
      numeric_grade
STUDENT_ID SECTION_ID GR NUMERIC_GRADE
---------- ---------- -- -------------
       102         86 FI            85
       102         86 HM            82
       102         86 HM            90
       102         86 HM            99
```

4 rows selected.

d) Based on question c, explain the result of the row with the student_id 102 and the section_id 89.

Answer: This record is not returned because unlike the ALL operator, the ANY operator returns false.

The following example illustrates the effect of no records in the subquery on the ANY operator. The student 102 enrolled in section_id 89 has no homework grades, and, therefore, does not appear in question c's result set.

```
SELECT student_id, section_id, grade_type_code,
      numeric_grade
  FROM grade
 WHERE student_id = 199
   AND section_id = 84
   AND grade_type_code IN ('HM', 'FI')
STUDENT_ID SECTION_ID GR NUMERIC_GRADE
---------- ---------- -- -------------
       199         84 FI            99
```

1 row selected.

LAB 7.3 SELF-REVIEW QUESTIONS

In order to test your progress, you should be able to answer the following questions.

I) Are the operators NOT IN and <> ANY equivalent as illustrated in the following example?

```
SELECT 'TRUE'
  FROM dual
 WHERE 6 <> ANY (6, 9)
```

```
SELECT 'TRUE'
  FROM dual
 WHERE 6 NOT IN (6, 9)
```

    a) _____ Yes
    b) _____ No

2) The following queries are logically equivalent.

```
SELECT 'TRUE'
  FROM dual
 WHERE 6 IN (6, 9)
```

```
SELECT 'TRUE'
  FROM dual
 WHERE 6 = ANY (6,9)
```

    a) _____ True
    b) _____ False

3) The operators ANY and SOME are equivalent.
    a) _____ True
    b) _____ False

4) To perform any >=, <=, >, or < comparison with a subquery returning multiple rows, you need to use either the ANY, SOME, or ALL operator.
    a) _____ True
    b) _____ False

5) The ANY, SOME, and ALL operators do not work with multiple columns.
    a) _____ True
    b) _____ False

Quiz answers appear in Appendix A, Section 7.3.

**LAB
7.3**

C H A P T E R   7

TEST YOUR THINKING

1) Using a subquery construct, determine which sections the student Henry Masser is enrolled in.

2) Write the question for the following SELECT statement.

```
SELECT zip
  FROM zipcode z
 WHERE NOT EXISTS
       (SELECT '*'
          FROM student
         WHERE z.zip = zip)
   AND NOT EXISTS
       (SELECT '*'
          FROM instructor
         WHERE z.zip = zip)
```

3) Display the course id and course description of courses with no enrollment. Also include courses which have no section assigned.

4) Can the ANY and ALL operators be used on the DATE datatype? Write a simple query to prove your answer.

5) If you have a choice to write either a correlated subquery or a simple subquery, which one would you choose and why?

6) Write a SQL statement that shows you cannot use an ORDER BY clause in a subquery.

CHAPTER 8

SET OPERATORS

CHAPTER OBJECTIVES

In this chapter, you will learn about:

✔ The Power of UNION and UNION ALL   Page 224
✔ The MINUS and INTERSECT Set Operators   Page 233

Set operators combine two or more sets of data to produce a single result set. Oracle has four set operators: UNION, UNION ALL, MINUS, and INTERSECT. The UNION and UNION ALL operators combine results. The INTERSECT operator determines common rows. The MINUS operator shows differences between sets of rows. In this chapter you will use set operators to combine data from many tables throughout the schema.

L A B   8 . 1

THE POWER OF UNION AND UNION ALL

LAB OBJECTIVES

After this Lab, you will be able to:

✔   Use the UNION and UNION ALL Set Operators

The UNION operator is probably the most commonly used set operator. It combines two or more sets of data to produce a single set of data. Think of the UNION operator as two overlapping circles, as illustrated in Figure 8.1. The *union* of the two circles is everything from both circles. There are duplicates where they overlap, and there may even be duplicates within each set, but the final result shows these values only once.

The sets of data in a set operation are SELECT statements, as simple or as complex as SELECT statements can be written. When writing any set operation, there are two rules to remember:

- Each of the SELECT lists must contain the same number of columns.
- The matching columns in each of the SELECT lists must be the same datatype. (Oracle considers CHAR and VARCHAR2 to be datatype compatible.)

Figure 8.1

■ FOR EXAMPLE

Imagine you need to create a phone list of all instructors and students. The following set operation uses the UNION operator to combine instructor and student names and phone numbers from the instructor and student tables into a single result set.

```
SELECT first_name, last_name, phone
  FROM instructor
 UNION
SELECT first_name, last_name, phone
  FROM student
```

FIRST_NAME	LAST_NAME	PHONE
A.	Tucker	203-555-5555
Adele	Rothstein	718-555-5555
...		
Z.A.	Scrittorale	203-555-5555
Zalman	Draquez	718-555-5555

```
276 rows selected.
```

The same three columns are selected from each table, effectively *stacking* the columns one on top of the other in the result set. The results are automatically sorted by the order in which the columns appear in the SELECT list.

Notice the result returns 276 rows, even though there are 268 student rows and 10 instructor rows. What happened to the other two rows? The following query shows duplicate rows in the student table.

```
SELECT first_name, last_name, phone, COUNT(*)
  FROM student
 GROUP BY first_name, last_name, phone
HAVING COUNT(*) > 1
```

FIRST_NAME	LAST_NAME	PHONE	COUNT(*)
Kevin	Porch	201-555-5555	2
Thomas	Edwards	201-555-5555	2

```
2 rows selected.
```

Because the UNION operator eliminates duplicates, both of the duplicate student rows appear just once in the result of the UNION set operation.

To list all the instructors and students, including duplicates, there are two approaches. One approach is to add the id of the instructor and student to the set operation, plus a text literal such as 'instructor' and 'student'. The other approach is to use the UNION ALL operator. UNION ALL *includes* any duplicates when sets of data are added. Think again of the two overlapping circles shown in Figure 8.1. UNION ALL not only adds the two sets of data, but includes the overlapping duplicates as well. Duplicates that may exist within each set are also included.

```
SELECT first_name, last_name, phone
  FROM instructor
 UNION ALL
SELECT first_name, last_name, phone
  FROM student
FIRST_NAME LAST_NAME         PHONE
---------- ---------------- ----------
Fernand    Hanks            2125551212
Tom        Wojick           2125551212
...
Kathleen   Mastandora       718-555-5555
Angela     Torres           718-555-5555

278 rows selected.
```

Even though there are 276 *distinct* combinations of first_name, last_name, and phone between the instructor and student tables, UNION ALL results in all 278 combinations, which includes the duplicates in the student table. Also, the result set is no longer sorted; UNION ALL does not perform a sort.

ORDER BY AND SET OPERATIONS

Just like the result of any SELECT statement, the result of a set operation can be ordered using the ORDER BY clause. Instead of naming the column you want to sort the result by, refer to its position in the SELECT list instead. Consider what happens if you add the instructor and student ids to the previous example using UNION, and order the results by last_name:

```
SELECT instructor_id id, first_name, last_name, phone
  FROM instructor
 UNION
SELECT student_id, first_name, last_name, phone
  FROM student
 ORDER BY 3
```

```
ID FIRST_NAME LAST_NAME          PHONE
--------- ---------- ----------------- ------------
    119 Mardig     Abdou             718-555-5555
    399 Jerry      Abdou             718-555-5555
...
    184 Salewa     Zuckerberg        718-555-5555
    206 Freedon    annunziato        718-555-5555

278 rows selected.
```

The ORDER BY clause can also refer to a column alias, such as id used for the first column. However, referring to the column position in the ORDER BY clause is ANSI-standard, and is also independent of the column names in either SELECT statement.

With the addition of the instructor and student ids, the unique combination of those ids with first name, last name, and phone number now produces all 278 rows between the instructor and student tables.

The first columns in each of the individual SELECT statements, instructor_id and student_id, have different names but are the same datatype. Oracle uses the alias to name the column in the result set to a meaningful name for both instructor and student ids.

SQL will always take its cue from the topmost SELECT statement when naming columns in the result set. When you want the result set to display a specific column name that is not dependent on the names of columns listed in the topmost statement, you must use a column alias.

LAB 8.1 EXERCISES

8.1.1 USE THE UNION AND UNION ALL SET OPERATORS

a) What is wrong with the following set operation, and what do you have to change to make it work correctly?

```
SELECT instructor_id, last_name
  FROM instructor
 UNION
SELECT last_name, student_id
  FROM student
```

b) Explain the result of the following set operation, and why it works.

```
SELECT first_name, last_name,
       'Instructor' "Type"
  FROM instructor
 UNION
SELECT first_name, last_name,
       'Student'
  FROM student
```

_____

_____

c) Write a set operation, using the UNION set operator, to list all the zip codes in the instructor and student tables.

_____

_____

d) Write the question for the following set operation.

```
SELECT created_by
  FROM enrollment
 UNION
SELECT created_by
  FROM grade
 UNION
SELECT created_by
  FROM grade_type
 UNION
SELECT created_by
  FROM grade_conversion
CREATED_BY
----------------------
ARISCHER
BMOTIVAL
BROSENZW
CBRENNAN
DSCHERER
```

```
JAYCAF
MCAFFREY

7 rows selected.
```

_____

_____

e) Explain the result of the following set operation:

```
SELECT course_no, description
  FROM course
 WHERE prerequisite IS NOT NULL
 ORDER BY 1
 UNION
SELECT course_no, description
  FROM course
 WHERE prerequisite IS NULL
```

_____

_____

LAB 8.1 EXERCISE ANSWERS

8.1.1 ANSWERS

a) What is wrong with the following set operation, and what do you have to change to make it work correctly?

```
SELECT instructor_id, last_name
  FROM instructor
 UNION
SELECT last_name, student_id
  FROM student
```

Answer: The datatypes of columns must be the same for columns in the same position in each SELECT list of a set operation. Either the order of the columns in the first or the second statement must be switched for the statement to work correctly.

b)   Explain the result of the following set operation, and why it works.

```
SELECT first_name, last_name,
       'Instructor' "Type"
  FROM instructor
 UNION
SELECT first_name, last_name,
       'Student'
  FROM student
```

Answer: The result set displays the first and last names of instructors and students. The third column identifies what type of person it is, which also identifies from which table the record originates. 'Instructor' and 'Student' are both text literals and are in the same position in each SELECT list. Therefore, the two SELECT statements are row-compatible.

FIRST_NAME	LAST_NAME	Type
A.	Tucker	Student
Adele	Rothstein	Student
...		
Z.A.	Scrittorale	Student
Zalman	Draquez	Student

276 rows selected.

As your SELECT statements and set operations become more complex, it can be difficult to identify the data in your result sets accurately. This technique of identifying each row in the result set coming from one or the other set of data may be very useful.

c)   Write a set operation, using UNION, to list all the zip codes in the instructor and student tables.

Answer: Two SELECT statements are joined using the UNION set operator for a result set displaying zip codes from both tables, eliminating any duplicates.

```
SELECT zip
  FROM instructor
 UNION
SELECT zip
  FROM student
```

ZIP
01247
02124

```
...
43224
48104
```

149 rows selected.

    d)   Write the question for the following set operation.

```
SELECT created_by
  FROM enrollment
 UNION
SELECT created_by
  FROM grade
 UNION
SELECT created_by
  FROM grade_type
 UNION
SELECT created_by
  FROM grade_conversion
CREATED_BY
----------------
ARISCHER
BMOTIVAL
BROSENZW
CBRENNAN
DSCHERER
JAYCAF
MCAFFREY
```

7 rows selected.

       Answer: Create a list of users who created rows in the enrollment, grade, grade_type, and grade_conversion tables. Show each user name only once.

As mentioned in the beginning of this lab, set operators can be used with two or more sets of data. This exercise combines the data from four separate tables into a single result set, eliminating duplicates where they occur.

    e)   Explain the result of the following set operation:

```
SELECT course_no, description
  FROM course
 WHERE prerequisite IS NOT NULL
 ORDER BY 1
```

```
  UNION
SELECT course_no, description
  FROM course
 WHERE prerequisite IS NULL
```

Answer: Oracle returns an error message because the ORDER BY clause must be used at the end of a set operation.

```
ORA-00933: SQL command not properly ended
```

SQL always expects the ORDER BY clause to be the very last command in *any* SQL statement, including set operations. An ORDER BY clause logically has no purpose in the topmost statement; it is applied only to the single set of data in the result set, which is a combination of all data from all SELECT statements in a set operation.

LAB 8.1 SELF-REVIEW QUESTIONS

In order to test your progress, you should be able to answer the following questions.

1) It is redundant to use DISTINCT in a UNION set operation.
   a) _____ True
   b) _____ False

2) Each of the SELECT statements in a set operation must have an ORDER BY clause when you want the results to be ordered.
   a) _____ True
   b) _____ False

3) A UNION set operation always returns the same result set as an equijoin.
   a) _____ True
   b) _____ False

4) You cannot use UNION to join two tables that do not have a primary key/foreign key relationship.
   a) _____ True
   b) _____ False

5) There must be the same number of columns in each SELECT statement of a set operation.
   a) _____ True
   b) _____ False

Quiz answers appear in Appendix A, Section 8.1.

L A B   8 . 2

THE MINUS AND INTERSECT SET OPERATORS

LAB OBJECTIVES

After this lab, you will be able to:

✔ Use the MINUS Set Operator
✔ Use the INTERSECT Set Operator

The MINUS set operator subtracts one set of data from another, identifying what data exists in one table but not the other. The INTERSECT set operator is the *intersection* of sets of data, identifying data common to all of them.

THE MINUS OPERATOR

The following set operation lists instructors not currently teaching any classes (sections).

```
SELECT instructor_id
  FROM instructor
 MINUS
SELECT instructor_id
  FROM section
INSTRUCTOR_ID
-------------
          109
```

```
                 110
```

2 rows selected.

Looking at the statements separately, the first SELECT statement returns the complete list of instructors.

```
SELECT instructor_id
  FROM instructor
INSTRUCTOR_ID
-------------
          101
          102
          103
          104
          105
          106
          109
          108
          107
          110
```

10 rows selected.

The second SELECT statement returns a *distinct* list of instructors currently teaching.

```
SELECT DISTINCT instructor_id
  FROM section
INSTRUCTOR_ID
-------------
          101
          102
          103
          104
          105
          106
          107
          108
```

8 rows selected.

Subtracting the second from the first leaves a list of instructors *not* currently teaching.

Just like the UNION set operator, MINUS eliminates duplicates when evaluating sets of data. Notice DISTINCT is used in the preceding second SELECT statement when it is written separately. However, the UNION set operation does not use DISTINCT. The following set operation implies distinct values in both SELECT statements.

```
SELECT created_by
  FROM enrollment
 MINUS
SELECT created_by
  FROM course
CREATED_BY
------------------------------
JAYCAF

1 row selected.
```

Written separately, the two SELECT statements use DISTINCT:

```
SELECT DISTINCT created_by
  FROM enrollment
CREATED_BY
---------------------------
DSCHERER
JAYCAF

2 rows selected.

SELECT DISTINCT created_by
  FROM course
CREATED_BY
------------------------------
DSCHERER

1 row selected.
```

The second SELECT statement results in the *distinct* value 'DSCHERER'. This is subtracted from the result of the first statement, which are the *distinct* values 'JAYCAF' and 'DSCHERER'. This results in the value 'JAY-CAF' because 'JAYCAF' does not exist in the course table, only in the enrollment table.

> *Be careful when positioning the SELECT statements in a MINUS set operation because their order makes a big difference. Be sure to place the set you want to subtract from first.*

THE INTERSECT OPERATOR

When you use INTERSECT instead of MINUS in the previous statement, the result is quite different:

LAB 8.2

```
SELECT created_by
   FROM enrollment
INTERSECT
SELECT created_by
   FROM course
CREATED_BY
-------------------------------
DSCHERER


1 row selected.
```

The result set contains 'DSCHERER', which is the *distinct* value where the two sets overlap, or intersect. Unlike MINUS, the order of the SELECT statements in an INTERSECT set operation does not matter.

INTERSECT INSTEAD OF EQUIJOINS

The INTERSECT set operator can replace the equijoin, which you learned about in Chapter 6, "Equijoins." The equijoin produces a result set which is the intersection of two or more tables, the same result as with INTERSECT.

■ FOR EXAMPLE

Here is an equijoin that returns a list of course numbers for courses having sections:

```
SELECT DISTINCT c.course_no
   FROM course c, section s
 WHERE c.course_no = s.course_no
COURSE_NO
---------
       10
       20
...
      420
      450


28 rows selected.
```

This INTERSECT set operation returns the same result:

```
SELECT course_no
  FROM course
INTERSECT
SELECT course_no
  FROM section
COURSE_NO
---------
       10
       20
...
      420
      450
```

28 rows selected.

The drawback to using INTERSECT instead of an equijoin is the INTERSECT operates on all columns in each SELECT list of the set operation. Therefore, you cannot include columns that exist in one table and not the other.

LAB 8.2 EXERCISES

8.2.1   USE THE MINUS SET OPERATOR

a) Explain the result of the following set operation.

```
SELECT course_no, description
  FROM course
 MINUS
SELECT s.course_no, c.description
  FROM section s, course c
 WHERE s.course_no = c.course_no
```

_____

_____

b) Use the MINUS set operator to create a list of courses and sections having no students enrolled. Add a column to the result set with the title `Status`, and display the text `No Enrollments` in each row. Order the results by course, then section.

_____

_____

8.2.2 USE THE INTERSECT SET OPERATOR

a) Use the INTERSECT set operator to list all zip codes that are in both the student and instructor tables.

_____

_____

b) Use the INTERSECT set operator to list student ids for students who are enrolled.

_____

_____

LAB 8.2 EXERCISE ANSWERS

8.2.1 ANSWERS

a) Explain the result of the following set operation.

```
SELECT course_no, description
  FROM course
 MINUS
SELECT s.course_no, c.description
  FROM section s, course c
 WHERE s.course_no = c.course_no
```

Answer: The set operation subtracts all courses having sections from all courses, resulting in the 2 courses without sections.

```
COURSE_NO DESCRIPTION
--------- ---------------------------------
       80 Structured Programming Techniques
      430 JDeveloper Techniques

2 rows selected.
```

Another way to formulate the query is to write a subquery using the NOT IN or the NOT EXISTS operator:

```
SELECT course_no, description
  FROM course c
 WHERE NOT EXISTS
        (SELECT '*'
           FROM section
          WHERE c.course_no = course_no)
```

b) Use the MINUS set operator to create a list of courses and sections
having no students enrolled. Add a column to the result set with the
title Status, and display the text No Enrollments in each row.
Order the results by course, then section.

*Answer: The first SELECT statement is the set of all courses with sections. The second
SELECT statement subtracts the set of courses and sections having enrollments, leav-
ing the difference of courses and sections without enrollments.*

```
SELECT course_no, section_no, 'No Enrollments' "Status"
  FROM section
 MINUS
SELECT course_no, section_no, 'No Enrollments'
  FROM section s
 WHERE EXISTS (SELECT section_id
                 FROM enrollment e
                WHERE e.section_id = s.section_id)
 ORDER BY 1, 2
COURSE_NO SECTION_NO Status
--------- ---------- --------------
       25          9 No Enrollments
      124          4 No Enrollments
...
      220          1 No Enrollments
      350          3 No Enrollments
```

14 rows selected.

This statement uses a trick to display 'No Enrollments' in the result
set. Even though it is not a column in either table, as long as it is in the
first statement there is a column for it in the result set. And, as long as it
is in the second statement, it matches the first and, therefore, allows the
MINUS to work correctly, subtracting one set from a similar set. If it did
not exist in the second statement, no rows would be returned in the result set.

8.2.2 Answers

a) Use the INTERSECT set operator to list all zip codes that are in both the student and instructor tables.

Answer: INTERSECT is used to find the intersection of distinct zip codes in the instructor and student tables.

```
SELECT zip
  FROM instructor
INTERSECT
SELECT zip
  FROM student
ZIP
-----
10025
```

1 row selected.

Be careful when deciding to use INTERSECT versus UNION. The key phrase in the question asked is ". . . zip codes that are in both. . . ." INTERSECT achieves the intersection of both tables alone, while UNION returns zip codes in both tables.

b) Use the INTERSECT set operator to list student ids for students who are enrolled.

Answer: The intersection of student ids in the student and enrollment tables yields all students who are enrolled.

```
SELECT student_id
  FROM student
INTERSECT
SELECT student_id
  FROM enrollment
STUDENT_ID
----------
       102
       103
...
       282
       283
```

165 rows selected.

LAB 8.2 SELF-REVIEW QUESTIONS

In order to test your progress, you should be able to answer the following questions.

1) The following two select statements are equivalent and return the same rows.

```
SELECT student_id              SELECT student_id
  FROM enrollment                FROM student
MINUS                          MINUS
SELECT student_id              SELECT student_id
  FROM student                           FROM enrollment
```

    a) _____ True
    b) _____ False

2) The SELECT statements in an INTERSECT set operation can contain a correlated subquery.
    a) _____ True
    b) _____ False

3) The following SQL statement executes without an error.

```
SELECT TO_CHAR(1)
  FROM dual
MINUS
SELECT TO_NUMBER('1')
  FROM dual
```

    a) _____ True
    b) _____ False

4) It is redundant to use DISTINCT in either a MINUS or INTERSECT set operation.
    a) _____ True
    b) _____ False

Quiz answers appear in Appendix A, Section 8.2.

C H A P T E R   8

TEST YOUR THINKING

1) List all the zip codes in the zipcode table that are not used in the student or instructor tables. Write two different solutions, using set operators for both.

2) Write a SQL statement, using a set operator, to show which students enrolled in a section on the same day they registered.

3) Find the students that are not enrolled in any classes. Write three solutions: a set operation; a subquery; a correlated subquery.

4) Show the students who have received grades for their class. Write four solutions: a set operation; a subquery; a correlated subquery; and a join.

CHAPTER 9

COMPLEX JOINS

CHAPTER OBJECTIVES

In this chapter, you will learn about:

- ✔ Outer Joins   Page 244
- ✔ Self-Joins   Page 258

Outer joins and self-joins are extensions of the equijoin you learned about in Chapter 6, "Equijoins." The outer join includes the result rows returned by the equijoin, plus extra rows where no matches are found. The self-join, as implied by the name, joins a table to itself. This type of join is useful for tables with a self-referencing relationship, or when you want to determine data inconsistencies.

You will see the usefulness of these types of joins for analyzing and exploring the relationships within your data.

L A B   9 . 1

OUTER JOINS

LAB OBJECTIVES

After this lab, you will be able to:

✔ Write Outer Joins With Two Tables
✔ Write Outer Joins With Three Tables

The outer join is similar to the equijoin because it returns all the records the equijoin returns. But it also returns records that are in one of the tables with no matching records in another table.

■ FOR EXAMPLE

The following is an equijoin and its result. The SQL statement returns all the rows where a match for the course_no column is found in both the course and the section tables.

```
SELECT c.course_no, c.description,
       s.section_id, s.course_no
  FROM course c, section s
 WHERE c.course_no = s.course_no
 ORDER BY c.course_no
```

COURSE_NO	DESCRIPTION	SECTION_ID	COURSE_NO
10	DP Overview	80	10
20	Intro to Computers	81	20
...			
420	Database System Principles	108	420
450	DB Programming in Java	109	450

78 rows selected.

Some courses are not included in the result because there are no matching course numbers in the section table. To determine those courses not assigned to any sections, write a NOT EXISTS subquery, a NOT IN subquery, or use the MINUS operator.

```
SELECT course_no, description
  FROM course c
 WHERE NOT EXISTS
       (SELECT 'X'
          FROM section
         WHERE c.course_no = course_no)
COURSE_NO DESCRIPTION
--------- --------------------------------
       80 Structured Programming Techniques
      430 JDeveloper Techniques

2 rows selected.
```

These two courses are not returned in the previous equijoin because there are no matches for course numbers 80 and 430 in the section table. To include these courses in the result, write an outer join. Oracle uses the outer join operator '(+)' to indicate that NULLs are generated for nonmatching rows. All the columns in the section table without matches have a NULL value in the result set.

```
SELECT c.course_no, c.description,
       s.section_id, s.course_no
  FROM course c, section s
 WHERE c.course_no = s.course_no(+)
 ORDER BY c.course_no
```

COURSE_NO	DESCRIPTION	SECTION_ID	COURSE_NO
10	DP Overview	80	10
20	Intro to Computers	81	20
...			
80	Structured Programming Techniques		
...			
430	JDeveloper Techniques		
450	DB Programming in Java	109	450

```
80 rows selected.
```

Look closely at the result for course numbers 80 and 430. These courses have no sections assigned. For example, course_no 430 of the course table (c.course_no) contains the course_no value, but the course_no from the section table (s.course_no) contains a NULL. The outer join operator generates NULL values for the columns c.course_no and s.section_id where a match is not found.

Alternatively, you can achieve the same result with two SQL statements: an equijoin and a correlated subquery, with the results combined using the UNION ALL operator.

```
SELECT c1.course_no, SUBSTR(c1.description,1,20),
       s.section_id, s.course_no
  FROM course c1, section s
 WHERE c1.course_no = s.course_no
UNION ALL
SELECT c2.course_no, SUBSTR(c2.description,1,20),
       TO_NUMBER(NULL), TO_NUMBER(NULL)
  FROM course c2
 WHERE NOT EXISTS
       (SELECT 'X'
          FROM section
         WHERE c2.course_no = course_no)
```

In this example, the UNION ALL operator is used to combine the result of the equijoin (all courses with sections) with the result of the correlated subquery (courses for which no match is found in the section table). Duplicate rows are not returned between the previous two SELECT statements; in this example, each SELECT statement returns a different set. Therefore, it is more efficient to use UNION ALL rather than the UNION operator because the UNION ALL avoids the sort required by the UNION operator to eliminate the duplicates.

The TO_NUMBER datatype conversion is performed to match the datatypes of the columns in each of the SELECT statements in the set operation.

LAB 9.1 EXERCISES

9.1.1 WRITE OUTER JOINS WITH TWO TABLES

a) Explain why Oracle returns an error message when you execute the following SELECT statement.

```
SELECT c.course_no, s.course_no, s.section_id,
       c.description, s.start_date_time
  FROM course c, section s
 WHERE c.course_no(+) = s.course_no(+)
```

_____

_____

b) Show the description of *all* courses with the prerequisite course number 350. Include the location where the sections meet in the result. Return course rows even if no corresponding section is found.

_____

_____

c) Rewrite the following SQL statement using an outer join.

```
SELECT course_no, description
  FROM course c
 WHERE NOT EXISTS
       (SELECT 'X'
          FROM section
         WHERE c.course_no = course_no)
COURSE_NO DESCRIPTION
--------- -------------------------------
       80 Structured Programming Techniques
      430 JDeveloper Techniques
```

_____

_____

9.1.2 WRITE OUTER JOINS WITH THREE TABLES

a) Display the course number, description, cost, class location, and the instructor's last name for *all* the courses. Also include courses where no sections or instructors have been assigned.

_____

_____

b) For students with the student_id of 102 and 301, determine the sections they are enrolled in. Also show the numeric grades and grade types they received. Include a student in the result set even if the student is not enrolled or has not received any grade.

_____

_____

LAB 9.1 EXERCISE ANSWERS

9.1.1 ANSWERS

a) Explain why Oracle returns an error message when you execute the following SELECT statement.

```
SELECT c.course_no, s.course_no, s.section_id,
       c.description, s.start_date_time
  FROM course c, section s
 WHERE c.course_no(+) = s.course_no(+)
```

Answer: The outer join symbol should be used only on one side of the equation, not both.

```
ERROR at line 4:
ORA-01468: a predicate may reference only one outer-joined table
```

This SQL statement attempts to include rows from the course table for which no match exists in the section table, and include rows from the section table where no match is found in the course table. This is referred to as a *full outer join*; you want to include the rows from both tables, including those rows for which a match cannot be found in either table.

FULL OUTER JOIN

Oracle does not support a full outer join in a single SELECT statement. To accomplish a full outer join, you need to use the UNION operator. Because the UNION operator eliminates duplicate rows, include the primary key column section_id of the section table to ensure all rows are included.

```
SELECT c.course_no, s.course_no, s.section_id,
       c.description, s.start_date_time
```

```
  FROM course c, section s
 WHERE c.course_no = s.course_no(+)
UNION
SELECT c.course_no, s.course_no, s.section_id,
       c.description, s.start_date_time
  FROM course c, section s
 WHERE c.course_no(+) = s.course_no
```

The first SELECT statement performs an outer join on the section table; the second SELECT statement performs an outer join on the course table. The result of each query is combined, and duplicates eliminated with the UNION operator. This statement provides the result of a full outer join.

When you look at the relationship between the section and course tables, you notice a section cannot exist unless a corresponding course exists. Therefore, finding any sections for which no course exists is impossible unless the foreign key constraint is disabled or dropped. For information on how to create and drop foreign keys, see Chapter 11, "Create, Alter, and Drop Tables." To learn how to determine if the foreign keys are disabled or enabled, see Chapter 13, "The Data Dictionary and Dynamic SQL Scripts."

The full outer join returns 80 rows; this is equivalent to the first SELECT statement of the UNION. To fully illustrate the effects of an outer join, here are tables named t1 and t2, not found in the schema diagram, and the data in them. Table t1 has one numeric column named col1, and table t2 also consists of a numeric column named col2.

```
SELECT col1
  FROM t1
     COL1
---------
        1
        2
        3

SELECT col2
  FROM t2
     COL2
---------
        2
        3
        4
```

To write a full outer join to join tables t1 and t2, first write an outer join on table t2 with the following SELECT statement. This SELECT statement is also referred to as a *left outer join*. The result includes all the rows from table t1.

```
SELECT col1, col2
  FROM t1, t2
 WHERE t1.col1 = t2.col2(+)
      COL1      COL2
--------- ---------
        1
        2         2
        3         3
```

The next SELECT statement returns all the rows from t2, whether a match is found or not. This outer join is also referred to as a *right outer join*. All the rows on the right table are returned including nonmatching rows.

```
SELECT col1, col2
  FROM t1, t2
 WHERE t1.col1(+) = t2.col2
      COL1      COL2
--------- ---------
        2         2
        3         3
                  4
```

The full outer join includes all the rows from both tables, whether a match is found or not. The UNION operator eliminates the duplicate rows.

```
SELECT col1, col2
  FROM t1, t2
 WHERE t1.col1 = t2.col2(+)
UNION
SELECT col1, col2
  FROM t1, t2
 WHERE t1.col1(+) = t2.col2
      COL1      COL2
--------- ---------
        1
        2         2
        3         3
                  4
```

b) Show the description of *all* courses with the prerequisite course number 350. Include the location where the sections meet in the result. Return course rows even if no corresponding section is found.

Answer: To include all the courses with this prerequisite, include courses without any corresponding course number in the section table. This involves writing an outer join and applying the outer join operator to the course_no column of the section table. For any records where no match in the section table is found, NULL values are generated for the section columns.

```
SELECT c.course_no cno, s.course_no sno,
       c.description,
       c.prerequisite prereq,
       s.location loc, s.section_id
  FROM course c, section s
 WHERE c.course_no = s.course_no(+)
   AND c.prerequisite = 350
```

CNO	SNO	DESCRIPTION	PREREQ	LOC	SECTION_ID
430		JDeveloper Techniques	350		
450	450	DB Programming in Java	350	L507	109

2 rows selected.

Course number 430, JDeveloper Techniques, does not have a matching section. Therefore, you cannot determine the columns of the section table, such as location and section_id; NULL values are generated for these columns.

WHERE CONDITIONS ON OUTER JOINS

In the previous example, a condition in the WHERE clause is applied to the column prerequisite. This column is in the course table from which you want to include all the rows. However, the WHERE condition must be modified to apply a condition to the outer joined section table.

■ FOR EXAMPLE

The next query is a modified version of the previous query and shows classes that only meet in location L507. Observe the output of the query and compare it to the previous result.

```
SELECT c.course_no cno, s.course_no sno,
       c.description,
       c.prerequisite prereq,
       s.location loc, s.section_id
  FROM course c, section s
 WHERE c.course_no = s.course_no(+)
```

```
    AND c.prerequisite = 350
    AND s.location = 'L507'
CNO  SNO DESCRIPTION              PREREQ LOC  SECTION_ID
---- ---- ------------------------ ---- ----------

450  450 DB Programming in Java   350 L507        109
```

1 row selected.

What happened to course number 430? The course is no longer included in the result, even though the outer join operator is applied to return all the rows whether a match is found in the section table or not.

When a WHERE clause contains a condition that compares a column from the outer joined table to a literal, such as the text literal 'L507', you also need to include the outer join operator on the column. Otherwise, Oracle returns only the results of the equijoin, rather than generating NULLs for the columns. The following query adds the outer join symbol to the location column.

```
SELECT c.course_no cno, s.course_no sno,
       c.description,
       c.prerequisite prereq,
       s.location loc, s.section_id
  FROM course c, section s
 WHERE c.course_no = s.course_no(+)
   AND c.prerequisite = 350
   AND s.location(+) = 'L507'
CNO  SNO DESCRIPTION            PREREQ LOC  SECTION_ID
---- ---- ---------------------- ------ ---- ----------

430      JDeveloper Techniques    350
450  450 DB Programming in Java   350 L507        109
```

2 rows selected.

These two records satisfy the condition of the prerequisite. The outer join operator applied to the location column includes records where either a) the location equals L507, or b) the location is NULL, or c) the location is different from 'L507'. You will see an example shortly of why the location can be different.

Once you apply the outer join operator to a column on the outer joined table, you need to understand the order in which the conditions are processed. First, the records on the table where you want to include all the rows are processed. This is the condition prerequisite = 350.

Next, the matching records in the section table are identified. If a match is not found, the records with the prerequisite 350 are still returned. The next condition, `location(+) = 'L507'`, shows any records in the section table that satisfy this condition; otherwise, a NULL is returned.

What happens when you choose a different location, such as L210? Neither course meets in this location.

```
SELECT c.course_no cno, s.course_no sno,
       SUBSTR(c.description, 1,20),
       c.prerequisite prereq,
       s.location loc, s.section_id
  FROM course c, section s
 WHERE c.course_no = s.course_no(+)
   AND c.prerequisite = 350
   AND s.location(+) = 'L210'
CNO   SNO  DESCRIPTION              PREREQ LOC    SECTION_ID
----  ---- -------------------- ------ ---- ----------
 430       JDeveloper Techniques    350
 450       DB Programming in Java   350

2 rows selected.
```

Here you see both courses with this prerequisite. This contrasts with the earlier output because now both the location and section_id columns contain NULLs. When the WHERE clause is evaluated, the prerequisite condition is evaluated first, then matches are found in the section table with the condition `location(+) = 'L210'`. Since none of the sections match this location condition for this course number, NULLs are generated for the section_id and the location.

c) Rewrite the following SQL statement using an outer join.

```
SELECT course_no, description
  FROM course c
 WHERE NOT EXISTS
       (SELECT 'X'
          FROM section
         WHERE c.course_no = course_no)
COURSE_NO DESCRIPTION
--------- ---------------------------------
       80 Structured Programming Techniques
      430 JDeveloper Techniques

2 rows selected.
```

Answer: A NOT EXISTS condition can be rewritten as a join condition by querying the outer joined column for NULLs.

```
SELECT c.course_no, c.description
  FROM course c, section s
 WHERE c.course_no = s.course_no(+)
   AND s.course_no IS NULL
```

The first three lines of the query return all the courses, whether a section is found or not. The last line of the query identifies the rows that have a NULL value in the section's course_no column. There is no need to qualify the condition `s.course_no IS NULL` with an outer join operator as the condition is applied to the table from which you want to include all the rows.

9.1.2 ANSWERS

a) Display the course number, description, cost, class location, and the instructor's last name for *all* courses. Also include courses where no sections or instructors have been assigned.

Answer: This outer join involves three tables: the course, section, and instructor tables. You want to include all the courses from the course table, whether a section exists for it or not. Also, if no instructor is assigned to a section or no match is found, the rows in the section table should still be included.

The SELECT statement requires the outer join operator to be placed on the course_no column of the section table. This indicates you want to see all the courses, whether there are corresponding sections or not. The outer join operator is also applied to the instructor_id column of the instructor table. This directs Oracle to include rows from the section table even if it doesn't find a matching record in the instructor table.

```
SELECT c.course_no cou, c.description, c.cost,
       s.location, i.last_name
  FROM course c, section s, instructor i
 WHERE c.course_no = s.course_no(+)
   AND s.instructor_id = i.instructor_id(+)
 ORDER BY c.course_no
COU DESCRIPTION                 COST LOCA LAST_NAME
---- --------------------- --------- ---- ---------
  10 DP Overview                1195 L214 Wojick
  20 Intro to Computers         1195 L210 Schorin
  20 Intro to Computers         1195 L214 Pertez
  20 Intro to Computers         1195 L509 Morris
```

```
  20 Intro to Computers          1195 L210 Smythe
 ...
 430 JDeveloper Techniques       1195
 450 DB Programming in Java            L507 Hanks
```

80 rows selected.

The join between the section and instructor tables is defined with the following criteria:

```
AND s.instructor_id = i.instructor_id(+)
```

If you leave out the outer join operator on the instructor_id column, you get the result of an equijoin.

While you review the result, recall from the previous examples that course number 430 does not have a section assigned. Therefore, the column location is NULL. Also, the instructor's last name is NULL because there cannot be an instructor assigned if the row does not exist.

b) For students with the student_id of 102 and 301, determine the sections they are enrolled in. Also show the numeric grades and grade types they received. Include a student in the result set even if the student is not enrolled or has not received any grade.

Answer: Use the outer join operator on columns of the grade table and enrollment table. Otherwise, only the result of the equijoin is returned.

```
SELECT s.student_id, e.section_id, g.grade_type_code,
       g.numeric_grade
  FROM student s, enrollment e, grade g
 WHERE s.student_id IN (102, 301)
   AND s.student_id = e.student_id(+)
   AND e.student_id = g.student_id(+)
   AND e.section_id = g.section_id(+)
```

STUDENT_ID	SECTION_ID	GR	NUMERIC_GRADE
102	86	FI	85
102	86	HM	90
102	86	HM	99
102	86	HM	82
102	86	HM	82
102	86	MT	90
102	86	PA	85
102	86	QZ	90
102	86	QZ	84

```
102        86 QZ        97
102        86 QZ        97
102        89 FI        92
102        89 MT        91
301
```

14 rows selected.

The student with id 102 is enrolled and received grades. His rows are returned as part of an equijoin. However, student 301 is not enrolled in any section, and does not have any grades. Because the outer join operator is applied to both the section and the grade table, student 301 is included in the result. The condition s.student_id IN (102, 301) does not require an outer join operator because it is based on the student table and it is the table from which you want all the rows that satisfy this condition.

LAB 9.1 SELF-REVIEW QUESTIONS

In order to test your progress, you should be able to answer the following questions.

1) A WHERE clause containing an outer join (+) operator cannot contain another condition with the OR operator, as in this example:

```
SELECT *
  FROM course c, section s
 WHERE c.course_no = s.course_no(+)
    OR c.course_no = 100
```

    a) _____ True
    b) _____ False

2) A column with the outer join (+) operator may not use the IN operator, as in this example:

```
SELECT *
  FROM course c, section s
 WHERE c.course_no = s.course_no(+)
   AND c.course_no(+) IN (100, 200)
```

    a) _____ True
    b) _____ False

3) An outer join returns all rows that satisfy the join condition plus those records from another table for which no matches are found.

    a) _____ True

    b) _____ False

4) Which of the WHERE clauses results in this error message?

```
SELECT c.course_no, s.course_no,
       SUBSTR(c.description, 1,20), s.start_date_time
  FROM course c, section s
```

ORA-01468: a predicate may reference only one outer joined table

    a) _____ WHERE course_no = course_no

    b) _____ WHERE c.course_no(+) = s.course_no

    c) _____ WHERE c.course_no = s.course_no(+)

    d) _____ WHERE c.course_no(+) = s.course_no(+)

Quiz answers appear in Appendix A, Section 9.1.

L A B   9 . 2

SELF-JOINS

LAB OBJECTIVES

After this lab, you will be able to:

✔ Write Self-Joins and Detect Data Inconsistencies

Equijoins always join one or multiple tables. A self-join joins a table to itself by pretending there are different tables involved. This is accomplished by using table aliases. One table has one alias, and the same table another alias. For the purpose of executing the query, Oracle treats them as two different tables.

Self-joins are quite useful to perform comparisons and to check for inconsistencies in data. Sometimes a self-join is needed to report on recursive relationships. Chapter 15, "Advanced SQL Queries," covers detailed examples on hierarchical reporting of recursive relationships using the CONNECT BY operator.

■ FOR EXAMPLE

The prerequisite column is a foreign key to the primary key column course_no of the course table, reflecting a recursive relationship between the two columns. A prerequisite is valid only if it is also a valid course_no; otherwise the data manipulation operation on the table is rejected.

Many queries executed on the course table so far in this workbook typically only show the prerequisite number:

```
SELECT course_no, description, prerequisite
   FROM course
```

When you also want to show the description of the prerequisite, you need to write a self-join. This is accomplished by pretending to have two separate tables via table aliases, such as c1 and c2. Join the prerequisite column of table c1 with the course_no column of table c2. If matching records are found, the description of the prerequisite is displayed.

```
SELECT c1.course_no,
       c1.description course_descr,
       c1.prerequisite,
       c2.description pre_req_descr
  FROM course c1, course c2
 WHERE c1.prerequisite = c2.course_no
 ORDER BY 3
COURSE_NO COURSE_DESCR       PREREQUISITE PRE_REQ_DESCR
--------- ------------------ ------------ ------------------
      230 Intro to Internet          10 DP Overview
      100 Hands-On Windows           20 Intro to Computers
...
      450 DB Programming            350 JDeveloper Lab
      144 Database Design           420 Database Systems

26 rows selected.
```

Examine the first row, course_no 230, with the prerequisite course number of 10. The course description for course number 10 is DP Overview. This join works just like the equijoins you learned about in Chapter 6, "Equijoin." If a prerequisite is NULL or a match is not found, the self-join, just like the equijoin, does not return the record.

The self-join acts like other joins with primary key and foreign key columns, except in this table the relationship is to the table itself. The prerequisite column is a foreign key to the primary key course_no. The prerequisite comes from the child table, and the course_no from the parent table. Every course_no may have zero or one prerequisite. To qualify as a prerequisite, the prerequisite course number must be listed in the prerequisite column for at least one or multiple courses.

LAB 9.2 EXERCISES

9.2.1 WRITE SELF-JOINS AND DETECT DATA INCONSISTENCIES

a) For section_id 86, determine which students received a lower grade on their final than on their midterm. In your result, list the columns student_id, grade_type_code, and numeric_grade for the midterm and the final.

b) Formulate the question for the following query.

```
SELECT DISTINCT a.student_id, a.first_name, a.salutation
  FROM student a, student b
 WHERE a.salutation <> b.salutation
   AND b.first_name = a.first_name
   AND a.student_id <> b.student_id
 ORDER BY a.first_name
```

c) Display the student_id, last_name, and street address of students living at the same address and zip code.

d) Write a query showing the course number, course description, prerequisite, and description of the prerequisite. Include courses without any prerequisites. Note this requires a self-join and an outer join.

LAB 9.2 EXERCISE ANSWERS

9.2.1 ANSWERS

a)   For section_id 86, determine which students received a lower grade on their final than on their midterm. In your result, list the columns student_id, grade_type_code, and numeric_grade for the midterm and the final.

*Answer: Using a self-join, you can compare the grade for the midterm with the grade
for the final and determine if the final is lower than the midterm grade.*

```
SELECT fi.student_id, mt.numeric_grade,
       mt.grade_type_code,
       fi.numeric_grade, fi.grade_type_code
  FROM grade fi, grade mt
 WHERE fi.grade_type_code = 'FI'
   AND fi.section_id = 86
   AND mt.grade_type_code = 'MT'
   AND fi.section_id = mt.section_id
   AND fi.student_id = mt.student_id
   AND fi.numeric_grade < mt.numeric_grade
```

STUDENT_ID	NUMERIC_GRADE	GR	NUMERIC_GRADE	GR
102	90	MT	85	FI
108	91	MT	76	FI
211	92	MT	77	FI

3 rows selected.

Notice three students have a lower grade in the final than the grade they
achieved in the midterm. Using a self-join allows you to easily determine
this query and accomplish the correct result. Imagine you're actually
joining to a different table, even though it really is the same table. Visualize one table as the midterm table and the other as the final table, and
the formulation of your SQL statement falls into place.

Start with the table representing the final grade for section_id 86. Then
compare the result with the table representing the midterm grade
(grade_type_code = 'MT'). Also join the columns student_id and
section_id to make sure you match the same individuals and section.
Lastly, compare the numeric grades between the midterm and final.

Alternatively, the same solution can be obtained using the ANY operator
and a correlated subquery discussed in Chapter 7, "Subqueries."

```
SELECT student_id, section_id, numeric_grade
  FROM grade g
 WHERE grade_type_code = 'FI'
   AND section_id = 86
   AND numeric_grade < ANY
       (SELECT numeric_grade
          FROM grade
         WHERE grade_type_code = 'MT'
```

```
        AND g.section_id = section_id
        AND g.student_id = student_id)
```

b) Formulate the question for the following query.

```
SELECT DISTINCT a.student_id, a.first_name, a.salutation
  FROM student a, student b
 WHERE a.salutation <> b.salutation
   AND a.first_name = b.first_name
   AND a.student_id <> b.student_id
 ORDER BY a.first_name
```

Answer: Determine the students who might have inconsistent salutations for their respective first names.

This self-join is used to check for errors and inconsistency of data. A number of students have different salutations for the same first name. For example, Kevin is both a female and male name. The same holds true for Daniel, Roger, and some other students as well.

```
STUDENT_ID FIRST_NAME                       SALUT
---------- ------------------------------   -----
       124 Daniel                           Mr.
       242 Daniel                           Mr.
       315 Daniel                           Ms.
...
       272 Kevin                            Ms.
       341 Kevin                            Mr.
       368 Kevin                            Mr.
       238 Roger                            Mr.
       383 Roger                            Ms.
```

17 rows selected.

The query self-joins by the first name and shows only those having a different salutation for the same name. Because there are multiple names for each table alias, this results in a Cartesian product. Eliminate any records where the student_ids are identical with the condition `a.student_id <> b.student_id`. Duplicate rows are also eliminated using DISTINCT.

c) Display the student_id, last_name, and street address of students living at the same address and zip code.

Answer: The self-join compares the street address and the zip code.

```
SELECT DISTINCT a.student_id, a.last_name,
       a.street_address
  FROM student a, student b
 WHERE a.street_address = b.street_address
   AND a.zip = b.zip
   AND a.student_id <> b.student_id
 ORDER BY a.street_address
```

**LAB
9.2**

```
STUDENT_ID LAST_NAME               STREET_ADDRESS
---------- --------------------    --------------------
       390 Greenberg               105-34 65th Ave.  #6B
       392 Saliternan              105-34 65th Ave.  #6B
       234 Brendler                111 Village Hill Dr.
       380 Krot                    111 Village Hill Dr.
...
       217 Citron                  PO Box 1091
       182 Delbrun                 PO Box 1091

22 rows selected.
```

The condition a.student_id <> b.student_id eliminates the student itself from the result.

You can also expand the query to include the city and state information for the particular zip code by joining to a third table, the zipcode table.

```
SELECT DISTINCT b.student_id id, b.last_name,
       b.street_address ||' '|| city || ', '
       || state address
  FROM student a, student b, zipcode z
 WHERE a.street_address = b.street_address
   AND a.zip = b.zip
   AND a.student_id <> b.student_id
   AND z.zip = b.zip
 ORDER BY address
```

```
 ID LAST_NAME      ADDRESS
---- -----------    ---------------------------------------
 390 Greenberg      105-34 65th Ave.  #6B Forest Hills, NY
 392 Saliternan     105-34 65th Ave.  #6B Forest Hills, NY
...
 217 Citron         PO Box 1091 Ft. Lee, NJ
 182 Delbrun        PO Box 1091 Ft. Lee, NJ

22 rows selected.
```

Alternatively, you can determine the results with a subquery.

```
SELECT DISTINCT student_id id, last_name,
       street_address ||' '|| city || ', '
       || state address
  FROM student s, zipcode z
 WHERE s.zip = z.zip
   AND (street_address, s.zip) IN
       (SELECT street_address, zip
          FROM student
         GROUP BY street_address, zip
        HAVING COUNT(*) > 1)
 ORDER BY address
```

d) Write a query showing the course number, course description, pre-requisite, and description of the prerequisite. Include courses without any prerequisites. Note this requires a self-join and an outer join.

Answer: The SELECT statement joins the courses and their corresponding prerequisites. It also includes those courses that do not have any prerequisites using an outer join, and generates a NULL for the prerequisite description column.

```
SELECT c1.course_no,
       SUBSTR(c1.description, 1,15) course_descr,
       C1.prerequisite,
       SUBSTR(c2.description,1,15) pre_req_descr
  FROM course c1, course c2
 WHERE c1.prerequisite = c2.course_no(+)
 ORDER BY 1
```

COURSE_NO	COURSE_DESCR	PREREQUISITE	PRE_REQ_DESCR
10	DP Overview		
20	Intro to Comput		
25	Intro to Progra	140	Structured Anal
...			
145	Internet Protoc	310	Operating Syste
146	Java for C/C++		
147	GUI Programming	20	Intro to Comput
...			
430	JDeveloper Tech	350	JDeveloper Lab
450	DB Programming	350	JDeveloper Lab

30 rows selected.

LAB 9.2 SELF-REVIEW QUESTIONS

In order to test your progress, you should be able to answer the following questions.

1) A self-join requires you to always join the foreign key with the primary key in the same table.
   a) _____ True
   b) _____ False

2) Self-joins work only when you have a recursive relationship in your table.
   a) _____ True
   b) _____ False

3) You cannot use subqueries or ORDER BY clauses with self-joins.
   a) _____ True
   b) _____ False

4) A self-join joins a table to itself.
   a) _____ True
   b) _____ False

5) You need to use a table alias to be able to write a self-join.
   a) _____ True
   b) _____ False

Quiz answers appear in Appendix A, Section 9.2.

C H A P T E R   9

TEST YOUR THINKING

1) Write a query that shows all the instructors that live in the same zip code.

2) Are any of the rooms overbooked? Determine if any sections meet at the same date, time, and location.

3) Determine if there is any scheduling conflict between instructors: are any instructors scheduled to teach one or more sections at the same date and time?

4) Show the course number, description, course cost, and section_id for courses that cost 1195 or more. Include courses that have no corresponding section.

5) Write a query that lists the section numbers and students_ids of students enrolled in classes held in location 'L210'. Include sections for which no students are enrolled.

CHAPTER 10

INSERT, UPDATE, AND DELETE

CHAPTER OBJECTIVES

In this chapter, you learn about:

✔ Manipulating Data and Transaction Control   Page 268

In Chapters 1 through 9 you learned what data is, and how to present data. In this chapter, you learn how to manipulate the data in tables with the INSERT, UPDATE, and DELETE statements, also known as Data Manipulation Language (DML). These statements give you the ability to create, change, or delete data from a table.

L A B   1 0 . 1

MANIPULATING DATA AND TRANSACTION CONTROL

LAB OBJECTIVES

After this lab, you will be able to:

✔ Insert Data
✔ Update Data
✔ Delete Data

INSERTING DATA

The INSERT statement inserts data into a table. It can insert one row or multiple rows into a single table at one time.

INSERTING AN INDIVIDUAL ROW

The following INSERT statement inserts a row into the zipcode table.

```
INSERT INTO zipcode
VALUES
   ('11111', 'Westerly', 'MA',
   USER, TO_DATE('18-JAN-2000', 'DD-MON-YYYY'),
   USER, SYSDATE)
```

When the statement is executed, Oracle responds with this message:

```
1 row created.
```

The INSERT INTO keywords always precede the name of the table into which you want to insert data. The VALUES keyword precedes a set of parentheses that encloses the values you want to insert. For each of the seven columns of the zipcode table there are seven corresponding values with matching datatypes in the insert statement separated by commas. The values in the list are in the same order as the columns when you DESCRIBE the zipcode table. Text literals are enclosed with single quotes, and dates require the TO_DATE function with the format mask if the date is not in the default format.

The INSERT statement uses the SYSDATE function to insert the current date and time into the modified_date column. The USER function is another function similar to SYSDATE, because it does not take a parameter. It returns the schema name of the user logged in; in this case, the value STUDENT. This value is inserted in the created_by and modified_by columns. You see the result of the USER function in the following example.

```
SELECT USER
  FROM dual
USER
--------------------
STUDENT


1 row selected.
```

Note, the SQL*Plus SHOW USER command also returns the schema name of the user logged in, but you cannot use this in an INSERT statement.

Not all columns of the zipcode table require values, only columns defined as NOT NULL. When you are not inserting data into all columns of a table, you must explicitly name the columns to insert data into. The following statement inserts values into just five of the seven columns in the zipcode table; no data is inserted into the city and state columns.

```
INSERT INTO zipcode
  (zip, created_by, created_date,
  modified_by, modified_date)
VALUES
  ('11111', USER, SYSDATE, USER, SYSDATE)
```

Alternatively, the statement can be written to not explicitly list the columns, and to insert NULL values in the columns instead.

```
INSERT INTO zipcode
VALUES
  ('11111', NULL, NULL, USER, SYSDATE, USER, SYSDATE)
```

INSERTING MULTIPLE ROWS

Another method for inserting data is to select data from another table, inserting one or multiple rows at a time. Suppose there is a table called intro_course in the student schema with columns similar to the course table, that is, the corresponding columns have a compatible datatype and column length. They do not have to have the same column names or column order. The following INSERT statement inserts data into the intro_course table based on rows in the course table where the courses have no prerequisite.

```
INSERT INTO intro_course
  (course_no, description_tx, cost, prereq_no,
   created_by, created_date, modified_by,
   modified_date)
SELECT course_no, description, cost, prerequisite,
       created_by, created_date, 'Melanie',
       TO_DATE('01-JAN-2001', 'DD-MON-YYYY')
  FROM course
 WHERE prerequisite IS NULL
```

TRANSACTION CONTROL

Just as important as manipulating data is controlling *when* the manipulation becomes permanent. DML statements are controlled within the context of a *transaction*. A transaction is a DML statement or group of DML statements that logically belong together. The group of statements is defined by the two commands COMMIT and ROLLBACK, in conjunction with the SAVEPOINT command.

COMMIT

The COMMIT command makes the change to the data permanent. It also allows other users and their sessions, or another SQL*Plus session on your computer, to see the data. The session issuing the DML command can always see the changes, but others only after you COMMIT. SQL statements, such as DDL and DCL statements, implicitly issue a COMMIT to the database; there is no need to issue a COMMIT command. This also means any work you have done previously is committed and cannot be undone. You learn about DDL commands in Chapter 11, "Create, Alter, and Drop Tables," and DCL commands in Chapter 14, "Security."

ROLLBACK

The ROLLBACK command undoes any DML statements back to the last COMMIT command issued.

■ FOR EXAMPLE

The following SQL statements all constitute a single transaction.

```
INSERT INTO zipcode
   (zip, city, state,
   created_by, created_date, modified_by, modified_date)
VALUES
   ('22222', NULL, NULL,
   USER, SYSDATE, USER, SYSDATE)
1 row created.

INSERT INTO zipcode
   (zip, city, state,
   created_by, created_date, modified_by, modified_date)
VALUES
   ('33333', NULL, NULL,
   USER, SYSDATE, USER, SYSDATE)
1 row created.

INSERT INTO zipcode
   (zip, city, state,
   created_by, created_date, modified_by, modified_date)
VALUES
   ('44444', NULL, NULL,
   USER, SYSDATE, USER, SYSDATE)
1 row created.
```

Now query the zipcode table for the values inserted.

```
SELECT zip, city, state
  FROM zipcode
 WHERE zip IN ('22222', '33333', '44444')
ZIP    CITY                      ST
-----  ------------------------- --
22222
33333
44444

3 rows selected.
```

Then, issue the ROLLBACK command, and perform the same query.

```
ROLLBACK
Rollback complete.
```

```
SELECT zip, city, state
  FROM zipcode
 WHERE zip IN ('22222', '33333', '44444')
```
no rows selected

The values inserted are no longer in the zipcode table; the ROLLBACK command prevents the values inserted by all three statements from being committed to the database. If a COMMIT command is issued between the first and second statements, the value '22222' would be found in the zipcode table, but not the values '33333' and '44444'.

SAVEPOINT

The SAVEPOINT command allows you to save the result of DML transactions temporarily. The ROLLBACK command can then refer back to a particular SAVEPOINT, and roll back the transaction up to that point; any statements issued after the SAVEPOINT are rolled back.

■ FOR EXAMPLE

Here are the same three DML statements used previously, but with SAVEPOINT commands issued in between.

```
INSERT INTO zipcode
  (zip, city, state,
   created_by, created_date, modified_by, modified_date)
VALUES
  ('22222', NULL, NULL,
   USER, SYSDATE, USER, SYSDATE)
```
1 row created.

```
SAVEPOINT zip22222
```
Savepoint created.

```
INSERT INTO zipcode
  (zip, city, state,
   created_by, created_date, modified_by, modified_date)
VALUES
  ('33333', NULL, NULL,
   USER, SYSDATE, USER, SYSDATE)
```
1 row created.

```
SAVEPOINT zip33333
```
Savepoint created.

```
INSERT INTO zipcode
```

```
  (zip, city, state,
   created_by, created_date, modified_by, modified_date)
VALUES
  ('44444', NULL, NULL,
   USER, SYSDATE, USER, SYSDATE)
```
1 row created.

Now query the zipcode table for the values inserted.

```
SELECT zip, city, state
  FROM zipcode
 WHERE zip IN ('22222', '33333', '44444')
```
ZIP   CITY   ST
----- ------------------------- --
22222
33333
44444

3 rows selected.

Then, issue the command ROLLBACK TO SAVEPOINT zip33333, and perform the same query.

```
ROLLBACK TO SAVEPOINT zip33333
```
Rollback complete.

```
SELECT zip, city, state
  FROM zipcode
 WHERE zip IN ('22222', '33333', '44444')
```
ZIP   CITY   ST
----- ------------------------- --
22222
33333

2 rows selected.

All statements issued after the zip33333 savepoint are rolled back. When you rollback to the previous savepoint, the same result occurs, and so on.

```
ROLLBACK TO SAVEPOINT zip22222
```
Rollback complete.

```
SELECT zip, city, state
  FROM zipcode
 WHERE zip IN ('22222', '33333', '44444')
```

**LAB
10.1**

```
ZIP    CITY                    ST
-----  ----------------------- --
22222
```

1 row selected.

> The three statements still constitute a single transaction, however it is possible to mark parts of the transaction with a SAVEPOINT in order to control when a statement is rolled back with the ROLLBACK TO SAVEPOINT command.

> It is important to control DML statements using COMMIT, ROLLBACK, and SAVEPOINT. If the three previous statements logically belong together—in other words, one does not make sense without the others occurring—then another session should not see the results until all three are committed at once. Until the user performing the inserts issues a COMMIT command, no other database users or sessions are able to see the changes. A typical example of such a transaction is the transfer from a savings account to a checking account; unless both data manipulations are successful, the change does not become permanent and visible to other sessions.

UPDATING DATA

> Updating data in a database manipulates existing data. An UPDATE statement can change only one table at a time. The following UPDATE statement updates the final grade column in the enrollment table to 90 for all students who enrolled in January 1999.

```
UPDATE enrollment
   SET final_grade = 90
 WHERE enroll_date >= TO_DATE('01/01/1999', 'MM/DD/YYYY')
   AND enroll_date < TO_DATE('02/01/1999', 'MM/DD/YYYY')
11 rows updated.
```

> The keyword UPDATE always precedes the name of the table updated, and the SET keyword precedes the column or columns changed. An UPDATE statement can update all rows in a table at once, or just certain rows when restricted with a WHERE clause as in the previous example.

> An UPDATE statement can also update columns with a NULL value. The following UPDATE statement sets the final_grade column to NULL for all rows in the enrollment table.

```
UPDATE enrollment
   SET final_grade = NULL
```

Note the IS NULL operator is used only in a WHERE clause, not in the SET clause of an UPDATE statement.

An update can occur based on data from other tables using a subquery. The following statement updates the final grade column to 90 and the modified_date column to March 13, 2000 for those sections taught by the instructor Hanks.

```
UPDATE enrollment e
   SET final_grade = 90,
       modified_date = TO_DATE('13-MAR-2000', 'DD-MON-YYYY')
 WHERE EXISTS
       (SELECT *
          FROM section s, instructor i
         WHERE e.section_id = s.section_id
           AND s.instructor_id = i.instructor_id
           AND i.last_name = 'Hanks')
```

As you see, you can use any of the SELECT statements you learned about to restrict the result set. In this example, a correlated subquery identifies the rows to be updated. A column from the outer table, in this case enrollment, is referenced in the subquery through the column e.section_id. Every row of the enrollment table is updated where a corresponding section_id is returned by the subquery. Just like other correlated subqueries, every row in the outer table, here the enrollment table, is examined and evaluated against the inner query. The update occurs where the correlated subquery evaluates to true.

DELETING DATA

Data is removed from a table with the DELETE statement. It can delete all rows or just specific rows. The following statement deletes all rows in the grade_conversion table.

```
DELETE FROM grade_conversion
```
15 rows deleted.

When a ROLLBACK command is issued, the DELETE command is undone and the rows are back in the grade_conversion table.

```
ROLLBACK
```
Rollback complete.

```
SELECT COUNT(*)
  FROM grade_conversion
```
COUNT(*)
```
---------
       15
```

1 row selected.

A DELETE statement may also delete rows in other tables without your knowledge. For example, if a foreign key constraint specifies the ON DELETE CASCADE option, a delete of a parent row automatically deletes the associated child rows.

If a foreign key constraint does not specify ON DELETE CASCADE, you will not be able to delete any parent row, if any child records exist. In the following example, an attempt is made to delete the zip code 10025. Because the zip column of the zipcode table is referenced as a foreign key column in the student table, you cannot delete the row, because students exist with this zip code in the student table.

```
DELETE FROM zipcode
  WHERE zip = '10025'
```
DELETE FROM zipcode
```
            *
```
ERROR at line 1:
ORA-02292: integrity constraint (STUDENT.INST_ZIP_FK)
violated - child record found

You learn more about foreign keys and the effect of DML statements in the Chapter 11, "CREATE, ALTER, and DROP Tables."

THE TRUNCATE COMMAND

The TRUNCATE command deletes all rows from a table, just like the DELETE command. However, the TRUNCATE command does not allow a WHERE clause, and automatically issues a COMMIT; all rows are deleted without the ability to roll back the change.

```
TRUNCATE TABLE class
```
Table truncated.

The TRUNCATE statement works more quickly than a DELETE statement to remove all rows from a table because the database does not have to store the undo information in case a ROLLBACK command is issued.

Oracle places a lock on a row whenever the row is manipulated through a DML statement. This prevents other users from manipulating the row until it is either committed or rolled back.

LAB 10.1 EXERCISES

10.1.1 INSERT DATA

a) Write and execute an INSERT statement to insert a row into the grade_type table for a grade type of 'Extra Credit', identified by a code of 'EC'. Issue a COMMIT command afterward.

_____

_____

b) Explain what is wrong with the following INSERT statement. Hint: It is not the value `course_no_seq.NEXTVAL`, which inserts a value from a sequence, thus generating a unique number.

```
INSERT INTO course
   (course_no, description, cost)
VALUES
   (course_no_seq.NEXTVAL, 'Intro to Linux', 1295)
```

_____

_____

c) Make students with the first name of Yvonne into instructors by inserting their records into the instructor table. Hint: Use instructor_id_seq.NEXTVAL to generate the instructor ids. Once the insert is successful, issue a ROLLBACK command.

_____

_____

10.1.2 UPDATE DATA

a) Using an UPDATE statement, change the location to B111 for all sections where the location is currently L210.

_____

_____

b) Update the modified_by column with the user login name, and update the modified_date column with a date of March 31, 2001 using the TO_DATE function for all the rows updated in Exercise a.

_____

_____

c) Write and execute an UPDATE statement to update the phone numbers of instructors from 2125551212 to 212-555-1212 and the modified_by and modified_date columns with the user logged in and today's date respectively. Write a SELECT statement to prove the update worked correctly. Do *not* issue a COMMIT command.

_____

_____

d) Start another SQL*Plus session on your computer, and login as STUDENT with the password LEARN while your current session is still open. Execute the same SELECT statement you executed in Exercise c to prove your update worked correctly. Explain what data you see and why.

_____

_____

10.1.3 DELETE DATA

a) Delete all rows from the grade table. Then SELECT all the data from the table, issue a ROLLBACK command, and explain your observations.

_____

_____

b) If TRUNCATE is used in Exercise a instead of DELETE, how would this change your observations? Caution: Do not actually execute the TRUNCATE statement unless you are prepared to reload the data.

_____

_____

c) Delete the row inserted in Exercise 10.1.1a in the grade_type table.

_____

_____

d) Formulate the question for the following query.

```
DELETE FROM enrollment
 WHERE student_id NOT IN
       (SELECT student_id
          FROM student s, zipcode z
         WHERE s.zip = z.zip
           AND z.city = 'Brooklyn'
           AND z.state = 'NY')
```

_____

_____

LAB 10.1 EXERCISE ANSWERS

10.1.1 ANSWERS

a) Write and execute an INSERT statement to insert a row into the grade_type table for a grade type of 'Extra Credit', identified by a code of 'EC'. Issue a COMMIT command afterward.

Answer: All columns of the grade_type table are identified as NOT NULL, so the IN-SERT statement needs to list all the columns and corresponding values.

```
INSERT INTO grade_type
  (grade_type_code, description,
   created_by, created_date, modified_by, modified_date)
VALUES
  ('EC', 'Extra Credit',
   USER, SYSDATE, USER, SYSDATE)
1 row created.
```

```
COMMIT
Commit complete.
```

It is not necessary to explicitly list the columns of the grade_type table because values are supplied for all columns. However, it is best to name all the columns, because if additional columns are added in the future or the order of columns in the table changes, the INSERT statement will fail. This is particularly important when the INSERT statement is used in a program for subsequent and repeated use.

b) Explain what is wrong with the following INSERT statement. Hint: It is not the value course_no_seq.NEXTVAL, which inserts a value from a sequence, thus generating a unique number.

```
INSERT INTO course
  (course_no, description, cost)
VALUES
  (course_no_seq.NEXTVAL, 'Intro to Linux', 1295)
```

Answer: The INSERT statement fails because it does not insert values into the NOT NULL columns created_by, created_date, modified_by, and modified_date in the course table.

```
INSERT INTO course
            *
ERROR at line 1:
```

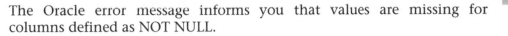

```
ORA-01400: mandatory (NOT NULL) column is missing or NULL during
insert
```

The Oracle error message informs you that values are missing for columns defined as NOT NULL.

Notice the value supplied for the course_no column, `course_no_seq.NEXTVAL`, is not a text literal, number, or date. It is a value generated from a *sequence* called course_no_seq. A sequence is an Oracle database object that generates sequential numbers to ensure uniqueness whenever it is used, most commonly for generating primary keys. The word `NEXTVAL` indicates to Oracle to select the next value in the sequence. You learn more about sequences in Chapter 12, "Views, Indexes, and Sequences."

c) Make students with the first name of Yvonne into instructors by inserting their records into the instructor table. Hint: Use instructor_id_seq.NEXTVAL to generate the instructor ids. Once the insert is successful, issue a ROLLBACK command.

Answer: An INSERT statement selects values from all columns of the student table for students with a first name of Yvonne and inserts them into the instructor table.

```
INSERT INTO instructor
 (instructor_id,
  salutation, first_name, last_name,
  street_address, zip, phone,
  created_by, created_date, modified_by, modified_date)
SELECT instructor_id_seq.NEXTVAL,
       salutation, first_name, last_name,
       street_address, zip, phone,
       USER, SYSDATE, USER, SYSDATE
  FROM student
 WHERE first_name = 'Yvonne'
3 rows created.


ROLLBACK
Rollback complete.
```

10.1.2 ANSWERS

a) Using an UPDATE statement, change the location to B111 for all sections where the location is currently L210.

Answer: The UPDATE statement updates the location column in 10 rows of the section table.

```
UPDATE section
   SET location = 'B111'
 WHERE location = 'L210'
```
10 rows updated.

The statement updates the section table by replacing the same values being restricted in the WHERE clause. Without the WHERE clause, all rows in the section table are updated, not just 10 rows. For example, if you want to make sure all students have their last names begin with a capital letter, issue the following UPDATE statement.

```
UPDATE student
   SET last_name = INITCAP(last_name)
```

b) Update the modified_by column with the user login name, and update the modified_date column with a date of March 31, 2001 using the TO_DATE function for all the rows updated in Exercise a.

Answer: The modified_by column is updated with the USER function to reflect an update by the user logged in, namely STUDENT, and the modified_date column is updated using the TO_DATE function. The update is based on the previously updated location.

```
UPDATE section
   SET modified_by = USER,
       modified_date = TO_DATE('31-MAR-2001', 'DD-MON-YYYY')
 WHERE location = 'B111'
```
10 rows updated.

Instead of writing them as single UPDATE statements, Exercises a and b can be combined in a single UPDATE statement with the columns updated separated by commas.

```
UPDATE section
   SET location = 'B111',
       modified_by = USER,
       modified_date = TO_DATE('31-MAR-2001', 'DD-MON-YYYY')
 WHERE location = 'L210'
```

c) Write and execute an UPDATE statement to update the phone numbers of instructors from 2125551212 to 212-555-1212 and the modified_by and modified_date columns with the user logged in and today's date respectively. Write a SELECT statement to prove the update worked correctly. Do *not* issue a COMMIT command.

Answer: A single UPDATE statement updates three columns in ten rows simultaneously in the instructor table. The modified_by column is updated with the USER func-

*tion, and the modified_date column is updated with the SYSDATE function, entering
today's date into the column.*

```
UPDATE instructor
   SET phone = '212-555-1212',
       modified_by = USER,
       modified_date = SYSDATE
 WHERE phone = '2125551212'

10 rows updated.

SELECT instructor_id, phone, modified_by, modified_date
   FROM instructor
INSTRUCTOR_ID PHONE         MODIFIED_BY MODIFIED_
------------- ------------- ----------- ---------
          101 212-555-1212  STUDENT     12-MAR-00
          102 212-555-1212  STUDENT     12-MAR-00
...
          109 212-555-5555  STUDENT     12-MAR-00
          110 212-555-5555  STUDENT     12-MAR-00

10 rows selected.
```

d) Start another SQL*Plus session on your computer, and login as STU-
DENT with the password LEARN while your current session is still open.
Execute the same SELECT statement you executed in Exercise c to
prove your update worked correctly. Explain what data you see and why.

*Answer: The session does not reflect the changes made. Any other database user or
session cannot see the updated values in the instructor table until a COMMIT command is issued in the original session.*

```
SELECT instructor_id, phone, modified_by, modified_date
   FROM instructor
INSTRUCTOR_ID PHONE           MODIFIED_BY  MODIFIED_
------------- --------------- ------------ ---------
          101 2125551212      ESILVEST     02-JAN-99
          102 2125551212      ESILVEST     02-JAN-99
...                                 .
          109 2125555555      ESILVEST     02-JAN-99
          110 2125555555      ARISCHER     11-MAR-99

10 rows selected.
```

READ-CONSISTENCY OF DATA

Whenever a database user changes data with a DML operation, Oracle keeps track of the old values. If the user rolls back the transaction with the ROLLBACK command, Oracle reads the old values from the *rollback segment* that stores the values and returns the data to the previous state.

Oracle guarantees a *read-consistent* view of all data by using data from rollback segments. For example, if one user updates values but does not COMMIT them, another user will still see the old values, which are retrieved from the rollback segments. Another user will not see the data until the user performing the change makes it permanent by issuing a COMMIT.

The SQL*Plus command AUTOCOMMIT can be set to automatically commit every statement issued during a SQL*Plus session by typing SET AUTOCOMMIT ON *or* SET AUTOCOMMIT IMMEDIATE. *This means a ROLLBACK command issued during that session has no effect because every transaction is automatically committed.*

10.1.3 ANSWERS

a) Delete all rows from the grade table. Then SELECT data from the table, issue a ROLLBACK command, and explain your observations.

Answer: A DELETE statement deletes all rows in the grade table. A subsequently issued SELECT statement shows no rows in the table. Issuing a ROLLBACK command returns the rows. You can verify this by issuing another SELECT statement against the table.

```
DELETE FROM grade
2004 rows deleted.

SELECT *
  FROM grade
no rows selected

ROLLBACK
Rollback complete.
```

b) If TRUNCATE is used in Exercise a instead of DELETE, how does this change your observations? Caution: Do not execute the TRUNCATE statement unless you are prepared to reload the data.

Answer: When TRUNCATE is used the data cannot be rolled back; the ROLLBACK statement has no effect. A subsequent SELECT statement reflects no rows in the grade_conversion table.

```
TRUNCATE TABLE grade
Table truncated.


ROLLBACK
Rollback complete.


SELECT COUNT(*)
  FROM grade
COUNT(*)
---------
        0

1 row selected.
```

Notice, when the ROLLBACK command is issued, Oracle returns the `Rollback complete` *message. This is misleading, because in this case a rollback did not occur; the data is permanently deleted. Be sure to use caution when using TRUNCATE.*

c) Delete the row inserted in Exercise 10.1.1a in the grade_type table.

Answer: A DELETE statement is written for the row where the grade type code is 'EC'.

```
DELETE FROM grade_type
 WHERE grade_type_code = 'EC'
1 row deleted.
```

d) Formulate the question for the following query.

```
DELETE FROM enrollment
 WHERE student_id NOT IN
       (SELECT student_id
          FROM student s, zipcode z
         WHERE s.zip = z.zip
           AND z.city = 'Brooklyn'
           AND z.state = 'NY')
```

Answer: Delete enrollments for all students except those who live in Brooklyn, NY.

The DELETE statement narrows down the records in the WHERE clause using a NOT IN subquery to find students who do not live in Brooklyn, NY. Alternatively, the DELETE statement can be rewritten as a correlated subquery using the NOT EXISTS operator, which under certain circumstances can execute faster.

```
DELETE FROM enrollment e
 WHERE NOT EXISTS
       (SELECT 'x'
          FROM student s, zipcode z
         WHERE s.zip = z.zip
           AND s.student_id = e.student_id
           AND z.city = 'Brooklyn'
           AND z.state = 'NY')
```

Because the student_id in the student table is defined as NOT NULL, the NOT IN and NOT EXISTS statements are equivalent. For more information on the differences between NOT IN and NOT EXISTS see Chapter 7, "Subqueries," and Chapter 16, "SQL Optimization."

LAB 10.1 SELF-REVIEW QUESTIONS

In order to test your progress, you should be able to answer the following questions.

1) A DML command automatically issues a COMMIT.
   a) _____ True
   b) _____ False

2) The TRUNC function and the TRUNCATE command are the same; they both COMMIT data to the database.
   a) _____ True
   b) _____ False

3) An INSERT statement can only insert one row at a time into a table.
   a) _____ True
   b) _____ False

4) It is possible to restore rows deleted with a DELETE statement.
   a) _____ True
   b) _____ False

5) There is no error in the following UPDATE statement.

```
UPDATE grade_type
   SET description = 'Exams'
 WHERE grade_type_code IN ('FI', 'MT')
```

a) _____ True

b) _____ False

Quiz answers appear in Appendix A, Section 10.1.

CHAPTER 10

TEST YOUR THINKING

1) Write and execute two INSERT statements to insert rows into the zipcode table for the following two cities: Newton, MA 02199; Cleveland, OH 43011. After your INSERT statements are successful, make the changes permanent.

2) Make yourself a student by writing and executing an INSERT statement to insert a row into the student table with data about you. Use one of the zip codes you inserted in Exercise 1. Only insert values into the columns student_id (use a value of '900'), first_name, last_name, zip, registration_date (use a date that is five days after today), created_by, created_date, modified_by, and modified_date. Issue a COMMIT command afterwards.

3) Write an UPDATE statement to update the data about you in the student table. Update the columns salutation, street_address, phone, and employer. Be sure to update the modified_date column also, and make the changes permanent.

4) Delete the row in the student table and the two rows in the zipcode table you created. Be sure to issue a COMMIT command afterwards.

CHAPTER 11

CREATE, ALTER, AND DROP TABLES

CHAPTER OBJECTIVES

In this chapter, you will learn about:

✔ Creating and Dropping Tables   Page 290

✔ Altering Tables and Manipulating Constraints   Page 306

In this chapter, you use Data Definition Language (DDL) to create, alter, and drop tables. You also learn to create and manipulate *integrity constraints* on a table to enforce business rules and data integrity.

L A B   1 1 . 1

CREATING AND DROPPING TABLES

LAB OBJECTIVES

After this lab, you will be able to:

✔   Create and Drop Tables
✔   Create Constraints

CREATING TABLES

Tables are created beginning with the CREATE TABLE command. Tables can be created in one of two ways. The first method is to specify the columns and their datatypes explicitly; the second method is to create a table based on an existing table.

■ *FOR EXAMPLE*

The following statement creates a table called toy, consisting of three columns.

```
CREATE TABLE toy
   (description          VARCHAR2(15) NOT NULL,
    last_purchase_date   DATE,
    remaining_quantity   NUMBER(6))
```

A table name must be unique within a database schema; no other database object, such as another table or an index, can have the same name. All database object names must not be longer than 30 characters. The table name should describe the nature of the data contained in it, and for consistency, choose either singular or plural names. The new table is empty because no data has yet been inserted into it.

A column name must be unique within a table, not exceed 30 characters, and should be descriptive of the values stored in the column. A column is defined by a name, datatype, and length, where appropriate. In the previous CREATE TABLE statement, a NOT NULL constraint is specified for the description column. Each column definition is separated by a comma. Spaces in table and column names are not permitted.

DDL commands cannot be rolled back, and they COMMIT any previously issued DML statements.

COMMON DATATYPES

Character data can be stored in columns of datatype VARCHAR2, CHAR, LONG, or CLOB. When creating or altering a table, the VARCHAR2 and CHAR datatypes require a column length. The maximum length of a VARCHAR2 column is 4,000 characters. A fixed length CHAR column stores at most 2,000 characters. The LONG datatype stores up to 2 gigabytes of data in a single column. In the future, Oracle recommends the use of the CLOB datatype instead of LONG. CLOBs store up to 4 gigabytes of data.

The NUMBER datatype does not require a precision and scale and it can store up to 38 decimal digits of precision. The definition of NUMBER(5,2) on a column allows you to store values between –999.99 and 999.99. A number such as 1,000 is rejected because it exceeds the precision, and a value such as 80.999 is rounded to 81.00. Note that in the student schema, the zip column of the zipcode table is stored as a VARCHAR2 rather than a NUMBER datatype, because it requires leading zeros.

The DATE datatype stores the century, year, month, day, hour, minute and second. It has its own internal format, which can be displayed using different format masks.

Oracle also allows you to store binary information in the database in BLOBs, RAW, LONG RAW, and BFILE, which points to a binary operating system file.

Tables can also be created with storage parameters, specifying how much space to allocate for the table, and where to place it.

CREATING TABLES BASED ON OTHER TABLES

Another method of creating a table is to base it on another table or tables. You can choose to include the data or not. The following example creates a table called jan_99_enrollment based on the January 1999 enrollments in the enrollment table.

```
CREATE TABLE jan_99_enrollment AS
SELECT *
  FROM enrollment
 WHERE enroll_date >= TO_DATE('01/01/1999',
       'MM/DD/YYYY')
   AND enroll_date < TO_DATE('02/01/1999',
       'MM/DD/YYYY')
Table created.
```

The database feedback **Table created** confirms the jan_99_enrollment table is successfully created. Notice the columns and their datatypes when you DESCRIBE the new table.

```
DESC jan_99_enrollment
```

Name	Null?	Type
STUDENT_ID	NOT NULL	NUMBER(8)
SECTION_ID	NOT NULL	NUMBER(8)
ENROLL_DATE	NOT NULL	DATE
FINAL_GRADE		NUMBER(3)
CREATED_BY	NOT NULL	VARCHAR2(30)
CREATED_DATE	NOT NULL	DATE
MODIFIED_BY	NOT NULL	VARCHAR2(30)
MODIFIED_DATE	NOT NULL	DATE

The new table has the same columns, datatypes, and lengths as the enrollment table on which it is based. A SELECT statement on the new table confirms the data was inserted into the table based on the SELECT statement of the CREATE TABLE statement.

```
SELECT student_id, section_id, enroll_date
  FROM jan_99_enrollment
```

STUDENT_ID	SECTION_ID	ENROLL_DA
102	89	30-JAN-99
102	86	30-JAN-99
...		
109	101	30-JAN-99

```
    109              99 30-JAN-99
```

`11 rows selected.`

You can use the same syntax to create a table without data. The following example creates a table based on the columns of the enrollment table.

```
CREATE TABLE jan_99_enrollment AS
SELECT *
  FROM enrollment
 WHERE 1 = 2
```

Instead of the WHERE clause restricting specific rows from the enrollment table, here no rows are returned. The value 1 never equals 2, therefore, the WHERE clause evaluates to false for every row in the enrollment table. A new, yet empty, table is created.

 If a SELECT statement in a CREATE TABLE statement joins two tables or more, it is best not to use the asterisk wildcard in the SELECT list. The tables being joined may contain columns with the same name, resulting in an error message when Oracle attempts to create two columns with the same name in one table.

INTEGRITY CONSTRAINTS

When creating tables, you typically create them with *integrity constraints*. These constraints enforce the business rules of a system. For instance, "The salary of an employee may not be a negative number," can be enforced with a check constraint on the salary column. Constraints ensure the data integrity and data consistency among all applications. They also ease the burden of programming the business rules in individual programs, because the work is performed by the database.

■ *FOR EXAMPLE*

The following CREATE TABLE statement creates a table with several types of constraints.

```
CREATE TABLE tab1
   (col1   VARCHAR2(10) PRIMARY KEY,
    col2   NUMBER(4) NOT NULL,
    col3   VARCHAR2(5) REFERENCES zipcode(zip)
           ON DELETE CASCADE,
    col4   DATE DEFAULT SYSDATE,
```

```
col5   VARCHAR2(5) UNIQUE,
col6   NUMBER(2) UNIQUE,
col7   NUMBER CHECK(col7 < 100))
```

THE PRIMARY KEY CONSTRAINT

The first column of the table, col1, has a PRIMARY KEY constraint. This ensures all values in this column are NOT NULL and are unique. This is enforced by a unique index automatically created by Oracle. Indexes are discussed in Chapter 12, "Views, Indexes, and Sequences." When tab1 is created, Oracle also creates a name for this constraint, which looks something like this: SYS_C0030291. This constraint name is not terribly meaningful because it does not identify the table the constraint was created for, or the constraint type. You learn how to name constraints shortly.

THE NOT NULL CHECK CONSTRAINT

The next column, col2, contains a check constraint you are already familiar with, namely NOT NULL. Any inserts or changes to data changing the values in this column to NULL are rejected.

THE FOREIGN KEY CONSTRAINT

The column col3 contains a FOREIGN KEY constraint. The keyword REFERENCES, followed by the zipcode table and the zip column in the zipcode table in parentheses, indicates col3 is a foreign key to the zip column of the zipcode table. The FOREIGN KEY constraint indicates the *domain* of values for col3; in other words, the only valid values for the col3 column are zip codes found in the zip column of the zipcode table.

If you do not specify the column in the referencing table, Oracle assumes you are referring to the primary key of the referenced table. When defining a FOREIGN KEY constraint on a table, the column name does not have to be the same as the column it references, but its datatype and length must agree. Note: A foreign key can also reference the unique constraint of a parent table.

The ON DELETE CASCADE clause indicates that when a parent row is deleted, the corresponding row or rows in this child table will be deleted also. In this case, if a row in the zipcode table is deleted, any rows with the same zip code are deleted from the tab1 table. If you do not specify the ON DELETE CASCADE clause, the delete is said to be restricted. This means a parent row cannot be deleted if child rows exist.

THE UNIQUE CONSTRAINT

The columns col5 and col6 each have a UNIQUE constraint, indicating every value must be unique. Oracle automatically creates a unique index when a UNIQUE constraint is specified.

THE CHECK CONSTRAINT

The column col7 has a CHECK constraint, constraining the column to only values less than 100.

THE DATA DEFAULT

The column col4 specifies a DEFAULT option, which is not a constraint. When a row is inserted into tab1 and no value is supplied for col4, SYSDATE is inserted by default. As long as its default value's datatype matches the datatype of the column itself, a default value can be specified for any column except the column or columns of the primary key.

NAMING CONSTRAINTS

It is best to always name constraints. Following is an example of how to name constraints in a CREATE TABLE statement.

```
CREATE TABLE tab1
   (col1   VARCHAR2(10),
    col2   NUMBER(4) NOT NULL,
    col3   NUMBER(6),
    col4   DATE DEFAULT SYSDATE,
    col5   VARCHAR2(5),
    col6   NUMBER(2),
    col7   NUMBER,
    CONSTRAINT tab1_pk PRIMARY KEY(col1),
    CONSTRAINT tab1_zipcode_fk FOREIGN KEY(col3)
      REFERENCES zipcode(zip),
    CONSTRAINT tab1_uk UNIQUE(col5, col6),
    CONSTRAINT tab1_col7_chk CHECK(col7 < 100))
```

Four constraints are listed at the end of the CREATE TABLE statement, separated by commas. Each of the constraint names consists of the name of the table and an abbreviation identifying the type of constraint. The foreign key constraint contains the name of the parent and child tables. The last constraint, a CHECK constraint called tab1_col7_chk, contains the name of the column. Note that the unique constraint is now enforced for the values of the combined columns col5 and col6.

It is best to name constraints explicitly, for clarity and to manipulate them more easily, as you see in Lab 11.2. Also, when a SQL operation, such as an INSERT statement, violates a constraint, Oracle returns an error message with the name of the constraint, making it easy to identify the source of the error.

RENAMING TABLES

Tables can be renamed with the RENAME command, as in the following statement.

```
RENAME jan_99_enrollment TO jan_99
Table renamed.
```

Constraint names and dependent database objects, such as indexes and triggers, are not renamed when the table name is changed.

DROPPING TABLES

Tables can be dropped when they are no longer needed, using the DROP TABLE command.

```
DROP TABLE jan_99
Table dropped.
```

When you drop a table, the table as well as its data is removed from the database. Any indexes or triggers on the table are automatically dropped. Database objects that depend on the table, such as a view referencing the table, become invalid. You learn about views and indexes in Chapter 12.

Other tables may be dependent on the dropped table as a domain for a foreign key reference. For example, if you drop the zipcode table, an Oracle error message occurs because there are other tables with a foreign key referencing the zip column of the zipcode table. One solution is to disable or drop the foreign key constraints with an ALTER TABLE command on these dependent tables which you will learn in Lab 11.2. Another is to let Oracle drop the foreign key constraints with the CASCADE CONSTRAINTS option. Caution: Do not actually execute the following statement unless you are prepared to reload the data from the zipcode table and add the foreign key constraints on the student and instructor tables.

```
DROP TABLE zipcode CASCADE CONSTRAINTS
```

LAB 11.1 EXERCISES

11.1.1   CREATE AND DROP TABLES

a) Explain the error(s) in the following CREATE TABLE statement, if any. If there are errors, rewrite the statement correctly.

```
CREATE TABLE student candidate
   (name      VARCHAR2(25)
   address   VARCHAR2(20)
   city      VARCHAR2
   zip       NUMBER)
```

_____

_____

b) Write and execute a CREATE TABLE statement to create an empty table called new_student containing the following columns: first name, last name, the description of the first course the student takes, and the date the student registered in the program. Determine the datatype and length necessary for each column based on the tables in the student schema. DESCRIBE the table when you have finished.

_____

_____

c) Execute the following CREATE TABLE statement and explain the result.

```
CREATE TABLE school_program AS
SELECT last_name||', '||first_name name
  FROM student
UNION
SELECT last_name||', '||first_name
  FROM instructor
```

_____

_____

d) Rename the school_program table you created in Exercise c to a table called school_program2. Then, drop both the school_program and school_program2 tables, and explain your observations.

_____

_____

11.1.2 CREATE CONSTRAINTS

a) Execute the following SQL statements to create an empty table called course2, and insert two rows into course2, respectively. What do you observe about the values of the course_no column in the course2 table?

```
CREATE TABLE course2 AS
SELECT *
  FROM course
 WHERE 1 = 2
Table created.

INSERT INTO course2
   (course_no, description, cost, prerequisite,
    created_by, created_date, modified_by, modified_date)
VALUES
   (999, 'Teaching SQL - Part 1', 1495, NULL,
    'AMORRISON', SYSDATE, 'AMORRISON', SYSDATE)
1 row created.

INSERT INTO course2
   (course_no, description, cost, prerequisite,
    created_by, created_date, modified_by, modified_date)
VALUES
   (999, 'Teaching SQL - Part 2', 1495, NULL,
    'AMORRISON', SYSDATE, 'AMORRISON', SYSDATE)
1 row created.
```

_____

_____

b) Identify the constraints in the following CREATE TABLE statement, and explain their purpose.

```
CREATE TABLE extinct_animal
   (name            VARCHAR2(30) NOT NULL,
```

```
species            VARCHAR2(30) NOT NULL,
native_country  VARCHAR2(20)
  REFERENCES country(country_name),
remaining          NUMBER(2),
CONSTRAINT extinct_animal_pk PRIMARY KEY(name, species),
CONSTRAINT extinct_animal_remaining_chk
  CHECK (remaining BETWEEN 0 and 10))
```

_____

_____

c) Rewrite and execute the following CREATE TABLE statement to give the PRIMARY KEY and FOREIGN KEY constraints a name.

```
CREATE TABLE former_student
  (studid    NUMBER(8) PRIMARY KEY,
   first     VARCHAR2(25),
   last      VARCHAR2(25),
   enrolled  VARCHAR2(1) DEFAULT 'N',
   zip       VARCHAR2(5) REFERENCES zipcode(zip))
```

_____

_____

d) Rewrite the solution to Exercise c to add a UNIQUE constraint on the first and last columns.

_____

_____

LAB 11.1 EXERCISE ANSWERS

11.1.1 ANSWERS

a) Explain the error(s) in the following CREATE TABLE statement, if any. If there are errors, rewrite the statement correctly.

```
CREATE TABLE student candidate
  (name      VARCHAR2(25)
   address   VARCHAR2(20)
   city      VARCHAR2
   zip       NUMBER)
```

Answer: One error is the table name contains spaces. Another is that the length of the city column is not specified. Also, commas are required to separate the column definitions.

```
CREATE TABLE student_candidate
  (name      VARCHAR2(25),
   address   VARCHAR2(20),
   city      VARCHAR2(15),
   zip       NUMBER)
```

b) Write and execute a CREATE TABLE statement to create an empty table called new_student containing the following columns: first name, last name, the description of the first course the student takes, and the date the student registered in the program. Determine the datatype and length necessary for each column based on the tables in the student schema. DESCRIBE the table when you have finished.

Answer: The table contains the four columns first_name, last_name, description, and registration_date. The first three are of datatype VARCHAR2, and registration_date is of datatype DATE.

```
CREATE TABLE new_student
  (first_name         VARCHAR2(25),
   last_name          VARCHAR2(25),
   description        VARCHAR2(50),
   registration_date  DATE)
```

```
DESC new_student
```

Name	Null?	Type
FIRST_NAME		VARCHAR2(25)
LAST_NAME		VARCHAR2(25)
DESCRIPTION		VARCHAR2(50)
REGISTRATION_DATE		DATE

c) Execute the following CREATE TABLE statement and explain the result.

```
CREATE TABLE school_program AS
SELECT last_name||', '||first_name name
  FROM student
UNION
SELECT last_name||', '||first_name
  FROM instructor
```

Answer: The statement creates a table called school_program with student and instructor names combined. The first and last names are concatenated into one column.

```
DESC school_program
Name                                Null?      Type
--------------------------------    --------   ------------
NAME                                           VARCHAR2(52)
```

Notice the length of the name column in the new table: It is long enough to accommodate the combined length of first and last names, plus a comma and a space.

d) Rename the school_program table you created in Exercise c to a table called school_program2. Then drop both the school_program and school_program2 tables, and explain your observations.

Answer: The RENAME and DROP TABLE commands are used. The school_program table no longer exists because it is renamed to school_program2, so it cannot be dropped.

```
RENAME school_program TO school_program2
Table renamed.

DROP TABLE school_program
DROP TABLE school_program
          *
ERROR at line 1:
ORA-00942: table or view does not exist

DROP TABLE school_program2
Table dropped.
```

11.1.2 Answers

a) Execute the following SQL statements to create an empty table called course2, and insert two rows into course2, respectively. What do you observe about the values of the course_no column in the course2 table?

```
CREATE TABLE course2 AS
SELECT *
  FROM course
 WHERE 1 = 2
Table created.

INSERT INTO course2
  (course_no, description, cost, prerequisite,
   created_by, created_date, modified_by, modified_date)
```

```
VALUES
   (999, 'Teaching SQL - Part 1', 1495, NULL,
   'AMORRISON', SYSDATE, 'AMORRISON', SYSDATE)
```
1 row created.

```
INSERT INTO course2
   (course_no, description, cost, prerequisite,
   created_by, created_date, modified_by, modified_date)
VALUES
   (999, 'Teaching SQL - Part 2', 1495, NULL,
   'AMORRISON', SYSDATE, 'AMORRISON', SYSDATE)
```
1 row created.

> *Answer: When a table is created from another table, the primary key constraint is not preserved.*

When a table is created from another table, constraints are not automatically preserved in the new table, except for the NOT NULL constraint. The course_no column is the primary key in the course table, and, therefore, prevents duplicate values. But, when the course2 table is created from the course table, a primary key constraint is not created so the course_no column in the course2 table allows duplicate values to be inserted.

After creating a table based on another, you must *alter* the table to add constraints. Altering tables is discussed in Lab 11.2.

b)   Identify the constraints in the following CREATE TABLE statement, and explain their purpose.

```
CREATE TABLE extinct_animal
   (name             VARCHAR2(30) NOT NULL,
   species           VARCHAR2(30) NOT NULL,
   native_country  VARCHAR2(20)
     REFERENCES country(country_name),
   remaining         NUMBER(2),
   CONSTRAINT extinct_animal_pk PRIMARY KEY(name, species),
   CONSTRAINT extinct_animal_remaining_chk
     CHECK (remaining BETWEEN 0 and 10))
```

> *Answer: The name and species columns each have a NOT NULL constraint. The native_country column has a foreign key constraint to constrain the column to values only from the country_name column in a table called country. There is a concatenated PRIMARY KEY constraint called extinct_animal_pk, consisting of the name and species columns. The CHECK constraint on the column called extinct_animal_remaining_chk checks whether a number inserted or updated is between the values 0 and 10 inclusively.*

The NOT NULL constraint on the name and species columns is optional because the columns are defined as a primary key.

When a primary key on a table consists of more than one column, the constraint must be written on a separate line of the CREATE TABLE statement.

c) Rewrite and execute the following CREATE TABLE statement to give the PRIMARY KEY and FOREIGN KEY a name.

```
CREATE TABLE former_student
  (studid    NUMBER(8) PRIMARY KEY,
   first     VARCHAR2(25),
   last      VARCHAR2(25),
   enrolled  VARCHAR2(1) DEFAULT 'N',
   zip       VARCHAR2(5) REFERENCES zipcode(zip))
```

Answer: The constraints are moved to the end of the CREATE TABLE statement where they are created with specific names.

```
CREATE TABLE former_student
  (studid    NUMBER(8),
   first     VARCHAR2(25),
   last      VARCHAR2(25),
   enrolled  VARCHAR2(1) DEFAULT 'N',
   zip       VARCHAR2(5),
   CONSTRAINT former_student_pk PRIMARY KEY(studid),
   CONSTRAINT former_student_zipcode_fk FOREIGN KEY(zip)
     REFERENCES zipcode(zip))
```

In previous examples, the CONSTRAINT keyword and name of the constraint are not always used when creating constraints. However, here is an example of what occurs when a constraint is violated and the constraint is not explicitly named.

```
INSERT INTO former_student
  (studid, first, last, enrolled, zip)
VALUES
  (101, 'Alex', 'Morrison', NULL, '10005')
1 row created.

INSERT INTO former_student
  (studid, first, last, enrolled, zip)
VALUES
  (101, 'Alex', 'Morrison', NULL, '11717')
```

```
INSERT INTO former_student
            *
ERROR at line 1:
ORA-00001: unique constraint (STUDENT.SYS_C001293) violated
```

From the error message, it is impossible to determine the type of constraint, and on which column or columns; you can only determine that the constraint is in the STUDENT schema. You need to look up the name of the constraint in the Oracle data dictionary to determine the reason for the error. The system-generated name is not informative; therefore, always name your constraints. The Oracle data dictionary is discussed in Chapter 13, "The Data Dictionary and Dynamic SQL Scripts."

d) Rewrite the solution to Exercise c to add a UNIQUE constraint on the first and last columns.

Answer: The constraint is added to the end of the CREATE TABLE statement with a specific name.

```
CREATE TABLE former_student
   (studid    NUMBER(8),
    first     VARCHAR2(25),
    last      VARCHAR2(25),
    enrolled  VARCHAR2(1) DEFAULT 'N',
    zip       VARCHAR2(5),
    CONSTRAINT former_student_pk PRIMARY KEY(studid),
    CONSTRAINT former_student_zipcode_fk FOREIGN KEY(zip)
      REFERENCES zipcode(zip),
    CONSTRAINT former_student_uk UNIQUE(first, last))
```

 A UNIQUE constraint prevents duplicate values from being inserted into a column. It is different from a PRIMARY KEY constraint because a UNIQUE constraint allows NULL values.

LAB 11.1 SELF-REVIEW QUESTIONS

In order to test your progress, you should be able to answer the following questions.

1) The primary key of the following CREATE TABLE statement is a concatenated primary key.

```
CREATE TABLE class_roster
   (class_id        NUMBER(3),
    class_name      VARCHAR2(20) UNIQUE,
```

```
first_class       DATE NOT NULL,
num_of_students   NUMBER(3),
CONSTRAINT class_roster_pk
 PRIMARY KEY(class_id, class_name))
```

    a) _____ True
    b) _____ False

2) It is possible to create one table from three different tables in a single CREATE TABLE statement.
    a) _____ True
    b) _____ False

3) The CASCADE CONSTRAINTS keywords in a DROP TABLE statement drop all referencing child tables.
    a) _____ True
    b) _____ False

4) Every column of a table can have one or more constraints.
    a) _____ True
    b) _____ False

5) You cannot create a table from another table if it has no rows.
    a) _____ True
    b) _____ False

Quiz answers appear in Appendix A, Section 11.1.

L A B   1 1 . 2

ALTERING TABLES AND MANIPULATING CONSTRAINTS

LAB OBJECTIVES

After this lab, you will be able to:

✔ Alter Tables and Manipulate Constraints

Once a table is created, you sometimes find you must change its characteristics. The ALTER TABLE command, in conjunction with the ADD, DROP, and MODIFY clauses, allows you to do this. You can add or delete a column, change the length, datatype, or default value of a column, or add, drop, enable, or disable a table's integrity constraints.

ADDING COLUMNS

Following is a list of the columns of the toy table created in Lab 11.1.

```
DESC toy
Name                                   Null?      Type
-------------------------------- -------- ----
DESCRIPTION                            NOT NULL VARCHAR2(15)
LAST_PURCHASE_DATE                                DATE
REMAINING_QUANTITY                                NUMBER(6)
```

The following statement alters the toy table to add a new column called manufacturer.

```
ALTER TABLE toy
   ADD (manufacturer VARCHAR2(30) NOT NULL)
Table altered.
```

The `Table altered` command indicates the successful completion of the operation. When the column is added, it is defined as datatype and length VARCHAR2(30). The column also has a NOT NULL constraint. When you issue another DESCRIBE command, you see the new column.

```
DESC toy
Name                              Null?      Type
------------------------------    --------   ----
DESCRIPTION                       NOT NULL   VARCHAR2(15)
LAST_PURCHASE_DATE                           DATE
REMAINING_QUANTITY                           NUMBER(6)
MANUFACTURER                      NOT NULL   VARCHAR2(30)
```

Alternatively, you can add the column and name the constraint as in the following example.

```
ALTER TABLE TOY
   ADD (manufacturer VARCHAR2(30)
     CONSTRAINT toy_manufacturer_nn NOT NULL)
```

You can only add a column together with a NOT NULL constraint if the table contains no data. Otherwise, add the column first without the NOT NULL constraint, then update the column with data and change the column definition to a NOT NULL constraint with the MODIFY clause of the ALTER TABLE statement. You learn about modifying columns shortly.

DROPPING COLUMNS

Columns can also be dropped from a table with the ALTER TABLE command using the DROP COLUMN clause. The following drops the last_purchase_date column from the toy table.

```
ALTER TABLE toy
   DROP COLUMN last_purchase_date
Table altered.
```

Instead of dropping a column, you can mark it as unused with the SET UNUSED clause of the ALTER TABLE statement

```
ALTER TABLE toy
  SET UNUSED last_purchase_date
```
Table altered.

This clause is useful if you want to make the column no longer visible but do not want to physically remove it yet. When you drop another column or issue the ALTER TABLE command with the DROP UNUSED COLUMNS clause, the column is physically removed from the database. Changing a column to unused instead of dropping it is quicker, because it does not demand a lot of system resources. When the database system resources are less in demand, you can then physically remove the column.

MODIFYING COLUMNS

You can also modify the datatype, length, and column default of existing columns with the ALTER TABLE statement. There are a number of restrictions, as you see in the lab exercises.

The following statement changes the length of the description column from 15 to 25 characters.

```
ALTER TABLE toy
  MODIFY (description VARCHAR2(25))
```
Table altered.

The following statement modifies the datatype of the remaining_quantity column from NUMBER to VARCHAR2, and makes the column NOT NULL simultaneously.

```
ALTER TABLE toy
  MODIFY (remaining_quantity VARCHAR2(6) NOT NULL)
```
Table altered.

You can also execute the statements individually.

```
ALTER TABLE toy
  MODIFY (remaining_quantity VARCHAR2(6))
```
Table altered.

```
ALTER TABLE toy
  MODIFY (remaining_quantity NOT NULL)
```
Table altered.

Other database objects, such as views and stored PL/SQL objects, may be dependent on the table, making them invalid when the table is altered. These objects need to be recompiled.

ADDING, DROPPING, DISABLING AND ENABLING CONSTRAINTS

ADDING CONSTRAINTS

When the toy table was created, no primary key was specified. The following statement alters the toy table to add a primary key constraint based on the description column.

```
ALTER TABLE toy
  ADD PRIMARY KEY(description)
```
Table altered.

The same statement can be rewritten with a constraint name.

```
ALTER TABLE toy
  ADD CONSTRAINT toy_pk PRIMARY KEY(description)
  USING INDEX TABLESPACE store_idx
  STORAGE (INITIAL 1 M
        NEXT 500 K)
```
Table altered.

The statement also specifies the tablespace where the index is stored. For performance reasons, you typically separate indexes and data by storing them on separate tablespaces on different physical devices. The index is created in a tablespace called store_idx. Other characteristics of a table, such as its storage parameters, determining the size of a table, can also be specified with the ALTER TABLE command. In the previous example, the index gets 1 megabyte of space allocated for it, regardless of whether any entries exist or not. After this space is used, the subsequent amount of space allocated is 500 kilobytes.

Any of the constraints you learned in Lab 11.1 can be added to a table with the ALTER TABLE . . . ADD command.

Constraint names cannot exceed 30 characters and must be unique within the user's schema.

DROPPING CONSTRAINTS

Constraints can also be dropped by specifying the constraint name explicitly, as in this example.

```
ALTER TABLE toy
  DROP CONSTRAINT toy_pk
```
Table altered.

Alternatively, you can drop the primary key with the following statement.

```
ALTER TABLE toy
  DROP PRIMARY KEY
```

DISABLING AND ENABLING CONSTRAINTS

Constraints can be *enabled* or *disabled* as necessary with the ALTER TABLE command. By default, when a constraint is created it is enabled, unless you explicitly disable it. You may want to disable constraints when loading large amounts of data at once to decrease the load time. The following statement disables an existing primary key constraint on the toy table.

```
ALTER TABLE toy
  DISABLE CONSTRAINT toy_pk
```
Table altered.

Note, when primary key or unique constraints are disabled, any associated indexes are dropped and are automatically recreated when the constraint is enabled.

Naming constraints helps when you want to disable or enable them. Once data is loaded, you can enable the primary key again with either of the following statements.

```
ALTER TABLE toy
  ENABLE PRIMARY KEY
  USING INDEX TABLESPACE store_idx
  STORAGE (INITIAL 1 M
        NEXT 500 K)
```
Table altered.

```
ALTER TABLE toy
  ENABLE CONSTRAINT toy_pk
  USING INDEX TABLESPACE store_idx
  STORAGE (INITIAL 1 M
        NEXT 500 K)
```
Table altered.

If you don't specify the tablespace name when you enable the index, the index will be stored on your default tablespace. If you do not specify the size of your index, Oracle uses the default storage values from the tablespace. Storage parameters are only relevant with primary and unique constraints because they create indexes.

The following statement disables the foreign key constraint between the course and the section tables.

```
ALTER TABLE section
  DISABLE CONSTRAINT sect_crse_fk
```
Table altered.

DETERMINE WHICH ROWS VIOLATE CONSTRAINTS

When a constraint is reenabled, Oracle checks to see if all the rows satisfy the condition of the constraint. If some rows violate the constraint, Oracle issues an error message. In the following example, a course number was added to the section table but the course table has no such course_no. Therefore, the Foreign Key constraint cannot be enabled.

```
ALTER TABLE section
  ENABLE CONSTRAINT sect_crse_fk
```
ALTER TABLE section
*
ERROR at line 1:
ORA-02298: cannot validate (STUDENT.SECT_CRSE_FK) - parent keys not
found

There are a variety of ways to determine the offending rows. For example, you can issue the following statement to display the rows:

```
SELECT course_no
  FROM section
 MINUS
SELECT course_no
  FROM course
```

To determine which rows violate the primary key constraint, you can issue the following SQL statement:

```
SELECT section_id, COUNT(*)
  FROM section
 GROUP BY section_id
HAVING COUNT(*) > 1
```

THE WHOLE TRUTH

Oracle also allows you to record all the rows violating constraints in an EXCEPTIONS table with the Oracle script utlexcpt.sql found in the %ORACLE_HOME%\rdbms\admin directory. For example, in an Oracle 8i Windows NT installation, the default directory is c:\oracle\ora81\rdbms\admin.

As part of the ENABLE clause of the ALTER TABLE statement, Oracle also provides a NOVALIDATE option, allowing only subsequent DML operations on the table to comply with the constraint; existing data can violate the constraint.

LAB 11.2 EXERCISES

11.2.1 ALTER TABLES AND MANIPULATE CONSTRAINTS

a) Alter the table called new_student you created in Exercise 11.1.1 b to add four columns called phone, num_courses with datatype and length NUMBER(3), created_by, and created_date. Determine the other column datatypes and lengths based on the student table. The phone and num_courses columns should allow NULL values; the created_by and created_date columns should not allow NULL values, and their values should default to the schema user logged in and today's date, respectively. DESCRIBE the table when you have finished.

_____

_____

b) Execute the following INSERT statement to insert a row into the new_student table. Then alter the table to change the phone column from NULL to NOT NULL. What do you observe?

```
INSERT INTO new_student
   (first_name, last_name, description, registration_date)
VALUES
   ('Joe', 'Fisher', 'Intro to Linux', SYSDATE)
```

_____

_____

c) Alter the new_student table to change the registration_date column from DATE datatype to VARCHAR2 datatype. What do you observe?

_____

_____

d) Alter the new_student table to create a primary key consisting of the first_name and last_name columns.

e) Alter the new_student table to change the length of the last_name column from 25 to 20. What do you observe?

f) Disable the primary key constraint on the new_student table, and write an INSERT statement, with the values Joe Fisher for the first and last name, to prove it is successful. Then enable the constraint again and describe the result.

g) Drop all the tables created throughout the labs. The table names are: student_candidate, new_student, course2, extinct_animal, and former_student.

LAB 11.2 EXERCISE ANSWERS

11.2.1 ANSWERS

a) Alter the table called new_student you created in Exercise 11.1.1 b to add four columns called phone, num_courses with datatype and length NUMBER(3), created_by, and created_date. Determine the other column datatypes and lengths based on the student table. The phone and num_courses columns should allow NULL values; the created_by and created_date columns should not allow NULL values, and their values should default to the schema user logged in and today's date, respectively. DESCRIBE the table when you have finished.

Answer: The four columns are added with a single ALTER TABLE...ADD command, separated by commas. The created_by column has a NOT NULL constraint and a DE-

FAULT clause to default the column to the value of the current user; the created_date column also has a NOT NULL constraint and a DEFAULT clause to default the column to the value SYSDATE.

```
ALTER TABLE new_student
  ADD (phone VARCHAR2(15),
       num_courses NUMBER(3),
       created_by VARCHAR2(30) DEFAULT USER NOT NULL,
       created_date DATE DEFAULT SYSDATE NOT NULL)
```
Table altered.

```
DESC new_student
```

Name	Null?	Type
FIRST_NAME		VARCHAR2(25)
LAST_NAME		VARCHAR2(25)
DESCRIPTION		VARCHAR2(50)
REGISTRATION_DATE		DATE
PHONE		VARCHAR2(15)
NUM_COURSES		NUMBER(3)
CREATED_BY	NOT NULL	VARCHAR2(30)
CREATED_DATE	NOT NULL	DATE

A column or columns can be added to a table regardless of whether the table contains data or not. However, you cannot add columns with a NOT NULL constraint, if the column contains NULL values. This can be achieved only by first adding the column with the NULL constraint, updating the column with values, then altering the table to modify the column to add the NOT NULL constraint.

CHANGING COLUMN DEFAULT VALUES

A column with a DEFAULT option can also be changed to remove the default restriction for new rows with the following statement.

```
ALTER TABLE new_student
  MODIFY (created_by VARCHAR2(30) DEFAULT NULL,
          created_date DATE DEFAULT NULL)
```
Table altered.

b) Execute the following INSERT statement to insert a row into the new_student table. Then alter the table to change the phone column from NULL to NOT NULL. What do you observe?

```
INSERT INTO new_student
  (first_name, last_name, description, registration_date)
```

```
VALUES
  ('Joe', 'Fisher', 'Intro to Linux', SYSDATE)
```

> *Answer: The column cannot be modified to have a NOT NULL constraint because there is already a row in the table containing a NULL value in the column.*

**LAB
11.2**

```
ALTER TABLE new_student
  MODIFY (phone NOT NULL)
MODIFY (phone NOT NULL)
       *
ERROR at line 2:
ORA-01449: column contains NULL values; cannot alter to NOT NULL
```

Just as you are unable to add a column with a NOT NULL constraint to a table, you cannot modify an existing column to NOT NULL if it contains NULL values. You must first add data to the column, then modify the column to add the constraint.

```
UPDATE new_student
  SET phone = '917-555-1212'
1 row updated.

ALTER TABLE new_student
  MODIFY (phone NOT NULL)
Table altered.

DESC new_student
Name                             Null?     Type
-------------------------------- --------- ----
FIRST_NAME                                 VARCHAR2(25)
LAST_NAME                                  VARCHAR2(25)
DESCRIPTION                                VARCHAR2(50)
REGISTRATION_DATE                          DATE
PHONE                            NOT NULL  VARCHAR2(15)
NUM_COURSES                                NUMBER(3)
CREATED_BY                       NOT NULL  VARCHAR2(30)
CREATED_DATE                     NOT NULL  DATE
```

The column can also be changed from NOT NULL to NULL with the following statement.

```
ALTER TABLE new_student
  MODIFY (phone NULL)
Table altered.
```

```
DESC new_student
Name                               Null?    Type
-------------------------------- -------- ----
FIRST_NAME                                 VARCHAR2(25)
LAST_NAME                                  VARCHAR2(25)
DESCRIPTION                                VARCHAR2(50)
REGISTRATION_DATE                          DATE
PHONE                                      VARCHAR2(15)
NUM_COURSES                                NUMBER(3)
CREATED_BY                        NOT NULL VARCHAR2(30)
CREATED_DATE                      NOT NULL DATE
```

c) Alter the new_student table to change the registration_date column from DATE datatype to VARCHAR2 datatype. What do you observe?

Answer: A column's datatype cannot be changed when there is data in the column.

```
ALTER TABLE new_student
  MODIFY (registration_date VARCHAR2(12))
MODIFY (registration_date VARCHAR2(12))
        *
ERROR at line 2:
ORA-01439: column to be modified must be empty to change datatype
```

CHANGING A COLUMN'S DATATYPE

It is possible to change a column's datatype under two sets of circumstances. The first is when changing from one datatype to a compatible datatype, such as VARCHAR2 to CHAR. The second is when the column is empty, as in the following example.

```
UPDATE new_student
   SET registration_date = NULL
1 row updated.

ALTER TABLE new_student
  MODIFY (registration_date VARCHAR2(12))
Table altered.
```

d) Alter the new_student table to create a primary key consisting of the first_name and last_name columns.

Answer: The new_student table is altered to add a PRIMARY KEY constraint consisting of the two columns, separated by commas inside the parentheses.

```
ALTER TABLE new_student
  ADD CONSTRAINT new_student_pk
    PRIMARY KEY(first_name, last_name)
Table altered.
```

The ADD PRIMARY KEY keywords are used to add the primary key constraint. You cannot use the MODIFY clause to modify the individual columns of the primary key.

The following statement adds a unique constraint to the description column.

```
ALTER TABLE new_student
  ADD CONSTRAINT new_student_uk UNIQUE(description)
Table altered.
```

e) Alter the new_student table to change the length of the last_name column from 25 to 20. What do you observe?

Answer: The length of a column cannot be decreased when there is data in the column.

```
ALTER TABLE new_student
  MODIFY (last_name VARCHAR2(20))
MODIFY (last_name VARCHAR2(20))
      *
ERROR at line 2:
ORA-01441: column to be modified must be empty to decrease column
length
```

INCREASING AND DECREASING THE COLUMN WIDTH

For columns containing data, the length of the column can always be increased, as in the following example, but never decreased.

```
ALTER TABLE new_student
  MODIFY (last_name VARCHAR2(30))
Table altered.
```

The num_courses column does not yet have data in it, and the following statement successfully decreases the length of the column.

```
ALTER TABLE new_student
  MODIFY (num_courses NUMBER(2))
Table altered.
```

f) Disable the primary key constraint on the new_student table, and write an IN-SERT statement with the values Joe Fisher for the first and last name. Then enable the constraint again and describe the result.

Answer: The values Joe Fisher exist twice in the first_name and last_name columns, respectively, so a primary key constraint cannot be enabled on the table.

```
ALTER TABLE new_student
  DISABLE PRIMARY KEY
```
Table altered.

```
INSERT INTO new_student
  (first_name, last_name, phone, created_by, created_date)
VALUES
  ('Joe', 'Fisher', '718-555-1212', USER, SYSDATE)
```
1 row created.

```
ALTER TABLE new_student
  ENABLE PRIMARY KEY
```
ALTER TABLE new_student
*
ERROR at line 1:
ORA-02437: cannot enable (STUDENT.SYS_C001265) - primary key violated

It is dangerous to disable a table's primary key, because the integrity of the data may be violated. The only time you may want to disable constraints is when you are performing large data loads. If the constraints are enabled, each row must be evaluated to ensure it does not violate any of the constraints, slowing down the data loading process. Constraints can be disabled temporarily, the data loaded, then enabled again.

In Chapter 13 you learn how to do this easily for many constraints at once by generating a SQL statement to generate other SQL statements. The chapter also teaches you how to query the Oracle Data Dictionary for what constraints exist, and their status, such as enabled or disabled.

g) Drop all the tables created throughout the labs. The table names are: student_candidate, new_student, course2, extinct_animal, and former_student.

Answer: Use the DROP TABLE command to remove the tables from the schema.

```
DROP TABLE student_candidate
```
Table dropped.

```
DROP TABLE new_student
```
Table dropped.

```
DROP TABLE course2
```
Table dropped.

```
DROP TABLE extinct_animal
```
Table dropped.

```
DROP TABLE former_student
```
Table dropped.

LAB 11.2 SELF-REVIEW QUESTIONS

In order to test your progress, you should be able to answer the following questions.

1) The following ALTER TABLE statement contains an error.

```
ALTER TABLE new_student
  DROP CONSTRAINT PRIMARY_KEY
```

    a) _____ True
    b) _____ False

2) The ADD and MODIFY keywords can be used interchangeably in an ALTER TABLE statement.
    a) _____ True
    b) _____ False

3) You can add a NOT NULL constraint on a column providing all the rows in the column contain data.
    a) _____ True
    b) _____ False

4) A constraint must have a name in order for it to be disabled.
    a) _____ True
    b) _____ False

5) A column's datatype can be changed *only* when the column contains no data.
    a) _____ True
    b) _____ False

6) The following statement constrains values in the phone column of the student table to a particular format.

```
ALTER TABLE student
  ADD CONSTRAINT student_phone_chk CHECK
    (TRANSLATE (phone,'1234567890-', '9999999999-') = '999-999-9999')
```

    a) _____ True
    b) _____ False

Quiz answers appear in Appendix A, Section 11.2.

C H A P T E R   1 1

TEST YOUR THINKING

1) Create a table called temp_student with the following columns and constraints: a column studid for student id that is NOT NULL and is the primary key; a column first_name for student first name; a column last_name for student last name; a column zip that is a foreign key to the zip column in the zipcode table; a column registration_date that is NOT NULL and has a CHECK constraint to restrict the registration date to dates after January 1st, 2000.

2) Write an INSERT statement violating at least two of the constraints for the temp_student table you just created. Write another INSERT statement that succeeds when executed, and commit your work.

3) Alter the temp_student table to add two more columns called employer and employer_zip. The employer_zip column should have a foreign key constraint referencing the zip column of the zipcode table. Update the employer column, and alter the table once again to make the employer column NOT NULL.

CHAPTER 12

VIEWS, INDEXES, AND SEQUENCES

CHAPTER OBJECTIVES

In this chapter, you will learn about:

✔ Creating and Modifying Views   Page 322

✔ Indexes   Page 335

✔ Sequences   Page 347

Views, indexes, and sequences are important for the security, efficiency and integrity of a database.

Views are significant in a database because they allow you to look at the data differently, and because they also hide certain information from the user.

Indexes are required for good performance of any database. A well-thought-out indexing strategy entails the careful placement of indexes on relevant columns.

Sequences generate unique values, and are used mainly for creating primary key values.

L A B   1 2 . 1

CREATING AND MODIFYING VIEWS

LAB OBJECTIVES

After this lab, you will be able to:

✔ Create, Alter, and Drop Views
✔ Understand the Data Manipulation Rules for Views

A SELECT statement can be stored as a view. The view is a virtual table consisting of columns and rows, but it is only the query that is stored, not a physical table with data. A view's SELECT statement may reference one or multiple tables. These tables are called base tables. The base tables are typically actual tables or other views.

The data retrieved from the view can be just certain columns, or certain rows from the base tables that are restricted with the SELECT column list and/or the WHERE clause. In a view you can also give a column a different name from the one in the base table. A view looks just like any other table. You can describe it and also issue INSERT, UPDATE, and DELETE statements to a certain extent.

Views are useful for security reasons because they can hide data. They also simplify the writing of queries. You can query a single view instead of writing a complicated SQL statement joining many tables. The complexity of the underlying SQL statement is hidden from the user, and contained only in the view.

■ FOR EXAMPLE

The following statements create a view and describe the new view, respectively.

```
CREATE OR REPLACE VIEW course_no_cost AS
SELECT course_no, description, prerequisite
  FROM course
View created.


DESC course_no_cost
```

Name	Null?	Type
COURSE_NO	NOT NULL	NUMBER(38)
DESCRIPTION	NOT NULL	VARCHAR2(50)
PREREQUISITE		NUMBER(38)

The view named course_no_cost hides a number of columns that exist in the course table. You do not see the cost column, or the created_date, created_by, modified_date, and modified_by columns. The main purpose of this view is security. You can grant access just to the view course_no_cost instead of to the course table itself. For more information on granting access privileges to database objects, see Chapter 14, "Security."

The following demonstrates a view with column names different from the column names in the base tables. Here the view named stud_enroll shows a listing of the student_id, the last name of the student in capital letters, and the number of classes the student is enrolled in. The column student_id from the student table is renamed in the view to stud_id using a column alias. When a column contains an expression, a column alias is required as in the two expressions in the stud_enroll view, namely the student last name in caps and the count of classes enrolled.

```
CREATE OR REPLACE VIEW stud_enroll AS
SELECT s.student_id stud_id,
       UPPER(s.last_name) last_name,
       COUNT(*) num_enrolled
  FROM student s, enrollment e
 WHERE s.student_id = e.student_id
 GROUP BY s.student_id, UPPER(s.last_name)
```

The OR REPLACE keywords are useful in case the view already exists. It allows you to replace the view with a different SELECT statement without having to drop the view first. This also means you do not have to re-grant privileges to the view; the rights to the view are retained by those who have already been granted privileges.

LAB 12.1 EXERCISES

12.1.1   CREATE, ALTER, AND DROP VIEWS

a) Create a view called long_distance_student with all the columns in the student table plus the city and state columns from the zipcode table. Exclude students from New York, New Jersey, and Connecticut.

_____

_____

b) Create a view named cheap_course showing all columns of the course table where the course cost is 1095 or less.

_____

_____

c) Issue the INSERT statement below. What do you observe when you query the cheap_course view?

```
INSERT INTO cheap_course
  (course_no, description, cost,
   created_by, created_date, modified_by,
   modified_date)
VALUES
  (900, 'Expensive', 2000,
   'ME', SYSDATE, 'ME', SYSDATE)
```

_____

_____

d) Drop the views named long_distance_student and cheap_course.

_____

_____

e) Using the following statement, create a table called test_tab, and build a view over it. Then, add a column to the table and attempt to access the view. What do you observe? Drop the table and view after you complete the exercise.

```
CREATE TABLE test_tab
  (col1 NUMBER)
```

_____

_____

12.1.2   UNDERSTAND THE DATA MANIPULATION RULES FOR VIEWS

a) Create a view called busy_student based on the following query. Update the number of enrollments for student id 124 to five through the busy student view. Record your observation.

```
SELECT student_id, COUNT(*)
  FROM enrollment
 GROUP BY student_id
HAVING COUNT(*) > 2
```

_____

_____

b) Create a view listing the addresses of students. Include the columns student_id, first_name, last_name, street_address, city, state, and zip. Using the view, update the last name of student_id 237 from Frost to O'Brien. Then, update the state for the student from NJ to CT. What do you notice for the statements you issue?

_____

_____

LAB 12.1 EXERCISE ANSWERS

12.1.1 ANSWERS

a) Create a view called long_distance_student with all the columns in the student table plus the city and state columns from the zipcode table. Exclude students from New York, New Jersey, and Connecticut.

Answer: To select all columns from the student table, use the wildcard symbol. For the columns city and state in the view, join to the zipcode table. With this view definition you see only records where the state is not equal to New York, Connecticut, or New Jersey.

```
CREATE OR REPLACE VIEW long_distance_student AS
SELECT s.*, city, state
  FROM student s, zipcode z
 WHERE s.zip = z.zip
   AND state NOT IN ('NJ','NY','CT')
View created.
```

You can issue a query against the view or DESCRIBE the view. As you observe, you can restrict the columns and/or the rows of the view.

```
SELECT state, first_name, last_name
  FROM long_distance_student
ST FIRST_NAME                   LAST_NAME
-- ------------------------    -----------
MA James E.                     Norman
MA George                       Kocka
...
OH Phil                         Gilloon
MI Roger                        Snow

10 rows selected.
```

You might want to validate the view by querying for students living in New Jersey.

```
SELECT *
  FROM long_distance_student
 WHERE state = 'NJ'

no rows selected
```

As you see, there are none because the view's defining query excludes these records.

b) Create a view named cheap_course showing all columns of the course table where the course cost is 1095 or less.

Answer: The view restricts the rows to courses with a cost of 1095 or less.

```
CREATE OR REPLACE VIEW cheap_course AS
SELECT *
  FROM course
 WHERE cost <= 1095
```

c) Issue the INSERT statement below. What do you observe when you query the cheap_course view?

```
INSERT INTO cheap_course
  (course_no, description, cost,
   created_by, created_date, modified_by,
   modified_date)
VALUES
  (900, 'Expensive', 2000,
   'ME', SYSDATE, 'ME', SYSDATE)
```

Answer: You can insert records through the view, violating the view's defining query condition.

A cost of 2000 is successfully inserted into the course table through the view, even though this is higher than 1095, which is the defining condition of the view.

You can query the cheap_view to see if the record is there. The course was successfully inserted in the course table, but it does not satisfy the view's definition.

```
SELECT course_no, cost
  FROM cheap_course
COURSE_NO        COST
---------  ---------
      135       1095
      230       1095
      240       1095

3 rows selected.
```

A view's WHERE clause works for any query, but not for DML statements. The course number 900 is not visible through the cheap_course view, but insert, update, or delete operations are permitted despite the conflicting WHERE condition. To change this security-defying behavior, create the view with the WITH CHECK OPTION constraint. But first undo the INSERT statement with the ROLLBACK command, because any subsequent DDL command, such as the creation of a view, automatically commits the record.

```
ROLLBACK
```
Rollback complete.

```
CREATE OR REPLACE VIEW cheap_course AS
SELECT *
  FROM course
 WHERE cost <= 1095
WITH CHECK OPTION CONSTRAINT check_cost
```
View created.

It is a good habit to name constraints. You understand the benefit of well-named constraints when you query the Oracle data dictionary, or when you violate constraints with data manipulation statements.

The following error message appears when inserts, updates, and deletes issued against a view violate the view's defining query. The previous INSERT statement would now be rejected with the error message below.

ORA-01402: view WITH CHECK OPTION where-clause violation

What happens if you attempt to insert a record with a value of NULL for the course cost? Again, Oracle rejects the row because the condition is not satisfied. The NULL value is not less than or equal to 1095.

d) Drop the views named long_distance_student and cheap_course.

Answer: Just like other operations on data objects, the DROP keyword removes a database object from the database.

```
DROP VIEW long_distance_student
```
View dropped.

```
DROP VIEW cheap_course
```
View dropped.

Remember, any DDL operation, such as the creation of a view, cannot be rolled back, and any prior DML operations, such as inserts, updates, and deletes are automatically committed.

e) Using the following statement, create a table called test_tab, and build a view over it. Then, add a column to the table and attempt to access the view. What do you observe? Drop the table and view after you complete the exercise.

```
CREATE TABLE test_tab
  (col1 NUMBER)
```

Answer: The view becomes invalid after the underlying table is altered.

```
CREATE OR REPLACE VIEW test_tab_view AS
SELECT *
  FROM test_tab
View created.
```

After the table creation, the view is created. Here, the name test_tab_view is used. Then add an additional column to the table; here it is named col2.

```
ALTER TABLE test_tab
  ADD (col2 NUMBER)
Table altered.
```

You would expect the SQL*Plus DESCRIBE command on the view to show the additional column, but it shows an error. Whenever there is any database change to the underlying base table, the view becomes invalid.

```
DESC test_tab_view
ERROR:
ORA-24372: invalid object for describe
```

The next time you attempt to access the view through a SQL statement, not a SQL*Plus statement such as DESCRIBE, Oracle automatically attempts to revalidate the view by *compiling* it. Access the view by issuing a SELECT statement against it to see if it causes any errors.

```
SELECT *
  FROM test_tab_view

no rows selected
```

You can explicitly issue the COMPILE command to make sure the view is valid. The command to compile is:

```
ALTER VIEW test_tab_view COMPILE
```
View altered.

A subsequently issued DESCRIBE of the view reveals another interesting fact.

```
DESC test_tab_view
```

Name	Null?	Type
COL1		NUMBER

Where is the new column that was added? Whenever a view is created with the wildcard (*) character, Oracle stores the individual column names in the definition of the view. Altering the table by adding or dropping columns invalidates the view. In this case, the view is automatically recompiled and working, but the new column is missing. You need to re-issue the creation of the view statement for the view to include the new column.

```
CREATE OR REPLACE VIEW test_tab_view AS
SELECT *
  FROM test_tab
```
View created.

Now, when DESCRIBE is issued on the view, the new column is included.

```
DESC test_tab_view
```

Name	Null?	Type
COL1		NUMBER
COL2		NUMBER

Drop the no longer needed table and notice the effect on the view.

```
DROP TABLE test_tab
```
Table dropped.

```
ALTER VIEW test_tab_view COMPILE
```
Warning: View altered with compilation errors.

Oracle invalidates the view because the base table no longer exists. Any subsequent attempt to access the view or to compile it returns an error.

```
SELECT *
  FROM test_tab_vicw
ERROR at line 2:
ORA-04063: view "STUDENT.TEST_TAB_VIEW" has errors
```

Drop the view to restore the student schema to its previous state.

```
DROP VIEW test_tab_view
View dropped.
```

12.1.2 ANSWERS

a) Create a view called busy_student based on the following query. Update the number of enrollments for student id 124 to five through the busy_student view. Record your observation.

```
SELECT student_id, COUNT(*)
  FROM enrollment
 GROUP BY student_id
HAVING COUNT(*) > 2
```

Answer: The UPDATE operation fails. Data manipulation operations on a view impose a number of restrictions.

To create the view, you need to give the COUNT(*) expression a column alias; otherwise, this error occurs:

```
ERROR at line 2:
ORA-00998: must name this expression with a column alias
```

```
CREATE OR REPLACE VIEW busy_student AS
SELECT student_id, COUNT(*) enroll_num
  FROM enrollment
 GROUP BY student_id
HAVING COUNT(*) > 2
View created.
```

This SQL statement shows an alternate syntax for naming columns in a view.

```
CREATE OR REPLACE VIEW busy_student
     (student_id, enroll_num) AS
SELECT student_id, COUNT(*)
  FROM enrollment
```

```
 GROUP BY student_id
HAVING COUNT(*) > 2
```

You can now attempt to update the enrollment table using the view with the UPDATE statement below.

```
UPDATE busy_student
   SET enroll_num = 5
 WHERE student_id = 124
```
ORA-01732: data manipulation operation not legal on this view

For a view to be updateable it needs to conform to a number of rules: The view may not contain an expression, aggregate function, set operator, DISTINCT keyword, GROUP BY clause, or ORDER BY clause. Columns containing an expression are also not updateable. That is, no insert, update, or delete operation is permitted that references the column. Special rules apply to views containing join conditions, as you see in the next exercise.

b) Create a view listing the addresses of students. Include the columns student_id, first_name, last_name, street_address, city, state, and zip. Using the view, update the last name of student_id 237 from Frost to O'Brien. Then, update the state for the student from NJ to CT. What do you notice for the statements you issue?

Answer: Not all updates to views containing joins are allowed.

For a join view to be updateable, the DML operation may affect only the child base table, and the child's primary key must be included in the view's definition. In this case, the child table is the student table and the primary key is the student_id.

```
CREATE OR REPLACE VIEW student_address AS
SELECT student_id, first_name, last_name,
       street_address, city, state, s.zip szip,
       z.zip zzip
  FROM student s, zipcode z
 WHERE s.zip=z.zip
```
View created.

Now update the last name to O'Brien with the following statement.

```
UPDATE student_address
   SET last_name = 'O''Brien'
 WHERE student_id = 237
```
1 row updated.

To indicate a single quote, prefix the single quote with another single quote. See Chapter 13, "The Data Dictionary and Dynamic SQL Scripts" for more examples.

Since the test was successful, rollback the UPDATE in order to retain the current data in the table.

```
ROLLBACK
```
Rollback complete.

As you can see, you are able to update the child table student. Now update the column state in the parent table zipcode.

```
UPDATE student_address
   SET state = 'CT'
 WHERE student_id = 237
```
ORA-01779: cannot modify a column which maps to a nonkey-preserved table

The understanding of a key-preserved table is essential to understanding the restrictions on join views. A table is considered key-preserved if every key of the table can also be a key of the result of the join. In this case, the student table is the key-preserved or child table. If you are in doubt which table is the key-preserved table, query the Oracle data dictionary table user_updatable_columns. The result shows you which columns are updateable. Also, note the student table's zip column is updateable, but not the zip column from the zipcode table. Only the student's zip code is considered key-preserved.

```
SELECT column_name, updatable
  FROM user_updatable_columns
 WHERE table_name = 'STUDENT_ADDRESS'
```

COLUMN_NAME	UPD
STUDENT_ID	YES
FIRST_NAME	YES
LAST_NAME	YES
STREET_ADDRESS	YES
CITY	NO
STATE	NO
SZIP	YES
ZZIP	NO

8 rows selected.

The data dictionary is covered in greater detail in Chapter 13.

LAB 12.1 SELF-REVIEW QUESTIONS

In order to test your progress, you should be able to answer the following questions.

1) Views are useful for security and to simplify the writing of queries.

    a) _____ True

    b) _____ False

2) Under what circumstances can views become invalid? Check all that apply.

    a) _____ The datatype of a column changes.

    b) _____ The underlying table(s) are dropped.

    c) _____ Views never become invalid, they automatically recompile.

3) Identify the error in the view definition below.

```
CREATE OR REPLACE VIEW my_student
      (studid, slname, szip) AS
SELECT student_id, last_name, zip
  FROM student
 WHERE student_id BETWEEN 100 AND 200
```

    a) _____ Line 1

    b) _____ Line 2

    c) _____ Line 4

    d) _____ Line 1, 2, 4

    e) _____ No error

4) A view may contain an ORDER BY statement.

    a) _____ True

    b) _____ False

5) An UPDATE to the state column in the zipcode table is permitted using the following view.

```
CREATE OR REPLACE VIEW my_zipcode AS
SELECT zip, city, state, created_by,
      created_date, modified_by,
      TO_CHAR(modified_date, 'DD-MON-YYYY') modified_date
  FROM zipcode
```

    a) _____ True

    b) _____ False

Quiz answers appear in Appendix A, Section 12.1.

L A B   1 2 . 2

INDEXES

LAB OBJECTIVES

After this lab, you will be able to:

✔ Create B-Tree Indexes
✔ Understand When Indexes Are Useful

To achieve good performance for data retrieval and data manipulation statements, you need to understand Oracle's use of indexes. Just like the index in the back of a book, Oracle uses indexes to look up data quickly. If the appropriate index does not exist on a table, Oracle needs to examine every row. This is called a *full table scan*.

If the index speeds up query time, you may wonder why not just index every column in the table? When you retrieve a large number of rows in a table, it may be more efficient to read the entire table rather than look up the values from the index. It also takes a significant amount of time and storage space to build and maintain an index. For each DML statement that changes a value in an indexed column, the index needs to be maintained. Therefore, you only want to index columns frequently used in the WHERE clause of SQL statements, as well as foreign key columns. Oracle automatically creates a unique index to enforce the primary key constraint and the unique constraint.

Oracle provides two popular types of indexes, B-tree indexes and bitmapped indexes.

The B-tree (balanced tree) index is by far the most common type of index, and it is used throughout this workbook. It performs best when there are many distinct values on a column or columns. If you have several *low-selectivity* columns, you can also consider combining them into one *composite index,* also called a *concatenated index.*

A bitmapped index is typically used on columns with a very low selectivity, that is, columns with very few distinct values. For example, a column like gender, with four distinct values of female, male, unknown, and not applicable (in case of a legal entity such as a corporation) in a table with a million rows has a very low selectivity. This column is a good candidate for a bitmapped index.

■ FOR EXAMPLE

To find all the classes held in location L206, write the following query.

```
SELECT course_no, section_no, start_date_time, location
  FROM section
 WHERE location = 'L206'
COURSE_NO SECTION_NO START_DAT LOCATION
--------- ---------- --------- --------
      120          2 24-JUL-99 L206

1 row selected.
```

Because there is no index on the column location, Oracle reads every record to determine if any row in the location column is equal to the value L206. Generally, this takes some time, particularly if the table has many records. To speed up the query retrieval, create an index on the column location.

```
CREATE INDEX sect_location_i
  ON section(location)
Index created.
```

Even when you create an index on one or multiple columns of a table, Oracle may not be able to use it. This is the case if you modify a column with a function, as in the following SQL query.

```
SELECT course_no, section_no, start_date_time, location
  FROM section
 WHERE UPPER(location) = 'L206'
```

However, starting in Oracle version 8.1, columns modified by functions can use indexes if you create a function-based index instead, as in the following example.

```
CREATE INDEX sect_location_i
  ON section(UPPER(location))
```

For function-based indexes to work, you must also set two Oracle initialization parameters in the oracle.ini file. Alternatively, you can

Issue two ALTER SESSION commands in SQL*Plus: ALTER SESSION SET query_rewrite enabled = TRUE and ALTER SESSION SET query_rewrite_integrity = TRUSTED.

To drop an index, use the DROP INDEX command.

```
DROP INDEX sect_location_i
```
Index dropped.

The Whole Truth

To optimize performance, you typically separate indexes from data by placing them in separate *tablespaces* residing on different physical drives. To create an index and place it in a tablespace called index_tx use the following syntax:

```
CREATE INDEX sect_location_i
  ON section(location)
    TABLESPACE index_tx
```

In Chapter 16, "SQL Optimization," you learn to verify that SQL statements issued actually use an index.

THE ROWID PSEUDOCOLUMN

Every row in the database has a unique address called the ROWID. The address determines exactly where the row is located. Indexes store the ROWID to retrieve rows quickly. The ROWID consists of several components: the data object number, the number of the *data block* of the file, the number of rows within the data block, and the *data file* number. The data block and the data file define the physical storage characteristics of data in the Oracle database.

```
SELECT ROWID, student_id, last_name
  FROM student
 WHERE student_id = 123
```
ROWID   STUDENT_ID LAST_NAME
------------------- ---------- ---------
AAADA1AABAAARAIAAD   123 Radicola

1 row selected.

The ROWID is unique, and the fastest way to access a row. You can use the ROWID in update statements to directly access the row, rather than searching the index. For example, since the ROWID of the student named Radicola is already selected, an update to the name of the student can find the row in the table immediately without having to scan the entire table or use an index.

```
UPDATE student
   SET last_name = 'Radicolament'
 WHERE student_id = 12
   AND ROWID = 'AAADA1AABAAARAIAAD'
   AND last_name = 'Radicola'
```

It is also good practice to include the old values in the WHERE clause of the UPDATE to ensure that another session or user has not changed the name in the meantime.

Note: Never use the ROWID as a table's primary key, because a ROWID may change if you delete and reinsert a row; you cannot update the ROWID.

A *pseudocolumn* is not an actual column, but it acts like one. You learn about other Oracle pseudocolumns, namely NEXTVAL, CURRVAL, ROWNUM, and LEVEL shortly.

At times you may want to enforce a unique combination of the values in a table, for example, the course_no and section_no columns. You can create a unique constraint on the table which automatically creates a unique index, or use the CREATE UNIQUE INDEX command. Oracle recommends using a constraint and not using the CREATE UNIQUE INDEX syntax.

LAB 12.2 EXERCISES

12.2.1 CREATE B-TREE INDEXES

a) Create an index on the phone column of the student table. Drop the index after you successfully create it to return the student schema to its original state.

_____

_____

b) Create a composite index on the first and last name columns of the student table. Drop the index when you have finished.

c) Create an index on the description column of the course table. Note that queries against the table often use the UPPER function. Drop the index after you successfully create it.

d) Execute the following SQL statements. Explain the reason for the error.

```
CREATE TABLE test (col1 NUMBER)
CREATE INDEX test_col1_i ON test(col1)
DROP TABLE test
DROP INDEX test_col1_i
```

12.2.2 UNDERSTAND WHEN INDEXES ARE USEFUL

a) Would you create a B-tree index on a frequently accessed column with few distinct values? Explain.

b) List the advantages and disadvantages of indexes on performance.

c) Assume an index exists on the column enroll_date in the enrollment table. Change the following query so it uses the index.

```
SELECT student_id, section_id,
       TO_CHAR(enroll_date,'DD-MON-YYYY')
  FROM enrollment
 WHERE TO_CHAR(enroll_date,'DD-MON-YYYY') = '12-MAR-1999'
```

LAB 12.2 EXERCISE ANSWERS

12.2.1 ANSWERS

a) Create an index on the phone column of the student table. Drop the index after you successfully create it to return the student schema to its original state.

Answer: To create the index on the table, issue a CREATE INDEX statement.

```
CREATE INDEX stu_phone_i
  ON student(phone)
Index created.
```

Include the name of the table and the indexed column(s) in the index name; this allows you to identify the indexed columns in a particular table without querying the data dictionary. But remember, no database object's name, such as an index, may be longer than 30 characters.

To drop the index, simply issue the DROP INDEX command.

```
DROP INDEX stu_phone_i
Index dropped.
```

b) Create a composite index on the first and last name columns of the student table. Drop the index when you have finished.

Answer: There are two possible solutions for creating a composite index using the first and last name columns.

A composite or concatenated index is an index that consists of more than one column. Depending on how you access the table, you need to order the columns in the index accordingly.

To determine the best column order in the index, determine the selectivity of each column. That means determining how many distinct values each column has. You also need to determine what types of queries to write against the table. All this information helps you choose the best column order for the index.

SOLUTION 1: THE INDEX IS CREATED IN THE ORDER FIRST_NAME, LAST_NAME.

```
CREATE INDEX stu_first_last_name_i
  ON student(first_name, last_name)
```

This index is used in a SQL statement only if you refer to *both* columns or only the first_name column in a WHERE clause. Oracle can access the index only if the WHERE clause lists the *leading column* of the index. The leading column, also called the *leading edge*, of the above index is the first_name column. If the WHERE clause in a SQL statement lists only the last_name column, the SQL statement cannot access the index. For example, the following two WHERE clauses do *not* use the index.

```
WHERE last_name = 'Smith'
WHERE last_name LIKE 'Sm%'
```

SOLUTION 2: THE INDEX IS CREATED IN THE ORDER LAST_NAME, FIRST_NAME. THE LAST_NAME COLUMN IS THE LEADING COLUMN OF THE INDEX.

```
CREATE INDEX stu_last_first_name_i
  ON student(last_name, first_name)
```

This index is used in a SQL statement if you query *both* columns or only the last_name column. If a WHERE clause in a SQL statement lists only the first_name column, Oracle does not use the index because it is not the leading column of the index.

COMPOSITE INDEXES VERSUS INDIVIDUAL INDEXES

An alternative to the composite index is to create two separate indexes: one for the first_name and one for the last_name column.

```
CREATE INDEX stu_first_name_i
  ON student(first_name)
```
Index created.

```
CREATE INDEX stu_last_name_i
  ON student(last_name)
```
Index created.

A SQL statement with one of the columns in the WHERE clause typically uses the appropriate index. In the case where both columns are used in the WHERE clause, Oracle typically merges the two indexes together to retrieve the rows. You may wonder, Why, then, have concatenated indexes at all? A composite index outperforms individual column indexes, provided all the columns are referenced in the WHERE clause.

The database designer, together with the application developer, decides how to structure the indexes to make them most useful, based on the SQL statements issued. To verify that Oracle actually uses the index you can look at the *explain plan* of the SQL statement. This topic is covered in Chapter 16.

■ FOR EXAMPLE

Assume that on a given table you create a composite index on columns A, B, and C in this order. To make use of the index, specify in the WHERE clause either column A, or columns A and B, or columns A, B, and C, or A and C. Queries listing column C only, or B only, or B and C only do not use the index. You always need to specify the leading column of the index for Oracle to find the index entry. To determine the best order, think about the types of queries issued and the selectivity of each column. The following three indexes cover all the query possibilities of at least one of the columns. The leading column always varies and, therefore, covers all the possibilities with the least amount of storage and the best overall performance.

```
CREATE INDEX test_table_a_b_c ON test_table(a, b, c)
CREATE INDEX test_table_b_c ON test_table(b, c)
CREATE INDEX test_table_c ON test_table(c)
```

NULLS AND INDEXES

NULL values are only stored in composite indexes where at least the first column of the index contains a value. The following query does not make use of the index on the first_name column.

```
SELECT student_id, first_name
  FROM student
 WHERE first_name IS NULL
```

c) Create an index on the description column of the course table. Note that queries against the table often use the UPPER function. Drop the index after you successfully create it.

Answer: A function-based index is created on the description column.

```
CREATE INDEX crse_description_i
  ON course(UPPER(description))
```

A function-based index stores the indexed values and uses the index based on the following SELECT statement, which retrieves the course number for the course called Hands-On Windows. If you don't know in what case the description was entered into the course table, you may want to apply the UPPER function to the column.

```
SELECT course_no, description
  FROM course
 WHERE UPPER(description) = 'HANDS-ON WINDOWS'
```

Any queries modifying a column with a function in the WHERE clause do not make use of an index unless you create a function-based index.

An index like the following cannot be used for the previously issued SQL statement.

```
CREATE INDEX crse_description_i
  ON course(description)
```

To restore the schema to its previous state, drop the index.

```
DROP INDEX crse_description_i
```
Index dropped.

d) Execute the following SQL statements. Explain the reason for the error.

```
CREATE TABLE test (col1 NUMBER)
CREATE INDEX test_col1_i on test(col1)
DROP TABLE test
DROP INDEX test_col1_i
```

Answer: Dropping a table automatically drops any associated index. There is no need to drop the index separately.

```
DROP INDEX test_col1_i
            *
```
ERROR at line 1:
ORA-01418: specified index does not exist

**LAB
12.2**

a) Would you create a B-tree index on a frequently accessed column with few distinct values? Explain.

Answer: It may be advantageous to create a B-tree index even on a low-selectivity column.

Assume you have an employee table with a column named gender that you consider indexing. Also assume that 90% of your employees are male and 10% female. You frequently query for female employees. In this case, the index is helpful and improves the performance of your query. A query for male employees might also access the index, even though a full table scan of the table is more efficient than looking up all the values in the index.

b) List the advantages and disadvantages of indexes on performance.

Answer: Advantages: Adding an index on a table increases the performance of SQL statements using the indexed column(s) in the WHERE clause, provided only a small percentage of the rows are accessed. Should you access many rows in the table, accessing the entire table via a full table scan probably yields better performance. Disadvantages: Adding indexes may increase the time required for insert, update, and delete operations. Indexes also require additional disk space.

Periodically, you need to rebuild indexes to compact the data and balance the index tree. This is particularly important after data is subject to a large number of DML operations. Oracle provides the index rebuild option.

```
ALTER INDEX stu_zip_fk_i REBUILD
Index altered.
```

When you load or update large amounts of data, you may want to consider dropping certain indexes to improve the performance of the load. After the operation is complete, recreate the indexes.

c) Assume an index exists on the column enroll_date in the enrollment table. Change the following query so it uses the index.

```
SELECT student_id, section_id,
       TO_CHAR(enroll_date,'DD-MON-YYYY')
  FROM enrollment
 WHERE TO_CHAR(enroll_date,'DD-MON-YYYY') = '12-MAR-1999'
```

Answer: When you modify an indexed column with a function, such as the function TO_CHAR in the WHERE clause, the SQL statement is not able to access the index. The exception is when you create a function-based index on the column.

```
SELECT student_id, section_id,
       TO_CHAR(enroll_date,'DD-MON-YYYY')
  FROM enrollment
 WHERE enroll_date = TO_DATE('12-MAR-1999','DD-MON-YYYY')
```

In this case you do not need a function-based index. The SQL statement is changed so it does not modify the indexed column with a function. Refer to Chapter 4, "Date and Conversion Functions," about the dangers of using TO_CHAR with a DATE column in the WHERE clause.

LAB 12.2 SELF-REVIEW QUESTIONS

In order to test your progress, you should be able to answer the following questions.

1) For the following query, choose which index(es), if any, probably yield the best performance.

```
SELECT student_id, last_name, employer, phone
  FROM student
 WHERE employer = 'FGIC'
   AND phone = '201-555-5555'
```

    a) _____ Index on employer
    b) _____ Index on phone
    c) _____ Index in the order employer, phone
    d) _____ Index in the order phone, employer
    e) _____ No index

2) You should always index as many columns as possible.
    a) _____ True
    b) _____ False

3) Frequently queried columns and foreign keys should almost always be indexed.
    a) _____ True
    b) _____ False

4) Disabling a primary key or unique constraint drops the unique index.
    a) _____ True
    b) _____ False

5) The following query uses the index on the zip column of the instructor table.

```
SELECT instructor_id, last_name, first_name, zip
  FROM instructor
 WHERE zip IS NULL
```

    a) _____ True
    b) _____ False

6) The following SQL statement benefits from an index on the column instructor_id.

```
UPDATE instructor
   SET phone = '212-555-1212'
 WHERE instructor_id = 123
```

      a) _____ True

      b) _____ False

Quiz answers appear in Appendix A, Section 12.2.

L A B   1 2 . 3

SEQUENCES

LAB OBJECTIVES

After this lab, you will be able to:

✔   Create and Use Sequences

Sequences are Oracle database objects allowing you to generate unique integers. Recall the student table with the primary key column student_id. The value of student_id is a synthetic key generated from a sequence. This key is useful to the system but usually has no meaning for the user, is not subject to changes, and is never NULL.

Assume a student is uniquely identified by the first name, last name, and address. These columns are also called the *alternate key*. If you choose these columns as the primary key, imagine a scenario where a student's name or address changes. This requires a large amount of updates in many tables because all the foreign key columns need to be changed, involving a lot of customized programming. Instead, a synthetic column is created and populated by a sequence. This synthetic key is not subject to change and the users rarely see this column.

Sequences assure that no user gets the same value from the sequence, thus guaranteeing unique values. Sequences are typically incremented by 1, but other increments can be specified. You can also start sequences at a specific number.

Because you still need to enforce your users' business rule and prevent duplicate student entries, consider creating a unique constraint on the alternate key.

■ FOR EXAMPLE

To create a sequence named student_id_seq_new, issue the CREATE SEQUENCE command.

```
CREATE SEQUENCE student_id_seq_new START WITH 1 NOCACHE
```
Sequence created.

> To base the name of the sequence on the name of the column for which you want to use it is helpful for identification, but it does not associate the sequence with a particular column or table. The START WITH clause starts the sequence with the number 1. The NOCACHE keyword indicates the sequence numbers should not be kept in memory, so that if the system crashes you will not lose any cached numbers. However, losing numbers is not a reason for concern because there are many more available from the sequence. It is useful to leave the sequence numbers in the cache only if you access the sequence frequently.

> To increment the sequence and display the unique number, use the NEXTVAL *pseudocolumn*. The following SQL statement takes the next value from the sequence. Because the sequence was just created and starts with the number 1, it takes the number 1 as the first available value.

```
SELECT student_id_seq_new.NEXTVAL
   FROM dual
```
NEXTVAL
```
----------
          1
```

1 row selected.

> Typically, you use NEXTVAL in INSERT and UPDATE statements. To display the current value of the sequence after it is incremented, use the CURRVAL pseudocolumn.

LAB 12.3 EXERCISES

12.3.1 CREATE AND USE SEQUENCES

a) Describe the effects of the following SQL statement on the sequence section_id_seq.

```
INSERT INTO section
   (section_id, course_no, section_no,
    start_date_time, location,
    instructor_id, capacity, created_by,
    created_date, modified_by, modified_date)
```

```
VALUES
  (section_id_seq.NEXTVAL, 122, 5,
   TO_DATE('15-MAY-1999', 'DD-MON-YYYY'), 'R305',
   106, 10, 'ARISCHERT',
   SYSDATE, 'ARISCHERT', SYSDATE)
```

_____

_____

b) Write a SQL statement to increment the sequence student_id_
seq_new with NEXTVAL, and then issue a ROLLBACK command.
Determine the effect on the sequence number.

_____

_____

c) Drop the sequence student_id_seq_new.

_____

_____

LAB 12.3 EXERCISE ANSWERS

12.3.1 ANSWERS

a) Describe the effects of the following SQL statement on the sequence
section_id_seq.

```
INSERT INTO section
  (section_id, course_no, section_no,
   start_date_time, location,
   instructor_id, capacity, created_by,
   created_date, modified_by, modified_date)
VALUES
  (section_id_seq.NEXTVAL, 122, 5,
   TO_DATE('15-MAY-1999', 'DD-MON-YYYY'), 'R305',
   106, 10, 'ARISCHERT',
   SYSDATE, 'ARISCHERT', SYSDATE)
```

*Answer: The sequence is accessible from within an INSERT statement. The sequence
is incremented with the next value and this value is inserted in the table.*

b) Write a SQL statement to increment the sequence student_id_new_seq with NEXTVAL, and then issue a ROLLBACK command. Determine the effect on the sequence number.

Answer: Once a sequence is incremented the ROLLBACK command does not restore the number.

```
SELECT student_id_new_seq.NEXTVAL
  FROM dual
  NEXTVAL
---------
        2

1 row selected.


ROLLBACK
Rollback complete.


SELECT student_id_new_seq.NEXTVAL
  FROM dual
  NEXTVAL
---------
        3

1 row selected.
```

If there are any gaps in the primary key sequence numbers it really doesn't matter, because the numbers have no meaning to the user and there are many more numbers available from the sequence. One of the unique properties of sequences is no two users receive the same number.

c) Drop the sequence student_id_seq_new.

Answer: Just as with other database objects, you use the DROP command to drop a sequence.

```
DROP SEQUENCE student_id_seq_new
Sequence dropped.
```

LAB 12.3 SELF-REVIEW QUESTIONS

In order to test your progress, you should be able to answer the following questions.

1) Sequences are useful for generating unique values.
   a) _____ True
   b) _____ False

2) A student's social security number is a good choice for a primary key value instead of a sequence.
   a) _____ True
   b) _____ False

3) The default increment of a sequence is 1.
   a) _____ True
   b) _____ False

4) When you drop a table the associated sequence is also dropped.
   a) _____ True
   b) _____ False

5) The statement below creates a sequence employee_id_seq which starts at the number 1000.

```
CREATE SEQUENCE employee_id_seq START WITH 1000
```
   a) _____ True
   b) _____ False

Quiz answers appear in Appendix A, Section 12.3.

C H A P T E R   1 2

TEST YOUR THINKING

1) Who can update the salary column through the my_employee view? Hint: The USER function returns the name of the currently logged in user.

```
CREATE OR REPLACE VIEW my_employee AS
SELECT employee_id, employee_name, salary, manager
  FROM employee
 WHERE manager = USER
  WITH CHECK OPTION CONSTRAINT my_employee_ck_manager
```

2) Which columns in a table should you consider indexing?

3) Explain the purpose of the Oracle SQL command below.

```
ALTER INDEX crse_crse_fk_i rebuild
```

4) Are NULLs stored in an index? Explain.

C H A P T E R   1 3

THE DATA DICTIONARY AND DYNAMIC SQL SCRIPTS

CHAPTER OBJECTIVES	
In this chapter, you will learn about:	
✔ The Oracle Data Dictionary Views	Page 354
✔ Dynamic SQL Scripts	Page 370

The Oracle data dictionary is a set of tables and views that contains data about the database; it is also sometimes referred to as the *catalog*. The data dictionary is used internally by Oracle for many purposes, for example to determine if a SQL statement contains valid column and table names, or to determine the privileges of an individual user. It is very useful to query the data dictionary since it contains a wealth of information about the database.

Dynamic SQL scripts expand your knowledge of SQL*Plus and its capabilities as a SQL execution environment. In many situations you can simplify the writing of SQL statements and the administration of the database by writing SQL scripts that execute other SQL statements.

L A B   1 3 . 1

THE ORACLE DATA DICTIONARY VIEWS

LAB OBJECTIVES

After this lab, you will be able to:

✔ Query the Data Dictionary

The data dictionary has two distinct sets of views: the *static* data dictionary views and the *dynamic* data dictionary views, also referred to as dynamic performance views or as v$tables (V-Dollar tables).

The static data dictionary stores details about database objects, such as tables, indexes, and views. It also contains information about referential integrity constraints and indexed columns. Whenever a new object is added, or an object is changed, data about the object is recorded in the data dictionary.

Most of the static dictionary views begin with the prefix *user_*, *all_*, or *dba_*. The user_ views show information belonging to the user querying the data dictionary. For example, when you login as STUDENT, the views beginning with the user_ prefix show all the objects belonging to the STUDENT schema.

The all_ views show the same information, plus any information granted to the STUDENT user by another user, and public objects. You learn how to grant and receive access rights in Chapter 14, "Security." The dba_views show all objects, but you need DBA (database administrator) privileges to be able to query these views.

The dynamic views begin with v$ and are typically used by the database administrator to monitor the system. They are called dynamic because they are continuously updated by the database but never by the user.

The collection of the static and dynamic data dictionary tables and views, along with a description of each, is listed in the view called dictionary, also known as the *synonym* dict. A synonym is another name for a database object; instead of using dictionary, you can refer to its shorter synonym dict. You learn about synonyms and their use in Chapter 14. Take a look at the columns of the dict view by issuing the SQL*Plus DESCRIBE command.

```
DESC dict
Name                                Null?     Type
-------------------------------     --------  --------------
TABLE_NAME                                    VARCHAR2(30)
COMMENTS                                      VARCHAR2(4000)
```

The column table_name contains a list of all the individual data dictionary tables and views accessible to you, together with a brief description.

■ FOR EXAMPLE

To find information about sequences in the database, you can query the dict view. The column table_name stores the names of the data dictionary tables and views in uppercase. The following query results in all data dictionary views with the letters SEQ in their name.

```
SELECT table_name, comments
  FROM dict
 WHERE table_name LIKE '%SEQ%'
```

```
TABLE_NAME       COMMENTS
--------------   ------------------------------------------------
ALL_SEQUENCES    Description of SEQUENCEs accessible to the user
DBA_SEQUENCES    Description of all SEQUENCEs in the database
USER_SEQUENCES   Description of the user's own SEQUENCEs
SEQ              Synonym for USER_SEQUENCES

4 rows selected.
```

Four different data dictionary views contain information about sequences. Note that if you do not have DBA access privileges, you may not see the dba_sequences view. To display the columns of the seq view, issue the DESCRIBE command at the SQL*Plus prompt.

```
DESC SEQ
Name                              Null?     Type
------------------------------- -------- ---------
SEQUENCE_NAME                   NOT NULL VARCHAR2(30)
MIN_VALUE                                NUMBER
MAX_VALUE                                NUMBER
INCREMENT_BY                    NOT NULL NUMBER
CYCLE_FLAG                                VARCHAR2(1)
ORDER_FLAG                                VARCHAR2(1)
CACHE_SIZE                      NOT NULL NUMBER
LAST_NUMBER                     NOT NULL NUMBER
```

To find out which individual sequences are in the student schema, query the view.

```
SELECT sequence_name
  FROM seq
SEQUENCE_NAME
-------------------------------
COURSE_NO_SEQ
INSTRUCTOR_ID_SEQ
SECTION_ID_SEQ
STUDENT_ID_SEQ

4 rows selected.
```

If you are unclear about the meaning of the different columns in the seq view, query yet another view named dict_columns for a description of each column.

```
SELECT column_name, comments
  FROM dict_columns
 WHERE table_name = 'USER_SEQUENCES'
COLUMN_NAME       COMMENTS
---------------   ------------------------------------
SEQUENCE_NAME     SEQUENCE name
MIN_VALUE         Minimum value of the sequence
...
CACHE_SIZE        Number of sequence numbers to cache
LAST_NUMBER       Last sequence number written to disk

8 rows selected.
```

LAB 13.1 EXERCISES

13.1.1 QUERY THE DATA DICTIONARY

a) Execute the following SQL statement. Describe the result of the query, and name the different object types.

```
SELECT object_name, object_type
  FROM user_objects
```

_____

_____

b) Based on the user_objects view, what information is stored in the columns created, last_ddl_time, and status?

_____

_____

c) Name the data dictionary view listing tables only in the student schema.

_____

_____

d) Query the data dictionary view user_tab_columns for the section table and describe the information found in the columns data_type, data_length, nullable, and data_default.

_____

_____

e) Show a list of all indexes and their columns for the enrollment table.

_____

_____

f) Display a list of all the sequences in the student schema and the current value of each.

_____

_____

g) Execute the following two SQL statements. The first statement creates a view, the second queries the data dictionary view called user_views. What information is stored in the text column of user_views? Drop the view afterward.

```
CREATE OR REPLACE VIEW my_test AS
SELECT first_name, instructor_id
  FROM instructor

SELECT view_name, text
  FROM user_views
 WHERE view_name = 'MY_TEST'
```

_____

_____

h) Execute the following query. What do you observe?

```
SELECT constraint_name, table_name, constraint_type
  FROM user_constraints
```

_____

_____

i) What columns are listed in the data dictionary view user_cons_columns?

_____

_____

j) Execute the following SQL statement. Describe the result.

```
SELECT username
  FROM all_users
```

_____

_____

k) Execute the following query. What do you observe about the result?

```
SELECT segment_name, segment_type, bytes/1024
  FROM user_segments
 WHERE segment_name = 'STUDENT'
   AND segment_type = 'TABLE'
```

_____

_____

l) Describe the columns of the data dictionary view user_tab_privs.

_____

_____

LAB 13.1 EXERCISE ANSWERS

13.1.1 ANSWERS

a) Execute the following SQL statement. Describe the result of the query, and name the different object types.

```
SELECT object_name, object_type
  FROM user_objects
```

Answer: The query returns a list of all the objects owned by the current user. The object types listed are table, sequence, and index.

```
OBJECT_NAME                         OBJECT_TYPE
--------------------------------    -----------
COURSE                              TABLE
...
```

```
COURSE_NO_SEQ                    SEQUENCE
...
ZIP_PK                           INDEX
```

36 rows selected.

Depending on the objects created in your individual schema, you see different results. Most likely, you see a list of tables, indexes, and sequences, but the list can also include views, procedures, packages, functions, synonyms, triggers, and other object types.

The all_objects view is different from the user_objects view because it includes an additional column called owner. It identifies the name of the schema in which the object is stored. The user_objects view shows only those objects in the user's own schema.

The columns owner and object_name represent the unique identifier of the all_objects data dictionary view. There can be objects with the same name in other schemas, but within a schema, the object name has to be unique.

b) Based on the user_objects view, what information is stored in the columns created, last_ddl_time, and status?

Answer: The created column shows when an object was created in the schema. The last_ddl_time column indicates when an object was last modified via a Data Definition Language command, such as when a column was added to a table, or a view was recompiled. The status column indicates whether an object is valid or invalid.

The resulting output may vary depending on the objects in your schema.

```
SELECT object_name, created, last_ddl_time, status
  FROM user_objects
OBJECT_NAME              CREATED    LAST_DDL_  STATU
--------------------     ---------  ---------  -----
COURSE                   14-AUG-99  23-OCT-99  VALID
...
ZIP_PK                   14-AUG-99  14-AUG-99  VALID
```

36 rows selected.

A view may become invalid if the underlying table is modified or dropped. Other objects, such as PL/SQL procedures, packages, or functions may become invalid if dependent objects are modified, and these objects subsequently need to be recompiled.

If you are unclear about the meaning of a particular column, refer to the dict_columns view for information.

```
SELECT column_name, comments
  FROM dict_columns
 WHERE table_name = 'USER_OBJECTS'
   AND column_name IN ('STATUS', 'LAST_DDL_TIME',
                       'CREATED')
COLUMN_NAME         COMMENTS
-----------------   ----------------------------------
CREATED             Timestamp for the creation of the object
LAST_DDL_TIME       Timestamp for the last DDL change (including
                    GRANT and REVOKE) to the object
STATUS              Status of the object

3 rows selected.
```

c) Name the data dictionary view listing tables only in the student schema.

Answer: The view is user_tables.

```
SELECT table_name
  FROM user_tables
TABLE_NAME
-----   -----------
COURSE
...
ZIPCODE

10 rows selected.
```

d) Query the data dictionary view user_tab_columns for the grade table and describe the information found in the columns data_type, data_length, nullable, and data_default.

Answer: The column data_type shows the datatype of the column, data_length shows the length of the column in bytes, and there is either a 'Y' or 'N' in the column nullable indicating whether or not NULL values are allowed in the column. The column data_default shows the default value for the column, if any.

```
SELECT table_name, column_name, data_type, data_length,
       nullable, data_default
```

```
  FROM user_tab_columns
 WHERE table_name = 'GRADE'
```

TABLE_NA	COLUMN_NAME	DATA_TYP	DATA_LENGTH	N	DATA_
GRADE	STUDENT_ID	NUMBER	22	N	
...					
GRADE	NUMERIC_GRADE	NUMBER	22	N	0
...					
GRADE	MODIFIED_BY	VARCHAR2	30	N	
GRADE	MODIFIED_DATE	DATE	7	N	

10 rows selected.

Note the zero value in the last column named data_default. This means the column called numeric_grade has a column default value of zero. This value is inserted into a table's row if the numeric_grade column is not specified during an INSERT operation. For example, the following INSERT statement does not list the numeric_grade column and, therefore, the numeric_grade column is zero.

```
INSERT INTO GRADE
   (student_id, section_id, grade_type_code,
    grade_code_occurrence,
    created_by, created_date,
    modified_by, modified_date)
VALUES
   (102,89, 'FI',
    2,
    'ARISCHERT', SYSDATE,
    'ARISCHERT', SYSDATE)
```
1 row created.

e) Show a list of all indexes and their columns for the enrollment table.

Answer: The data dictionary view user_ind_columns lists the desired result.

```
SELECT index_name, table_name, column_name,
       column_position
  FROM user_ind_columns
 WHERE table_name = 'ENROLLMENT'
 ORDER BY 1, 4
```

INDEX_NAME	TABLE_NAME	COLUMN_NAM	COLUMN_POSITION
ENR_SECT_FK_I	ENROLLMENT	SECTION_ID	1
ENR_PK	ENROLLMENT	STUDENT_ID	1

```
ENR_PK              ENROLLMENT SECTION_ID                      2
```

3 rows selected.

The enrollment table has two indexes: enr_sect_fk_i and enr_pk. The first index consists of the column section_id. The second index, a unique index created by the primary key constraint, has the columns student_id and section_id in that order. The column_position shows the order of the columns within the index.

f) Display a list of all the sequences in the student schema and the current value of each.

Answer: The user_sequence data dictionary view shows the sequence name and the current value of the sequence.

The resulting output may vary depending on the sequences in your schema.

```
SELECT sequence_name, last_number
  FROM user_sequences
SEQUENCE_NAME                      LAST_NUMBER
-------------------------------- -----------
COURSE_NO_SEQ                              451
INSTRUCTOR_ID_SEQ                          111
SECTION_ID_SEQ                             157
STUDENT_ID_SEQ                             400
```

4 rows selected.

g) Execute the following two SQL statements. The first statement creates a view, the second queries the data dictionary view called user_views. What information is stored in the text column of user_views? Drop the view afterward.

```
CREATE OR REPLACE VIEW my_test AS
SELECT first_name, instructor_id
  FROM instructor

SELECT view_name, text
  FROM user_views
 WHERE view_name = 'MY_TEST'
```

Answer: The text column of the user_views data dictionary view stores the view's defining SQL statement.

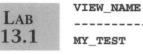

```
VIEW_NAME   TEXT
----------  --------------------------------
MY_TEST     SELECT first_name, instructor_id
              FROM instructor
```

1 row selected.

DROP VIEW my_test
View dropped.

From Chapter 12, "Views, Indexes, and Sequences," recall the definition of a view as a stored query. The query is stored in the column named text of user_views.

The text column in the user_views data dictionary is of the LONG datatype. By default, SQL*Plus does not display more than 80 characters of a LONG. You can increase this length with the SQL*Plus SET LONG command. You can also wrap whole words using the SQL*Plus FORMAT COLUMN command with the WORD_WRAPPED option.

h) Execute the following query. What do you observe?

```
SELECT constraint_name, table_name, constraint_type
  FROM user_constraints
```

Answer: The output shows the constraints on the various tables. The foreign key constraint is listed as constraint type R (Referential Integrity constraint), the NOT NULL and check constraints are shown as constraint type C, and the primary key constraints are displayed as constraint type P. The section table has a unique constraint listed as constraint type U.

CONSTRAINT_NAME	TABLE_NAME	C
CRSE_CRSE_FK	COURSE	R
...		
SYS_C001441	GRADE	C
ENR_STU_FK	ENROLLMENT	R
...		
SECT_SECT2_UK	SECTION	U
...		
ZIP_PK	ZIPCODE	P
...		
ZIP_MODIFIED_BY_NNULL	ZIPCODE	C

94 rows selected.

Note, any constraint not explicitly named receives a system-assigned name, such as the constraint called SYS_C001441.

The user_constraints view contains more useful columns in addition to the ones shown in the previous query, particularly for referential integrity constraints.

■ FOR EXAMPLE

Query the table for the foreign key constraint called enr_stu_fk. The foreign key constraint (constraint_type R) shows the name of the table and the primary key the foreign key value references. The constraint enr_stu_fk is enforced on the enrollment table and refers to the student table's primary key constraint named stu_pk.

```
SELECT r_owner, r_constraint_name, delete_rule
  FROM user_constraints
 WHERE constraint_name = 'ENR_STU_FK'
```

R_OWNER	R_CONSTRAINT_NAME	DELETE_RU
STUDENT	STU_PK	NO ACTION

1 row selected.

The delete rule on the enr_stu_fk constraint specifies NO ACTION, which means any delete of a student record (parent record) is prevented if dependent enrollment rows (child records with the same student_id) exist. This is in contrast to a CASCADE, which means if a parent record is deleted the children are automatically deleted.

The referential integrity constraints avoid the creation of orphan rows, meaning enrollment records without corresponding students. Also, the parent table may not be dropped unless the foreign key constraint is dropped. To disable constraints use the ALTER TABLE command. Alternatively, the parent table may be dropped using the DROP TABLE command with the CASCADE CONSTRAINTS clause, automatically dropping the foreign key constraints.

OTHER CONSTRAINT TYPES

In addition to the constraint types mentioned, Oracle lists additional constraint types in the data dictionary, if they are used. These are the view constraint with check option (V), and the view constraint with the read-only option (O).

i) What columns are listed in the data dictionary view user_cons_columns?

Answer: The columns are owner, constraint_name, table_name, column_name, and position.

This data dictionary view shows which columns are referenced in a constraint. A query against the view illustrates this by showing the primary key constraint enr_pk consisting of the two columns student_id and section_id.

```
SELECT constraint_name, column_name
  FROM user_cons_columns
 WHERE constraint_name = 'ENR_PK'
CONSTRAINT_NAME                 COLUMN_NAME
------------------------------- -----------
ENR_PK                          STUDENT_ID
ENR_PK                          SECTION_ID

2 rows selected.
```

j) Execute the following SQL statement. Describe the result.

```
SELECT username
  FROM all_users
```

Answer: It shows a list of all the users in the database.

The resulting output may vary, depending on your database.

```
USERNAME
---------------------------
SYS
SYSTEM
...
SCOTT
...
STUDENT

15 rows selected.
```

Note that there are two users named SYS and SYSTEM. The SYS user is the *owner* of the Oracle data dictionary. The default password for this user is typically change_on_install. This password should be changed as soon as the database installation is complete. Never log in as this "super user" unless you are an experienced Oracle DBA, or are instructed by Oracle to do so. Otherwise, you may inadvertently perform actions that could adversely affect the database. The SYSTEM user has DBA privileges, but does not own the data dictionary. Always change the default password, manager, to another password. Be sure to keep track of all these passwords.

Another useful view is the USER_USERS view. Following is a query displaying information about the current user or schema. It shows your login name and the name of the tablespace on which tables or indexes you create are stored, unless you explicitly specify another tablespace. It also shows when your account was created.

```
SELECT username, default_tablespace, created
  FROM user_users
```

USERNAME	DEFAULT_TABLESPACE	CREATED
STUDENT	USERS	14-AUG-99

1 row selected.

k) Execute the following query. What do you observe about the result?

```
SELECT segment_name, segment_type, bytes/1024
  FROM user_segments
 WHERE segment_name = 'STUDENT'
   AND segment_type = 'TABLE'
```

Answer: The query shows the size of the student table.

SEGMENT_NA	SEGMENT_TYPE	BYTES/1024
STUDENT	TABLE	60

1 row selected.

The most common segment types are tables and indexes. The user_segment table shows the storage in bytes for a particular segment. Dividing the bytes by 1024 displays the size in kilobytes (KB).

l) Describe the columns of the data dictionary view user_tab_privs.

Answer: The view shows the columns grantee, owner, table_name, grantor, privilege, and grantable. For a description of each column, query the dict_columns view.

```
SELECT column_name, comments
  FROM dict_columns
```

```
   WHERE table_name = 'USER_TAB_PRIVS'
COLUMN_NAM COMMENTS
---------- ----------------------------------------
GRANTEE    Name of the user to whom access was granted
OWNER      Owner of the object
TABLE_NAME Name of the object
GRANTOR    Name of the user who performed the grant
PRIVILEGE  Table Privilege
GRANTABLE  Privilege is grantable
```

6 rows selected.

If any grants were issued on any object to which you have access, such as SELECT, INSERT, UPDATE, DELETE, INDEX, REFERENCE or EXECUTE, you see the object listed in the data dictionary view user_tab_privs.

The REFERENCE privilege is used when you want to reference another user's table with a foreign key constraint. The INDEX privilege allows you to create indexes on tables owned by another user. The grantable column shows if you can grant the privilege to another user. For more information on granting and revoking privileges, see Chapter 14.

LAB 13.1 SELF-REVIEW QUESTIONS

In order to test your progress, you should be able to answer the following questions.

1) The data dictionary contains data about the database.
   a) _____ True
   b) _____ False

2) The data dictionary view user_objects stores information about tables, indexes, and sequences.
   a) _____ True
   b) _____ False

3) The dynamic data dictionary is updated only by the Oracle database.
   a) _____ True
   b) _____ False

4) The all_tables data dictionary view shows all the tables in the entire database.
   a) _____ True
   b) _____ False

5) The obj view is a public synonym for the user_objects view.
   a) _____ True
   b) _____ False

Quiz answers appear in Appendix A, Section 13.1.

L A B   1 3 . 2

DYNAMIC SQL SCRIPTS

LAB OBJECTIVES

After this lab, you will be able to:

✔ Write Dynamic SQL Statements
✔ Write Dynamic SQL Scripts

So far, you have executed many SQL statements in the SQL*Plus environment. In this lab, you learn how to write SQL statements that create and execute other SQL statements.

SQL*PLUS SUBSTITUTION VARIABLES

You probably find yourself executing the same command over and over again, sometimes just with slight modifications. Instead of editing the SQL statement each time, you can substitute part of the SQL statement with a *variable*. When the statement is executed, you supply the appropriate value for the variable.

■ *FOR EXAMPLE*

The variable in the following statement is named v_course_no. You identify a variable by prefixing an arbitrary variable name with an ampersand (&) symbol. When you execute the statement, SQL*Plus prompts you for a value and the supplied value is assigned to the variable.

```
SELECT course_no, description
  FROM course
 WHERE course_no = &v_course_no
Enter value for v_course_no: 204
old   3:   WHERE course_no = &v_course_no
new   3:   WHERE course_no = 204
```

```
COURSE_NO DESCRIPTION
--------- ------------------------------
      204 Intro to SQL
```

1 row selected.

If you want to re-execute the statement in the buffer, use the forward slash (/) and you are prompted for a value for the v_course_no substitution variable each time.

You can use a substitution variable in any SQL statement executed within the SQL*Plus environment, for example, against the data dictionary.

To determine if the name of a particular database object is valid, or to determine its type, you can execute a SQL statement against the data dictionary view user_objects. Instead of repeatedly editing the same statement, use a variable to substitute the value of the object.

```
SELECT object_name, object_type, status
  FROM obj
 WHERE object_name LIKE UPPER('&v_object_name')
Enter value for v_object_name: student
old    3:   WHERE object_name LIKE UPPER('&v_object_name')
new    3:   WHERE object_name LIKE UPPER('student')


OBJECT_NAME                     OBJECT_TYPE         STATUS
------------------------------- ------------------- ------
STUDENT                         TABLE               VALID
```

1 row selected.

To save the file, issue the SAVE command or save it in your text editor. You can then execute the file repeatedly with the START or the @ command.

GENERATE DYNAMIC SQL

Dynamic SQL allows you to execute SQL commands built at runtime. Dynamic SQL is often executed in Oracle's PL/SQL language, but can also be generated and executed in SQL*Plus using SQL*Plus scripts. These scripts are often referred to as *SQL To Generate SQL* scripts or *Master/Slave* scripts. Using SQL*Plus you can automatically generate SQL statements and spool them to a file for use. The SPOOL command captures all the output from the SQL*Plus prompt in a file.

For example, you made some database changes to tables, causing other database objects, such as views, to become invalid. To compile the views, you can repeatedly type the ALTER VIEW command for each invalid view, or you can wait for the user to access the views and let Oracle compile them. However, it is best to compile them after the table changes to make sure there are no errors. This is best achieved by writing a script to generate the ALTER VIEW statement for each invalid view. The following SQL statement generates the dynamic SQL.

```
SELECT 'ALTER VIEW '|| object_name || ' COMPILE;'
  FROM user_objects
 WHERE object_type = 'VIEW'
   AND status <> 'VALID'
```

If you have any invalid views, your result may look like this:

```
'ALTERVIEW'||OBJECT_NAME||'COMPILE;'
----------------------------------------
ALTER VIEW CAPACITY_V COMPILE;
ALTER VIEW CT_STUDENT_V COMPILE;
ALTER VIEW NJ_STUDENT_V COMPILE;
ALTER VIEW NY_STUDENT_V COMPILE;

4 rows selected.
```

The text literal or constant 'ALTER VIEW' is concatenated with the view name, and then with the text literal ' COMPILE ;'. You can spool the result into a file using the SPOOL command.

LAB 13.2 EXERCISES

13.2.1 WRITE DYNAMIC SQL STATEMENTS

a) Execute the following statements. What result do you see when you substitute the variable with the value `enr_pk`?

```
COL column_name FORMAT A20
COL owner FORMAT A10
COL constraint_name HEADING 'Constraint|Name' FORMAT A20
UNDEFINE vname
SELECT t.constraint_type, c.column_name,
       t.constraint_name, t.owner
  FROM all_constraints t, all_cons_columns c
 WHERE t.owner = c.owner
```

```
   AND t.constraint_name - c.constraint_name
   AND t.constraint_name LIKE UPPER('%&vname%')
ORDER BY position
```

b) Execute the SQL*Plus command `SET VERIFY OFF`. Reexecute the SQL statement from Exercise a by entering the forward slash. What do you observe?

c) Enter the following SQL statement into a text file named s_query.sql. Don't forget to end the statement with a semicolon or a forward slash on a separate line. Save the file and execute it at the SQL*Plus prompt with the command `@s_query 252`. What result do you see?

```
SELECT last_name, student_id
  FROM student
 WHERE student_id = &1
```

d) Execute the following SQL*Plus commands and the SQL statement which determines the maximum and minimum value of a column in a table. When prompted for the value of the vcol variable, enter the value `cost`, for the vtable variable enter `course`. Describe your observation about the SQL*Plus prompts.

```
UNDEFINE vcol
UNDEFINE vtable
SET VERIFY OFF
SELECT MIN(&vcol), MAX(&vcol)
  FROM &vtable
```

e) Enter all the following commands in a file named maxval.sql, then execute the script. For the column name supply the value `capacity`, and for the table name enter the value `section`. What do you observe?

```
PROMPT Determine the maximum and minimum value of a column
ACCEPT vcol CHAR PROMPT 'Enter the column name: '
ACCEPT vtable CHAR PROMPT 'Enter the corresponding table name: '
SET VERIFY OFF
SELECT MIN(&vcol), MAX(&vcol)
   FROM &vtable
```


13.2.2 WRITE DYNAMIC SQL SCRIPTS

The following SQL statement disables the foreign key constraint on the zip column of the student table.

```
ALTER TABLE student DISABLE CONSTRAINT stu_zip_fk
```

Disabling the constraint allows entering of child values where no corresponding parent exists. This means you can insert or update a zip code in the student table that does not have a corresponding value in the zipcode table. There are times when you want to disable constraints temporarily, such as when you must bulk load or update data quickly. Afterward you enable the constraints again. The following exercises show you how to disable and enable constraints using a dynamic SQL script.

a) Execute the following SQL statement to generate other SQL statements. What do you observe?

```
SELECT 'ALTER TABLE ' || table_name
  FROM user_constraints
 WHERE constraint_type = 'R'
```

---

b) Expand the SQL statement in Exercise a by adding the constraint name dynamically. The resulting output should look like this:

```
ALTER TABLE COURSE DISABLE CONSTRAINT CRSE_CRSE_FK;
...
ALTER TABLE SECTION DISABLE CONSTRAINT SECT_CRSE_FK;
ALTER TABLE SECTION DISABLE CONSTRAINT SECT_INST_FK;
ALTER TABLE STUDENT DISABLE CONSTRAINT STU_ZIP_FK;

11 rows selected.
```

c) Save the SQL statement in Exercise b to a file named disable_fk.sql. Add the following SQL*Plus statements at the beginning of the file. Note that the double dashes represent single line comments.

```
-- File Name: disable_fk.sql
-- Purpose: Disable Foreign Key constraints.
-- Created Date: Place current date here
-- Author: Put your name here
SET PAGESIZE 0
SET LINESIZE 80
SET FEEDBACK OFF
SET TERM OFF
SPOOL disable_fk.out
```

Add a semicolon at the end of the SQL statement and the following SQL*Plus commands afterward.

```
SPOOL OFF
SET PAGESIZE 20
SET LINESIZE 100
SET FEEDBACK ON
SET TERM ON
```

Save the file and run the disable_fk.sql file at the SQL*Plus prompt with the @ command. Describe the output from the spooled file named disable_fk.out.

d) Write a dynamic SQL script enabling the foreign key constraints.

_____

_____

e) Explain each line in the following SQL script and then describe the purpose of the script in one sentence.

```
01 /*
02 ------------------------------------------------
03 File name:   rows.sql
04 Purpose:
05 Created by:  H. Ashley on January 7, 2000
06 Modified by: A. Christa on September 29, 2001
07 ------------------------------------------------
08 */
09 SET TERM OFF
10 SET PAGESIZE 0
11 SET FEEDBACK OFF
12 SPOOL temp
13 SELECT 'SELECT ' || '''' || table_name || '''' ||
14        ', COUNT(*) '||CHR(10) ||
15        ' FROM '|| LOWER(table_name) || ';'
16   FROM user_tables;
17 SPOOL OFF
18 SET FEEDBACK 1
19 SET PAGESIZE 20
20 SET TERM ON
21 @temp.lst
22 HOST DEL temp.lst
```

_____

_____

LAB 13.2 EXERCISE ANSWERS

13.2.1 ANSWERS

a) Execute the following statements. What result do you see when you substitute the variable with the value `enr_pk`?

```
COL column_name FORMAT A20
```

```
COL owner FORMAT A10
COL constraint_name HEADING 'Constraint|Name' FORMAT A20
UNDEFINE vname
SELECT t.constraint_type, c.column_name,
       t.constraint_name, t.owner
  FROM all_constraints t, all_cons_columns c
 WHERE t.owner = c.owner
   AND t.constraint_name = c.constraint_name
   AND t.constraint_name LIKE UPPER('%&vname%')
 ORDER BY position
```

> *Answer: The old and new substitution values for the vname variable are displayed. After the value is entered, the SQL statement displays constraints with a similar name.*

The number 6, after the old and new values, represents the line number of the substitution variable within the SQL statement.

```
Enter value for vname: enr_pk
old   6:     AND t.constraint_name LIKE UPPER('%&vname%')
new   6:     AND t.constraint_name LIKE UPPER('%enr_pk%')


                          Constraint
C COLUMN_NAME             Name                  OWNER
- -------------------- -------------------- --------
P STUDENT_ID             ENR_PK                STUDENT
P SECTION_ID             ENR_PK                STUDENT

2 rows selected.
```

The result includes the constraint type; in this example it is the primary key constraint. Additionally, you see the individual primary key columns student_id and section_id. Also, note the substitution value can be entered in either lower or upper case; the UPPER function in the SQL statement converts it into upper case.

The query that provides this result joins the table constraints (all_constraints) and column constraints (all_cons_columns) via the owner and constraint_name columns. These two columns represent the unique identifier of the all_constraints view. Although a view cannot have a primary key or unique constraint, the view's underlying data dictionary tables have these columns as a unique identifier.

The UNDEFINE command deletes any previous reference to the vname SQL*Plus variable. A variable is typically defined when you explicitly use the DEFINE command, the ampersand (&), the double ampersand (&&),

or the ACCEPT command. You learn about the double ampersand and the ACCEPT command shortly. The value of the variable is retained until you UNDEFINE the variable, or use the variable with a single ampersand, or use the variable with the ACCEPT command, or exit SQL*Plus.

The SQL*Plus FORMAT command shows the use of the COL HEADING command. The vertical pipe permits splitting of a column name across multiple lines.

SUPPRESSING THE USE OF SUBSTITUTION VARIABLES

There are times when you don't want the ampersand to be an indicator in SQL*Plus that a substitution variable follows, but a literal ampersand instead.

■ FOR EXAMPLE

```
UPDATE student
   SET employer = 'Soehner & Peter'
 WHERE student_id = 135
Enter value for peter:
```

SQL*Plus thinks you want to use a substitution parameter rather than the literal ampersand. To remedy this, use the SET DEFINE command to turn the use of substitution parameters on or off.

```
SET DEFINE OFF
UPDATE student
   SET employer = 'Soehner & Peter'
 WHERE student_id = 135
1 row updated.
SET DEFINE ON
```

Lastly, issue a ROLLBACK command to undo the change of employer and set it back to the original value.

```
ROLLBACK
Rollback complete.
```

b) Execute the SQL*Plus command SET VERIFY OFF. Reexecute the SQL statement from Exercise a by entering the forward slash. What do you observe?

Answer: The VERIFY command suppresses the listing of the OLD and NEW substitution values.

Reset it back to its SQL*Plus default with the SET VERIFY ON command.

c)   Enter the following SQL statement into a text file named s_query.sql. Don't forget to end the statement with a semicolon or a forward slash on a separate line. Save the file and execute it at the SQL*Plus prompt with the command `@s_query 252`. What result do you see?

```
SELECT last_name, student_id
  FROM student
 WHERE student_id = &1
```

Answer: The result displays the last name of the student with the student_id of 252.

```
old    3:   WHERE student_id = &1
new    3:   WHERE student_id = 252


LAST_NAME                      STUDENT_ID
------------------------       ----------
Barogh                                252


1 row selected.
```

You can pass parameters (arguments) when running a script file in SQL*Plus. This works only if your substitution variable is a numeral. The &1 parameter is substituted with the first parameter passed; in this example with the value 252. If you include another parameter, such as &2, you can pass a second argument, and so on.

d)   Execute the following SQL*Plus commands and the SQL statement which determines the maximum and minimum value of a column in a table. When prompted for the value of the vcol variable, enter the value `cost`, for the vtable variable enter `course`. Describe your observation about the SQL*Plus prompts.

```
UNDEFINE vcol
UNDEFINE vtable
SET VERIFY OFF
SELECT MIN(&vcol), MAX(&vcol)
  FROM &vtable
```

*Answer: When a variable with the same name is preceded multiple times using an ampersand (&), SQL*Plus prompts you for each one.*

```
Enter value for vcol: cost
Enter value for vcol: cost
Enter value for vtable: course


MIN(COST) MAX(COST)
```

```
--------- ---------
     1095      1595
```

1 row selected.

To avoid being re-prompted, define the variable with a double ampersand (&&.)

```
UNDEFINE vcol
UNDEFINE vtable
SET VERIFY OFF
SELECT MIN(&&vcol), MAX(&&vcol)
  FROM &vtable
```
Enter value for vcol: cost
Enter value for vtable: course

```
MIN(COST) MAX(COST)
--------- ---------
     1095      1595
```

1 row selected.

Note that, until you exit SQL*Plus, the && variable is defined with the entered value, so any subsequent execution of the statement has the value for the variable vcol already defined without re-prompting. Another execution will now prompt only for the table name because the vtable variable has only one & symbol.

Enter value for vtable: section
SELECT MIN(cost), MAX(cost)
                     *

ERROR at line 1:
ORA-00904: invalid column name

The value section was entered as the table name, but the v_col variable retained the value cost, so the statement resulted in an error; the cost column is not a valid column on the section table. It can also be confusing to use the && if you forget you defined the variable because you are not prompted again. Undefine the vcol variable and rerun the statement.

```
UNDEFINE vcol
/
```
Enter value for vcol: capacity
Enter value for vtable: section

```
MIN(CAPACITY) MAX(CAPACITY)
------------- -------------
          10            25
```

1 row selected.

 To display the values defined and their associated values, use the DEFINE command.

e) Enter all the following commands in a file named maxval.sql, then execute the script. For the column name supply the value capacity, and for the table name enter the value section. What do you observe?

```
PROMPT Determine the maximum and minimum value of a column
ACCEPT vcol CHAR PROMPT 'Enter the column name: '
ACCEPT vtable CHAR PROMPT 'Enter the corresponding table name: '
SET VERIFY OFF
SELECT MIN(&vcol), MAX(&vcol)
  FROM &vtable
```

Answer: The PROMPT command prompts the user for input.

```
@maxval
```
Determine the maximum and minimum value of a column
Enter the column name: capacity
Enter the corresponding table name: section

```
MIN(CAPACITY) MAX(CAPACITY)
------------- -------------
          10            25
```

1 row selected.

Notice the ACCEPT SQL*Plus command defines a variable which can then be referenced with the ampersand symbol. The SQL*Plus ACCEPT command allows for datatype checking of the entered value. In this example, SQL*Plus verifies that the entered value is either a number or a character.

Other valid datatypes used with the ACCEPT command are NUMBER and DATE.

13.2.2 ANSWERS

a) Execute the following SQL statement to generate other SQL statements. What do you observe?

```
SELECT 'ALTER TABLE ' || table_name
  FROM user_constraints
 WHERE constraint_type = 'R'
```

Answer: The statement generates a list of all the tables with foreign key constraints together with a literal.

```
'ALTERTABLE'||TABLE_NAME
-----------------------------------
ALTER TABLE COURSE
...
ALTER TABLE SECTION
ALTER TABLE SECTION
ALTER TABLE STUDENT

11 rows selected.
```

Note there are multiple rows with the same table name because a table may have multiple foreign keys.

b) Expand the SQL statement in Exercise a by adding the constraint name dynamically. The resulting output should look like this:

```
ALTER TABLE COURSE DISABLE CONSTRAINT CRSE_CRSE_FK;
...
ALTER TABLE SECTION DISABLE CONSTRAINT SECT_CRSE_FK;
ALTER TABLE SECTION DISABLE CONSTRAINT SECT_INST_FK;
ALTER TABLE STUDENT DISABLE CONSTRAINT STU_ZIP_FK;

11 rows selected.
```

Answer: The disable clause is added to the statement by concatenating the text literal 'DISABLE CONSTRAINT' with the constraint name and then with another text literal containing the semicolon.

```
SELECT 'ALTER TABLE ' || table_name ||
       ' DISABLE CONSTRAINT '|| constraint_name||';'
  FROM user_constraints
 WHERE constraint_type = 'R'
```

```
'ALTERTABLE'||TABLE_NAME||'DISABLECONSTRAINT'||CONSTRAIN
---------------------------------------------------------
ALTER TABLE COURSE DISABLE CONSTRAINT CRSE_CRSE_FK;
...
ALTER TABLE SECTION DISABLE CONSTRAINT SECT_CRSE_FK;
ALTER TABLE SECTION DISABLE CONSTRAINT SECT_INST_FK;
ALTER TABLE STUDENT DISABLE CONSTRAINT STU_ZIP_FK;
```

11 rows selected.

    c)   Save the SQL statement in Exercise b to a file named disable_fk.sql. Add the following SQL*Plus statements at the beginning of the file. Note that the double dashes represent single line comments.

```
-- File Name: disable_fk.sql
-- Purpose: Disable Foreign Key constraints.
-- Created Date: Place current date here
-- Author: Put your name here
SET PAGESIZE 0
SET LINESIZE 80
SET FEEDBACK OFF
SET TERM OFF
SPOOL disable_fk.out
```

        Add a semicolon at the end of the SQL statement and the following SQL*Plus commands afterwards.

```
SPOOL OFF
SET PAGESIZE 20
SET LINESIZE 100
SET FEEDBACK ON
SET TERM ON
```

        Save the file and run the disable_fk.sql file at the SQL*Plus prompt with the @ command. Describe the output from the spooled file named disable_fk.out.

        Answer: The spooled file contains a list of all SQL statements necessary to disable the foreign constraints.

After editing the file, the disable_fk.sql script should look similar to the following:

```
-- File Name: disable_fk.sql
-- Purpose: Disable Foreign Key constraints.
-- Created Date: Place current date here
```

```
-- Author: Put your name here
SET PAGESIZE 0
SET LINESIZE 80
SET FEEDBACK OFF
SET TERM OFF
SPOOL disable_fk.out
SELECT 'ALTER TABLE ' || table_name || CHR(10)||
       '        DISABLE CONSTRAINT '|| constraint_name||';'
  FROM user_constraints
 WHERE constraint_type = 'R';
SPOOL OFF
SET PAGESIZE 20
SET LINESIZE 100
SET FEEDBACK ON
SET TERM ON
```

Executing the script disable_fk.sql with the @ command results in the disable_fk.out file, which looks like the following:

```
ALTER TABLE COURSE
      DISABLE CONSTRAINT CRSE_CRSE_FK;
...
ALTER TABLE STUDENT
      DISABLE CONSTRAINT STU_ZIP_FK;
```

You can now execute the commands in the file by typing @disable_fk.out at the SQL*Plus prompt. You need to specify the extension here because the file does not have the default .SQL extension.

Note the SQL statement contains the function CHR(10). This column function automatically returns a new line in the result.

COMMON SQL*PLUS COMMANDS IN SQL*PLUS SCRIPTS

The SQL*Plus commands before and after the SQL statement in the script change the settings of the SQL*Plus environment.

The SPOOL command together with a filename spools any subsequently issued SQL*Plus or SQL command to a file named disable_fk.out. If you don't add an extension, the default extension is typically .LST. The following command creates a file named temp.lst. If a file with the same name already exists, it is overwritten without warning.

```
SPOOL temp
```

To show the file name you're currently spooling to, use the SPOOL command.

```
SPOOL
```
currently spooling to temp.lst

To end the spooling and close the file, enter this command:

```
SPOOL OFF
```

Just as with other file names, you can add a path to store the file in a directory other than your default directory. To learn how to change your default directory, see the companion Web site for this book located at:

```
http://www.phptr.com/Morrison
```

The PAGESIZE 0 command suppresses the column headings.

The FEEDBACK command returns the number of records returned by a query. Because you don't want to see this in the resulting file you subsequently execute, issue either the command SET FEEDBACK 0 or the command SET FEEDBACK OFF.

The SET TERMOUT OFF or SET TERM OFF command controls the display of output generated by the commands. The OFF setting suppresses the output from the screen only when the command is executed from a script file.

The SET LINESIZE command determines the total number of characters SQL*Plus displays in one line before beginning a new line. Setting it to 80 makes it easy to read the spooled output in a text editor.

You want to reset all the SQL*Plus environmental variables to their previous settings. To see the current settings of all environmental variables, use the SHOW ALL command at the SQL*Plus prompt.

DOCUMENTING YOUR SCRIPT

You can document your scripts by using comments. You can begin a single line comment with two hyphens (--). A multiline comment begins with a slash and an asterisk (/*) and ends with an asterisk and a slash (*/). In SQL*Plus scripts, you can also use the REMARK (REM) command.

```
/* This is a multi-line
comment */
-- A single-line comment, it ends with a line break.
REM Another single-line comment, only used in SQL*Plus.
```

d) Write a dynamic SQL script enabling the foreign key constraints.

Answer: The spooled file contains a list of all SQL statements necessary to enable the foreign key constraints.

```
-- File Name: enable_fk.sql
-- Purpose: Enable Foreign Key constraints.
-- Created Date: Place current date here
-- Author: Put your name here
SET PAGESIZE 0
SET LINESIZE 80
SET FEEDBACK OFF
SET TERM OFF
SPOOL enable_fk.out
SELECT 'ALTER TABLE ' || table_name || CHR(10)||
       '        ENABLE CONSTRAINT '|| constraint_name||';'
  FROM user_constraints
 WHERE constraint_type = 'R';
SPOOL OFF
SET PAGESIZE 20
SET LINESIZE 80
SET FEEDBACK ON
SET TERM ON
```

e) Explain each line in the following SQL script and then describe the purpose of the script in one sentence.

```
01 /*
02 -----------------------------------------------------
03 File name:   rows.sql
04 Purpose:
05 Created by:  H. Ashley on January 7, 2000
06 Modified by: A. Christa on September 29, 2001
07 -----------------------------------------------------
08 */
09 SET TERM OFF
10 SET PAGESIZE 0
11 SET FEEDBACK OFF
12 SPOOL temp
13 SELECT 'SELECT ' || '''' || table_name || '''' ||
```

```
14            ',  COUNT(*) '||CHR(10) ||
15              '  FROM '|| LOWER(table_name) || ';'
16    FROM user tables;
17 SPOOL OFF
18 SET FEEDBACK 1
19 SET PAGESIZE 20
20 SET TERM ON
21 @temp.lst
22 HOST DEL temp.lst
```

> *Answer: The purpose of the script is to display a list of all user accessible tables, together with a row count for each.*

The script dynamically generates these statements and spools them to the resulting temp.lst file as follows.

```
SELECT 'course', COUNT(*)
  FROM course;
...
SELECT 'zipcode', COUNT(*)
  FROM zipcode;
```

The temp.lst file is then executed with the @temp.lst command and a count of all rows for each table is displayed.

```
'STUDEN   COUNT(*)
-------  ----------
student        268

1 row selected.
...
'ZIPCOD   COUNT(*)
-------  ----------
zipcode        227

1 row selected.
```

Lines 1 through 8 show a multiline comment; the comment starts with a /* and ends with */. Line 9 listing the command SET TERM OFF turns the output to the screen off. Line 10 sets the PAGESIZE to zero, line 11 avoids any FEEDBACK, and line 12 spools the result of all subsequent statements to the temp.lst file in the current directory. Line 13 shows an example of the literal SELECT concatenated with four single quotes. The four single quotes result in a single quote in the spooled file, and the table name is concatenated between the single quotes.

USING QUOTES IN SQL

As you see in many SQL statements, a single quote is used to enclose a text literal.

```
SELECT last_name
  FROM student
 WHERE last_name = 'Smith'
```

If you want to query, insert, update, or delete a value containing a single quote, prefix the quote with another quote.

```
SELECT last_name
  FROM student
 WHERE last_name = 'O''Neil'
```

To replicate a single quote in a dynamic SQL script, you need four quotes: two individual quotes to represent a single quote, and two quotes to surround the text literal.

Line 14 displays the COUNT function to count rows. The CHR(10) function results in a new line in the spooled file. This concatenation is then further combined with the literal FROM in line 15 together with the table name in lower case and a semicolon.

Line 16 shows the query is issued against the user_tables data dictionary view. Line 17 ends the spooling to the file. Lines 18, 19, and 20 reset the SQL*Plus settings to their defaults. Line 21 runs the spooled temp.lst file. Line 22 uses the HOST command to execute the operating system DEL (Delete) command to delete the temp.lst file. Instead of the HOST command, you can also use a $ (NT, VMS operating systems) or a ! (Unix operating system). Note the delete command is really not necessary because the file is overwritten the next time you run the script. But it demonstrates the use of an NT operating system command within SQL*Plus.

LAB 13.2 SELF-REVIEW QUESTIONS

In order to test your progress, you should be able to answer the following questions.

1) The following statements are SQL*Plus commands, not SQL commands.
```
SET FEEDBACK ON
SET HEADING ON
COL student FORMAT A20
START
DEFINE v_stud_id
```
      a) _____ True
      b) _____ False

2) What is the result of the following SELECT statement?

```
SELECT 'HELLO ' || CHR(10) || 'THERE'
  FROM dual
```

a) _____

HELLO THERE

b) _____

HELLO
THERE

c) _____ Invalid query

3) Dynamic SQL scripts are useful for generating SQL statements.
    a) _____ True
    b) _____ False

4) The $ command and the HOST command are equivalent in SQL*Plus.
    a) _____ True
    b) _____ False

5) The following SELECT statement returns a single quote.

```
SELECT ''''
  FROM dual
```

    a) _____ True
    b) _____ False

Quiz answers appear in Appendix A, Section 13.2.

C H A P T E R   1 3

TEST YOUR THINKING

1) Formulate the question that is answered by the following query.

```
SELECT table_name, column_name, comments
  FROM user_col_comments
```

2) Describe the differences between the views user_users, all_users, and dba_users.

3) Name the underlying data dictionary views for the public synonyms tabs and cols.

4) Write a dynamic SQL script to drop all views in the student schema. If there are no views, create some to test your script.

CHAPTER 14

SECURITY

CHAPTER OBJECTIVES

In this chapter, you will learn about:

✔ Users, Privileges, Roles, and Synonyms   Page 392

Protecting the data in a database is done by implementing security via users, roles, and privileges, also known as Data Control Language (DCL). Every database user has certain *system privileges* that determine the type of actions a user can perform, such as create tables, drop views, or create other users.

The owner of database objects can control exactly who can access what objects, and to what extent; these privileges are referred to as *object privileges*. System and object privileges can be grouped together into a *role*.

L A B   1 4 . 1

USERS, PRIVILEGES, ROLES, AND SYNONYMS

LAB OBJECTIVES

After this lab, you will be able to:

✔ Create Users, and Grant and Revoke Privileges
✔ Create and Use Synonyms
✔ Create User-Defined Roles

CREATING USERS

To log into the Oracle database, a user must have a user name and password. A user name is created with the CREATE USER command. To establish a connection to the database, for example using SQL*Plus, the user must be granted certain system privileges. These privileges are granted individually, or collectively in the form of roles.

■ *FOR EXAMPLE*

To create a new user, first login as the user SYSTEM; the default password is MANAGER. Note the default password is typically changed by the database administrator to another password.

Instead of logging out of SQL*Plus and starting another session, you can login with the CONNECT command at the SQL*Plus prompt. The CONNECT command can be abbreviated to CONN, followed by the user id, a forward slash, and the password:

```
CONN system/manager
```
Connected.

When you connect as another user while you are running a SQL*Plus session, you are no longer logged in as the previous user.

The Whole Truth

You can also use the CONNECT command to supply a *host string* identifying the name of the database you want to connect to. For example, to connect to a database named scratchy, you enter:

```
CONN system/manager@scratchy
```

The host string is found in the tnsnames.ora file listing the server name and the database instance name.

While logged in as the user SYSTEM, the following statement creates a new user called MUSIC with a password of LISTEN.

```
CREATE USER music IDENTIFIED BY listen
   DEFAULT TABLESPACE user_data
   TEMPORARY TABLESPACE temp_data
```
User created.

In preparation for creating users in your database, you must first determine what default and temporary tablespaces exist in your Oracle database. See the readme.txt file, which is part of the installation files, on the companion Web site located at: http://www.phptr.com/Morrison/ for instructions on how to do this.

Users cannot create other users unless they have the authority to do so. In this example, the user SYSTEM is a DBA (Database Administrator) with the privilege to perform this action.

The **User created** message indicates the successful creation of the user. The keywords DEFAULT TABLESPACE indicate where objects created by the user are stored. Here the tablespace is called user_data. The TEMPORARY TABLESPACE keywords indicate where any sorting of data that cannot be performed in memory is temporarily stored. If a default and temporary tablespace are not specified when a user is created, the SYSTEM tablespace is used as the default.

 Do NOT use the SYSTEM tablespace to store any user objects. The SYSTEM tablespace should be used by Oracle only to store Oracle system related objects.

SYSTEM PRIVILEGES

Although the user music is created, the user cannot start a SQL*Plus session, as you see from the following error message.

```
CONN music/listen
```
ERROR: ORA-01045: user MUSIC lacks CREATE SESSION privilege; logon denied

The user lacks the CREATE SESSION privilege to login to the database.

THE GRANT COMMAND

A privilege is given to a user with the GRANT command. Privileges can be granted individually, or through a role. A role is a collection of privileges. When a user is granted a role, the user acquires all the privileges defined within the role. The following statement uses two predefined Oracle roles, CONNECT and RESOURCE, to grant a number of system privileges to the new user.

```
GRANT CONNECT, RESOURCE TO music
```
Grant succeeded.

The CONNECT role includes the CREATE SESSION privilege and allows the user to start a SQL*Plus session, as well as create views and sequences among other operations. The RESOURCE role allows the user to create tables and indexes on any tablespace.

Another Oracle role, DBA, grants all system privileges. This role is usually granted only to a user who performs database administration tasks. The user SYSTEM has DBA privileges.

You can grant users the privilege to extend privileges to others if you receive them with the WITH ADMIN option. For example, the user music can now grant the CONNECT role to other users:

```
GRANT CONNECT TO music WITH ADMIN OPTION
```
Grant succeeded.

You can see which system privileges you have been granted through a role by querying the Oracle data dictionary view ROLE_SYS_PRIVS. You see individually granted system privileges in the data dictionary view USER_SYS_PRIVS.

THE REVOKE COMMAND

Privileges can be taken away with the REVOKE command, as in the following statement. Here the RESOURCE role is revoked from the user named music.

```
REVOKE RESOURCE FROM music
```
Revoke succeeded.

ALTERING AND DROPPING USERS

If a user's password needs to change, or a different default tablespace needs to be specified, the user can be altered. The following statement changes music's password from listen to tone, and changes the default tablespace from user_data to users.

```
ALTER USER music IDENTIFIED BY tone
   DEFAULT TABLESPACE users
```
User altered.

A user is dropped with the following command.

```
DROP USER music
```
User dropped.

The DROP USER command drops the user if the user does not own any objects. If you want to also drop the objects owned by the user, execute the DROP USER command with the CASCADE keyword: DROP USER music CASCADE. *If the objects and their data need to be preserved, be sure to first back up the data using the Oracle EXPORT utility program or any other reliable method.*

OBJECT PRIVILEGES

Object privileges grant certain privileges on specific objects such as tables, views, or sequences. You grant object privileges to other users when you want them to have access to objects you created. You can also grant users access to objects you do not own, if the object's owner gave you permission to extend rights to others.

■ *FOR EXAMPLE*

The following statement connects as the student user and grants SELECT privileges on the course table to the new user music.

```
CONN student/learn
Connected.
```

```
GRANT SELECT ON course TO music
Grant succeeded.
```

In this case, student is the *grantor*, and music is the *grantee*, the recipient of the privileges. In addition to SELECT, other object privileges can be granted on a table, such as INSERT, UPDATE, DELETE, ALTER, INDEX and REFERENCES. The ALTER privilege allows another user to change table definitions with the ALTER table command; the INDEX privilege allows the creation of indexes on the table, and the REFERENCES privilege allows the table to be referenced with a foreign key constraint. You can also grant all object privileges at once with the GRANT ALL command. The following SQL statement grants all object privileges on the course table to the music user. It also passes on to the music user the ability to grant these privileges to yet other users using the WITH GRANT OPTION.

```
GRANT ALL ON course TO music WITH GRANT OPTION
Grant succeeded.
```

Here, music is the grantee, but can become a grantor, if the privilege is passed on to another user.

GRANTING PRIVILEGES ON COLUMNS

You can grant INSERT, UPDATE, or REFERENCE privileges on individual columns on a table. For example, to grant update on the columns cost and description of the course table, execute the following command.

```
GRANT UPDATE (cost, description) ON course TO music
Grant succeeded.
```

> **THE WHOLE TRUTH**
>
> Object privileges can be assigned to other database objects such as sequences, packages, procedures and functions. SELECT and ALTER privileges can be granted on sequences. Packages, procedures, and functions require the EXECUTE privilege if other users want to run these stored programs.
>
> Also note that if an object such as a table is dropped and then recreated, the grants need to be reissued. This is not the case if the object is replaced with the CREATE OR REPLACE keywords available for views and stored programs.

REVOKING PRIVILEGES

Object privileges can also be revoked, as in the following statement.

```
REVOKE UPDATE ON course FROM music
Revoke succeeded.
```

Object privileges granted using the WITH GRANT OPTION are revoked if the grantor's object privilege is revoked. For example, assume user1 is granted SELECT privilege WITH GRANT OPTION and grants the same privilege to user2. If the SELECT privilege is revoked from user1, then the revoke cascades to user2. However, revoking system privileges does not have a cascading effect.

REFERENCING OBJECTS IN OTHER SCHEMAS

The music user still has the SELECT privilege on the course table, and may be able to SELECT from it as you see in the following SQL statement issued by the music user.

```
CONN music/tone
Connected.

SELECT description
  FROM course
  FROM course
     *
ERROR at line 2:
ORA-00942: table or view does not exist
```

Even though the user music is granted the SELECT privilege on the course table, music does not own the course table and must qualify the name of the schema where the object exists.

```
SELECT description
  FROM student.course
DESCRIPTION
---------------------------
DP Overview
Intro to Computers
...
JDeveloper Techniques
DB Programming in Java

30 rows selected.
```

The course table is now qualified with the name of the user who owns the course table, namely student. When any query, DML, or DDL statement is issued in Oracle, the database assumes the object being referenced is in the user's own schema, unless it is otherwise qualified.

PRIVATE SYNONYMS

Instead of qualifying the name of an object with the object owner's name, a *synonym* can be used. A synonym is a way to alias an object with another name. You can create *private* and *public* synonyms. A private synonym is a synonym in a user's schema; public synonyms are visible to everyone. You learn about public synonyms shortly.

The following CREATE SYNONYM statement creates a private synonym called course in the music schema for the course table located in the student schema.

```
CREATE SYNONYM course FOR student.course
Synonym created.
```

Now, instead of selecting from the table qualified with the schema name, you can specify the synonym instead.

```
SELECT description
  FROM course
DESCRIPTION
---------------------------
DP Overview
Intro to Computers
```

...
JDeveloper Techniques
DB Programming in Java

30 rows selected.

The SELECT statement is resolved by looking at the synonym course which points to the course table located in the student schema.

Whenever any statement is executed, Oracle looks in the current schema for the object. If there is no object of that name in the current schema, Oracle checks for a public synonym of that name.

When a synonym is created, the validity of the underlying object is not checked.

PUBLIC SYNONYMS

All synonyms are private unless the keyword PUBLIC is specified. Public synonyms are visible to all users of the database. However, this does not automatically grant any object privileges to the underlying objects. Grants still need to be issued to either individual users, or to PUBLIC by referring to either the public synonym or the underlying object. For the user music, the following statements create a table, create a public synonym for the table, and grant the SELECT privilege on the table to the user student.

```
CREATE TABLE instrument
  (instrument_id  NUMBER(10),
   description  VARCHAR2(25))
```
Table created.

```
CREATE PUBLIC SYNONYM instrument FOR instrument
```
Synonym created.

```
GRANT SELECT ON instrument TO student
```
Grant succeeded.

Now the user student can perform queries against the public synonym or table instrument located in the music schema. The user student, or for that matter any other user, does not need to prefix the instrument table with the owner. However, users other than the user student do not have access to the table. If you want every user in the database system to have SELECT privileges, you can grant the SELECT privilege to PUBLIC:

```
GRANT SELECT ON instrument TO PUBLIC
```

The ability to create public synonyms is typically granted to users with DBA privileges. To complete the exercises in this chapter for public synonyms, have your system administrator grant the user student this privilege, or login as SYSTEM and grant the system privilege CREATE PUBLIC SYNONYM with the following statement: GRANT CREATE PUBLIC SYNONYM TO student.

Private and public synonyms can be dropped with the DROP [PUBLIC] SYNONYM command, followed by the name of the synonym.

USER-DEFINED ROLES

In addition to Oracle's predefined roles, *user-defined* roles can be created to customize a grouping of either system and/or object privileges. There may be different types of users for a given system. Sometimes, there are users who only view data, so those users only need SELECT privileges. There are other users who maintain the data, so they typically need a combination of SELECT, INSERT, UPDATE, and DELETE privileges on certain tables and columns.

■ *FOR EXAMPLE*

The following statement creates a role for users who only need to read the data in the student schema.

```
CREATE ROLE read_data_only
```
Role created.

The role still does not have any privileges associated with it. The following SELECT statement generates other statements, granting SELECT privileges on all of the user student's tables to the new role read_data_only.

```
SELECT 'GRANT SELECT ON '||table_name||
       ' TO read_data_only;'
  FROM user_tables
```

When the statement is executed from a script that in turn executes each resulting statement, the role now has a collection of privileges. The next step is to grant the role to users so these users have the privileges defined by the role. The following statement grants all the users in the database this role by granting the read_data_only role to PUBLIC.

```
GRANT read_data_only TO PUBLIC
```
Grant succeeded.

Now each user of the database has SELECT privileges on all of the user student's tables. All privileges defined by the role can be revoked in a single statement, as in the following.

```
REVOKE read_data_only FROM PUBLIC
```
Revoke succeeded.

If you want none of the users to have the SELECT privilege to the course table anymore, you can revoke this privilege from the role only and all users that have been granted the role will no longer have access to the table.

The ability to create roles is only allowed by users with DBA privileges, or by individual users granted the CREATE ROLE privilege. To complete the exercises in this chapter for user-defined roles, have your database administrator grant this privilege to the student user, or login as SYSTEM and grant this system privilege by executing the following statement: GRANT CREATE ROLE TO student.

Roles can be dropped with the DROP ROLE command, followed by the name of the role.

LAB 14.1 EXERCISES

14.1.1 CREATE USERS, AND GRANT AND REVOKE PRIVILEGES

The text [default_tablespace] **and** [temporary_tablespace] in the following exercise solutions is where the name of the appropriate tablespaces in your database should appear in your answers.

a) Login to SQL*Plus as SYSTEM/MANAGER and create a user called TEACHER with a password of SUBJECT, with the appropriate default and temporary tablespaces for your database. Using Oracle roles, grant enough privileges to the new user to start a SQL*Plus session, create a table, and create a view. Login to SQL*Plus as the new user and create a table called account with these three columns:

account_num as the primary key column, and the columns account_type, and account_status. Determine appropriate datatypes for the columns. Insert a row with the values 1001, Checking, and Active, respectively. Create a view based on the account table called account_status with the account_num and status columns.

_____

_____

b) While logged in as the new user teacher created in Exercise a, execute the following SELECT statements against data dictionary views. What do these views tell you about the new user?

```
SELECT username, granted_role, admin_option
  FROM user_role_privs

SELECT *
  FROM session_privs
```

_____

_____

c) While logged in as the user teacher, grant SELECT privileges for the account table to the student user, and allow the student user to grant the same privilege to another user. Then, login as the student user, and execute the following three statements. What do you observe?

```
SELECT *
  FROM teacher.account

INSERT INTO teacher.account
  (account_num, type , status)
VALUES
  (1002, 'Savings', 'Active')

SELECT *
  FROM teacher.account_status
```

_____

_____

d) Connect as SYSTEM/MANAGER and change the password for the user teacher from subject to class. Login as teacher, and revoke the SELECT privileges from student on the account table.

_____

_____

14.1.2 CREATE AND USE SYNONYMS

a) While logged in as the student user, create a private synonym called course for the course table. Explain your observations.

_____

_____

b) Explain the result of the following SELECT statement.

```
SELECT 'CREATE PUBLIC SYNONYM '||table_name||
       ' FOR '||table_name||';'
  FROM user_tables
```

_____

_____

14.1.3 CREATE USER-DEFINED ROLES

a) While logged in as the student user, create a role called student_admin. Grant INSERT and UPDATE privileges on the course table to the role. Then, grant the role to TEACHER.

_____

_____

b) Execute the following SELECT statement and describe the result.

```
SELECT *
  FROM user_tab_privs_made
```

_____

_____

LAB 14.1 EXERCISE ANSWERS

14.1.1 ANSWERS

a) Login to SQL*Plus as SYSTEM/MANAGER and create a user called TEACHER with a password of SUBJECT, with the appropriate default and temporary tablespaces for your database. Using Oracle roles, grant enough privileges to the new user to start a SQL*Plus session, create a table, and create a view. Login to SQL*Plus as the new user and create a table called account with these three columns: account_num as the primary key column, and the columns account_type, and account_status. Determine appropriate datatypes for the columns. Insert a row with the values 1001, Checking, and Active, respectively. Create a view based on the account table called account_status with the account_num and status columns.

Answer: The CONNECT command is used to connect as the system user. The CREATE USER command and the GRANT commands are used to create the new user and grant system privileges to the user. The CONNECT command is used again to connect as the new user, and the CREATE TABLE and CREATE OR REPLACE VIEW commands are used to create two new objects for the new user.

```
CONN system/manager
Connected.

CREATE USER teacher IDENTIFIED BY subject
  DEFAULT TABLESPACE [default_tablespace]
  TEMPORARY TABLESPACE [temporary_tablespace]
User created.

GRANT CONNECT, RESOURCE to TEACHER
Grant succeeded.

CONN teacher/subject
Connected.

CREATE TABLE account
  (account_num  NUMBER(15),
   type         VARCHAR(10),
   status       VARCHAR(6),
   CONSTRAINT account_pk PRIMARY KEY(account_num))
Table created.

INSERT INTO account
  (account_num, type, status)
```

```
VALUES
  (1001, 'Checking', 'Active')
1 row created.

CREATE OR REPLACE VIEW account_status AS
SELECT account_num, status
  FROM account
View created.
```

b) While logged in as the new user teacher created in Exercise a, execute the following SELECT statements against data dictionary views. What do these views tell you about the new user?

```
SELECT username, granted_role, admin_option
  FROM user_role_privs

SELECT *
  FROM session_privs
```

> *Answer: The query against the user_role_privs view shows what Oracle roles the user teacher has been granted, and whether the user has been granted the administration option on those roles. The query against the session_privs view shows the privileges the user of the current session has, in this case the user teacher.*

```
SELECT username, granted_role, admin_option
  FROM user_role_privs
```

USERNAME	GRANTED_ROLE	ADM
TEACHER	CONNECT	NO
TEACHER	RESOURCE	NO

```
2 rows selected.

SELECT *
  FROM session_privs
```

PRIVILEGE

CREATE SESSION
ALTER SESSION
UNLIMITED TABLESPACE
CREATE TABLE
CREATE CLUSTER
CREATE SYNONYM
CREATE VIEW
CREATE SEQUENCE
CREATE DATABASE LINK

```
CREATE PROCEDURE
CREATE TRIGGER
```

11 rows selected.

The user can also be given the ability to grant these same privileges to another user in turn, with the following statement.

```
GRANT CONNECT, RESOURCE TO music WITH ADMIN OPTION
```
Grant succeeded.

The user music, or *grantee*, can now grant the same system privileges to another user, becoming the *grantor*. When you reexecute the query against the user_role_privs view, you now see 'YES' in the admin_option column.

```
SELECT username, granted_role, admin_option
  FROM user_role_privs
```

USERNAME	GRANTED_ROLE	ADM
TEACHER	CONNECT	YES
TEACHER	RESOURCE	YES

2 rows selected.

To grant these privileges, however, music must first be granted the system privilege to create other users.

```
GRANT CREATE USER TO music
```
Grant succeeded.

The ability to create users can be granted through the Oracle predefined DBA role, or individually as in the previous statement.

c) While logged in as the user teacher, grant SELECT privileges for the account table to the student user, and allow the student user to grant the same privilege to another user. Then, login as the student user, and execute the following three statements. What do you observe?

```
SELECT *
  FROM teacher.account

INSERT INTO teacher.account
```

```
        (account_num, type, status)
VALUES
        (1002, 'Savings', 'Active')

SELECT *
  FROM teacher.account_status
```

> *Answer: The first statement selects data from the account table created by teacher. The second statement attempts to insert a row into the account table, but the student user does not have the privilege to do this. The third statement attempts to access the account_status view created by teacher, but the student user has not been granted SELECT privileges on the view.*

```
GRANT SELECT ON account TO student WITH GRANT OPTION
```
Grant succeeded.

```
CONN student/learn
```
Connected.

```
SELECT *
  FROM teacher.account
```
ACCOUNT_NUM TYPE   STATUS
----------- ----------   ------
         1001 Checking   Active

1 row selected.

```
INSERT INTO teacher.account
        (account_num, type, status)
VALUES
        (1002, 'Savings', 'Active')
```
INSERT INTO teacher.account
                        *

ERROR at line 1:
ORA-01031: insufficient privileges

```
SELECT *
  FROM teacher.account_status
```
  FROM teacher.account_status
              *

ERROR at line 2:
ORA-00942: table or view does not exist

d) Connect as SYSTEM/MANAGER and change the password for the user teacher from subject to class. Login as teacher, and revoke the SELECT privileges from student on the account table.

Answer: The ALTER USER command is used to change the password from subject to class. The REVOKE SELECT ON...FROM command is used to revoke SELECT privileges on the account table from the student user.

```
CONN system/manager
Connected.

ALTER USER teacher identified by class
User altered.

CONN teacher/class
Connected.

REVOKE SELECT ON account FROM student
Revoke succeeded.
```

14.1.2 ANSWERS

a) While logged in as the student user, create a private synonym called course for the course table. Explain your observations.

Answer: Two objects with the same name cannot exist in the same schema.

```
CREATE SYNONYM course FOR course
CREATE SYNONYM course FOR course
*
ERROR at line 1:
ORA-01471: cannot create a synonym with same name as object
```

It is not necessary to create private synonyms for objects you already own. However, it is possible to do so, but the synonym must have a different name from the underlying object. Within one schema, all object names must be unique, regardless of the type of object.

b) Explain the result of the following SELECT statement.

```
SELECT 'CREATE PUBLIC SYNONYM '||table_name||
       ' FOR '||table_name||';'
  FROM user_tables
```

Answer: The SELECT statement generates other SELECT statements dynamically. Each statement generated creates a public synonym for each table owned by the current user.

When you create public synonyms for other users to see your objects, you typically do it for many objects in your schema. Using a SELECT statement to generate other statements is the fastest way to do this.

 Public synonyms are not owned by the user who creates them, so there is no conflict between the public synonym name and the name of the object on which it is based.

14.1.3 ANSWERS

a) While logged in as the student user, create a role called student_admin. Grant INSERT and UPDATE privileges on the course table to the role. Then, grant the role to TEACHER.

Answer: First, the CREATE ROLE command is used to create the role. Then a GRANT command is used to grant insert and update privileges, separated by commas, to the role. Then another GRANT statement grants the role to the user TEACHER.

```
CREATE ROLE student_admin
Role created.

GRANT INSERT, UPDATE ON course TO student_admin
Grant succeeded.

GRANT student_admin TO TEACHER
Grant succeeded.
```

The WITH ADMIN OPTION can be used to pass on the ability to grant the privileges being granted. The following statement is the same as the previous GRANT statement, but also gives the ability to the TEACHER user to pass on the privileges being granted.

```
GRANT student_admin TO TEACHER WITH ADMIN OPTION
Grant succeeded.
```

Now the user TEACHER can pass this same set of privileges on to other users.

b) Execute the following SELECT statement and describe the result.

```
SELECT *
  FROM user_tab_privs_made
```

Answer: The result shows the details of all grants made on tables by the student user: the recipient of the grant (the grantee); the table on which the grant was based; the grantor, or the user who granted the privilege; the privilege granted on the table; and whether the privilege is grantable to other users.

The results vary depending on the privileges you have granted, and have been granted by other users.

```
GRANTEE            TABLE_NAME  GRANTOR     PRIVILEGE   GRA
---------------    ----------  ----------  ----------  ---
STUDENT_ADMIN      COURSE      STUDENT     INSERT      NO
STUDENT_ADMIN      COURSE      STUDENT     UPDATE      NO

2 rows selected.
```

You can see that the student_admin role is the grantee of INSERT and UP-DATE privileges on the course table, and the student user is the grantor.

The data dictionary view, called dict, can be queried to list several other data dictionary views containing information about the roles created and privileges granted in a system.

LAB 14.1 SELF-REVIEW QUESTIONS

In order to test your progress, you should be able to answer the following questions.

1) A user's objects must be dropped in a separate statement before the user can be dropped.
   a) _____ True
   b) _____ False

2) The SQL*Plus CONNECT command is not the same as the CONNECT role.
   a) _____ True
   b) _____ False

3) The following statement contains an error.

   REVOKE resource, SELECT ON course FROM music
   a) _____ True
   b) _____ False

4) System privileges cannot be granted through a role.

   a) _____ True

   b) _____ False

5) Dropping a role drops the underlying object the role's privileges are based on.

   a) _____ True

   b) _____ False

Quiz answers appear in Appendix A, Section 14.1.

CHAPTER 14

TEST YOUR THINKING

To complete the exercises below, create a new user called SCHOOL with the password PROGRAM, and grant CONNECT and RESOURCE privileges to it. Then, login as the student user. Using your knowledge of generating SQL statements dynamically, the following exercises should all be included in a single file.

1) Create two roles: one called registrar, the other called instructor.

2) Create a view called current_regs reflecting all students that registered today. Grant SELECT privileges on the new view to the registrar role.

3) Create a view called roster, reflecting all students taught by the instructor Marilyn Frantzen. Grant SELECT privileges on the new view to the instructor role.

4) Grant the registrar and instructor roles to the new user called school.

5) Start a SQL*Plus session as the user school, and select from the two views created previously.

CHAPTER 15

ADVANCED SQL QUERIES

CHAPTER OBJECTIVES

In this chapter, you will learn about:

- ✔ DECODE Magic and In-Line Views   Page 414
- ✔ Hierarchical Queries   Page 429

This chapter revisits some of the concepts discussed in prior chapters, namely the DECODE function and aggregate functions. You learn how these individual topics are combined to solve more complex queries.

In Lab 15.2 you use the CONNECT BY clause and the PRIOR operators for *hierarchical queries*. These operators allow you to graphically display a hierarchy, and reveal the relationship of records within a table.

L A B   1 5 . 1

DECODE MAGIC AND IN-LINE VIEWS

LAB OBJECTIVES

After this lab, you will be able to:

✔ Transpose a Result Set Using the DECODE Function
✔ Understand the Danger of Aggregate
    Functions and Write In-Line Views

TRANSPOSE RESULTS WITH THE DECODE FUNCTION

The DECODE function allows you to perform powerful *if then else* comparisons to transpose the results of queries. For example, the following query returns a listing of the number of courses held for each day of the week. The day of the week is formatted using the DY format mask.

```
SELECT TO_CHAR(start_date_time, 'DY') Day, COUNT(*)
  FROM section
 GROUP BY TO_CHAR(start_date_time, 'DY')
DAY  COUNT(*)
---  ---------
FRI        15
MON         5
...
TUE         4
WED        17

7 rows selected.
```

If you want to transpose the result and show it horizontally, with the days of the week as columns and a count below, you nest the DECODE function within the COUNT function.

```
SELECT  COUNT(DECODE(
        TO_CHAR(start_date_time, 'DY'), 'MON', 1)) MON,
        COUNT(DECODE(
        TO_CHAR(start_date_time, 'DY'), 'TUE', 1)) TUE,
        COUNT(DECODE(
        TO_CHAR(start_date_time, 'DY'), 'WED', 1)) WED,
        COUNT(DECODE(
        TO_CHAR(start date_time, 'DY'), 'THU', 1)) THU,
        COUNT(DECODE(
        TO_CHAR(start_date_time, 'DY'), 'FRI', 1)) FRI,
        COUNT(DECODE(
        TO_CHAR(start_date_time, 'DY'), 'SAT', 1)) SAT,
        COUNT(DECODE(
        TO_CHAR(start_date_time, 'DY'), 'SUN', 1)) SUN
  FROM section
```

MON	TUE	WED	THU	FRI	SAT	SUN
5	4	17	12	15	18	7

1 row selected.

Recall the syntax of the DECODE function:

```
DECODE(if_expr, equals_search, then_result, [, else_default])
```

Note: Search and result values can be repeated.

When each row of the expression TO_CHAR(start_date_time, 'DY') is evaluated, it returns the day of the week in the format DY, which is MON for Monday, TUE for Tuesday, and so on. If the DECODE expression is equal to the search value, the result value of 1 is returned. Because no else condition is specified, a NULL value is returned.

The COUNT function with an argument does not count NULL values; NULLs are counted only with the wildcard COUNT(*). Therefore, when the COUNT function is applied to the result of either NULL or 1, it only counts those records with NOT NULL values.

AGGREGATE FUNCTIONS AND JOINS

Many SQL statements perform joins, together with aggregate functions. When you join tables together, some values are repeated as a result. If you apply an aggregate function to a repeating value, the result of the calculation may be incorrect. The following example shows a listing of the total capacity for courses with enrolled students.

```
SELECT s.course_no, SUM(s.capacity)
  FROM enrollment e, section s
 WHERE e.section_id = s.section_id
 GROUP BY s.course_no
COURSE_NO SUM(S.CAPACITY)
--------- ---------------
       10              15
       20             175
...
      420              50
      450              25
```

25 rows selected.

To illustrate that the result is incorrect, look at the value for the capacity column of course_no 20. The following query shows the capacity for each section, resulting in a total capacity of 80 students, rather than 175 students.

```
SELECT section_id, capacity
  FROM section
 WHERE course_no = 20
SECTION_ID  CAPACITY
----------  ---------
        81        15
        82        15
        83        25
        84        25
```

4 rows selected.

A closer look at the result of the join without the aggregate function reveals the problem.

```
SELECT s.section_id, s.capacity, e.student_id,
       s.course_no
  FROM enrollment e, section s
```

```
WHERE e.section_id = s.section_id
  AND s.course_no = 20
ORDER BY section_id
```

SECTION_ID	CAPACITY	STUDENT_ID	COURSE_NO
81	15	103	20
81	15	104	20
81	15	240	20
82	15	244	20
82	15	245	20
83	25	124	20
83	25	235	20
84	25	158	20
84	25	199	20

9 rows selected.

For each enrolled student, the capacity record is repeated as the result of the join. This is correct, because for every row in the enrollment table, the corresponding section_id is looked up in the section table. But when the SUM aggregate function is applied to the capacity, every record is added to the total capacity for each course. Instead, the query needs to be written as follows.

```
SELECT course_no, SUM(capacity)
  FROM section s
 WHERE EXISTS
       (SELECT NULL
          FROM enrollment e, section sect
         WHERE e.section_id = sect.section_id
           AND sect.course_no = s.course_no)
 GROUP BY course_no
```

COURSE_NO	SUM(CAPACITY)
10	15
20	80
...	
420	25
450	25

25 rows selected.

The EXISTS operator checks to see if the course_no exists in the subquery. If it exists, the course has enrollment records for the particular course. The outer query sums up the values for every row of the section table.

The EXISTS operator solves this particular problem, but not all queries can be solved this way; some may need to be written using *in-line views*.

IN-LINE VIEWS

In-line views, also referred to as *queries in the FROM clause*, allow you to treat a query as a virtual table or view. The following example illustrates this concept.

```
SELECT e.student_id, e.section_id, s.last_name
  FROM (SELECT student_id, section_id, enroll_date
          FROM enrollment
         WHERE student_id = 123) e,
        student s
 WHERE e.student_id = s.student_id
```

STUDENT_ID	SECTION_ID	LAST_NAME
123	87	Radicola

1 row selected.

The in-line view is written in the FROM clause of the query, and receives an alias called e. The result of this query is evaluated and then joined to the student table. The in-line view acts just like a virtual table, or, for that matter, like a view built from the query. The difference between a view and an in-line view is the in-line view does not need to be created and stored in the data dictionary.

In-line view queries may look very complicated, but are very easy to understand. They allow you to break down complex problems into simple queries. The following query uses two in-line views to return the actual number of enrollments for course number 20, and joins this result to the capacity of the course. The actual and potential revenue is then computed by multiplying the course cost with the enrollment and capacity of the course.

```
SELECT enr.num_enrolled "Enrollments",
       enr.num_enrolled * cour.cost "Actual Revenue",
       cap.capacity "Total Capacity",
       cap.capacity * cour.cost "Potential Revenue"
  FROM (SELECT COUNT(*) num_enrolled
          FROM enrollment e, section s
         WHERE s.course_no = 20
           AND s.section_id = e.section_id) enr,
       (SELECT SUM(capacity) capacity
```

```
        FROM section
      WHERE course_no = 20) cap,
    course cour
 WHERE cour.course_no = 20
```

Enrollments	Actual Revenue	Total Capacity	Potential Revenue
9	10755	80	95600

1 row selected.

The easiest way to understand the query is to look at the result set for each in-line view. The first query, referenced with the alias enr, returns the number of students enrolled in course number 20. It requires a join between the enrollment and the section table, because the number of students enrolled per section is in the enrollment table, and the course_no column is found in the section table. The column joining the two tables is the section_id. The query returns one row.

```
SELECT COUNT(*) num_enrolled
  FROM enrollment e, section s
 WHERE s.course_no = 20
   AND s.section_id = e.section_id
```

NUM_ENROLLED

          9

1 row selected.

The second query, with the alias cap, uses the aggregate function SUM to add all the values in the capacity column for course number 20. This result returns one row.

```
SELECT SUM(capacity) capacity
  FROM section
 WHERE course_no = 20
```

CAPACITY

       80

1 row selected.

The last table in the FROM clause of the query is the course table. This table holds the course cost to compute the actual revenue and the potential revenue. The query also retrieves one row.

Note, the results of the in-line views (enr, cap) and the course table are not joined together, thus creating a Cartesian product. Because a multiplication of 1*1*1 results in one row, this query returns the one row for course number 20. A join condition is not required in this case.

TOP-N QUERY

An example of a top-n query is a query allowing you to determine the top three students for a particular section. The ROWNUM pseudocolumn, together with an in-line view, helps achieve this result. Recall a pseudocolumn is not a real column in a table; it just appears to be.

The ROWNUM pseudocolumn returns a number indicating the order in which Oracle returns the rows. You can use ROWNUM to limit the number of rows returned, as in the following example.

```
SELECT last_name, first_name
  FROM student
 WHERE ROWNUM <=5
```

LAST_NAME	FIRST_NAME
Eakheit	George
Millstein	Leonard
Cadet	Austin V.
Zapulla	Tamara
Goldsmith	Jenny

5 rows selected.

To determine the three highest final examination grades of section 101, combine the ROWNUM pseudocolumn together with an in-line view as follows.

```
SELECT ROWNUM, numeric_grade
  FROM (SELECT DISTINCT numeric_grade
          FROM grade
         WHERE section_id = 101
           AND grade_type_code = 'FI'
         ORDER BY numeric_grade DESC)
 WHERE ROWNUM <= 3
```

ROWNUM	NUMERIC_GRADE
1	99
2	92

```
     3                91
```

3 rows selected.

The in-line view selects the distinct numeric_grades for all final examinations where section_id equals 101. This result is ordered by the numeric_grade in descending order, with the highest numeric_grade listed first. The outer query uses the ROWNUM to return only the first three.

LAB 15.1 EXERCISES

15.1.1 TRANSPOSE A RESULT SET USING THE DECODE FUNCTION

a) The following query result is a listing of all the distinct course costs and a count of each. Write the query to achieve the result.

```
   1095        1195        1595       NULL
--------- --------- --------- ---------
      3          25           1          1
```

1 row selected.

_____

_____

b) Build upon Exercise a to include a range so the output looks like the following. Hint: Use the SIGN function.

```
1500 OR LESS MORE THAN 1500
------------ --------------
        29             1
```

1 row selected.

15.1.2 UNDERSTAND THE DANGER OF AGGREGATE FUNCTIONS AND WRITE IN-LINE VIEWS

a) Display the course number, description, and capacity of all the sections for each course. Include the number of students enrolled and the percentage the course is filled. The result should look similar to the following output.

COURSE_NO	TOTAL_CAPACITY	TOTAL_STUDENTS	Filled Percentage
240	25	13	52
230	27	14	51.85
...			
450	25	1	4
134	65	2	3.08

25 rows selected.

---

b) Determine the top five courses with the largest number of enrollments.

LAB 15.1 EXERCISE ANSWERS

15.1.1 ANSWERS

a) The following query result is a listing of all the distinct course costs and a count of each. Write the query to achieve the result.

1095	1195	1595	NULL
3	25	1	1

1 row selected.

Answer: The answer requires the use of the DECODE function nested inside the aggregate function COUNT.

```
SELECT COUNT(DECODE(cost, 1095, 1)) "1095",
       COUNT(DECODE(cost, 1195, 1)) "1195",
       COUNT(DECODE(cost, 1595, 1)) "1595",
       COUNT(DECODE(cost, NULL, 1)) "NULL"
  FROM course
```

The following query achieves the same result, but the rows are not transposed horizontally.

```
SELECT COST, COUNT(*)
  FROM COURSE
 GROUP BY COST
     COST   COUNT(*)
--------- ----------
     1095          3
     1195         25
     1595          1
                   1
```

4 rows selected.

The transposed result uses the COUNT function to count the row only if it meets the search criteria of the DECODE function. The first column of the SELECT statement tests for courses with a cost of 1095. If this expression is equal to 1095, then the DECODE function returns the value 1, otherwise it returns a NULL value. The COUNT function counts NOT NULL values; the NULL values are not included. Note that this is different from the way the COUNT(*) function works, which includes NULL values in the count.

The last column in the SELECT statement tests for courses with a NULL cost. If this condition of a NULL course cost is true, the DECODE function returns a 1 and the row is included in the count.

You can also expand on the previous example to show all the course costs by prerequisite. Here, two courses with prerequisite 25 have a course cost of 1095 and 1195, respectively.

```
SELECT prerequisite,
       COUNT(DECODE(cost, 1095, 1)) "1095",
       COUNT(DECODE(cost, 1195, 1)) "1195",
       COUNT(DECODE(cost, 1595, 1)) "1595",
       COUNT(DECODE(cost, NULL, 1)) "NULL"
  FROM course
 GROUP BY prerequisite
```

PREREQUISITE	1095	1195	1595	NULL
10	1	0	0	0
20	0	5	0	0
25	1	1	0	0

. . .

350	0	1	0	1
420	0	1	0	0
	0	4	0	0

17 rows selected.

b) Build upon Exercise a to include a range so the output looks like the following. Hint: Use the SIGN function.

```
1500 OR LESS MORE THAN 1500
------------ --------------
         29              1
```

1 row selected.

Answer: The SIGN function is nested within the DECODE function to compare the values.

```
SELECT COUNT(DECODE(SIGN(NVL(cost, 0) -1500), 1, NULL, 'A'))
       "1500 OR LESS",
       COUNT(DECODE(SIGN(NVL(cost,0) -1500), 1, 'A', NULL))
       "MORE THAN 1500"
  FROM course
```

To evaluate the function, read it from the inside out. Look at the first column of the SELECT statement. First, the NVL function is evaluated; if the cost equals NULL, a zero is substituted. The result of the expression NVL(cost, 0) – 1500 returns either a zero, a negative number, or a positive number. The SIGN function is applied to this expression, and the SIGN function returns a 1 if the result of the expression NVL(COST, 0) – 1500 is positive. If the result is negative, the SIGN function returns a –1; if the result is zero, the SIGN function returns a zero. Based on the return value of the SIGN function, the DECODE function compares it to the search criteria.

For example, look at the first column, which counts the courses with a cost of 1500 or less. If the course cost of the row equals 1095, then the result of the expression 1095 – 1500 equals –405, a negative number. The SIGN function returns a –1. Therefore, the else condition of the DECODE function is executed which returns the value 'A'. The COUNT function counts this record, because it is a NOT NULL value.

If the cost is greater than 1500, the expression SIGN(NVL(cost, 0) – 1500) returns a positive number, for which you find the search value of 1; then the resulting return value of the DECODE function is a NULL value. This row is not included in the count.

For the second column, which lists the costs greater than 1500, the same logic is repeated, but the search and resulting condition of the DECODE change accordingly.

Alternatively, you can write this with a SUM function to achieve the same result. Note that with the SUM function, the substitution value of the DECODE matters because it is added up. This is in contrast to the COUNT function, where only the NOT NULL values are counted, but the actual value does not matter.

```
SELECT SUM(DECODE(SIGN(NVL(cost, 0) -1500), 1, NULL, 1))
       "1500 OR LESS",
       SUM(DECODE(SIGN(NVL(cost, 0) -1500), 1, 1, NULL))
       "MORE THAN 1500"
  FROM course
```

15.1.2 Answers

a) Display the course number, description, and capacity of all the sections for each course. Include the number of students enrolled and the percentage the course is filled. The result should look similar to the following output.

COURSE_NO	TOTAL_CAPACITY	TOTAL_STUDENTS	Filled Percentage
240	25	13	52
230	27	14	51.85
...			
450	25	1	4
134	65	2	3.08

25 rows selected.

Answer: The query uses an in-line view to retrieve the total capacity for each course, the number of students enrolled, and the percentage filled, and orders it by the percentage filled in descending order.

```
SELECT a.course_no, total_capacity, total_students,
       ROUND(100/total_capacity*total_students, 2)
       "Filled Percentage"
  FROM (SELECT COUNT(*) total_students, s.course_no
          FROM enrollment e, section s
         WHERE e.section_id = s.section_id
         GROUP BY s.course_no) a,
```

```
(SELECT SUM(capacity) total_capacity, course_no
   FROM section
  GROUP BY course_no) b
WHERE b.course_no = a.course_no
ORDER BY "Filled Percentage" DESC
```

It helps to build the query step-by-step by looking at the individual queries. The first query, with the column alias a, returns the total number of students enrolled for each course.

```
SELECT COUNT(*) total_students, s.course_no
  FROM enrollment e, section s
 WHERE e.section_id = s.section_id
 GROUP BY s.course_no
```

TOTAL_STUDENTS	COURSE_NO
1	10
9	20
...	
2	420
1	450

25 rows selected.

The second query, with the alias b, returns the total capacity for each course.

```
SELECT SUM(capacity) total_capacity, course_no
  FROM section
 GROUP BY course_no
```

TOTAL_CAPACITY	COURSE_NO
15	10
80	20
...	
25	420
25	450

28 rows selected.

Then, the two queries are joined by the common column, the course_no. The outer query references the columns total_students and total_capacity. The ROUND function computes the percentage filled up to a two-digit precision after the comma. The result is ordered by this percentage.

b) Determine the top five courses with the largest number of enrollments.

Answer: This question is solved with an in-line view and the ROWNUM pseudocolumn.

```
SELECT ROWNUM Ranking, course_no, num_enrolled
  FROM (SELECT COUNT(*) num_enrolled, s.course_no
          FROM enrollment e, section s
         WHERE e.section_id = s.section_id
         GROUP BY s.course_no
         ORDER BY 1 DESC)
 WHERE ROWNUM <= 5
```

RANKING	COURSE_NO	NUM_ENROLLED
1	25	45
2	122	24
3	120	23
4	140	15
5	230	14

```
5 rows selected.
```

LAB 15.1   SELF-REVIEW QUESTIONS

In order to test your progress, you should be able to answer the following questions.

1) Always evaluate the result of a join first, before applying an aggregate function.
   a) _____ True
   b) _____ False

2) What value does the following expression return?

```
DECODE(SIGN(100-500), 1, 50, -1, 400, NULL)
```

   a) _____ −400
   b) _____ 50
   c) _____ 400
   d) _____ −1
   d) _____ NULL

3) In-line views are stored in the data dictionary.
   a) _____ True
   b) _____ False

4) The ROWNUM is an actual column in a table.
   a) _____ True
   b) _____ False

5) The ORDER BY clause is allowed in an in-line view.
   a) _____ True
   b) _____ False

Quiz answers appear in Appendix A, Section 15.1.

LAB 15.2

HIERARCHICAL QUERIES

LAB OBJECTIVES

After this Lab, you will be able to:

✔ Restrict the Result Set in Hierarchical Queries
✔ Move Up and Down the Hierarchy Tree

A recursive relationship, also called a self-referencing relationship, exists on the course table of the student schema. This recursive relationship is between the columns course_no and prerequisite. It is just like any other parent-child table relationship, except the relationship is with itself. The prerequisite column is a foreign key referencing its own table's primary key. Only valid course numbers can be entered as prerequisites. Any attempt to insert or update the prerequisite column to a value for which no course_no exists is rejected. A course can have one or no prerequisite. For a course to be considered a prerequisite, it must appear at least once in the prerequisite column.

This relationship between the child and parent can be depicted as a hierarchy, or *tree*, using Oracle's CONNECT BY clause and the PRIOR operator. In the following result, you see how Oracle allows you to visualize the relationship of the courses having the course number 310, Operating Systems, as their prerequisite.

```
310  Operating Systems
  130  Intro to Unix
    132  Basics of Unix Admin
      134  Advanced Unix Admin
        135  Unix Tips and Techniques
    330  Network Administration
  145  Internet Protocols
```

Reading from the outside in, first the student needs to take Operating Systems, then decide on either Intro to Unix or Internet Protocols. If the student completes the Intro to Unix course, he or she may choose between the Basics of Unix Admin class and the Network Administration class. If the student completes the Basics of Unix Admin, he or she may enroll in Advanced Unix Admin. After completion of this course, the student may enroll in Unix Tips and Techniques.

You can also travel the hierarchy in the reverse direction. If a student wants to take course number 134, Advanced Unix Administration, you can determine the required prerequisite courses until you reach the first course required.

In the business world, you may often encounter hierarchical relationships, such as the relationship between a manager and employees. Every employee may have at most one manager (parent), and to be a manager (parent) one must manage one or multiple employees (children). The root of the tree is the company's president; the president does not have a parent, and, therefore, shows a NULL value in the parent column.

THE CONNECT BY CLAUSE AND THE PRIOR OPERATOR

To accomplish the hierarchical display, you need to construct a query with the CONNECT BY clause and the PRIOR operator. You identify the relationship between the parent and the child by placing the PRIOR operator before the parent column. To find the children of a parent, Oracle evaluates the PRIOR expression for the parent row. Rows for which the condition is true are the children of the parent. With the following CONNECT BY clause, you can see the order of courses and the sequence in which they need to be taken.

```
CONNECT BY PRIOR course_no = prerequisite
```

The course_no column is the parent, and the prerequisite column is the child. The PRIOR operator is placed in front of the parent column, course number. Depending on which column you prefix with the PRIOR operator, you can change the direction of the hierarchy.

THE START WITH CLAUSE

The START WITH clause determines the *root rows* of the hierarchy. The records for which the START WITH clause is true are first selected. All children are retrieved from these records going forward. Without this clause, Oracle uses all rows in the table as root rows.

The following query selects the parent course number 310, its children rows, and for each child its respective descendents. The LPAD function, together with the LEVEL pseudocolumn, accomplishes the indentation.

```
SELECT LPAD(' ', 3*(LEVEL-1)) ||course_no
       || ' ' ||description
  FROM course
 START WITH course_no = 310
CONNECT BY PRIOR course_no = prerequisite
LPAD('',3*(LEVEL-1))||COURSE_NO||''||DESCRIPTION
-------------------------------------------------
310  Operating Systems
   130   Intro to Unix
      132   Basics of Unix Admin
         134   Advanced Unix Admin
            135   Unix Tips and Techniques
      330   Network Administration
   145   Internet Protocols

7 rows selected.
```

UNDERSTANDING LEVEL AND LPAD

The pseudocolumn LEVEL returns the number 1 for the root of the hierarchy, 2 for the child, and so on. The LPAD function allows you to visualize the hierarchy by indenting it with spaces. The length of the padded characters is calculated with the LEVEL function.

In Chapter 9, "Complex Joins," you learned about self-joins. You may wonder how they compare to the hierarchical query. There are some fundamental differences: Only the hierarchical query with the CONNECT BY clause allows you to visually display the hierarchy; the self-join shows you the prerequisite in a vertical fashion only.

LAB 15.2 EXERCISES

15.2.1 RESTRICT THE RESULT SET IN HIERARCHICAL QUERIES

a) Show the course number and course description of courses with course number 310 as a prerequisite. Make these records the root of your hierarchical query. Display all the courses that can be taken after these root courses have been completed as child records. Include the LEVEL pseudocolumn as an additional column.

_____

_____

b) Modify the following query, using a WHERE clause to eliminate only the course number 132, Basics of Unix Administration. What do you observe about their respective children?

```
SELECT LEVEL, LPAD(' ', 3*(LEVEL-1)) ||course_no
       || ' ' ||description hierarchy
  FROM course
 START WITH course_no = 310
CONNECT BY PRIOR course_no = prerequisite
```

_____

_____

c) Execute the following query. What do you observe about the result?

```
SELECT LEVEL, LPAD(' ', 6*(LEVEL-1)) ||course_no
       || ' ' ||description hier
  FROM course
 START WITH course_no = 310
CONNECT BY PRIOR course_no = prerequisite
   AND LEVEL <= 3
```

_____

_____

d) Display the unrestricted hierarchy of the course table listing all the courses and prerequisites.

_____

_____

15.2.2   MOVE UP AND DOWN THE HIERARCHY TREE

a) Execute the following query placing the PRIOR operator on the prerequisite column. How does the result compare to the previously issued queries?

```
SELECT LEVEL, LPAD(' ', 6*(LEVEL-1)) ||course_no
       || ' ' ||description hierarchy
  FROM course
 START WITH course_no = 132
CONNECT BY course_no = PRIOR prerequisite
```

_____

_____

b) Write the SQL statement to display the following result.

```
LEVEL HIERARCHY
----- -------------------------------------
    5 310   Operating Systems
    4    130   Intro to Unix
    3       132   Basics of Unix Admin
    2          134   Advanced Unix Admin
    1             135   Unix Tips and Techniques

5 rows selected.
```

_____

_____

LAB 15.2 EXERCISE ANSWERS

15.2.1 ANSWERS

a) Show the course number and course description of courses with course number 310 as a prerequisite. Make these records the root of your hierarchical query. Display all the courses that can be taken after these root courses have been completed as child records. Include the LEVEL pseudocolumn as an additional column.

Answer: The START WITH clause starts the hierarchy at the prerequisite course number 310. The PRIOR operator identifies the course_no as the parent record for which all the children are retrieved.

```
SELECT LEVEL, LPAD(' ', 6*(LEVEL-1)) ||course_no
       || ' ' ||description hierarchy
  FROM course
 START WITH prerequisite = 310
CONNECT BY PRIOR course_no = prerequisite
```

```
    LEVEL HIERARCHY
--------- ---------------------------------------------
        1 130    Intro to Unix
        2       132    Basics of Unix Admin
        3              134    Advanced Unix Admin
        4                     135    Unix Tips and Techniques
        2       330    Network Administration
        1 145    Internet Protocols
```

6 rows selected.

The START WITH condition returns two records, one for the Intro to Unix class, the second for Internet Protocols. These are the root records from the hierarchy.

```
START WITH prerequisite = 310
```

The PRIOR operator in the CONNECT BY clause identifies the course_no as the parent. Children records are those records with the same course number in the prerequisite column. The following two CONNECT BY clauses are equivalent.

```
CONNECT BY PRIOR course_no = prerequisite
```

Or:

```
CONNECT BY prerequisite = PRIOR course_no
```

Shortly you see examples where the PRIOR operator is on the prerequisite column instead.

Lastly, you need to add the LEVEL function as a single column to display the hierarchy level of each record. If you also want to show the hierarchy visually with indents, the combination of LEVEL and LPAD does the trick. Recall the syntax of LPAD:

```
LPAD(char1, n [, char2])
```

The LPAD function uses the first argument as a literal. If char2 is not specified, by default it will be filled from the left with blanks up to the length shown as parameter n. The following SELECT clause indents each level with six additional spaces. Obviously, you may choose any number of spaces you like.

```
SELECT LEVEL, LPAD(' ', 6*(LEVEL-1)) ||course_no
       || ' ' ||description hierarchy
```

The length for the first level is 0 (Level 1 – 1 = 0), therefore this level is not indented. The second level is indented by six spaces (6*(2 – 1)=6), the next by twelve (6*(3 – 1) = 12), and so on. The resulting padded spaces are then concatenated with the course number and course description.

b) Modify the following query, using a WHERE clause to eliminate only the course number 132, Basics of UNIX Administration. What do you observe about their respective children?

```
SELECT LEVEL, LPAD(' ', 3*(LEVEL-1)) ||course_no
       || ' ' ||description hierarchy
  FROM course
 START WITH course_no = 310
CONNECT BY PRIOR course_no = prerequisite
```

Answer: The child records from course number 132 are not eliminated. The children of course number 132, which are course number 134 and course number 135, still appear on the result set.

```
SELECT LEVEL, LPAD(' ', 3*(LEVEL-1)) ||course_no
       || ' ' ||description hierarchy
  FROM course
 WHERE course_no <> 132
 START WITH course_no = 310
CONNECT BY PRIOR course_no = prerequisite
```

```
LEVEL HIERARCHY
--------- ----------------------------------------
      1 310   Operating Systems
      2    130   Intro to Unix
      4          134   Advanced Unix Admin
      5             135   Unix Tips and Techniques
      3       330   Network Administration
      2    145   Internet Protocols
```

6 rows selected.

LAB
15.2

    c)   Execute the following query. What do you observe about the result?

```
SELECT LEVEL, LPAD(' ', 6*(LEVEL-1)) ||course_no
       || ' ' ||description hier
  FROM course
 START WITH course_no = 310
CONNECT BY PRIOR course_no = prerequisite
   AND LEVEL <= 3
```

        Answer: The LEVEL pseudocolumn restricts the rows in the CONNECT BY clause.

```
LEVEL HIER
--------- ----------------------------------------
      1 310   Operating Systems
      2    130   Intro to Unix
      3          132   Basics of Unix Admin
      3          330   Network Administration
      2    145   Internet Protocols
```

5 rows selected.

From the previous exercise you learned that the WHERE clause eliminates only the particular row but not its children. You restrict child rows with conditions in the CONNECT BY clause. Here the PRIOR operator applies to the parent row, and the other side of the equation applies to the child record. A qualifying child needs to have the correct parent, and it must have a LEVEL number of 3 or less.

    d)   Display the unrestricted hierarchy of the course table listing all the courses and prerequisites.

        Answer: This query does not contain a START WITH clause.

```
SELECT LEVEL, LPAD(' ', 3*(LEVEL-1)) ||course_no
       || ' ' ||description hier
```

```
   FROM course
CONNECT BY PRIOR course_no = prerequisite
```

```
   LEVEL HIER
--------- -------------------------------------------
      1 10   DP Overview
      2    230   Intro to Internet
      ...
      1 310   Operating Systems
      2    130   Intro to Unix
      3      132   Basics of Unix Admin
      4        134   Advanced Unix Admin
      5       135   Unix Tips and Techniques
      3        330   Network Administration
      2    145   Internet Protocols
      1 330   Network Administration
      ...
      1 130   Intro to Unix
      2    132   Basics of Unix Admin
      3      134   Advanced Unix Admin
      4     135   Unix Tips and Techniques
      2    330   Network Administration
      1 132   Basics of Unix Admin
      2    134   Advanced Unix Admin
      3        135   Unix Tips and Techniques
      1 134   Advanced Unix Admin
      2     135   Unix Tips and Techniques
      1 135   Unix Tips and Techniques
      1 350   JDeveloper Lab
      ...
      1 430   JDeveloper Techniques
      1 450   DB Programming in Java
```

107 rows selected.

Though such a query is not very useful, it helps to understand why the records appear multiple times. When the START WITH clause is not specified, every record in the table is considered the root of the hierarchy. Therefore, for every record in the table, the hierarchy is displayed and the courses repeated multiple times.

For example, the course number 135, Unix Tips and Techniques, is returned five times. From the root 310, Operating Systems, it is five levels deep in the hierarchy. It is repeated for the root course number 130, Intro to Unix, then for 132, Basics of Unix Admin, then for 134, Advanced Unix Admin, and lastly for itself.

15.2.2 ANSWERS

a) Execute the following query, placing the PRIOR operator on the prerequisite column. How does the result compare to the previously issued queries?

```
SELECT LEVEL, LPAD(' ', 6*(LEVEL-1)) ||course_no
       || ' ' ||description hierarchy
  FROM course
 START WITH course_no = 132
CONNECT BY course_no = PRIOR prerequisite
```

Answer: The prerequisite column becomes the parent, and the course_no the children records. This effectively reverses the direction of the hierarchy compared to the previously issued queries.

The result of the query shows all the prerequisites a student needs to take before enrolling in course number 132, Basics of Unix Administration.

```
LEVEL HIERARCHY
--------- ------------------------------------
    1 132   Basics of Unix Admin
    2      130   Intro to Unix
    3            310   Operating Systems
```

```
3 rows selected.
```

The student needs to take course number 310, Operating Systems, then course number 130, Intro to Unix, before taking the class Basics of Unix Admin.

b) Write the SQL statement to display the following result.

```
LEVEL HIERARCHY
----- ------------------------------------
    5 310   Operating Systems
    4    130   Intro to Unix
    3      132   Basics of Unix Admin
    2        134   Advanced Unix Admin
    1          135   Unix Tips and Techniques
```

```
5 rows selected.
```

Answer: The rows show you the prerequisite courses for 135 as a root, thus resulting in the use of the START WITH clause. The ORDER BY clause orders the result by the hierarchy level.

```
SELECT LEVEL, LPAD(' ', 2*(5-LEVEL)) ||course_no
       || ' ' ||description hierarchy
  FROM course
 START WITH course_no = 135
CONNECT BY course_no = PRIOR prerequisite
 ORDER BY LEVEL DESC
```

Because the result shows you the prerequisites, the PRIOR operator needs to be applied on the prerequisite column. Prerequisite becomes the parent column.

```
CONNECT BY course_no - PRIOR prerequisite
```

The ORDER BY clause orders the records by the hierarchy LEVEL in descending order.

The indentation with the LPAD function is different from previous examples. You now subtract the number five from each level and multiply the result by two, resulting in the largest indentation for the root.

LAB 15.2 SELF-REVIEW QUESTIONS

In order to test your progress, you should be able to answer the following questions.

1) Identify the error in the following statement.

```
1  SELECT LEVEL, LPAD(' ', (3*3)*(LEVEL-1)) ||c.course_no
2    FROM course c, section s
3   WHERE c.course_no = s.course_no
4   START WITH prerequisite = 310
5  CONNECT BY PRIOR c.course_no = prerequisite
```

    a) _____ Line 1
    b) _____ Line 2
    c) _____ Line 5
    d) _____ No error

2) The ORDER BY clause does not order the columns within a hierarchy, but does order the columns in the order stated in the ORDER BY clause.
    a) _____ True
    b) _____ False

3) Which column is the parent in the SQL statement below?

```
CONNECT BY PRIOR emp = manager
```

a) _____ The emp column
b) _____ The manager column
c) _____ None of the above

4) The CONNECT BY condition cannot contain a subquery.
a) _____ True
b) _____ False

Quiz answers appear in Appendix A, Section 15.2.

C H A P T E R   1 5

TEST YOUR THINKING

1) Write the question for the following query and answer.

```
SELECT COUNT(DECODE(SIGN(total_capacity-20),
            -1, 1, 0, 1)) "<=20",
       COUNT(DECODE(SIGN(total_capacity-21),
            0, 1, -1, NULL,
            DECODE(SIGN(total_capacity-30), -1, 1)))
            "21-30",
       COUNT(DECODE(SIGN(total_capacity-30), 1, 1)) "31+"
  FROM (SELECT SUM(capacity) total_capacity, course_no
          FROM SECTION
          GROUP BY COURSE_NO)

    <=20       21-30        31+
--------- --------- ---------
      2         10          16

1 row selected.
```

2) Determine the top three zip codes where most of the students live.

3) Insert the following record into the course table and execute the query. What error message do you get, and why? Rollback the INSERT statement after you issue the SELECT statement.

```
INSERT INTO course
   (course_no, description, prerequisite,
    created_by, created_date, modified_by, modified_date)
VALUES
   (1000, 'Test', 1000,
    'TEST', SYSDATE, 'TEST', SYSDATE)

SELECT course_no, prerequisite
  FROM course
```

(continued)

```
 START WITH course_no = 1000
CONNECT BY PRIOR course_no = prerequisite

ROLLBACK
```

4) Name other hierarchical relationships you are familiar with.

SQL OPTIMIZATION

CHAPTER OBJECTIVES

In this chapter, you will learn about:

✔ The Oracle Optimizer and Writing   Page 444
   Effective SQL Statements

Throughout this book you find alternate SQL statements for many solutions. This chapter focuses on determining the most effective SQL statement to efficiently and quickly return results. You gain an overview of the workings of the Oracle Optimizer and an understanding of SQL performance tuning techniques. The list of tuning suggestions in this chapter is by no means comprehensive, but merely a starting point. After you understand how to read the execution steps of SQL statements, you learn to focus on tuning problem areas with alternate SQL statements.

L A B   1 6 . 1

THE ORACLE OPTIMIZER AND WRITING EFFECTIVE SQL STATEMENTS

LAB OBJECTIVES

After this lab, you will be able to:

✔ Analyze Tables and Indexes
✔ Read the Explain Plan
✔ Understand Join Operations and Alternate SQL Statements

Poor performance of a system is often caused by poor database design, improper tuning of the Oracle server, and/or poorly written SQL statements. A well-thought-out database design has the greatest positive impact on database performance, followed by effectively written SQL statements, and then by tuning the Oracle server itself. This chapter focuses on writing effective SQL statements only. The Oracle optimizer is part of the Oracle software; it examines each SQL statement and chooses the best *execution plan* for it. The execution plan consists of a sequence of steps that are necessary to execute your SQL statement. Oracle has two optimizers: the *rule-based* optimizer and the *cost-based* optimizer.

THE RULE-BASED AND COST-BASED OPTIMIZERS

The rule-based optimizer is the optimizer employed by Oracle since its beginning. It considers a number of rules in SQL statements and ranks them. The condition with the highest rank is the first executed. For example, if a WHERE clause condition contains a column with a unique index as well as a non-indexed column, the optimizer creates a plan to process the condition with the unique index first because it has a higher ranking.

The cost-based optimizer takes *statistics* into consideration, rather than rigid rules only. It considers the number of rows in the table and the selectivity of columns, among other factors, to determine the best execution path. These statistics are collected with the ANALYZE command and stored in a number of data dictionary views, such as user_tables, user_tab_columns, and user_indexes. You can choose to compute exact statistics or estimate a sample size. Tables should be analyzed regularly, particularly if the number of records in the table and/or the distribution of the values in the columns change significantly. The syntax to analyze the table, together with the associated indexes to compute the exact statistics, is as follows:

```
ANALYZE TABLE student COMPUTE STATISTICS
Table analyzed.
```

The choice of optimizer is determined by the database instance level, or the session level (ALTER SESSION command), or by a *hint* that overrides the default optimizer. You can set the optimizer to CHOOSE mode, causing Oracle to choose the cost-based optimizer if statistics are collected for any of the tables involved in the SQL statement; otherwise, the rule-based optimizer is used.

TIMING THE EXECUTION OF A STATEMENT

If a SQL statement does not perform well, you need a baseline to compare the execution time of other alternative SQL statements. This is simply accomplished in SQL*Plus by executing the SQL*Plus command SET TIMING ON. This command returns the execution time in milliseconds, that is 1/1000th of a second, for every executed SQL statement on most operating systems except VMS.

Note that repeated executions of the same or similar statements take less time than the initial execution because the data no longer needs to be retrieved from disk since it is cached in memory.

```
SET TIMING ON
SELECT COUNT(*)
```

```
FROM student
COUNT(*)
---------
     268
```

```
1 row selected.
 real: 30
```

Tuning a SQL statement is effective only if your SQL statement executes against realistic data volumes and column distributions similar to what is expected in a production environment. For instance, the execution plan for a join involving two tables varies if the data in the test environment is 100 rows, but in production it is 50,000 rows. The Oracle optimizer also evolves with each subsequent version of the Oracle database, so having a test environment that closely resembles your production environment greatly aids in this process.

THE EXPLAIN PLAN

The optimizer creates the explain plan. It shows the individual steps the Oracle database executes to process a statement. You read the explain plan from the inside out, meaning the most-indented step is performed first. If two steps have the same level of indentation, the step listed first is the first executed. Following is a SQL statement and its execution plan. You learn how to obtain an explain plan shortly.

```
SELECT student_id, last_name
  FROM student
 WHERE student_id = 123
Execution Plan
-------------------------------------------------------
0 SELECT STATEMENT Optimizer=CHOOSE
   (Cost=2 Card=1 Bytes=40)
1    0   TABLE ACCESS (BY INDEX ROWID) OF 'STUDENT'
          (Cost=2 Card=1 Bytes=40)
2    1     INDEX (UNIQUE SCAN) OF 'STU_PK' (UNIQUE)
            (Cost=1 Card=1)
```

The first step performed is a lookup of the value 123 in the index stu_pk. Using the index entry, the row is retrieved from the student table via the ROWID.

Notice the optimizer is in CHOOSE mode—that is, the Optimizer chooses between the rule-based or cost-based optimizer based on whether any of the tables involved are analyzed. In this example, the cost-based optimizer is used, because you see in parentheses the `cost` for each step of the statement. This cost helps you determine how involved each step is so you can focus on tuning the steps with the highest cost. The cost is estimated using estimated amounts of memory, input/output, and CPU time required to execute the statement. The `card` parameter shows the cardinality of the step, that is, how many rows the optimizer expects to process at this step. Lastly, the `bytes` parameter shows the size in bytes expected for the step. The numbers on the far left side indicate the parent step number and the number of each individual step.

USING AUTOTRACE

There are various ways to display an explain plan. The simplest way is to use the AUTOTRACE command in SQL*Plus. Other popular ways to obtain an explain plan include the EXPLAIN PLAN FOR command and the Oracle TKPROF utility.

To enable the AUTOTRACE facility you need to have access to the plustrace role. If the role is not already enabled, run the following script in SQL*Plus when logged in as the SYS user. The default password for the SYS user is typically change_on_install. The script is usually found in the \admin directory; the location varies depending on the operating system, Oracle version, and individual installation. You typically find it on NT in the %ORACLE_HOME%\rdbms\admin directory or on Unix in the $ORACLE_HOME/rdbms/admin directory. In the following example, the script is located on an NT machine in the directory e:\oracle\ora81\sqlplus\admin. First, start a SQL*Plus session as the user SYS, then run the script.

```
CONN sys/change_on_install
Connected.
@e:\oracle\ora81\sqlplus\admin\plustrce.sql
```

After the script executes successfully, grant the plustrace role to public. This makes the role accessible to everyone in the database, no matter who logs in.

```
GRANT plustrace TO PUBLIC
Grant succeeded.
```

Then, log back into the student schema.

```
CONN student/learn
Connected.
```

You also need a table called the `plan_table` in your schema. The script to create the table is named utlxplan.sql. In this example, the file is located on an NT machine in the directory e:\oracle\ora81\rdbms\admin. Again, run the file at the SQL*Plus prompt.

```
@e:\oracle\ora81\rdbms\admin\utlxplan.sql
```

Now you can enable the AUTOTRACE at the SQL*Plus prompt with the following command:

```
SET AUTOTTRACE EXPLAIN
```

This command does not show the result set of the SQL statement, only the plan.

Alternatively, to include the result set, execute the following command:

```
SET AUTOT ON
```

Each subsequently issued SQL statement shows the result plus additional summary statistics.

```
SELECT student_id, last_name
  FROM student
 WHERE student_id = 123
STUDENT_ID LAST_NAME
---------- -------------------------
       123 Radicola


1 row selected.

Execution Plan
----------------------------------------------------------
0      SELECT STATEMENT Optimizer=CHOOSE
       (Cost=2 Card=1 Bytes=40)
1    0    TABLE ACCESS (BY INDEX ROWID) OF 'STUDENT'
          (Cost=2 Card=1 Bytes=40)
2    1      INDEX (UNIQUE SCAN) OF 'STU_PK' (UNIQUE)
            (Cost=1 Card=2)

Statistics
----------------------------------------------------------
         0  recursive calls
         0  db block gets
         3  consistent gets
         0  physical reads
         0  redo size
      1158  bytes sent via SQL*Net to client
       703  bytes received via SQL*Net from client
         4  SQL*Net roundtrips to/from client
```

```
1   sorts (memory)
0   sorts (disk)
1   rows processed
```

To turn autotrace off, issue this command:

```
SET AUTOT OFF
```

HINTS

If you are not satisfied with the optimizer's plan, you can change it by using hints. Hints are directives to the optimizer. For example, you can ask to use a particular index, or to choose a specific join order. Because you know the distribution of the data best, sometimes you can come up with a better execution plan by overriding the default plan with specific hints. In certain instances this may result in a better plan. For example, if you know that a particular index is more selective for certain queries, you can ask the optimizer to use this index instead.

Following are examples of useful hints. The hint is always enclosed by either a multiline comment with a plus sign (/*+ */) or a single line comment with a plus sign (--+).

HINT	PURPOSE
FIRST_ROWS	This hint uses the cost-based optimizer to return the *first* row as quickly as possible.
ALL_ROWS	This hint uses the cost-based optimizer to return *all* rows as quickly as possible.
RULE	This hint chooses the rule-based optimizer. Note: All hints except for the RULE hint use the cost-based optimizer.
ORDERED	This hint joins the tables in the order listed in the FROM clause.
INDEX(tablename indexname)	The index hint asks the optimizer to perform an index scan on a specified index. Specify the name of the table on which the index is built. Note, if you use an alias on the table, you must use the alias name instead of the table name.
CHOOSE	This hint chooses between the cost-based optimizer or the rule-based optimizer, depending on the presence of statistics. If statistics are available, the cost-based optimizer then defaults to the ALL_ROWS costing model.

The following statement uses an index hint to scan the stu_zip_fk_i index on the student table. This index is actually a poorer choice than the stu_pk index, but the example demonstrates how you can override the optimizer's default plan.

```
SELECT /*+ INDEX (student stu_zip_fk_i) */ student_id,
       last_name
  FROM student
 WHERE student_id = 123
```

Execution Plan
```
--------------------------------------------------------
0   SELECT STATEMENT Optimizer=CHOOSE
    (Cost=79 Card=1 Bytes=40)
1    0   TABLE ACCESS (BY INDEX ROWID) OF 'STUDENT'
           (Cost=79 Card=1 Bytes=40)
2    1     INDEX (FULL SCAN) OF 'STU_ZIP_FK_I'
              (NON-UNIQUE) (Cost=4 Card=1)
```

INCORRECTLY SPECIFYING HINTS

If you incorrectly specify the hint, it is ignored by the optimizer and you are left to wonder why the hint does not work. Here is an example of the index hint specified incorrectly.

```
SELECT /*+ INDEX (student stu_zip_fk_i) */ student_id,
       last_name
  FROM student s
 WHERE student_id = 123
```

Execution Plan
```
--------------------------------------------------------
0   SELECT STATEMENT Optimizer=CHOOSE
    (Cost=2 Card=1 Bytes=40)
1    0   TABLE ACCESS (BY INDEX ROWID) OF 'STUDENT'
           (Cost=2 Card=1 Bytes=40)
2    1     INDEX (UNIQUE SCAN) OF 'STU_PK' (UNIQUE)
              (Cost=1 Card=1)
```

Instead of the table name student, the table alias s should be used because an alias is used in the FROM clause of the statement. This incorrect hint causes the optimizer to use a different index.

JOIN TYPES

Determining the type of join and the join order of tables has a significant impact on how efficiently your SQL statement executes. Oracle chooses one of four types of join operations: *Nested Loop Join, Sort-Merge Join, Hash Join,* or *Cluster Join.* This lab discusses only the first three, which are the most popular ones.

NESTED LOOP JOIN

With the nested loop join, the optimizer picks a *driving table* that is the first table in the join chain. In this example, assume the driving table is the student table. A full table scan is executed on the driving table, and for each row in the student table, the primary key index of the enrollment table is probed to see if the WHERE clause condition is satisfied. If so, the row is returned in the result set. This probing is repeated until all the rows of the driving table, in this case the student table, are tested.

The explain plan of a nested loop join looks like the following.

```
SELECT /*+ RULE */ *
  FROM enrollment e, student s
 WHERE s.student_id = e.student_id
Execution Plan
-----------------------------------------------------------
0       SELECT STATEMENT Optimizer=HINT: RULE
1    0    NESTED LOOPS
2    1      TABLE ACCESS (FULL) OF 'STUDENT'
3    1      TABLE ACCESS (BY INDEX ROWID) OF 'ENROLLMENT'
4    3        INDEX (RANGE SCAN) OF 'ENR_PK' (UNIQUE)
```

Note that the explain plan for a nested loop is read differently from the other explain plans because it contains a loop. The access to the enr_pk index, the most indented row, is not read first, but rather is probed for every row of the driving student table.

The nested loop join is typically the fastest join when the goal is to retrieve the first row as quickly as possible. It is also the best join when you access approximately 1–10% of the total rows from the tables involved. This percentage varies depending on the total number of rows returned, the parameters in your Oracle initialization file (init.ora), and on the Oracle version. But it gives you a general idea of when this join is useful.

The selection of the driving table is critical to good performance of the nested loop join. Making the driving table return the least number of rows is critical for probing fewer records in subsequent joins to other tables.

SORT-MERGE JOIN

To perform this join, a full table scan is executed on the enrollment table, the result is sorted by the joining column, then the student table is scanned and sorted. The two results are then merged, and the matching rows are returned for output. The first row is returned only after all the records from both tables are processed. This join is typically used when the majority of the rows are retrieved, when no indexes exist on the table to support the join condition, when the indexes are disabled, or when a sort-merge join hint is specified.

```
SELECT /*+ USE_MERGE (e, s)*/ *
  FROM enrollment e, student s
 WHERE s.student_id = e.student_id
Execution Plan
----------------------------------------------------------
0   SELECT STATEMENT Optimizer=CHOOSE
    (Cost=37 Card=226 Bytes=38420)
1     0   MERGE JOIN (Cost=37 Card=226 Bytes=38420)
2     1     SORT (JOIN) (Cost=10 Card=226 Bytes=10622)
3     2       TABLE ACCESS (FULL) OF 'ENROLLMENT'
                (Cost=2 Card=226 Bytes=10622)
4     1     SORT (JOIN) (Cost=27 Card=268 Bytes=32964)
5     4       TABLE ACCESS (FULL) OF 'STUDENT'
                (Cost=4 Card=268 Bytes=32964)
```

HASH JOIN

The hash join is available only in the cost-based optimizer and if the init.ora parameter HASH_JOIN_ENABLED is set to true. Oracle performs a full table scan on each of the tables and splits each into many partitions in memory. Oracle then builds a *hash table* from one of these partitions and probes it against the partition of the other table. The hash join typically outperforms the sort-merge join when the tables involved are relatively small.

```
SELECT /*+ ALL_ROWS */ *
  FROM enrollment e, student s
 WHERE s.student_id = e.student_id
Execution Plan
----------------------------------------------------------
0   SELECT STATEMENT Optimizer=HINT: ALL_ROWS
```

```
              (Cost=10 Card=226 Bytes=38420)
1      0    HASH JOIN (Cost=10 Card=226 Bytes=38420)
2      1       TABLE ACCESS (FULL) OF 'ENROLLMENT'
                  (Cost=2 Card=226 Bytes=10622)
3      1       TABLE ACCESS (FULL) OF 'STUDENT'
                  (Cost=4 Card=268 Bytes=32964)
```

LAB 16.1 EXERCISES

16.1.1   ANALYZE TABLES AND INDEXES

a) Analyze the table student, together with the associated indexes.

_____

_____

b) Create an index on the registration_date column of the student table. Check the data dictionary for the statistics for this index. Record your result. Drop the index afterward.

_____

_____

16.1.2   READ THE EXPLAIN PLAN

The following exercises assume the cost-based optimizer as your default optimizer and that your tables are analyzed. If they are not, execute the following PL/SQL procedure at the SQL*Plus prompt to generate statistics for your entire schema. See the *Oracle PL/SQL Interactive Workbook* (Ben Rosenzweig and Elena Silvestrova; Prentice Hall, 2000) for more on PL/SQL procedures.

```
EXECUTE DBMS_STATS.GATHER_SCHEMA_STATS('student')
PL/SQL procedure successfully completed.
```

a) Describe the result of the following query.

```
SELECT index_name, column_name, column_position
  FROM user_ind_columns
 WHERE table_name = 'STUDENT'
 ORDER BY 1, 3
```

b) Execute the SQL*Plus command SET AUTOT TRACE EXPLAIN at the SQL*Plus prompt. Then execute the SQL statement below. What do you observe about the use of the index?

```
SELECT *
  FROM student
 WHERE student_id <> 101
```

c) Create an index called stu_first_i on the first_name column of the student table. Analyze the index, then execute the following SQL statement and describe the result of the explain plan.

```
SELECT student_id, first_name
  FROM student
 WHERE first_name IS NULL
```

d) Execute the following SQL query and describe the result of the explain plan.

```
SELECT student_id, first_name
  FROM student
 WHERE UPPER(first_name) = 'MARY'
```

e) Execute the following SQL query and describe the result of the explain plan. Drop the index stu_first_i afterward.

```
SELECT student_id, first_name
  FROM student
 WHERE first_name LIKE '%oh%'
```

f) Execute the following SQL query and describe the result of the explain plan.

```
SELECT *
  FROM zipcode
 WHERE zip = 10025
```

g) Explain why the following query does not use an index. Note, to reset the AUTOTRACE facility, issue the SET AUTOTRACE OFF command.

```
SELECT *
  FROM grade
 WHERE grade_type_codc = 'HW'
```

16.1.3   UNDERSTAND JOIN OPERATIONS AND ALTERNATE SQL STATEMENTS

a) Given the following SELECT statement and the resulting explain plan, determine the driving table and the type of join performed.

```
SELECT --+ first_rows
       i.last_name, c.description, c.course_no
  FROM course c, section s, instructor i
 WHERE c.course_no = s.course_no
   AND s.instructor_id = i.instructor_id
   AND s.section_id = 133
Execution Plan
---------------------------------------------------------
0      SELECT STATEMENT Optimizer=HINT: FIRST_ROWS
       (Cost=4 Card=1 Bytes=119)
1    0   NESTED LOOPS (Cost=4 Card=1 Bytes=119)
```

```
2   1       NESTED LOOPS (Cost=3 Card=1 Bytes=92)
3   2         TABLE ACCESS (BY INDEX ROWID) OF 'SECTION'
                 (Cost=2 Card=1 Bytes=39)
4   3           INDEX (UNIQUE SCAN) OF 'SECT_PK' (UNIQUE)
                   (Cost=1 Card=1)
5   2         TABLE ACCESS (BY INDEX ROWID) OF 'COURSE'
                 (Cost=1 Card=30 Bytes=1590)
6   5           INDEX (UNIQUE SCAN) OF 'CRSE_PK' (UNIQUE)
7   1       TABLE ACCESS (BY INDEX ROWID) OF 'INSTRUCTOR'
                 (Cost=1 Card=10 Bytes=270)
8   7         INDEX (UNIQUE SCAN) OF 'INST_PK' (UNIQUE)
```

---

b) Execute the following SELECT statement under the rule-based optimizer using the RULE hint. Determine the driving table and the type of join performed.

```
SELECT /*+ RULE */ *
  FROM student s, enrollment e
 WHERE s.student_id = e.student_id
```

---

c) Reverse the order of the tables in the SELECT statement in Exercise b using the RULE hint. Determine the driving table.

---

d) Execute an explain plan for these alternate SQL statements. Describe your results.

```
SELECT /*+ RULE */ *
  FROM student
 WHERE student_id NOT IN
       (SELECT student_id
          FROM enrollment)

SELECT /*+ RULE */ *
```

```
     FROM student s
  WHERE NOT EXISTS
           (SELECT 'X'
              FROM enrollment
            WHERE s.student_id = student_id)

SELECT /*+ RULE */ student_id
  FROM student
 MINUS
SELECT student_id
  FROM enrollment
```

_____

_____

e) Show the explain plan for the following SELECT statements and describe the difference.

```
SELECT student_id, last_name, 'student'
  FROM student
UNION
SELECT instructor_id, last_name, 'instructor'
  FROM instructor

SELECT student_id, last_name, 'student'
  FROM student
UNION ALL
SELECT instructor_id, last_name, 'instructor'
  FROM instructor
```

_____

_____

LAB 16.1 EXERCISE ANSWERS

16.1.1 ANSWERS

a) Analyze the table student, together with the associated indexes.

Answer: Issue the ANALYZE TABLE command against the student table; this command gathers statistics about the table and any indexes associated with the table.

```
ANALYZE TABLE student COMPUTE STATISTICS
```
Table analyzed.

You can also use the option to estimate the statistics instead, which uses a default sample size of 1064 rows. Alternatively, you can specify a certain percentage of rows or a specific number of rows.

```
ANALYZE TABLE student ESTIMATE STATISTICS
```

Use the ESTIMATE STATISTICS option if the COMPUTE STATISTICS option takes too much time and does not change the result of the explain plan.

b) Create an index on the registration_date column of the student table. Check the data dictionary for the statistics for this index. Record your result. Drop the index afterward.

Answer: After the index is created, you also need to compute the statistics.

```
CREATE INDEX stu_reg_date_i
  ON student (registration_date)
```
Index created.

Now, check the statistics of the index:

```
SELECT distinct_keys, num_rows, sample_size,
       last_analyzed
  FROM user_indexes
 WHERE index_name = 'STU_REG_DATE_I'
```
DISTINCT_KEYS   NUM_ROWS SAMPLE_SIZE LAST_ANAL
------------- --------- ----------- ---------

1 row selected.

After you create an index, you also need to gather the statistics with the ANALYZE INDEX command in order for the previous statement to reflect them.

```
ANALYZE INDEX stu_reg_date_i COMPUTE STATISTICS
```
Index analyzed.

If you analyze the table, the index statistics are automatically gathered. But if you subsequently add indexes, you need to collect statistics on the indexes also, or re-analyze the table so the indexes on the table are recognized.

```
SELECT distinct_keys, num_rows, sample_size,
       last_analyzed
```

```
 FROM user_indexes
WHERE index_name = 'STU_REG_DATE_I'
DISTINCT_KEYS   NUM_ROWS  SAMPLE_SIZE LAST_ANAL
------------- --------- ----------- ---------
           14       268           0 01-JAN-00
```

1 row selected.

Alternatively, you can check the data dictionary view user_ind_columns.

ANALYZING THE ENTIRE SCHEMA

If you want to analyze all the tables and indexes in the schema, rather than writing a dynamic SQL script, you can execute the PL/SQL procedure gather_schema_stats and pass the schema name as a parameter.

```
EXECUTE DBMS_STATS.GATHER_SCHEMA_STATS('student')
```
PL/SQL procedure successfully completed.

Be sure to analyze your schema regularly as the distribution of the data may change the statistics, and, therefore, the optimizer's execution plan.

DELETING STATISTICS

To delete the statistics for tables or indexes and to use the rule-based optimizer, execute the following statement:

```
ANALYZE INDEX stu_reg_date_i DELETE STATISTICS
```
Index analyzed.

```
SELECT distinct_keys, num_rows, sample_size,
       last_analyzed
  FROM user_indexes
 WHERE index_name = 'STU_REG_DATE_I'
DISTINCT_KEYS   NUM_ROWS SAMPLE_SIZE LAST_ANAL
------------- --------- ----------- ---------
```

1 row selected.

Don't forget to drop the index to restore the schema to its original state.

```
DROP INDEX stu_reg_date_i
```
Index dropped.

16.1.2   ANSWERS

The following exercises assume the cost-based optimizer as your default optimizer and that your tables are analyzed. If they are not, execute the following PL/SQL procedure at the SQL*Plus prompt to generate statistics for your entire schema.

```
EXECUTE DBMS_STATS.GATHER_SCHEMA_STATS('student')
```

a)   Describe the result of the following query.

```
SELECT index_name, column_name, column_position
  FROM user_ind_columns
 WHERE table_name = 'STUDENT'
 ORDER BY 1, 3
```

> *Answer: The result of the query shows a listing of all indexes on the student table and the order in which the columns are indexed.*

INDEX_NAME	COLUMN_NAME	COLUMN_POSITION
STU_ZIP_FK_I	ZIP	1
STU_PK	STUDENT_ID	1

2 rows selected.

b)   Execute the SQL*Plus command SET AUTOT TRACE EXPLAIN at the SQL*Plus prompt. Then execute the SQL statement below. What do you observe about the use of the index?

```
SELECT *
  FROM student
 WHERE student_id <> 101
```

> *Answer: The index is not used in this query; every record is examined with the full table scan instead.*

Execution Plan
```
--------------------------------------------------------
0       SELECT STATEMENT Optimizer=CHOOSE
        (Cost=4 Card=267 Bytes=29370)
1   0     TABLE ACCESS (FULL) OF 'STUDENT'
            (Cost=4 Card=267 Bytes=29370)
```

Inequality conditions, such as <>, or !=, or any negation using NOT typically never make use of an index.

c) Create an index called stu_first_i on the first_name column of the student table. Analyze the index, then execute the following SQL statement and describe the result of the explain plan.

```
SELECT student_id, first_name
  FROM student
 WHERE first_name IS NULL
```

Answer: The query does not make use of the index on the first_name column because NULL values are not stored in the index. Therefore, a full table scan is executed.

```
Execution Plan
-------------------------------------------------------
0        SELECT STATEMENT Optimizer=CHOOSE
         (Cost=4 Card=1 Bytes=41)
1    0     TABLE ACCESS (FULL) OF 'STUDENT'
              (Cost=4 Card=1 Bytes=41)
```

If you expect to execute this query frequently and want to avoid a full table scan, you may want to consider adding a row with a default value for first_name such as 'Unknown'. When this value is inserted in the index, a subsequently issued query, such as the following, uses the index.

```
SELECT student_id, first_name
  FROM student
 WHERE first_name = 'Unknown'
```

The index is not useful, though, if you expect a significant number of the values to be 'Unknown'. In this case, retrieving values through the index rather than the full table scan takes longer.

 Concatenated indexes store NULLs unless the leading column contains a NULL.

d) Execute the following SQL query and describe the result of the explain plan.

```
SELECT student_id, first_name
  FROM student
 WHERE UPPER(first_name) = 'MARY'
```

Answer: The query does not make use of the index on the first_name column.

```
Execution Plan
-------------------------------------------------------
0        SELECT STATEMENT Optimizer=CHOOSE
         (Cost=4 Card=3 Bytes=123)
```

```
1    0    TABLE ACCESS (FULL) OF 'STUDENT'
              (Cost=4 Card=3 Bytes=123)
```

The UPPER function can be used in the SQL statement if you are unsure in which case the first name was entered. The query returns records with the values of MARY, Mary, or combinations thereof. Each time you modify an indexed column, the use of the index is disabled. The solution is to create a function-based index. For more information on this topic, refer to Chapter 12, "Views, Indexes, and Sequences."

e) Execute the following SQL query and describe the result of the explain plan. Drop the index stu_first_i afterward.

```
SELECT student_id, first_name
  FROM student
 WHERE first_name LIKE '%oh%'
```

Answer: The query does not make use of the index on the first_name column.

Execution Plan

```
----------------------------------------------------
0       SELECT STATEMENT Optimizer=CHOOSE
           (Cost=4 Card=14 Bytes=574)
1    0    TABLE ACCESS (FULL) OF 'STUDENT'
              (Cost=4 Card=14 Bytes=574)
```

The following WHERE clause does take advantage of the index, because Oracle can find entries in the index.

```
WHERE first_name LIKE 'Joh%'
```
Execution Plan

```
----------------------------------------------------
0       SELECT STATEMENT Optimizer=CHOOSE
           (Cost=4 Card=2 Bytes=82)
1    0    TABLE ACCESS (BY INDEX ROWID) OF 'STUDENT'
              (Cost=4 Card=2 Bytes=82)
2    1      INDEX (RANGE SCAN) OF 'STU_FIRST_I'
                (NON-UNIQUE) (Cost=2 Card=2)
```

Drop the index from the schema afterward to restore the schema to its original state.

```
DROP INDEX stu_first_i
```
Index dropped.

f) Execute the following SQL query and describe the result of the explain plan.

```
SELECT *
  FROM zipcode
 WHERE zip = 10025
```

Answer: The query does not make use of the primary key index on the zip column.

```
Execution Plan
----------------------------------------------------------
0          SELECT STATEMENT Optimizer=CHOOSE
           (Cost=2 Card=3 Bytes=24)
1     0    TABLE ACCESS (FULL) OF 'ZIPCODE'
           (Cost=2 Card=3 Bytes=24)
```

The full table access is used because the datatypes between the zip column and the number literal do not agree. The zip column is of VAR-CHAR2 datatype in order to store leading zeros for zip codes such as '00706', and the literal is a NUMBER. This query is an example of when Oracle performs an implicit conversion. In this case, Oracle converts the zip column to a NUMBER and, therefore, disables the use of the index. If the WHERE clause is written as follows, it uses the index.

```
WHERE zip = '10025'
Execution Plan
----------------------------------------------------------
0          SELECT STATEMENT Optimizer=CHOOSE
           (Cost=2 Card=1 Bytes=48)
1     0    TABLE ACCESS (BY INDEX ROWID) OF 'ZIPCODE'
           (Cost=2 Card=1 Bytes=48)
2     1      INDEX (UNIQUE SCAN) OF 'ZIP_PK' (UNIQUE)
             (Cost=1 Card=2)
```

g) Explain why the following query does not use an index. Note, to reset the AUTOTRACE facility, issue the SET AUTOTRACE OFF command.

```
SELECT *
  FROM grade
 WHERE grade_type_code = 'HW'
```

Answer: The grade_type_code column is not the leading column on any index of the grade table.

```
Execution Plan
--------------------------------------------------------
0        SELECT STATEMENT Optimizer=CHOOSE
         (Cost=2 Card=3 Bytes=144)
1    0     TABLE ACCESS (FULL) OF 'ZIPCODE'
           (Cost=2 Card=3 Bytes=144)
```

The following query shows the indexes on the grade table. As you see, the grade_type_column is a column in two different indexes but is never the leading column, nor are any of the leading columns in the WHERE clause of the query.

```
SELECT index_name, column_name, column_position
  FROM user_ind_columns
 WHERE table_name = 'GRADE'
 ORDER BY 1, 3
```

INDEX_NAME	COLUMN_NAME	COLUMN_POSITION
GR_GRTW_FK_I	SECTION_ID	1
GR_GRTW_FK_I	GRADE_TYPE_CODE	2
GR_PK	STUDENT_ID	1
GR_PK	SECTION_ID	2
GR_PK	GRADE_TYPE_CODE	3
GR_PK	GRADE_CODE_OCCURRENCE	4

6 rows selected.

The following query makes use of the index gr_grtw_fk_i because the leading edge of the index is in the WHERE clause.

```
SELECT *
  FROM grade
 WHERE grade_type_code = 'HW'
   AND section_id = 123
```

And this query uses the index gr_pk.

```
SELECT *
  FROM grade
 WHERE grade_type_code = 'HW'
   AND section_id = 123
   AND student_id = 567
```

a) Given the following SELECT statement and the resulting explain plan, determine the driving table and the type of join performed.

```
SELECT --+ first_rows
       i.last_name, c.description, c.course_no
  FROM course c, section s, instructor i
 WHERE c.course_no = s.course_no
   AND s.instructor_id = i.instructor_id
   AND s.section_id - 133
```

Execution Plan

```
--------------------------------------------------------
0          SELECT STATEMENT Optimizer=HINT: FIRST_ROWS
           (Cost=4 Card=1 Bytes=119)
1      0     NESTED LOOPS (Cost=4 Card=1 Bytes=119)
2      1      NESTED LOOPS (Cost=3 Card=1 Bytes=92)
3      2       TABLE ACCESS (BY INDEX ROWID) OF 'SECTION'
               (Cost=2 Card=1 Bytes=39)
4      3         INDEX (UNIQUE SCAN) OF 'SECT_PK' (UNIQUE)
                 (Cost=1 Card=1)
5      2       TABLE ACCESS (BY INDEX ROWID) OF 'COURSE'
               (Cost=1 Card=30 Bytes=1590)
6      5         INDEX (UNIQUE SCAN) OF 'CRSE_PK' (UNIQUE)
7      1      TABLE ACCESS (BY INDEX ROWID) OF 'INSTRUCTOR'
              (Cost=1 Card=10 Bytes=270)
8      7        INDEX (UNIQUE SCAN) OF 'INST_PK' (UNIQUE)
```

Answer: The driving table of this nested loop join is the section table.

The following steps are performed by this query: The index sect_pk is probed for the section_id of 133 and one record in the section table is accessed. Then, the index crse_pk on the course table is checked for the course_no matching the row. The row is retrieved for the description and course_no. Finally, the instructor index inst_pk is used to find a match for the instructor_id from the initial row in the section table, and then the corresponding record in the instructor table is retrieved.

b) Execute the following SELECT statement under the rule-based optimizer using the RULE hint. Determine the driving table and the type of join performed.

```
SELECT /*+ RULE */ *
  FROM student s, enrollment e
 WHERE s.student_id = e.student_id
```

Answer: Oracle performs a nested loop join because indexes exist on the tables. The driving table is the enrollment table.

Execution Plan

```
--------------------------------------------------------
0        SELECT STATEMENT Optimizer=HINT: RULE
1    0     NESTED LOOPS
2    1       TABLE ACCESS (FULL) OF 'ENROLLMENT'
3    1       TABLE ACCESS (BY INDEX ROWID) OF 'STUDENT'
4    3         INDEX (UNIQUE SCAN) OF 'STU_PK' (UNIQUE)
```

The nested loop join performs a full table scan on the enrollment table; for every row retrieved, the nested loop checks if a corresponding student exists in the stud_pk index. If the row exists, the row is then retrieved from the student table. The rule-based optimizer does not recognize that a full table scan with a hash or sort-merge join is more efficient than looking at the rows through the index.

Comparing the execution time of the nested loop to the sort-merge join or the hash join does not show a great variance, but if you are joining larger tables, the differences are significant.

c) Reverse the order of the tables in the SELECT statement in Exercise b using the RULE hint. Determine the driving table.

Answer: The driving table is the student table.

```
SELECT /*+ RULE */ *
  FROM enrollment e, student s
 WHERE s.student_id = e.student_id
```
Execution Plan

```
--------------------------------------------------------
0     SELECT STATEMENT Optimizer=HINT: RULE
1   0     NESTED LOOPS
2   1       TABLE ACCESS (FULL) OF 'STUDENT'
3   1       TABLE ACCESS (BY INDEX ROWID) OF 'ENROLLMENT'
4   3         INDEX (RANGE SCAN) OF 'ENR_PK' (UNIQUE)
```

The optimizer chooses the join order based on the order of the tables listed in the FROM clause, provided the WHERE clause conditions of the tables are equivalent. For the rule-based optimizer, the last table listed in the FROM clause is the driving table, as long as the indexes in the WHERE clause have the same ranking.

For the cost-based optimizer, given that the conditions in the WHERE clause are equivalent, it chooses the first table listed in the FROM clause. With the cost-based optimizer you can influence the join order with the ORDERED hint.

**LAB
16.1**

d) Execute an explain plan for these alternate SQL statements. Describe your results.

```
SELECT /*+ RULE */ *
  FROM student
 WHERE student_id NOT IN
       (SELECT student_id
           FROM enrollment)


SELECT /*+ RULE */ *
  FROM student s
 WHERE NOT EXISTS
       (SELECT 'X'
           FROM enrollment
          WHERE s.student_id = student_id)


SELECT /*+ RULE */ student_id
  FROM student
MINUS
SELECT student_id
  FROM enrollment
```

Answer: The NOT IN subquery does not take advantage of the index on the enrollment table, but the NOT EXISTS query does. The MINUS operator has a different explain plan.

```
SELECT /*+ RULE */ *
  FROM student
 WHERE student_id NOT IN
       (SELECT student_id
           FROM enrollment)
```
Execution Plan
```
---------------------------------------------------------
0        SELECT STATEMENT Optimizer=HINT: RULE
1     0     FILTER
2     1        TABLE ACCESS (FULL) OF 'STUDENT'
3     1        TABLE ACCESS (FULL) OF 'ENROLLMENT'
```

The NOT IN operator under the rule-based optimizer is very inefficient and is best replaced with a NOT EXISTS. Note that the cost-based optimizer for subqueries has greatly improved the notorious slowness of the NOT IN operator and optimizes the results.

```
SELECT /*+ RULE */ *
  FROM student s
```

```
WHERE NOT EXISTS
      (SELECT 'X'
         FROM enrollment
        WHERE s.student_id = student_id)
```
Execution Plan
```
----------------------------------------------------------
0       SELECT STATEMENT Optimizer=HINT: RULE
1   0     FILTER
2   1       TABLE ACCESS (FULL) OF 'STUDENT'
3   1       INDEX (RANGE SCAN) OF 'ENR_PK' (UNIQUE)
```

The NOT EXISTS operator takes advantage of the index on the enrollment table.

```
SELECT /*+ RULE */ student_id
  FROM student
MINUS
SELECT student_id
  FROM enrollment
```
Execution Plan
```
----------------------------------------------------------
0       SELECT STATEMENT Optimizer=HINT: RULE
1   0     MINUS
2   1       SORT (UNIQUE)
3   2         TABLE ACCESS (FULL) OF 'STUDENT'
4   1       SORT (UNIQUE)
5   4         TABLE ACCESS (FULL) OF 'ENROLLMENT'
```

The explain plan of the MINUS operator does not look very impressive, but can actually be one of the fastest ways to retrieve the result, especially when a large number of records are involved.

 Always tune your SQL statements with a representative data set. If the distribution of the data changes, so will the statistics, and the optimizer may favor a different execution plan.

e) Show the explain plan for the following SELECT statements and describe the difference.

```
SELECT student_id, last_name, 'student'
  FROM student
UNION
SELECT instructor_id, last_name, 'instructor'
  FROM instructor
```

```
SELECT student_id, last_name, 'student'
  FROM student
UNION ALL
SELECT instructor_id, last_name, 'instructor'
  FROM instructor
```

> *Answer: The UNION statement involves an additional sort, which is not performed on the UNION ALL statement.*

```
SELECT student_id, last_name, 'student'
  FROM student
UNION
SELECT instructor_id, last_name, 'instructor'
  FROM instructor
```

Execution Plan

```
--------------------------------------------------------

0       SELECT STATEMENT Optimizer=CHOOSE
        (Cost=14 Card=278 Bytes=7506)
1    0    SORT (UNIQUE) (Cost=14 Card=278 Bytes=7506)
2    1      UNION-ALL
3    2        TABLE ACCESS (FULL) OF 'STUDENT'
               (Cost=4 Card=268 Bytes=7236)
4    2        TABLE ACCESS (FULL) OF 'INSTRUCTOR'
               (Cost=1 Card=10 Bytes=270)
```

```
SELECT student_id, last_name, 'student'
  FROM student
UNION ALL
SELECT instructor_id, last_name, 'instructor'
  FROM instructor
```

Execution Plan

```
--------------------------------------------------------

0       SELECT STATEMENT Optimizer=CHOOSE
        (Cost=5 Card=278 Bytes=7506)
1    0    UNION-ALL
2    1      TABLE ACCESS (FULL) OF 'STUDENT'
             (Cost=4 Card=268 Bytes=7236)
3    1      TABLE ACCESS (FULL) OF 'INSTRUCTOR'
             (Cost=1 Card=10 Bytes=270)
```

Whenever possible, avoid any unnecessary sorts required by the use of UNION or DISTINCT.

LAB 16.1 SELF-REVIEW QUESTIONS

In order to test your progress, you should be able to answer the following questions.

1) The rule-based optimizer requires tables to be analyzed.
   a) _____ True
   b) _____ False

2) An ORDERED hint can influence the join order of SQL statements using the cost-based optimizer.
   a) _____ True
   b) _____ False

3) The join order of tables is important for good performance of the nested loop join.
   a) _____ True
   b) _____ False

4) An explain plan is read from the bottom to the top and then from the inside to the outside.
   a) _____ True
   b) _____ False

5) Incorrectly written hints are treated as comments and ignored.
   a) _____ True
   b) _____ False

Quiz answers appear in Appendix A, Section 16.1.

C H A P T E R 1 6

TEST YOUR THINKING

I) Given the following explain plan, describe the steps and their order of execution.

```
SELECT /*+ RULE */ c.course_no, c.description,
       i.instructor_id
  FROM course c, section s, instructor i
 WHERE prerequisite = 30
   AND c.course_no - s.course_no
   AND s.instructor_id = i.instructor_id
```

```
Execution Plan
-------------------------------------------------------
0       SELECT STATEMENT Optimizer=HINT: RULE
1    0    NESTED LOOPS
2    1     NESTED LOOPS
3    2       TABLE ACCESS (BY INDEX ROWID) OF 'COURSE'
4    3         INDEX (RANGE SCAN) OF 'CRSE_CRSE_FK_I' (NON-UNIQUE)
5    2       TABLE ACCESS (BY INDEX ROWID) OF 'SECTION'
6    5         INDEX (RANGE SCAN) OF 'SECT_CRSE_FK_I' (NON-UNIQUE)
7    1     INDEX (UNIQUE SCAN) OF 'INST_PK' (UNIQUE)
```

2) Describe the steps of the following execution plan.

```
UPDATE enrollment e
   SET final_grade =
       (SELECT NVL(AVG(numeric_grade),0)
          FROM grade
         WHERE e.student_id = student_id
           AND e.section_id = section_id)
 WHERE student_id = 1000
   AND section_id = 2000
0 rows updated.
Execution Plan
-------------------------------------------------------
0      UPDATE STATEMENT Optimizer=CHOOSE
          (Cost=2 Card=1 Bytes=47)
```

(continued)

```
1   0     UPDATE OF 'ENROLLMENT'
2   1        INDEX (UNIQUE SCAN) OF 'ENR_PK' (UNIQUE)
                 (Cost=1 Card=1 Bytes=47)
3   0     SORT (AGGREGATE)
4   3        TABLE ACCESS (BY INDEX ROWID) OF 'GRADE'
                 (Cost=3 Card=1 Bytes=39)
5   4           INDEX (RANGE SCAN) OF 'GR_PK' (UNIQUE)
                    (Cost=2 Card=1)
```

3) The following SQL statement has an error in the hint. Correct the statement so Oracle can use the hint.

```
SELECT /*+ INDEX (student stu_pk) */ *
  FROM student s
 WHERE last_name = 'Smith'
```

APPENDIX A

ANSWERS TO SELF-REVIEW QUESTIONS

CHAPTER 1

Lab 1.1 ■ Self-Review Answers

Question	Answer	Comments
1)	a	
2)	a	
3)	b	SQL is a language, not software like SQL*Plus.
4)	b	Most database systems are multiuser systems.

Lab 1.2 ■ Self-Review Answers

Question	Answer	Comments
1)	a, c	
2)	a	
3)	b	The number of rows are completely independent of the number of columns in a table.
4)	b	The section table has course_no and instructor_id columns as foreign keys.
5)	a	Each individual database system software may have limits constrained by the hardware and software. It is not uncommon to have tables exceeding 10 million rows.
6)	b	A primary key may never contain NULL values.

Lab 1.3 ■ Self-Review Answers

Question	Answer	Comments
1)	c	The table has at least three foreign key columns. Some foreign keys may consist of multiple columns.

2)	a	
3)	a	An example of a foreign key that allows NULLs is the zip code column on the instructor table.
4)	a	The prevention of orphan rows, thereby preserving the parent-child relationship between tables, is key to the success of a relational database design.

Lab 1.4 ■ Self-Review Answers

Question	Answer	Comments
1)	a	Do not confuse the DESC with the SQL command DESCENDING in the ORDER BY clause.
2)	b	The software to connect to the database is necessary, but a valid login id is also required.
3)	a	This command shows the same result as the SELECT USER FROM dual statement.
4)	b	SHOW RELEASE displays the version of the Oracle database, not the version of SQL*Plus.

CHAPTER 2

Lab 2.1 ■ Self-Review Answers

Question	Answer	Comments
1)	a	
2)	a	To show all the columns, it is easiest to use the asterisk wildcard character (*).
3)	b	The asterisk is used for the column list only.
4)	a	A column with the name courseno does not exist on the course table.

Lab 2.2 ■ Self-Review Answers

Question	Answer	Comments
1)	b	Only the most recent statement is saved in the buffer.
2)	a	The forward slash must be in a separate line and start at the first position.
3)	b	You can save a file anywhere you have permission to access the drive.
4)	b	The SQL*Plus START command can only execute files. The RUN command or the forward slash executes the contents of the buffer.

Lab 2.3 ■ Self-Review Answers

Question	Answer	Comments
1)	b	Comparison operators can compare multiple values, such as the IN operator that compares against a list of values.

2)	b	The BETWEEN operator is inclusive of the two values specified.
3)	a	Testing for NULLs must be done using the IS NULL operator.
4)	a	The LIKE operator cannot compare against a list of values.
5)	b	Alternatively, the <> operator or the WHERE clause NOT `state = 'NY'` can be used.

Lab 2.4 ■ Self-Review Answers

Question	Answer	Comments
1)	b	The order should be SELECT, FROM, WHERE, ORDER BY.
2)	b	The default ORDER BY sort order is ascending.
3)	a	

CHAPTER 3

Lab 3.1 ■ Self-Review Answers

Question	Answer	Comments
1)	b	For example, the INSTR function, which converts single values, takes two parameters, as well as optional parameters.
2)	a	
3)	a	Functions can be used in the SELECT clause, WHERE, or ORDER BY clauses. You will see the use of functions in other types of SQL statements in the following chapter.
4)	a	You may not apply a function in the FROM clause of a SQL statement.
5)	a	The RTRIM right trims characters. If a parameter is not specified, it trims spaces.
6)	c	The LENGTH function returns the length of a string.

Lab 3.2 ■ Self-Review Answers

Question	Answer	Comments
1)	a	
2)	b	Number functions take only the datatype NUMBER as a parameter.
3)	b	The ROUND function works on the DATE and the NUMBER datatypes. It can also take a string consisting of numbers as a parameter, providing it can be implicitly converted into a NUMBER datatype.
4)	b	This SELECT statement subtracts the capacity columns from each other.
5)	c	Most functions return a NULL with a NULL argument. Among the exceptions are DECODE, NVL, CONCAT, and REPLACE.

CHAPTER 4

Lab 4.1 ■ Self-Review Answers

Question	Answer	Comments
1)	d, e	The solution *d* results in an error, because 'A123' cannot be converted to a NUMBER. The solution *e* also results in an error because TO_CHAR expects a datatype NUMBER or DATE, but not a character datatype. Also, the literal 'A123' can not be implicitly converted into a NUMBER; therefore an error is returned.
2)	c, d, e	These are all valid, including *e*, but the solution *e* does not show all the digits because the passed parameter exceeds the specified precision. The solutions *a* and *b* are invalid NUMBER masks; solution *b* also misses a single quote at the end of the format mask.
3)	a	It is always best to explicitly specify the datatype and not to rely on Oracle's implicit conversion.
4)	a	Conversion functions operate on a single row at a time.

Lab 4.2 ■ Self-Review Answers

Question	Answer	Comments
1)	a	The TRUNC function, without a format model, sets the timestamp to midnight. TRUNC can also take a NUMBER datatype as a parameter.
2)	b	The TO_DATE function is required instead. For example, SELECT TO_DATE('01/12/2000','MM/DD/YYYY') FROM dual.
3)	d	The case is identical to the case of the format mask. The format mask DY returns MON, Day returns Monday, DAY returns MONDAY.
4)	e	The fill mode (fm) prevents any blank padding between December and 31. The date format element suffix *th* adds the ordinal number. A suffix of *sp* spells out the number. For example, the format mask 'fmMonth ddspth, yyyy' results in December thirty-first, 1999.

Lab 4.3 ■ Self-Review Answers

Question	Answer	Comments
1)	a	You need to supply a negative value as a parameter. For example, the following statement subtracts a month from the current date. SELECT ADD_MONTHS(SYSDATE, -1), SYSDATE FROM dual.
2)	a	You compute this by multiplying 24 hours by the 4 quarters of every hour. You can verify this with the following

query: `SELECT TO_CHAR(SYSDATE, 'HH24:MI'),`
`TO_CHAR(SYSDATE+1/96, 'HH24:MI') FROM`
`dual`.

3)   c   The NEXT_DAY function takes two parameters: a date and a day of the week. Sunday, January 9 is the next Sunday after January 2, 2000.

4)   c   The ROUND function rounds not just numbers, but also dates. If a format model is not specified, as in this example, it rounds to the nearest date. Because the time is before noon, it rounds to the current date. If the time is after noon, the next day is returned.

Lab 4.4 ■ Self-Review Answers

Question	Answer	Comments
1)	a	Any calculation with a NULL always yields NULL. If you want to avoid this behavior, use the NVL function to substitute another value.
2)	a	If the datatypes are different, Oracle attempts to convert the substitution expression's datatype to the input expression's datatype. If this is not possible, then the function returns an error. If the input expression is of a character datatype, the substitution expression's datatype is VARCHAR2.
3)	b	Only UPDATE statements update data in the database.
4)	a	DECODE lets you perform *if then else* comparisons.
5)	b	The DECODE function is allowed in any SQL statement where other column functions are allowed.

CHAPTER 5

Lab 5.1 ■ Self-Review Answers

Question	Answer	Comments
1)	c	Only AVG, COUNT, and SUM are aggregate functions. ROUND is a single-row function.
2)	c	The aggregate function MAX looks at the enrollment table for the most recently modified record. If a NULL value is returned, the value March 12, 2005 is substituted.
3)	a	Typically, aggregate functions work on groups of rows, but can also be applied to a single row. For example, the following two statements return the same result. `SELECT MAX(modified_date) FROM zipcode WHERE zip = '10025'; SELECT modified_date FROM zipcode WHERE zip = '10025'`.
4)	a	The asterisk is not a permissible argument for the AVG function.

5)   b   It computes the average capacity of the distinct capacities of the section table.

6)   b   The statement is correct and shows an example of an expression as an argument of an aggregate function. The capacity is multiplied by 1.5, then the aggregate function SUM is applied.

Lab 5.2 ■ Self-Review Answers

Question	Answer	Comments
1)	b	Only the section_id column. The other columns contain aggregate functions which are computed based on the grouping by section_id.
2)	a	It is syntactically correct to do this, but it is redundant because GROUP BY implies distinct values.
3)	a	Aggregate functions are not allowed in the WHERE clause unless they are part of a subquery.
4)	b	One row, because all the NULL values are grouped together. Although one NULL does not equal another, in a GROUP BY clause they are grouped together.
5)	a	You do not need to list the columns in the GROUP BY clause in the SELECT list.

CHAPTER 6

Lab 6.1 ■ Self-Review Answers

Question	Answer	Comments
1)	f	The alias is incorrect on the student table's zip column.
2)	d	Lines 2 and 5 are incorrect. In line 5 the stud.zip column does not exist; it needs to be changed to s.zip to correspond to the student alias s listed in the FROM clause. Line 2 lists a nonexistent szip column. Change it to s.zip for the query to work.
3)	b	The table alias is just another name to reference the table.
4)	a	The equijoin tests for equality of values in one or multiple columns.
5)	c	The column w.grade_type_code_cd is misspelled and needs to be changed to w.grade_type_code for the query to work.
6)	b	The NULL value from one table does not match the NULL value from another table; therefore the records are not included in the result.

Lab 6.2 ■ Self-Review Answers

Question	Answer	Comments
1)	b	This statement has the correct join criteria between the tables section, course, and instructor. Note, the course table

is not necessary to show the instructors assigned to sections.

2)	d	You get this error if you list two columns with the same name. Resolve it by prefixing the column with a table name or a table alias.
3)	b	Multicolumn joins need to have all the common columns listed. Some joins do not follow the primary/foreign key path, because either a foreign key relationship does not exist or a shortcut is used to obtain the information.
4)	a	The section_id column has the wrong table alias; change it to e.section_id or g.section_id instead.

CHAPTER 7

Lab 7.1 ■ Self-Review Answers

Question	Answer	Comments
1)	a	A subquery with the ORDER BY clause results in an error.
2)	b	Subqueries can also be used in other types of SQL statements, such as INSERT, DELETE, or UPDATE.
3)	a	The most-deeply-nested subquery is executed first. This is in contrast to the correlated subquery, which executes the outer query first, then repeatedly executes the inner subquery for every row of the outer query.
4)	a	The syntax of the SQL statement is incorrect. The subquery needs to be placed on the right side of the equal (=) sign.
5)	c	The IN operator allows multiple rows.
6)	a	You can compare column pairs by enclosing them in parentheses and comparing them to the subquery using the IN operator. Make sure the datatype and column pairs match on both sides of the IN operator.

Lab 7.2 ■ Self-Review Answers

Question	Answer	Comments
1)	a	The NOT EXISTS operator tests for NULL values, in contrast to the NOT IN operator which does not.
2)	a	For every row of the outer query, the inner query is executed.
3)	a	They result in the same output, although one may execute more efficiently than the other.
4)	b	The ORDER BY clause is never allowed in a subquery.
5)	b	The query looks only for enrolled students that have no corresponding record in the grade table for the particular section.

Lab 7.3 ■ Self-Review Answers

Question	Answer	Comments
1)	b	The first query tests if the number 6 is unequal to any of the values in the list. It is unequal to the number 9 and therefore the query returns the value True. The second query checks if the number 6 is not in the list of values. The value is included, and the query returns **no rows selected**.
2)	a	The two queries return the identical result.
3)	a	These operators can be used interchangeably.
4)	a	ANY, SOME, and ALL operators allow you to compare a list of values with the comparison operators. The IN operator tests only for equivalency.
5)	a	Only one column can be compared, not pairs of columns.

CHAPTER 8

Lab 8.1 ■ Self-Review Answers

Question	Answer	Comments
1)	a	The UNION set operator already performs a sort and only lists distinct values.
2)	b	The ORDER BY clause is always the last clause in a set operation.
3)	b	A UNION set operation does not eliminate rows; rather, it combines rows from each SELECT statement, eliminating duplicates only. An equijoin returns only rows where values from each table join.
4)	b	You can UNION any tables as long as you conform to the rules of the UNION operation; that is, the same number of columns and the same datatype.
5)	a	One of the rules of set operations is that the number of columns must be the same, as well as the datatypes of those columns.

Lab 8.2 ■ Self-Review Answers

Question	Answer	Comments
1)	b	The two SELECT statements are two different sets of data. Only one can be subtracted from the other for the desired, correct result.
2)	a	The SELECT statements in a set operation can be any SELECT statements.
3)	b	The datatype of the columns must agree.
4)	a	All set operators, except UNION ALL, eliminate duplicate values, so DISTINCT is not needed.

CHAPTER 9

Lab 9.1 ■ Self-Review Answers

Question	Answer	Comments
1)	a	The OR operator is not allowed in the outer join.
2)	a	The IN operator may not be used.
3)	a	The outer join operator indicates from which table you want to generate NULLs for nonmatching values.
4)	d	You cannot write a full outer join with two (+) outer join operators. You need to write two outer join statements and combine the result with the UNION set operator.

Lab 9.2 ■ Self-Review Answers

Question	Answer	Comments
1)	b	Joins do not have to follow the foreign/primary key path, but you have to carefully examine the result to make sure it is correct and does not result in a Cartesian product.
2)	b	You can join a table to itself without a recursive relationship, for example, to determine data inconsistencies.
3)	b	Such restrictions do not exist.
4)	a	
5)	a	Yes, to distinguish between the tables, an alias is required.

CHAPTER 10

Lab 10.1 ■ Self-Review Answers

Question	Answer	Comments
1)	b	
2)	b	The TRUNC function truncates a number or date. It does not delete records or issue a COMMIT.
3)	b	You can insert multiple rows by selecting from another table.
4)	a	If the rows have not been committed to the database, they can be restored.
5)	a	

CHAPTER 11

Lab 11.1 ■ Self-Review Answers

Question	Answer	Comments
1)	a	
2)	a	When the CREATE TABLE statement uses the AS SELECT keywords to select from another table or tables, the SELECT statement can contain a join of two or more tables.

3)	b	The foreign key constraints in the child tables are dropped, but not the child tables themselves.
4)	a	
5)	b	You can create a table from another regardless if the table has rows or not.

Lab 11.2 ■ Self-Review Answers

Question	Answer	Comments
1)	a	The syntax should not include both keywords CONSTRAINT and PRIMARY KEY. The correct syntax is either ALTER TABLE...DROP CONSTRAINT followed by the constraint name, or ALTER TABLE...DROP PRIMARY KEY.
2)	b	The ADD keyword is used to add columns or constraints to a table, while the MODIFY keyword is used to change characteristics of a column.
3)	a	If the column has no data, you can update the column with data, then add the NOT NULL constraint.
4)	b	The ALTER TABLE...DISABLE Primary KEY command is an example of the command used without the name of the constraint.
5)	b	A column's datatype can also be changed to a compatible datatype, such as from a VARCHAR2 to CHAR.
6)	a	The TRANSLATE function in the CHECK constraint checks if the format of a telephone number is correct when inserted or changed in the table. It also checks that the value contains only numbers and hyphens, and not letters.

CHAPTER 12

Lab 12.1 ■ Self-Review Answers

Question	Answer	Comments
1)	a	
2)	a, b	
3)	e	
4)	b	Views containing an ORDER BY clause are not allowed.
5)	a	Views must follow a number of rules to be updateable. This view allows inserts, updates, and deletes referencing the state column, but not to the modified_date column. If you are in doubt, query the data dictionary view user_updatable_columns.

Lab 12.2 ■ Self-Review Answers

Question	Answer	Comments
1)	c, d	A concatenated index typically outperforms individual column indexes. However, as with any query, you need to know how many rows you expect to retrieve with the cri-

		teria. If you retrieve a large number of records, the full table scan may outperform the retrieval from the index. If you create a concatenated index, choose the column order carefully. Make sure that your query accesses the leading column. If you have a choice, choose the most selective column first, that is, the column with the most distinct values.
2)	b	Indexes slow down DML operations. Retrieving data from an index may take more time if the retrieved data set is relatively large.
3)	a	These columns are often listed in the WHERE clause and therefore accessed frequently. Indexing these columns improves the performance of joins and other operations. Indexing foreign key columns also improves the locking of child records. If the foreign key columns are not indexed, locks are placed on the entire child table when a parent row is deleted or the columns referenced by the child table are updated. This then prevents any inserts, updates, and deletes on the child table. If you index the foreign key columns, locks are placed on the affected indexed child rows instead, thus not locking up the entire child table. This is more efficient and allows data manipulation of child rows not referenced by the updates and deletes of the parent table.
4)	a	
5)	b	NULLs are not stored in an index, therefore a search for NULL values will not use the index. However, a concatenated index will store NULLs as long as the leading column of the concatenated index is not NULL.
6)	a	Indexes are not only useful for SELECT statements, but also for UPDATE and DELETE statements to quickly locate the record. Note that INSERT, UPDATE, and DELETE operations on columns containing indexes are much slower, because the index needs to be updated with the changed or newly inserted values.

Lab 12.3 ■ Self-Review Answers

Question	Answer	Comments
1)	a	
2)	b	It is best to use a generated value for a primary key, such as from a sequence, because it is generic, is not subject to any change, and prevents duplicates or NULL values.
3)	a	
4)	b	These two objects are independent of each other. For example, you can use the same sequence for multiple tables.
5)	a	

CHAPTER 13

Lab 13.1 ■ Self-Review Answers

Question	Answer	Comments
1)	a	
2)	a	Other object types are also listed in this view.
3)	a	
4)	b	The all_tables view shows only the tables accessible to a user.
5)	a	

Lab 13.2 ■ Self-Review Answers

Question	Answer	Comments
1)	a	
2)	b	The CHR(10) function issues a line feed.
3)	a	
4)	a	Note that the $ command is not available on all operating systems.
5)	a	

CHAPTER 14

Lab 14.1 ■ Self-Review Answers

Question	Answer	Comments
1)	b	A user's objects can be dropped with the CASCADE keyword at the end of the DROP USER statement.
2)	a	
3)	a	System and object privileges cannot be granted or revoked in the same statement. However, system and object privileges, in separate statements, can be granted to or revoked from a single role, which can in turn be granted to a user.
4)	b	Both system and object privileges can be granted to a user through a role.
5)	b	Dropping a role has no effect on the underlying objects.

CHAPTER 15

Lab 15.1 ■ Self-Review Answers

Question	Answer	Comments
1)	a	
2)	c	
3)	b	In-line views, unlike regular views, are not stored in the data dictionary.

4)	b	It is a pseudocolumn, appearing as though it was an actual column in the table, but it is not.
5)	a	Like other views, this is allowed.

Lab 15.2 ■ Self-Review Answers

Question	Answer	Comments
1)	b	Joins are not allowed in hierarchical queries.
2)	a	
3)	a	The PRIOR operator determines the parent.
4)	a	

CHAPTER 16

Lab 16.1 ■ Self-Review Answers

Question	Answer	Comments
1)	b	
2)	a	
3)	a	The join order has a significant impact on performance.
4)	b	It is read from the inside to the outside. If two statements have the same level of indentation, the topmost statement is read first. The exception to this rule is the nested loop join.
5)	a	

APPENDIX B

SQL FORMATTING GUIDE AND SQL*PLUS COMMAND REFERENCE

SQL FORMATTING GUIDELINES

SQL formatting guidelines are a set of written instructions, similar to a style sheet in publishing, which helps programmers determine what the program code should look like. The main rule is *consistency;* once you have decided on the style, use it rigorously.

Why have guidelines? The major benefit of standardized formatting is ease of reading. This is particularly important if someone else has to maintain, upgrade, or fix your programs. The easier a program is to read, the easier it is to understand, and the faster changes can be made. This ultimately saves time and money.

CASE

SQL is case insensitive. However, there are guidelines to follow when writing SQL, for the sake of readability:

- Use UPPER case for SQL commands and keywords (SELECT, IN-SERT, UPDATE, DELETE, ALTER, etc.), datatypes (VARCHAR2,

DATE, NUMBER), functions (COUNT, TO_DATE, SUBSTR, etc.), and SQL*Plus commands (CONNECT, SET, etc.)

- Use lower case for column and tables names, as well as variable names.

FORMATTING SQL CODE

White space is important for readability. Put spaces on both sides of an equality sign or comparison operator. All examples in this workbook use a monospaced font (Courier) which makes the formatting easier to read. Proportionally-spaced fonts can hide spaces and make it difficult to line up clauses. Most text and programming editors by default use monospace fonts.

IN QUERIES

For SELECT statements, right-align keywords (SELECT, FROM, WHERE, the ORDER of ORDER BY), as in this example:

```
SELECT *
  FROM course
 WHERE prerequisite IS NULL
 ORDER BY course_no
```

IN DML STATEMENTS

For DML statements, right-align keywords (the INSERT of INSERT INTO, VALUES, SELECT). List columns on a separate line, indenting the open parenthesis two spaces. Align columns underneath each other, putting only a few columns on each line, as in this example:

```
INSERT INTO zipcode
  (zip, created_by, created_date,
   modified_by, modified_date)
VALUES
  ('11111', USER, SYSDATE,
   USER, SYSDATE)
```

IN DDL STATEMENTS

When using CREATE TABLE and defining columns, or using ALTER to alter a table, indent the second line and all other lines thereafter by two spaces, as in this example:

```
CREATE TABLE toy
  (description         VARCHAR2(15) NOT NULL,
```

```
last_purchase_date   DATE,
remaining_quantity   NUMBER(6))
```

When creating a table from another, right-align keywords (CREATE, SE-LECT, FROM, WHERE), as in this example:

```
CREATE TABLE jan_99_enrollment AS
SELECT *
  FROM enrollment
 WHERE 1 = 2
```

COMMENTS

Comments are very important when writing SQL code. Comments should explain the main sections of the program or SQL statement, and any major logic or business rules that are involved or non-trivial.

Suggestion: Use the '--' comments instead of the '/*' comments. It is easier to comment out a set of code for debugging using the '/*' comments if the code has only '--' comments. This is because you cannot embed '/*' comments within '/*' comments.

SQL*PLUS EDITING COMMANDS

SQL*PLUS ENVIRONMENT

SQL*Plus stores SQL and PL/SQL commands in the SQL*Plus buffer. However, it does not store SQL*Plus commands in the SQL*Plus buffer.

To edit SQL*Plus commands which have been entered at the SQL*Plus command prompt, simply backspace over the command. SQL and PL/SQL commands which have been stored in the SQL*Plus buffer may be edited from within SQL*Plus using the SQL*Plus editing commands listed in the following table:

SQL*Plus Editing Commands

Command	Abbreviation	Purpose
Append *text*	A *text*	add *text* at the end of a line
Change */old/new*	C */old/new*	change *old* to *new* in a line
Change */text*	C */text*	delete *text* from a line
Clear Buffer	CL Buff	delete all lines
Del	(none)	delete a line
Input	I	add one or more lines
Input *text*	I *text*	add a line consisting of *text*
List	L	list all lines in the SQL buffer
List *n*	L *n* or *n*	list 1 line
List *	L *	list the current line
List Last	L Last	list the last line
List *m n*	L *m n*	list a range of lines (*m* to *n*)

USING AN EDITOR WHICH IS EXTERNAL TO SQL*PLUS

If you have a set of commands (SQL*Plus, SQL, or a combination of the two) that may be used more than once, it is strongly recommended that you store them in a command script.

A command script is a text file which can be run from:

The SQL*Plus command prompt:

```
SQL> @create_table_cat[.sql]
```

The operating system command prompt:

```
C:\>sqlplus student/learn @c:\guest\create_table_cat[.sql]
```

USING AN EDITOR TO CREATE A COMMAND SCRIPT

To use your default operating system editor, type EDIT at the SQL*Plus prompt. EDIT loads the contents of the SQL*Plus buffer into the default editor.

Create a new file

```
SQL> EDIT
```

Load an already existing file

If a file already exists with the user-supplied filename, that file will be opened for editing. SQL*Plus will supply the extension .sql by default.

```
SQL> EDIT create_table_cat[.sql]
```

Change the default editor

To load the SQL*Plus buffer contents into a text editor other than the default, use the SQL*Plus DEFINE command to define a variable, _EDITOR, to hold the name of the editor.

```
SQL> DEFINE _EDITOR = ED
```

USING THE SQL*PLUS LINE EDITOR TO SAVE AND RETRIEVE FILES

SAVING A FILE

To save the current contents of the SQL*Plus buffer to a command script, use the SAVE command. An .sql extension is attached to the filename by default.

```
SQL> SAVE create_table_cat
```

To save the contents of the SQL*Plus buffer to a filename that already exists, use the SAVE command with the REPLACE option.

```
SQL> SAVE create_table_cat REPLACE
```

RETRIEVING A FILE

If you want to place the contents of a command script into the SQL*Plus buffer, use the SQL*Plus GET command.

```
SQL> GET create_table_cat
```

SQL*PLUS COMMAND REFERENCE

The following are just some of the commands available for use with SQL*Plus. Some of them are discussed in Chapter 2, "SQL: The Basics." This is not intended to be a thorough guide to SQL*Plus commands. Some of the commands take additional parameters. Some SQL*Plus commands can be toggled on or off, such as the ECHO and FEEDBACK commands, or from one value to another, such as with the LINESIZE command, all with the SET command. All of the current values of the commands can be viewed when you type SHOW ALL at the SQL*Plus prompt.

The letters appearing in square brackets are optional.

`@filename[.ext]`

The "at" symbol precedes a file name to start a SQL script. It is equivalent to the START command. An @@ runs a nested command file.

`&variablename`

The "ampersand" symbol is used as a substitution variable. Use the SET DEFINE OFF command to turn off the use of the ampersand as the substitution variable.

`&&variablename`

The double "ampersand" symbol is also a substitution variable, but it avoids reprompting. The variable is declared for the duration of the SQL*Plus session. Use UNDEFINE to undefine the variable and allow for reprompting.

`/`

The "forward slash" is entered at the SQL*Plus prompt to execute the current SQL statement in the buffer.

`ACC[EPT] variablename`

The ACCEPT command reads a line of input and stores it in a user variable.

`A[PPEND]`

The APPEND command appends text at the end of a line.

`C[HANGE]`

The CHANGE command changes text on the line indicated by following the CHANGE command with a forward slash, the old text, another forward slash, and the new text.

`CL[EAR] BUF[FER]`

The CLEAR BUFFER command clears all lines of a SQL statement from the buffer.

CL[EAR] COL[UMNS]

The CLEAR COLUMNS command clears all formatting of columns issued previously during the current session.

CL[EAR] SCR[EEN]

The CLEAR SCREEN command clears the entire screen of all commands.

COL[UMN]

The COLUMN command shows the display attributes for all columns. To show a specific column, use COLUMN column_name. To reset the attributes, use the COLUMN column_name CLEAR command. Also refer to the FORMAT command.

CONN[ECT]

When the CONNECT command is followed by a user id and password, it allows you to connect to the Oracle database as another user, and closes the active session for the current user. You can also use the DISCONNECT command to close an active session.

DEF[INE] [variablename]

The DEFINE command defines a SQL*Plus variable and stores it in a CHAR datatype variable. Without a variable name, it shows all the defined variables. SET DEFINE defines the substitution character—by default the ampersand symbol "&". SET DEFINE OFF turns the use of the substitution character off.

DEL

The DEL command deletes the current line in the buffer.

DESC[RIBE]

The DESCRIBE command describes the structure of a table or view, detailing its columns and their datatypes and lengths.

ED[IT] [filename.ext]

The EDIT command invokes the editor specified in SQL*Plus, opening a file with the current SQL statement. You can edit a specific file by executing the EDIT command followed by a filename.

`EXIT`

The EXIT command disconnects the current user from the database, and closes the SQL*Plus software.

`EXE[CUTE] statement`

The EXECUTE command executes a single PL/SQL statement.

`FOR[MAT] formatmodel`

The FORMAT command, together with the COLUMN command, specifies the display format of a column. For example, COL "Last Name" FORMAT A30, or COL cost FORMAT $999.99, or COL description FORMAT A20.

`HELP [topic]`

The HELP command accesses the SQL*Plus help system.

`HO[ST]`

The HOST command executes an operating system command. Depending on the operating system, ! or $ can be specified instead of the HOST command.

`I[NPUT]`

The INPUT command adds one or more lines to the current SQL statement.

`L[IST]`

The LIST command lists the contents of the buffer.

`PROMPT [text]`

The PROMPT command sends the specified message or a blank line to the user's screen.

`REM[ARK]`

The REMARK command begins a comment in a command file.

`REP[LACE]`

The REPLACE command is used in conjunction with the SAVE command to save a SQL statement to an existing file and overwrite it. The syntax is: SAVE [filename] REPLACE.

```
SAV[E] filename[.ext]
```

When followed by a file name, the SAVE command saves the file to the operating system. A directory can be specified.

```
SET AUTO[COMMIT]
```

The AUTOCOMMIT command can be set for a session to automatically commit all DML statements, rather than having to issue an explicit COMMIT command.

```
SET DEFINE [ON|OFF]
```

Turns the use of the substitution character on and off. See also DEFINE command.

```
SET ECHO {OFF|ON}
```

The ECHO command controls whether or not the START command lists each command in a SQL*Plus script as the command is executed.

```
SET FEED[BACK] {6|n|OFF|ON}
```

The FEEDBACK command displays the number of records returned by a query when a query selects at least *n* records.

```
SET LIN[ESIZE] {80|n}
```

The LINESIZE command sets the number of characters that SQL*Plus displays on a line before beginning a new line.

```
SET PAGES[IZE] {14|n}
```

The PAGESIZE command sets the number of lines from the top title to the end of the page. A value 0 suppresses SQL*Plus formatting information such as headings.

```
SET PAU[SE] {OFF|ON|text}
```

The PAUSE command allows control of scrolling and text displayed during pause.

```
SET SQL PROMPT
```

The SET SQL PROMPT command changes the SQL*Plus prompt.

```
SET TERM[OUT] {OFF|ON}
```

The TERMOUT command controls the display of output.

```
SET VER[IFY] {OFF|ON}
```

The VERIFY command controls whether SQL*Plus lists text of a command before and after SQL*Plus replaces substitution variables with values.

```
SHO[W] ALL
```

The SHOWALL command lists the value of all SQL*Plus system variables. The SHOW USER command is also useful to display the current login name.

```
SPO[OL] [filename[.ext]|OFF|OUT]
```

When you issue the SPOOL command followed by a file name, all commands subsequently issued in SQL*Plus are written to the file. The SPOOL OFF command stops writing to the file. If you do not specify an extension, the default extension is LIS or LST.

```
START filename[.ext]
```

When followed by a file name, the START command executes the file. This is the same as the @ symbol.

```
UNDEFINE variablename
```

The UNDEFINE command deletes a user variable that was explicitly defined with the DEFINE command or implicitly with the & or && substitution variables.

APPENDIX C

STUDENT DATABASE SCHEMA

TABLE AND COLUMN DESCRIPTIONS

Course

Information for a course.

Column Name	Null	Type	Comments
COURSE_NO	NOT NULL	NUMBER(8, 0)	The unique ID for a course.
DESCRIPTION	NULL	VARCHAR2(50)	The full name for this course.
COST	NULL	NUMBER(9,2)	The dollar amount charged for enrollment in this course.
PREREQUISITE	NULL	NUMBER(8, 0)	The ID number of the course which must be taken as a prerequisite to this course.
CREATED_BY	NOT NULL	VARCHAR2(30)	Audit column—indicates user who inserted data.
CREATED_DATE	NOT NULL	DATE	Audit column—indicates date of insert.
MODIFIED_BY	NOT NULL	VARCHAR2(30)	Audit column—indicates who made last update.
MODIFIED_DATE	NOT NULL	DATE	Audit column—date of last update.

Section

Information for an individual section (class) of a particular course.

Column Name	Null	Type	Comments
SECTION_ID	NOT NULL	NUMBER(8,0)	The unique ID for a section.
COURSE_NO	NOT NULL	NUMBER(8,0)	The course number for which this is a section.
SECTION_NO	NOT NULL	NUMBER(3)	The individual section number within this course.
START_DATE_TIME	NULL	DATE	The date and time on which this section meets.
LOCATION	NULL	VARCHAR2(50)	The meeting room for the section.
INSTRUCTOR_ID	NOT NULL	NUMBER(8,0)	The ID number of the instructor who teaches this section.
CAPACITY	NULL	NUMBER(3,0)	The maximum number of students allowed in this section.
CREATED_BY	NOT NULL	VARCHAR2(30)	Audit column—indicates user who inserted data.
CREATED_DATE	NOT NULL	DATE	Audit column—indicates date of insert.
MODIFIED_BY	NOT NULL	VARCHAR2(30)	Audit column—indicates who made last update.
MODIFIED_DATE	NOT NULL	DATE	Audit column—date of last update.

Student

Profile information for a student.

Column Name	Null	Type	Comments
STUDENT_ID	NOT NULL	NUMBER(8,0)	The unique ID for a student.
SALUTATION	NULL	VARCHAR2(5)	This student's title (Ms., Mr., Dr., etc.).
FIRST_NAME	NULL	VARCHAR2(25)	This student's first name.

LAST_NAME	NOT NULL	VARCHAR2(25)	This student's last name.
STREET_ADDRESS	NULL	VARCHAR2(50)	This student's street address.
ZIP	NOT NULL	VARCHAR2(5)	The postal zip code for this student.
PHONE	NULL	VARCHAR2(15)	The phone number for this student, including area code.
EMPLOYER	NULL	VARCHAR2(50)	The name of the company where this student is employed.
REGISTRATION_DATE	NOT NULL	DATE	The date this student registered in the program.
CREATED_BY	NOT NULL	VARCHAR2(30)	Audit column—indicates user who inserted data.
CREATED_DATE	NOT NULL	DATE	Audit column—indicates date of insert.
MODIFIED_BY	NOT NULL	VARCHAR2(30)	Audit column—indicates who made last update.
MODIFIED_DATE	NOT NULL	DATE	Audit column—date of last update.

Enrollment

Information for a student registered for a particular section (class).

Column Name	Null	Type	Comments
STUDENT_ID	NOT NULL	NUMBER(8,0)	The unique ID for a student.
SECTION_ID	NOT NULL	NUMBER(8,0)	The unique ID for a section.
ENROLL_DATE	NOT NULL	DATE	The date this student registered for this section.
FINAL_GRADE	NULL	NUMBER(3,0)	The final grade given to this student for all work in this section (class).
CREATED_BY	NOT NULL	VARCHAR2(30)	Audit column—indicates user who inserted data.
CREATED_DATE	NOT NULL	DATE	Audit column—indicates date of insert.

MODIFIED_BY	NOT NULL	VARCHAR2(30)	Audit column—indicates who made last update.
MODIFIED_DATE	NOT NULL	DATE	Audit column—date of last update.

Instructor

Profile information for an instructor.

Column Name	Null	Type	Comments
INSTRUCTOR_ID	NOT NULL	NUMBER(8)	The unique ID for an instructor.
SALUTATION	NULL	VARCHAR2(5)	This instructor's title (Mr., Ms., Dr., Rev., etc.).
FIRST_NAME	NULL	VARCHAR2(25)	This instructor's first name.
LAST_NAME	NULL	VARCHAR2(25)	This instructor's last name.
STREET_ADDRESS	NULL	VARCHAR2(50)	This instructor's street address.
ZIP	NULL	VARCHAR2(5)	The postal zip code for this instructor.
PHONE	NULL	VARCHAR2(15)	The phone number for this instructor, including area code.
CREATED_BY	NOT NULL	VARCHAR2(30)	Audit column—indicates user who inserted data.
CREATED_DATE	NOT NULL	DATE	Audit column—indicates date of insert.
MODIFIED_BY	NOT NULL	VARCHAR2(30)	Audit column—indicates who made last update.
MODIFIED_DATE	NOT NULL	DATE	Audit column—date of last update.

Zipcode

City, state, and zipcode information.

Column Name	Null	Type	Comments
ZIP	NOT NULL	VARCHAR2(5)	The zip code number, unique for a city and state.
CITY	NULL	VARCHAR2(25)	The city name for this zip code.

STATE	NULL	VARCHAR2(2)	The postal abbreviation for the US state.
CREATED_BY	NOT NULL	VARCHAR2(30)	Audit column—indicates user who inserted data.
CREATED_DATE	NOT NULL	DATE	Audit column—indicates date of insert.
MODIFIED_BY	NOT NULL	VARCHAR2(30)	Audit column—indicates who made last update.
MODIFIED_DATE	NOT NULL	DATE	Audit column—date of last update.

Grade_Type

Lookup table of a grade type (code) and its description.

Column Name	Null	Type	Comments
GRADE_TYPE_CODE	NOT NULL	CHAR(2)	The unique code which identifies a category of grade, (e.g., MT, HW).
DESCRIPTION	NOT NULL	VARCHAR2(50)	The description for this code (e.g., Midterm, Homework).
CREATED_BY	NOT NULL	VARCHAR2(30)	Audit column—indicates user who inserted data.
CREATED_DATE	NOT NULL	DATE	Audit column—indicates date of insert.
MODIFIED_BY	NOT NULL	VARCHAR2(30)	Audit column—indicates who made last update.
MODIFIED_DATE	NOT NULL	DATE	Audit column—date of last update.

Grade_Type_Weight

Information on how the final grade for a particular section is computed. For example, the midterm constitutes 50%, the quiz 10%, and the final examination 40% of the final grade.

Column Name	Null	Type	Comments
SECTION_ID	NOT NULL	NUMBER(8)	The unique ID for a section.

GRADE_TYPE_CODE	NOT NULL	CHAR(2)	The code which identifies a category of grade.
NUMBER_PER_SECTION	NOT NULL	NUMBER(3)	How many of these grade types can be used in this section; that is, there may be 3 quizzes.
PERCENT_OF _FINAL_GRADE	NOT NULL	NUMBER(3)	The percentage this category of grade contributes to the final grade.
DROP_LOWEST	NOT NULL	CHAR(1)	Is the lowest grade in this type removed when determining the final grade? (Y/N).
CREATED_BY	NOT NULL	VARCHAR2(30)	Audit column—indicates user who inserted data.
CREATED_DATE	NOT NULL	DATE	Audit column—indicates date of insert.
MODIFIED_BY	NOT NULL	VARCHAR2(30)	Audit column—indicates who made last update.
MODIFIED_DATE	NOT NULL	DATE	Audit column—date of last update.

Grade

The individual grades a student received for a particular section (class).

Column Name	Null	Type	Comments
STUDENT_ID	NOT NULL	NUMBER(8)	The unique ID for a student.
SECTION_ID	NOT NULL	NUMBER(8)	The unique ID for a section.
GRADE_TYPE_CODE	NOT NULL	CHAR(2)	The code which identifies a category of grade.
GRADE_CODE _OCCURRENCE	NOT NULL	NUMBER(38)	The sequence number of one grade type for one section. For example, there could be

			multiple assignments numbered 1, 2, 3, etc.
NUMERIC_GRADE	NOT NULL	NUMBER(3)	Numeric grade value, (e.g., 70, 75).
COMMENTS	NULL	VARCHAR2(2000)	Instructor's comments on this grade.
CREATED_BY	NOT NULL	VARCHAR2(30)	Audit column—indicates user who inserted data.
CREATED_DATE	NOT NULL	DATE	Audit column—indicates date of insert.
MODIFIED_BY	NOT NULL	VARCHAR2(30)	Audit column—indicates who made last update.
MODIFIED_DATE	NOT NULL	DATE	Audit column—date of last update.

Grade_Conversion

Converts a number grade to a letter grade.

Column Name	Null	Type	Comments
LETTER_GRADE	NOT NULL	VARCHAR(2)	The unique grade as a letter (A, A-, B, B+, etc.).
GRADE_POINT	NOT NULL	NUMBER(3,2)	The number grade on a scale from 0 (F) to 4 (A).
MAX_GRADE	NOT NULL	NUMBER(3)	The highest grade number which makes this letter grade.
MIN_GRADE	NOT NULL	NUMBER(3)	The lowest grade number which makes this letter grade.
CREATED_BY	NOT NULL	VARCHAR2(30)	Audit column—indicates user who inserted data.
CREATED_DATE	NOT NULL	DATE	Audit column—indicates date of insert.
MODIFIED_BY	NOT NULL	VARCHAR2(30)	Audit column—indicates who last made update.
MODIFIED_DATE	NOT NULL	DATE	Audit column—date of last update.

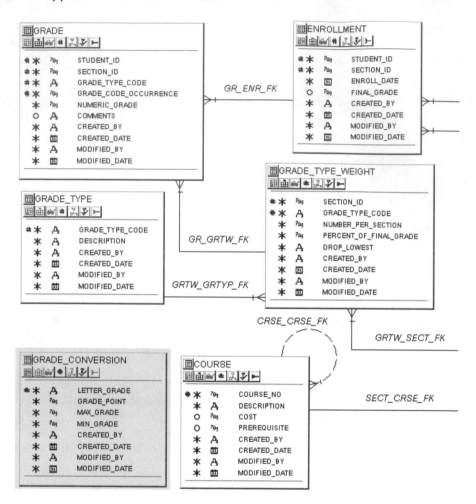

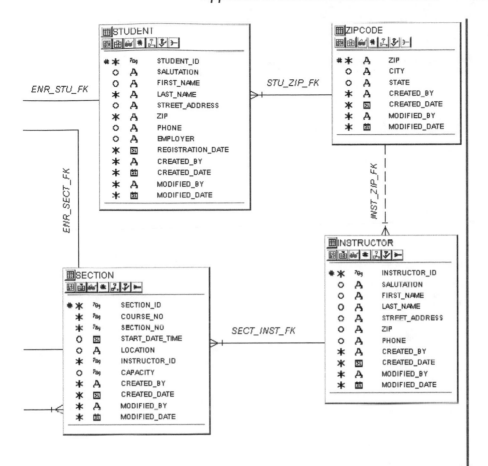

INDEX

A

ABS function, 83-84
ACCEPT command, 374, 378, 381
Add columns. See ALTER TABLE command, 482
Addition, 86
ADD_MONTHS function, 112, 115, 476
Advanced SQL Queries, 413
Aggregate function, 65, 127-28, 131, 134, 136, 138
    in equijoin statements, 414, 416, 421
    with joins, 185, 192-93, 207, 209
Alias
    column, 68
    column alias used in ORDER BY clause, 137
    column alias with AS keyword, 68, 137
    column with double quotes, 68
ALL operator. See Subqueries
    ALL operator, 181
ALL_ROWS hint, 449, 452
Alphanumeric data, 6
ALTER TABLE command, 296, 306-11, 313-19
ALTER USER command, 395, 408
ALTER VIEW command, 372
Alternate key, 347
ANALYZE INDEX command, 458-459
ANALYZE TABLE command, 444-45, 453, 457-58
AND operator, 48, 50-52, 54-55
    precedence, 51
ANSI, 7
ANY operator
    versus self-join, 261
ANY operator. See Subqueries
    ANY operator, 181
Argument
    definition, 65
Arithmetic operators, 86
ASC. See ORDER BY clause
    ascending, 61
Ascending. See ORDER BY clause
    ascending, 60
ASCII, 130
Asterisk
    in COUNT function, 128

in-line editor, 39
in SELECT statement, 30, 474
on schema diagram, 10
Audit columns, 13
AUTOT TRACE EXPLAIN, 454, 460
AUTOTRACE command, 447-48, 455, 463
AVG function, 130, 132-34, 141-42
    in subqueries, 191-92

B

Back end, 20
Back-up data, 395
Basc tables, 322
BETWEEN operator, 48-51, 56, 475
BFILE datatype, 291
BLOB datatype, 291
Boolean operator, 50
Buffer in SQL*Plus, 38-45, 474, 489
Business rules, 16, 289, 293

C

Cartesian product, 150, 153, 155, 159-60, 186
    avoid by writing a subquery, 159
CASCADE CONSTRAINTS in DROP TABLE command, 296, 305, 365
CASCADE delete in data dictionary, 365
Case
    for table and column names, 10
    in column alias, 68
    in format mask, 476
    in SQL statements, 487
Case sensitivity, 23, 30, 47
Catalog, 353
CHANGE command, 39, 42-43
CHAR datatype, 291
Character comparison, 107
Character function, 65-66, 74, 80
Character literal. See Literal
    text, 46
Check constraint, 294-95
Child table, 10
CHOOSE mode, 445-46
CHR function, 376, 384, 386-89, 484
Client/Server, 20-22
CLOB datatype, 291
Cluster Join, 451

Codd, 2
COL command, 372, 376-78, 388
Column
    add, 306
    change of datatype, 316
    decreasing column width, 317
    DEFAULT, 293, 295, 299, 303-04, 314
    definition, 2, 5
    drop, 306
    modify, 308, 315
    name restrictions, 291
Column alias
    set operators, 227
Column ambiguously defined, 151-52
COLUMN command, 35, 68
    clear, 35
    in SQL*Plus, 93
Column default
    in data dictionary, 362
Columns
    in data dictionary, 357, 361-62
Command Reference
    for SQL*Plus commands, 491
Comments, 385, 489
    on tables and columns, 390
COMMIT, 270, 272, 274, 276-78, 280, 282-84, 286, 288
    DDL commands, 291, 329
Common column in joins, 152, 155, 157, 161, 165, 170-73
Communication protocol, 20
Comparison operator, 27, 46, 48-50, 53-56, 60
    not equal, 57
Compiling views. See Views
    compiling, 329
Complex join, 147, 243
Computation, 89
COMPUTE STATISTICS, 445, 458
CONCAT function, 72
    NULLs, 475
Concatenation, 66, 72, 81
CONNECT BY clause, 258, 413, 429-40, 442
CONNECT command, 392-94, 396-397, 404, 407-08, 410
CONNECT role, 394, 404, 406, 410, 412
Constraint
    ADD, 309, 317
    check constraint. See Check constraint, 294
    column, 377
    create, 289
    DISABLE, 309-10, 318-19, 374
    DROP, 309, 319

ENABLE, 309, 318
    for column in data dictionary, 358, 366
    foreign key. See Foreign key constraint, 294
    in data dictionary, 358, 364-65, 374, 377, 382, 384, 386
    naming, 295
    NOVALIDATE, 312
    primary key. See Primary key constraint, 294
    resolving violation, 311
    unique. See Unique constraint, 295
    WITH CHECK OPTION. See View
        WITH CHECK OPTION, 328
Constraint types, 365
Correlated subqueries. See Subqueries
    correlated, 181
COS function, 84
Cost-based optimizer, 444-47, 449, 452-53, 460, 466-67
COUNT function, 128-30, 132-33, 136-38, 140-45
    in subqueries, 192-93, 196, 205-10
CREATE OR REPLACE VIEW. See View
    Create, Alter, and Drop Views, 404
CREATE ROLE command, 400-01, 409
CREATE SESSION privilege, 394, 405
CREATE SYNONYM command, 398, 405, 408
Create table
    based on other tables, 292
CREATE TABLE command, 290-93, 295, 297-305, 399, 404-05
CREATE USER command, 392-93, 404, 406
Crow's feet notation, 16
CURRVAL pseudocolumn, 338, 348

D

Data control language, 3, 7, 270
Data definition language, 3, 7, 270
Data dictionary, 249, 353-54, 357, 445
Data integrity. See also Integrity constraint, 293
Data manipulation in Views. See Views, 322
Data manipulation language, 2, 7, 267, 270, 272, 274, 284, 286
Database
    definition, 2
Database Management System, 2
Datatype, 46-47, 55
    choosing for table, 291
    definition, 6
    in functions, 130

Datatype conversion, 91, 93, 97, 108, 476
    explicit, 92, 99
    implicit, 463
    text literal to DATE, 99
    text literal to NUMBER, 94
Datatypes
    in set operations, 224, 229
Date
    comparison, 106
    functions, 91, 112
Date and time math, 91, 110-11, 113
Date and time stamp. See Time stamp, 98
DATE datatype, 98, 291
DATE format mask. See Format model
    DATE, 91
Day of the week, 101, 104, 108, 112
DBA role, 394, 406
DBMS
    definition, 2, 3
    See Data control language, 270
DCL
    definition, 3
    See Data control language, 270
DDL
    definition, 2
    See Data definition language, 270
DECODE function, 91, 116, 118-20, 122-
    24, 413-15, 421-25, 427, 441, 477
    NULLs, 475
Default mask. See Format model
    DATE, 103
Default tablespace. See Tablespace
    default, 393
DEFAULT value
    in column. See Column
        DEFAULT, 86, 295
DEFINE command, 23, 377-78, 381, 388
Definition of SQL, 1
DELETE, 7, 267, 275-77, 279, 284-86
    with subqueries, 182
DELETE STATISTICS, 459
DESC command. See DESCRIBE command,
    23
DESC. See ORDER BY clause
    descending, 58
Descending. See ORDER BY clause
    descending, 60
DESCRIBE SQL*Plus command, 23, 30
DICTIONARY, 355
DICT_COLUMNS, 356, 361, 367
Disable constraints. See ALTER TABLE
    command, 482
DISTINCT, 28, 30-33, 36, 56
    in SET operators, 480
    in subqueries, 195
    versus GROUP BY clause, 135, 478

    with aggregate function, 129
    with COUNT function, 132
    with primary key, 31
DISTINCT keyword in joins, 156, 159,
    171-72
Division, 86, 88
DML
    definition, 2
    See Data manipulation language,
        267
Domain, 15-19, 294, 296
Driving table, 451-52, 455-56, 465-66
DROP COLUMN clause, 307-308
DROP ROLE command, 401, 411
DROP TABLE command, 296, 301, 305-06
DROP UNUSED COLUMNS clause, 308
DROP USER command, 395, 484
Dual table, 70, 73-75, 78, 82-85, 87, 89-90
Dummy column. See Dual table, 70
Dynamic performance views, 354
Dynamic SQL Scripts, 353, 374

E

EDIT command, 40-41, 44
Editing
    a SQL statement, 27, 38, 41
Editor
    use in SQL*Plus, 39
    See Line editor, 38
Environmental variables, 24
Equal operator, 46, 54, 60
Equality
    testing for, 46
Equijoin, 6, 147, 150-52, 155, 160-61,
    243-46, 252, 255-56, 258-59, 478
    comparison to INTERSECT set opera-
        tor, 236
    multicolumn join criteria, 166, 168,
        172
    multitable, 160, 167, 169
    multitable equijoin, 163, 174
    skip primary key/foreign key path,
        160, 175-77
    WHERE clause, 154
    with NULLs, 152, 161, 478
ESTIMATE STATISTICS, 458
EXCEPTIONS table, 311
Execute SQL statement, 30
Execution order
    of WHERE, GROUP BY, and HAVING
        clause, 139
Execution plan, 444, 446, 459, 468, 471
EXISTS operator. See Subqueries
    EXISTS operator, 198
EXIT command, 24

Explain plan, 444, 446, 453
    for nested loop join, 451
EXPLAIN PLAN FOR command, 447
EXPORT utility, 395
Expression, 46, 51-52, 55
    definition, 46
    in Views, 323, 331-332

F

FEEDBACK command, 29, 375-76, 383-88
File
    saving, 474
File extension, 44
Fill mode, 104-105, 476
FIRST_ROWS hint, 449, 455, 465
Fm. See Fill mode, 476
Foreign key, 10-19, 26, 150, 152, 157, 159-60, 165-67, 175-77, 186
    multicolumn foreign key, 166
    skip in join statements, 160, 175-76
Foreign key constraint, 294
    delete restrict, 294
    disable, 249
    drop, 249
    ON DELETE CASCADE clause, 293-94
    rules, 294
FORMAT command, 35, 68, 364, 372, 376-78, 388
    SQL*Plus, 94
Format data, 93, 95
Format mask. See Format model, 98
Format model, 93, 97, 100
    DATE, 98-100, 109
    DATE default format mask, 98
    NUMBER, 94, 476
Formatting
    of SQL statements, 30
FROM clause, 33, 150
    definition, 28-29
    In-line views, 181
    order of tables in, 151
    Queries in the FROM clause. See In-Line view, 413
Front end, 20
Full outer join. See Outer joins
    Full outer join, 248
Full table scan, 335, 451-52, 460-61, 466
Function
    nested, 79-80, 89

G

GRANT command, 7, 394, 396-97, 399-401, 404, 406-407, 409
    on columns, 396

on stored objects, 397
    re-issuing if object is dropped, 397
    WITH ADMIN OPTION, 406, 409
    WITH GRANT OPTION, 396
Grantee, 396, 406, 410
Grantor, 396-397, 406, 410
GREATER THAN comparison, 48
GROUP BY
    and NULLs, 478
GROUP BY clause, 127, 135-45, 207
    common error, 137
    sorting of data, 137

H

Hash join, 451-52
Hash table, 452
HAVING clause, 127, 135, 138-43, 145, 207
    in subqueries, 192
HEADING command, 372, 377-78, 388
Hierarchical queries, 413, 429, 432
    joins, 485
Hint, 445, 449-52, 455-56, 465-68, 470-72
    incorrectly specifying, 450
HOST command, 376, 387-89
Host string, 393

I

If then else
    in TRANSLATE function, 73
Implicit conversion. See Datatype conversion, 106
IN operator, 49, 54, 60, 474-75
    in subqueries. See Subqueries returning multiple rows, 184
    versus OR operator, 54
In-line view, 181, 413-14, 418-21, 425, 427-28, 484
Index, 321, 335
    B-Tree, 335
    bitmapped, 335
    composite, 335, 339-42
    concatenated, 335, 482
    concatenated and NULLs, 461
    create, 336-37, 339-43
    data manipulation, 483
    disable use of index, 96, 102
    drop, 339-40, 343
    foreign key columns, 483
    function on indexed column, 337
    function-based, 343-44, 462
    leading column, 341-42, 461, 463-64
    merging of indexes, 342
    Nulls, 342, 483

performance, 344
rebuild, 344, 352
separate from data, 337
unique, 345, 445
unique on constraints, 335
when constraint is enabled or disabled, 310
INDEX hint, 449
Index tablespace. See Tablespace
index, 309
Indexed columns
in data dictionary, 362
Inequality conditions
use of index, 460
Init.ora, 451
INITCAP function, 74, 77, 282
Inner query. See Subqueries, 182
Input parameter
definition, 65
INSERT, 7, 267-72, 277, 280-81, 286, 288
individual row, 268
multiple rows, 270
with subqueries, 182
INSTR function, 69-70, 78-82, 475
Integrity constraint, 289, 293, 306
INTERSECT set operator, 223, 233, 236-38, 240-241
Invalid database object, 296, 308
Invalid number, 117
Invalid view, 329
IS NOT NULL operator, 52, 60
and Index. See Index, 483
IS NULL operator, 52, 56, 58-59, 132, 152, 154, 157, 169-70, 254, 475
and Index. See Index, 483
negation, 55

J

Join criteria, 151, 159, 166, 177
Join operations, 444, 455
Join types, 451

K

Key-preserved table, 333
Keys
Alternate. See Alternate key, 347
Foreign. See Foreign key, 14
Primary. See Primary key, 14
Synthetic. See Synthetic key, 14

L

LAST_DAY function, 112-14
Leading column. See Index
leading column, 341
Leading edge. See Index

leading column, 341
LENGTH function, 70-71, 75, 77-78, 81-82, 89, 475
LESS THAN comparison, 48
LEVEL pseudocolumn, 431-39
LIKE operator, 49-51, 54-56, 71, 74, 77, 81
Line editor, 38-39, 489, 491
LINESIZE command, 375, 383-86
LIST command, 39, 43
List of values
with the comparison operators. See Subqueries
ANY, ALL, SOME, 480
List of values. See IN operator, 474
Literal, 92
constant, 67
in outer join, 252
number, 95-96, 117, 205, 210
text, 46, 66-67, 70, 92-93, 98-99, 101-03, 107-09, 111, 113-14, 117
text conversion to DATE format, 100
Logical operator, 46, 50-54
Login to SQL*Plus, 20-22
Logout of SQL*Plus, 21
LONG datatype, 291
displaying in SQL*Plus, 364
LONG RAW datatype, 291
Low-selectivity, 335, 344
LOWER function, 66-67, 76-77, 82
LPAD function, 67-68, 79
with LEVEL function, 431-36, 438-39
LTRIM function, 75, 78-79

M

Manipulating data, 267
Master/Slave script, 371
Math
Dates. See Date and time math, 111
MAX function, 130-31, 133, 142-43, 145
in subqueries, 184-85, 187-88, 192-93, 196, 198-201, 218-19
MIN function, 130-131
in subqueries, 182-83, 190-91, 218-19
MINUS set operator, 223, 233, 235-39, 241, 245, 457, 467-68
duplicates, 235
MOD function, 84
Modify columns. See ALTER TABLE command, 482
MONTHS_BETWEEN function, 112, 114
Multi-column join. See Equijoin
multicolumn join criteria, 166, 479
Multiline comment, 386
Multiparameter function, 67

Multiple row function, 65
Multiplication, 86, 88, 97
Multiuser system, 473

N

Nested loop join, 451
Nesting
    of functions. See Function
        nested, 79
Net8, 20, 22
NEW_TIME function, 112, 114
NEXTVAL pseudocolumn, 277, 280-81, 338, 348-50
NEXT_DAY function, 477
NOCACHE
    in sequences, 348
NOT EXISTS operator, 245-47, 254
    comparison to MINUS set operator, 239
    in DELETE statement, 286
    See Subqueries NOT EXISTS opera-tor, 198
NOT IN operator
    in subqueries. See Subqueries
        returning multiple rows, 195
    SQL performance, 467
NOT NULL constraint. See Check con-straint, 303
NOT operator, 50, 475
Notepad
    as editor in SQL*Plus, 40
NOVALIDATE. See Constraint
    NOVALIDATE, 312
NULL
    and computation, 86
    as a return value in single row func-tion, 84
    comparison, 56
    definition, 10, 31, 52
    evaluating, 52
    in aggregate function, 130
    in computations, 477
    in concatenated index, 461
    in COUNT function, 129
    in equijoins, 152
    in functions, 475
    in Index. See Index
        NULLs, 483
    in INSERT statement, 269
    in SELECT statement, 31
    in UPDATE statement, 275
    in WHERE clause, 53
    Primary key, 10
    with DISTINCT, 31, 36
NULL value, 91, 116, 119, 121
    in computations, 116

Nulls
    indexes. See Indexes
        nulls, 342
NUMBER datatype, 291
Number function, 65, 83, 475
NVL function, 84, 91, 116-17, 119, 121, 124, 130, 132-33, 143, 477
    with aggregate function, 130

O

Object
    in data dictionary, 357, 359-60, 368-70, 372
Object privilege, 391, 396-97
ON DELETE CASCADE clause. See Foreign key constraint
    ON DELETE CASCADE clause, 294
OR operator, 50-52, 54-55, 60
    precedence, 51
Oracle Optimizer, 443
ORDER BY clause, 27, 58-62, 154-57, 175-76, 475
    ascending, 58-61
    column alias, 227
    column position, 227
    descending, 58-59, 61
    in SELECT statement, 59
    in SET operations, 226, 231-32, 480
    in subqueries. See Subqueries
        ORDER BY clause, 479
    sort order, 157
    subqueries. See Subqueries
        ORDER BY clause, 184
    using functions, 71
ORDERED hint, 449, 466, 470
Orphan rows, 15, 474
Outer join, 243-44, 246-47
    full outer join, 248-50, 481
    IN operator, 256, 481
    left outer join, 250
    OR operator, 256, 481
    right outer join, 250
    self-join, 264
    WHERE clause, 251
Outer query. See Subqueries, 182

P

PAGESIZE command, 375-76, 383-87
Parent table, 10
Parentheses, 49, 51-52, 54
    in computations, 86, 89
    in functions, 65, 80
    in nested functions, 80
    to indicate precedence, 51
Password, 20, 22
    changing, 393, 395, 404, 408

Pattern-matching, 49
Performance considerations, 96
Performance optimization, 186
Pipe symbol, 72, 81
PL/SQL, 23
Plustrace role, 447
Precedence
    of logical operators, 51
    of operators, 86
Primary key, 10-16, 18-19, 26, 31, 36, 150,
    157, 159, 165-67, 172-73, 175-77, 186
    composite, 13-14
    concatenated, 13
    definition, 10
    multicolumn primary key, 166, 173,
      175
    skip in join statements, 160, 175-76
Primary key constraint, 294
Primary key values
    generating from Sequence. See Se-
      quence, 483
PRIOR operator, 413, 429-440, 442, 485
Privileges. See GRANT or REVOKE com-
    mands, 396
Prompt, 22-23
PROMPT command, 374, 381
Pseudocolumn
    Rowid, 337
    ROWNUM, 485
PUBLIC
    granting to, 400-01
    revoking from, 401
    synonym. See Synonym
      PUBLIC, 399

Q

Quotes
    around text literal, 47
    single quotes, 333

R

RAW datatype, 291
RDBMS, 2, 20, 22
Read-consistency of data, 284
Recursive relationship. See Relationships
    between tables
      self-referencing, 258
Referential integrity, 1, 15, 17
Relational database management system,
    2
Relationships between tables, 1, 16-17
    mandatory relationship, 16
    many-to-many, 150, 159
    one-to-many, 16, 150, 165, 167
    one-to-one, 150, 165
    optional, 16

parent-child, 10, 474
schema diagram, 12
self-referencing, 16, 243, 258, 265,
    429, 481
RENAME command, 296, 301
Renaming table. See RENAME command,
    296
REPLACE function, 73-74, 82
    NULLs, 475
RESOURCE role, 394-95, 404-06, 412
Result set
    display of, 29
REVOKE command, 395, 397, 401, 408,
    410
    cascading of privileges, 397
Role, 391
    user-defined, 392, 400, 403
ROLLBACK, 270-75, 277, 279, 284-85
Rollback segments, 284
Root row, 432
    See START WITH operator, 430
ROUND function, 85-89, 97, 111, 142, 475
    versus TRUNC function, 85
    with DATE datatype, 88, 477
    with negative precision parameter,
      87
Rounding, 83, 94
Row
    definition, 2, 5
Rowid. See Pseudocolumn
    Rowid, 337
ROWNUM pseudocolumn, 420-21, 427-28
RPAD function, 67-68, 79, 81
RR year format, 103
RTRIM function, 75, 78-79, 82, 475
RULE hint, 449, 451, 456-57, 465-68, 471
Rule-based optimizer, 444-45, 449, 456,
    459, 465-67, 470
RUN command, 474

S

SAVEPOINT, 270, 272-74
Saving
    of files, 44
Schema, 447, 453, 459-60, 462
    referencing objects in other schemas,
      397
Schema diagram, 1, 9-14, 16, 26, 171
    description of relationships, 16
Security, 391
    of data, 7
    related views in data dictionary,
      395, 402-03, 405-06, 410
    views and security, 322
SELECT list
    asterisk, 30, 37

definition, 28-29
order of columns, 30, 37
wildcard, 30, 37
SELECT statement, 475
anatomy, 27-28
Self-join, 243, 258-65
together with outer join, 264
versus hierarchical query, 431
Sequence, 281, 321, 347
Create, 347
in data dictionary, 355-56, 358, 363, 368
increment, 350
Session, 24, 270, 274, 278, 283-84
SET
in UPDATE statement, 274
Set operators, 207, 223
column alias, 227
combining multiple, 231
datatype, 227
ORDER BY clause. See ORDER BY clause: in set operations, 226
rules, 224, 232
SET UNUSED clause, 307
SHOW ALL command, 385
SHOW command, 24
ALL, 24
RELEASE, 25, 474
USER, 25, 269
SIGN function, 84, 118-19, 421, 424-25, 427, 441
SIN function, 84
Single-quote
in a SQL script, 389
Single row function, 65, 70, 84, 91, 97, 127
Single-line comment, 385-86
Size of objects, 367
Sort order. See ORDER BY clause, 157
Sort-merge join, 451-52
Special Characters
!=, 48, 57
$ command. See HOST command, 484
& Symbol, 370, 377-80
&& Symbol, 377-78
(+). See outer join, 481
*/, 385, 489
--, 385, 489
--+, 4, 449, 465
/, 474
/*, 385, 489
/*+, 449-52, 456-57, 465-68, 471-72
<, 48, 5, 475
<=, 48
@ host string, 393

SPOOL command, 371-72, 375-76, 383-87
SQL commands
versus SQL*Plus commands, 24
SQL formatting guidelines, 487
SQL optimization, 443
SQL statement
execute, 30, 39, 44
formatting, 30, 67
versus SQL*Plus commands, 39
SQL to generate SQL script, 371
SQL*Net, 20, 22
SQL*Plus, 27, 29-30, 35-36, 38-44, 63
interaction with the database, 7
line editor, 40-41, 44, 63
number of rows returned, 29
SQL*Plus commands, 38
versus SQL commands, 30, 39
START command, 40-42, 44-45, 474
START WITH
in sequences, 348
START WITH clause, 430-39, 442
Statistics
deleting, 459
gathering, 453, 460
See Cost-based optimizer, 445
Storage parameters, 310
String, 66-71, 73-74, 76, 78-82, 89-90
See Literal
text, 46
Subqueries, 159, 182, 213
ALL operator, 181, 186, 213-18, 220-22
ANY operator, 186, 213-16, 219-22
SOME operator, 181, 186, 213-14, 216, 221
aggregate function, 186
ALL operator, 213
ALL operator and NULLs, 216
ALL operator versus NOT IN operator, 216
ANY operator, 213
ANY operator and NULLs, 216
ANY operator versus IN operator, 215
correlated, 181-82, 196-99, 201, 204-05, 207-08, 210-12, 217, 222, 275, 479
correlated update. See UPDATE
EXISTS operator, 198, 201-04, 208-10, 212
HAVING clause in correlated subquery, 207
inner query, 182-84, 188, 198-201, 209, 211-12
IN operator, 479
nesting, 183, 194

NOT EXISTS operator, 198, 202, 204, 210-12, 222, 479
NOT EXISTS with index, 457, 467-68
NOT IN operator, 479
NOT IN versus NOT EXISTS, 203
NULL keyword in correlated subqueries, 209
ORDER BY clause, 184, 196, 212, 479
outer query, 182, 185, 188, 195, 198-201, 207, 209, 211
returning multiple columns, 187, 190, 195-97, 479
returning multiple rows, 182, 184-86, 188-89, 193, 195, 197-98, 202-04, 206, 208, 211, 213-15
returning single row, 185
SOME operator, 213
table alias, 196, 199, 211
transformation to equijoin, 186, 194-95, 202-03, 207-08
WHERE and HAVING clause, 182, 188, 190, 192-93
Substitution value, 117-18
Substitution variables, 370
SUBSTR function, 69, 71, 75, 78-80, 82
Subtraction, 86
SUM function, 129-30, 133-34, 137-39, 141, 191-92
SUM function in join statements. See Aggregate function
in equijoin statements, 416
Synonym
private, 398-99, 403, 408
PUBLIC, 399-400, 403, 408
validity of underlying object, 399
Synthetic key, 13
SYS user, 366, 447
SYSDATE function, 110-11, 113, 115, 269, 295
as default value in column, 314
System privilege, 391, 394, 411
SYSTEM tablespace. See Tablespace SYSTEM, 394
SYSTEM user, 366, 392, 401

T

Table
definition, 2, 5
Table alias, 151-52, 156, 161, 177, 478-79
in self-join, 258, 262, 265, 481
in subquery. See Subquery
table alias, 196
Table name
restrictions, 290

Table privileges
in data dictionary, 359, 367-68
Tables
in data dictionary, 361, 376, 387-88
Tablespace, 337
default, 310, 367, 393, 395, 404
index, 309
SYSTEM, 394
temporary, 393, 404
TAN function, 84
Temporary tablespace. See Tablespace temporary, 393
TERM command, 375-76, 383-84, 386-87
Text constant, 46
See Literal text, 66
Text literal, 46-47
Time stamp, 98, 102, 106, 109, 111
Time. See Format model, 101
TIMING command, 445
TKPROF, 447
Tnsnames.ora file, 393
Top-n query, 420
TO_CHAR function, 93, 95, 98, 241
TO_DATE function, 93, 99, 101, 103, 105-06, 108, 110, 112-15, 476
TO_NUMBER function, 93, 96, 241, 246
Transaction Control, 267, 270
TRANSLATE function, 73, 84, 90
Transpose a result. See DECODE function, 414
Trigger, 13
TRUNC function, 102, 106-107, 109-110, 286, 476, 481
on NUMBER datatype, 85-86, 88
versus ROUND function, 85
with DATE datatype, 145
TRUNCATE, 276-77, 279, 285-86

U

UNDEFINE command, 372-73, 377, 379-80
UNION ALL set operator, 207, 223-24, 226-27, 230, 232, 246, 449, 452, 457, 469
versus UNION set operator, 246
duplicates, 224-26, 230, 232, 235
UNION set operator, 223-25, 227-29, 235, 246, 248-50, 457, 468-69, 480
ORDER BY clause, 226
Unique constraint, 294-295, 299, 304, 317, 335, 338, 345, 347, 352
Unique index
in primary key constraint, 294-95
in unique constraint, 295
UPDATE, 267, 274-75, 278, 281-83, 287-88
correlated subquery, 275

with subqueries, 182
UPDATE command, 7, 477
Updating a view. See View
data manipulation, 482
UPPER function, 74, 76-77, 79, 82
User
alter, 395
create, 392
drop, 395
USER function, 269, 352
User ID, 20

V

V$tables, 354
VALUES. See INSERT, 269
VARCHAR2 datatype, 291
literal text, 47
Variable
in SQL*Plus, 370
VERIFY, 373-74, 378-81
Version
of Oracle software, 22, 474
View, 321
compiling, 329-30
create, alter, and drop views, 322,
404
data manipulation, 322, 325, 327,
331-32, 482
data manipulation rules, 332

drop, 328, 390
granting of privileges, 323
in data dictionary, 358, 363-64
in-line view. See in-line view, 413
invalid, 329, 334, 360, 371-72, 380
renaming columns, 323, 331
violating query definition, 327
WITH CHECK OPTION, 328

W

WHERE clause, 27, 46, 53
comparison and logical operators, 27
the basics, 46
using functions, 71
WHERE-clause violation in views. See View
WITH CHECK OPTION, 328
Wildcard, 30, 37, 49
in COUNT function, 128
in Views, 326, 330
with LIKE operator, 49
WITH CHECK OPTION, 352
WORD_WRAPPED
in SQL*Plus, 364

Y

Year
four-digit year, 99
Year 2000, 103

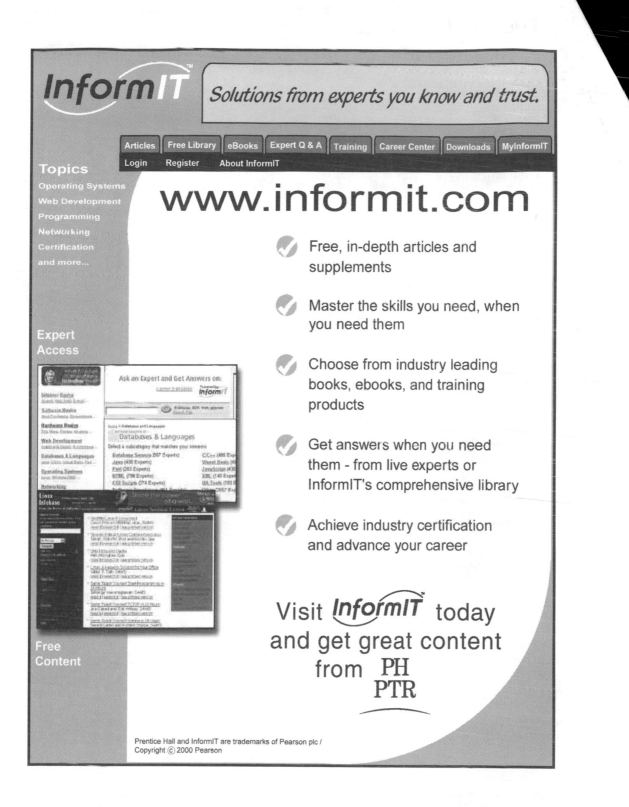